South Sudan's Fateful Struggle

South Sudan's Fateful Struggle

Building Peace in a State of War

STEVEN C. ROACH

OXFORD
UNIVERSITY PRESS

Oxford University Press is a department of the University of Oxford. It furthers
the University's objective of excellence in research, scholarship, and education
by publishing worldwide. Oxford is a registered trade mark of Oxford University
Press in the UK and certain other countries.

Published in the United States of America by Oxford University Press
198 Madison Avenue, New York, NY 10016, United States of America.

© Oxford University Press 2023

All rights reserved. No part of this publication may be reproduced, stored in
a retrieval system, or transmitted, in any form or by any means, without the
prior permission in writing of Oxford University Press, or as expressly permitted
by law, by license, or under terms agreed with the appropriate reproduction
rights organization. Inquiries concerning reproduction outside the scope of the
above should be sent to the Rights Department, Oxford University Press, at the
address above.

You must not circulate this work in any other form
and you must impose this same condition on any acquirer.

Library of Congress Cataloging-in-Publication Data
Names: Roach, Steven C., author.
Title: South Sudan's fateful struggle : building peace in a state of war /
Steven C. Roach, University of South Florida.
Other titles: Building peace in a state of war
Description: New York, NY : Oxford University Press, [2023] |
Includes bibliographical references and index. |
Contents: Introduction Building Peace in a State of War—Slave Soldiers, British Colonial Rule,
and Armed Resistance—A Divided Movement and a Framework for Peace—
The Troubled Transition—Kleptocracy and its Warring Contents—Impunity, Human Rights,
and the Struggle for Justice—Revitalizing the Peace Process—A Transitional Government
and the Prospects for Peace and National Unity.
Identifiers: LCCN 2022053512 (print) | LCCN 2022053513 (ebook) |
ISBN 9780190057848 (hardback) | ISBN 9780190057862 (epub)
Subjects: LCSH: Sudan—History—1881–1899. | Britons—Colonization—Sudan. |
Great Britain—Colonies—Africa—Cultural policy. | Sudan—Civilization.
Classification: LCC DT156.6 .R63 2023 (print) | LCC DT156.6 (ebook) | DDC 962.403—dc23
LC record available at https://lccn.loc.gov/2022053512
LC ebook record available at https://lccn.loc.gov/2022053513

DOI: 10.1093/oso/9780190057848.001.0001

Printed by Integrated Books International, United States of America

In Memory of my Mother

Contents

Preface		ix
Acknowledgments		xiii
List of Abbreviations		xv
	Introduction: Building Peace in a State of War	1
1.	Slave Soldiers, British Colonial Rule, and Armed Resistance	15
2.	The Divided Movement and a Framework for Peace	47
3.	The Troubled Transition	77
4.	Kleptocracy and Its Warring Contents	93
5.	Impunity, Human Rights, and the Struggle for Justice	115
6.	The Revitalized Peace Process and Civil Society's Challenge	147
7.	A Transitional Government and the Prospects for Peace and National Unity	171
Notes		191
References		221
Index		235

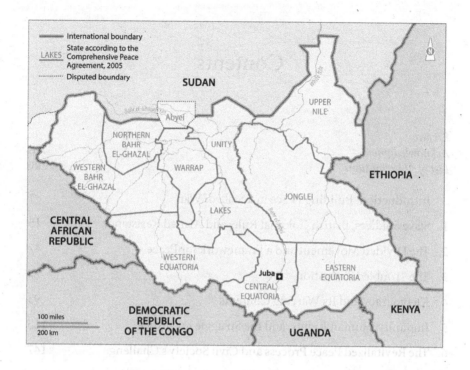

Preface

As one of Africa's most deeply divided countries, South Sudan is a story of both hope and unparalleled uncertainty. I had become interested in the country's politics in 2011, not long after it had gained independence from Sudan. Back then, I seemed to share the same hope and frustration of many international officials with the country's state of development and severe poverty.

When I first traveled to South Sudan in the summer of 2013, it was one week after President Salva Kiir had sacked several of his cabinet ministers, including Riek Machar, his Vice President. By this time, Kiir was struggling to contain the destabilizing effects of his austerity measures stemming from his disastrous decision to shut down the country's oil production. I had read about the country's corruption, but it was not until my first interview with the country's oil minister at the Rainbow Hotel that I felt it first-hand. I had asked a government minister about the oil money—whether it was being used for road construction (at the time there was only 60 km of paved road in the entire country). He paused, then grinned before abruptly getting out of his chair. He left without ever saying goodbye. I knew then that something was wrong.

It was not until mid-2013, with the results of outside investigations of the Dura scandal, that the true scale of corruption would become public. But the outbreak of the civil war in December 2013 had deflected attention away from government corruption, as reports of kleptocratic behavior and massive human rights abuses continued to emerge. None of the reports, though, altered my research focus on the country's sovereignty and troubled relations with Sudan. But, as the war dragged on, it was impossible to ignore the country's mounting problems of corruption, patronage, atrocities, and factionalism. It was becoming clear that, as guilty as Sudan was of meddling in the country's affairs, it was no longer the critical source of instability and insecurity. Rather, it was South Sudan's ruling elite.

By December 2015, I returned to Juba, four months after the signing of the Agreement on the Resolution of Conflict in South Sudan (ARCSS) in August 2015. The peace deal had led to renewed hope in peace and democracy. And I watched on local television as Kiir and the SPLM/A-IO delegation met in Juba to discuss the implementation of ARCSS, particularly the unified security forces. Kiir had recently adopted a Presidential decree that increased the number of states from 10 to 28. For the opposition, it was nothing more than a Dinka land grab—gerrymandering on a grand scale. Yet it seemed that both sides were

keener on the photo-op than getting anything done. At the very least, they looked stiff and unprepared to commit to the terms of ARCSS.

But nothing could prepare me for the renewed hostilities in August 2016, when I returned to Juba to conduct more interviews. Kiir had just driven out Machar, his Vice President (nearly killing him), to restart the civil war. I had conducted a couple of surveys and multiple interviews in December 2015, but the outbreak of war had driven officials into submission and silence. No one would talk with me. So I left the country with little to show for it. It was a disappointing outcome, but it deepened my interest in the country's factionalism, patronage, and the suffering of the people, who had seen their country hijacked by corrupt leaders. By now, the civil war had traumatized the entire country, and the government, in having weakened its opposition (SPLM-IO), seemed even more intent on using its power to oppress its people, as if somehow this would bring an end to the war.

After witnessing first-hand the brutality, I began to treat the civil war as a complicated extension of the South–South war. Yes, there may have been brief interludes of peace, but these were façades hiding a pernicious and entrenched reality: the totalizing effect of the state of war among the ruling elite. My assignment as Country Expert of the USAID Democracy, Human Rights, and Governance assessment team allowed me to talk with and interview many more government officials, civil society leaders, and civilians in Juba, Malakal, and Yambio. I saw how the war had razed large parts of Malakal to the ground and left the airport terminal building pock marked with bullet holes. With most, if not nearly all, affected civilians calling the United Nations PoC camp home, many were simply too traumatized to return to their homes (assuming they still had one). The national government had done little to help them. In fact, many army officers had taken residence at homes once occupied by civilians, and then refused to leave, despite efforts by local government officials to entice them to leave.

Meanwhile, in Juba, the mood had grown tense in early 2020. There was talk of yet another outbreak of war as the parties to the revitalized peace deal struggled to find common ground for approving a new transitional government of national unity. Kiir would eventually break the stalemate and keep the peace process on track. And it seemed this time all parties were more determined to finally implement the terms of the peace deal. But there was also a sense of guarded optimism in the new transitional government of national unity. After all, it was still the same ruling elite (albeit more diverse) attempting to transition the country to a peaceful and democratic government. For many, the new power-sharing arrangement was merely a critical extension of the status quo, and not the solution to the problem of violence. The question this raised was how enhanced power sharing could finally achieve what prior governments had not: national unity that was driven by the will of the people.

My research into this question was largely based on primary and secondary sources as well as interviews and conversations with a wide cross-section of South Sudanese. Many of the people expressed deep frustration with government officials over the failure of the state to deliver basic supplies to the people. Virtually no one I spoke to had received his or her wages/salary on time. The government was not only in arrears but, in most cases, four to five months behind in paying its workers. It had essentially grown insouciant toward its people. And yet in South Sudan, there are people working tirelessly for the cause of justice and democracy, including the chiefs, judges, and civil society members dedicated to promoting the rule of law, accountability, and national identity.

When I sat down to talk with several students on the campus of Juba University in 2015, many expressed a desire for what they called a true "nation-state," one that did not discriminate along tribal or ethnic lines. For them, ethnic identity was always a source of civic and cultural pride that would be realized in terms of a permanent constitution.

Accordingly, when I speak of South Sudan's fateful struggle, I am not trying to paint a bleak picture of its future, but rather, to expose the gross neglect of a people with the potential to shape the country's political destiny.

Acknowledgments

I would first like to express my gratitude to Derrick Hudson, a close friend and great colleague who inspired me to study and research South Sudan in 2011. Since that time, Derrick and I made three trips to South Sudan, collecting data and conducting interviews with numerous government officials. The work eventually culminated in a coedited book on the challenges of governance in South Sudan.

Between 2019 and 2020, I served as Country Expert for the United States Agency for International Development (USAID) Democracy, Governance, and Human Rights assessment team. I was part of a fantastic team that included Tye Ferrell, the team leader, and local analysts Lorne Merekaje and Patrick Riyuyo, whose insights into South Sudan's culture and politics proved invaluable. We visited several remote towns and saw first-hand the destructive effects of the civil war, particularly in Malakal. Kathy Stermer and Kelly Kimball of Tetra Tech provided wonderful technical support, and Kal Demerew, my PhD advisee, offered first-rate research assistance. There are many who either read or had some role in helping me to complete the manuscript, including Dave Atem, Mohamed Babiker, Andrew Dorman, Tye Ferrell, Phil Heenan, Derrick Hudson, Helena Hurd, Matthew Leriche, Francisco Gomes de Matos, Murid Partaw, Heidi Pettersson, Amir Hussein Radjy, Steve Tauber, James Wan, and Christopher Zambakari.

I had to work through many of life's obstacles to complete the book, so I am grateful to Dave McBride, my editor at Oxford University Press, for being so gracious and patient in moving the book from proposal phase to publication. I also would not have completed the manuscript had it not been for the love and dedication of my wife, Erica, and my two playful, spirited children, Emmett and Renée. Finally, during the writing of the book, my Mother passed away. She was an extraordinary person and devoted mother to me and my three siblings Dave, Justin, and Kristie. Her generosity, kindness, graciousness, and love will always remain a big part of my life. It is to her loving memory that I dedicate this book.

Abbreviations

ARCSS	Agreement on the Resolution of the Conflict in South Sudan
AU	African Union
AUCISS	African Union Commission of Inquiry on South Sudan
AUHLP	African Union High Level Panel
CMC	Crisis Management Committee
CPA	Comprehensive Peace Agreement
CRA	Compensation and Reparations Authority
CTHR	Commission for Truth, Healing and Reconciliation
DDR	Disarmament, Demobilization, and Reintegration
EPRDF	Ethiopian People's Revolutionary Democratic Front
FDP	Federal Democratic Party
GERD	Grand Ethiopian Renaissance Dam
GOS	Government of Sudan
GOSS	Government of Southern Sudan
GRSS	Government of the Republic of South Sudan
IDP	Internally Displaced Person
HCSS	Hybrid Court for South Sudan
IGAD	Intergovernmental Authority on Development
IMC	International Medical Corporation
IMF	International Monetary Fund
JMEC	Joint Monitoring Evaluation Commission
KPA	Khartoum Peace Agreement
LGA	Local Government Act
MSF	Médecins Sans Frontières (Doctors without Borders)
NAS	National Salvation Front
NCAC	National Constitutional Amendment Committee
NCP	National Congress Party
NCRC	National Constitutional Review Commission
NDI	National Democratic Institute
NGO	Nongovernmental Organization
NISS	National Intelligence Security Services
NIF	National Islamic Front
NMC	National Movement for Change
NSS	National Security Services
NUF	Necessary Unified Forces
PDM	People's Democratic Movement
POC	Protection of Civilians
PRMB	Petroleum Revenue Management Bill

xvi ABBREVIATIONS

PSA	Production Sharing Agreement
RARCSS	Revitalized Agreement on the Resolution of the Conflict in South Sudan
RJMEC	Reconstituted Joint Monitoring and Evaluation Commission
RTGONU	Revitalized Transitional Government of National Unity
SAF	Sudan Armed Forces
SANU	Sudan African National Union
SPDF	Sudan People's Defense Force
SSIM	Southern Sudan Independence Movement
SSDF	South Sudan Defense Forces
SPLM/A	Sudan People's Liberation Movement/Army
SPLM/DC	Sudan People's Liberation Movement/Democratic Change
SPLM-IO	Sudan People's Liberation Movement—In Opposition
SPLM/N	Sudan People's Liberation Movement/North
SRG	Southern Regional Government
SSAF	South Sudan Armed Forces
SSAR	South Sudan Autonomous Region
SSCC	South Sudan Churches Council
SSHRC	South Sudan Human Rights Commission
SSLM	South Sudan Liberation Movement
SSNMC	South Sudan National Movement for Change
SSOA	South Sudan Opposition Alliance
TGONU	Transitional Government of National Unity
TNLA	Transitional National Legislative Assembly
UDRA	United Democratic Republican Alliance
UN	United Nations
UNDP	United Nations Development Fund
UNMIS	United Nations Mission in Sudan
UNMISS	United Nations Mission in South Sudan
USAID	United States Agency for International Development

Introduction

Building Peace in a State of War

In December 2013, civil war broke out in South Sudan, forcing millions of South Sudanese to flee the country. This was not the outcome many expected. South Sudan, after all, had just declared independence from Sudan in 2011 and the Sudan People's Liberation Movement (SPLM), the country's dominant political organization, seemed poised to work with international leaders and donors to develop the country's infrastructure and institutions. But a series of events, which included the decision to shut off its oil pipelines and the abrupt dismissal of high-ranking cabinet officials in the summer of 2013, greatly destabilized the country. The civil war ended up devastating the country's economy and calling attention to its endless cycle of violence and pervasive corruption.

After the warring parties signed the Revitalized Agreement on the Resolution of the Conflict in South Sudan (R-ARCSS) in 2018, there was renewed hope for peace and democracy. Because the agreement was based on an expanded power-sharing arrangement, some felt that it would finally address the cycle of violence and set the country on a path toward peace and security. The feeling was that the inclusion of more parties would finally pressure the government to implement R-ARCSS. But the years of war had also left many either cynical or guardedly optimistic about the power-sharing arrangement. It was, after all, based on elite rule and largely excluded civil society actors and ordinary citizens from the peace process. The people, in short, were once again being asked to place their faith in a ruling elite that had repeatedly failed to broker the terms of peace and security. Beyond this, there was concern that the increased number of parties would lead to more demands and infighting that would delay the new peace process.

By mid-2022, the parties had yet to meet a series of deadlines of R-ARCSS, including adopting a permanent constitution. And in July 2022, the Revitalized Transitional Government of National Unity (RTGoNU) announced that national elections would be delayed until 2024. For many, the slow pace of implementation was proof that the ruling elite were never truly interested in peace and security, nor in unifying the nation (they still had not assembled a unified security force). The ruling elite still relied on tribal loyalties and the threat of violence to govern. And it was this brute form of governance that underscored a widespread public angst toward the ruling elite—an angst that was the product

South Sudan's Fateful Struggle. Steven C. Roach, Oxford University Press. © Oxford University Press 2023.
DOI: 10.1093/oso/9780190057848.003.0001

2 SOUTH SUDAN'S FATEFUL STRUGGLE

of years of war. In fact, South Sudan had been at war for over five of its 11 years of statehood, and 40 years since Sudan's independence in 1956. Even during the brief interludes of war, South Sudan's ruling elite had become increasingly corrupt and disorganized. Peace, it could be said, was never a time for reflection and true reform. Rather, it led to mounting tension and rash, fateful decisions as well as lax international monitoring.

What was easy to overlook, then, was how the effects of war had permeated society and the lives of its people and ruling elite. By reinforcing abusive norms and spurring ethnic division, infighting, and distrust, war informed a complex puzzle of achieving long-term peace and stability in South Sudan. A vital piece of this puzzle was the legacy of the 1991 rebellion inside the SPLM/A, which had divided the SPLA and represented the start of the South-South war. The 2005 Comprehensive Peace Agreement (CPA), it turned out, failed to address many of the deep-seated grievances fueled by the South–South war. And while it may have ended Sudan's second civil war between the North and the South, officials failed to fully appreciate the lingering effects of this brutal war, including rebel factionalism, corruption, and moral impunity, on society.

The years of war and party infighting has nonetheless produced a static dynamic of governance that has actively stymied a moral reckoning with the past and with genuine efforts at transitioning to peace and democracy. I argue that such a reckoning is necessary for successfully transitioning to democracy and long-term peace. Static governance, as we shall see, is ultimately about isolating the present from both the past and the future in order to maximize the use of fear (and the threats of violence or war) to maintain power and a semblance of order. Stealing by the national elite, for example, not only violates existing legal norms and justice for past crimes: it also deprives the country of the public investment needed to develop and stabilize it. A present isolated from the past and future is at its core a highly unstable and fragile dynamic. Yet it is precisely this inherent instability and uncertainty that motivate and enable the leaders to govern by brute force and to justify a militaristic approach to maintain order.

War in this sense becomes a totalizing and continuous event. The feeling that there is no apparent alternative to the abusive, warring ruling elite that continue to use their power to stymie peace indicates the extent to which the people and warring elite have internalized the effects of war and violence, starting with South Sudan's civil war (2013–2018) and stretching back to Sudan's two civil wars (1983–2005; 1955–1972) and British colonial rule (1898–1955).[1] The problem is that the ruling elite have erected few, if any, institutional barriers against the effects of their warlike traits. Instead, their brute governance was sown by divisions and unresolved grievances. When these divisions therefore culminated in the dramatic split within the SPLM/A in 1991, at the height of the second civil war in Sudan, they effectively blurred the line between enemy and ally, creating

BUILDING PEACE IN A STATE OF WAR   3

an environment of unshakeable distrust and brutality. The six-year interim period between Sudan's second civil war and South Sudan's statehood (2005–2011) did little to resolve these tensions and divisions. If anything, it was a time when the ruling elite's impulsive and kleptocratic behavior created the conditions for another civil war, this time in the new state of South Sudan.

In this book, I shall use the state of war metaphor rather loosely to describe the warlike state of the ruling elite and the underpinnings of their brute governance and lawlessness. For Thomas Hobbes, a seventeenth century jurist who popularized the term in his book *Leviathan*, the state of war was characterized as "solitary, nasty, brutish, and short," and a war of all against all.[2] Hobbes never addressed the role of culture in producing and maintaining the state of war; he of course was more interested in transcending it through a social contract based on the laws of nature. Yet in South Sudan, culture assumes an undeniable part in sowing the unruly behavior of the ruling elite. In particular, the harmful customs of child marriage and child conscription serve to reinforce a male patriarchy in which males tend to see themselves as the protectors and owners of women (i.e., the treatment of women as chattel or human property). For Susan Faludi, a feminist scholar, male masculinity and domination remains rooted in a primordial myth of protecting women, leading males to fantasize about becoming the hero of the tribe. Some of the male fighters in her view end up projecting this masculinity on the battlefield to profiteer from war, for example, by collecting booty.[3] In South Sudan, war profiteering eventually segued into kleptocratic state governance.

South Sudanese culture also reflects a prevailing desire and instinct to belong to a tribal group. Tribal bonds are rooted in longstanding customs, languages, and rituals and held together by the authority of chiefs. However, when they are politicized by local leaders or outside forces, they can fuel extreme violence and hatred.[4] The idea that tribal members will fight and die blindly for their tribal group points to the irrational and endless nature of such violence. In South Sudan, tribal loyalties are harnessed by the national elite to finance and extend such loyalty to national politics. The result has been a patchwork of patronage networks in which leaders use their personal wealth to pay soldiers and subordinates for political support. Such undying loyalty to former military leaders characterizes the unique role of militarization in South Sudan's politics. As early as the mid-1990s, the South Sudanese scholar Peter Adwok Nyaba argued that the militarism of the SPLM/A ultimately determined how it governed. In his view, this is why the SPLM never became a truly independent political body or a political organization capable of governing regional and state affairs. For it was still an organization whose leaders naturally defaulted to military training and status to resolve the country's problems, disputes, and issues. In short, militarism derived from years of unfettered warfare, which left soldiers and future political

4 SOUTH SUDAN'S FATEFUL STRUGGLE

leaders ill-prepared and unwilling to abide by civic rules and regulations. Having learned the personal rewards of violating rules and regulations, many impulsively took what they could get, given that the outbreak of war remained an imminent possibility.[5]

In the end, South Sudan's leaders were never prepared, much less trained to avoid war. Where the threat of war should have yielded restraint and risk aversion, it had become a source of the ruling elite's brute and militaristic approach to governance. The dichotomy between brutality and governance was not simply blurred: it had become mutually reinforcing. To understand the broader implications of this dynamic, South Sudan's armed factionalism and conflicts had come to symptomize the new nature of war in African countries in the 1990s, when more of the wars began to be conducted by predatory, nongovernment militias. These groups' main aim was not to topple the government per se, but to bargain economically and to extract rent and resources from it.[6] What this suggested was that armed factionalism in South Sudan was not something South Sudan's leaders could eliminate. They had to find a way to contain it. So they naturally drew on their militaristic mentality to contain the rebel factions, hoping that they could be reintegrated into the SPLM/A through various (perverse) incentives. These incentives included immunity from prosecution and economic rewards for fighting the opposition during the second civil war in Sudan. For Salva Kiir Mayardit, the current President of South Sudan, this entailed diverting state-controlled oil assets to pay militias, that is, the Padang militia, to fight the Sudan People's Liberation Movement in-Opposition (SPLM-IO). The endless nature of armed conflict, then, has continually disrupted and haunted the peace process in South Sudan. In some ways, it has superficialized the transition to peace and a national unity government by suggesting that the government can achieve long-term peace by successfully containing the militias (and their ability to destabilize the peace process), including the National Salvation Front (NAS), which continue to attack government forces.

South Sudan's endless conflicts has prompted some to re-evaluate the prospect for a new social contract. Luka Biong Deng Kuol, for example, argues that such failure reflects the leaders' disregard for the laws and rules of its constitution(s) and their exclusion of the people.[7] His idea is that the social contract needs to be resilient enough to promote justice and accountability. A resilient social contract in this sense reflects the important preconditions for an inclusive government, including further consultation with civil society groups and a more binding constitution that stipulates an effective checks-and-balances system.[8] Kuol assumes that the government repeatedly violated the social contract of the CPA, even though the CPA had been negotiated exclusively by John Garang de Marbior, the SPLM/A leader, Mohamed Taha, the Vice President of the Government of Sudan, and Troika officials. The SPLM/A leaders moreover had only consulted among

themselves, never with the people. In this way, the 2005 Interim Constitution of the Government of Southern Sudan (GoSS) was technically a contract arranged between international leaders and the SPLM, not the people and its leaders. This consequently ignored an essential premise of a social contract: that it must derive from the voluntary consent of the people who, in return for surrendering some of their civil freedoms, are assured that their civil rights will be protected by the leaders. South Sudan's contract, one could argue, was not a social contract between a consenting public and ruler; rather, it was a contract between a ruler and non-consenting public. All of this raises the question of why we should expect the transition from war to peace to occur when there are no realistic assurances of protecting the people's basic rights.

For many, this question cuts to a core challenge: the ongoing need to criminally punish the leaders. The CPA, for example, failed to address the issue of accountability for past human rights abuses. Many top officials, it seemed, feared that moral accountability would ultimately detract from promoting peace, security, and democracy in the region. The thinking was that for justice or accountability to have its desired effect on peace and stability, it would have to be administered by national authorities and reflect a strong national consensus. Yet the problem with this idea was that many of the future national leaders remained opposed to justice or national reconciliation through transitional justice mechanisms (e.g., a truth commission and hybrid war crimes court), even though such a process amounted to the most promising opportunity to break the national cycle of violence. Nonetheless, the Troika (the United States, Britain, and Norway), which led and oversaw the implementation of the CPA, did not wish to taint the reputation of Garang, the leader of the SPLM/A, who many US officials considered as a liberal reformer and the best hope for democratizing the South and containing Khartoum. Perhaps more importantly, administering a war crimes court usually comes with the spoils of war—when a victor is in a position to impose the terms of justice. Even if the SPLM had emerged victorious, there was little chance that they would investigate and prosecute the SPLM's commanders. What's more, implementing a hybrid war crimes court and a truth commission means deferring to the very national leaders who are negotiating the terms of peace. With enough internal and outside pressure, these leaders may agree to implement justice mechanisms, but only to the extent that it serves their own political interests. The result therefore is what we might call a partial process of moral reckoning that further divides the people and provides impunity for much of the ruling elite.

This is not to say that a robust process of moral accountability will finally break the cycle of violence in South Sudan. But it does suggest that without some comprehensive moral reckoning with past abuses, the abusive ruling elite will only be encouraged to thwart and delay the implementation of justice under R-ARCSS.

6   SOUTH SUDAN'S FATEFUL STRUGGLE

Ultimately, the leaders as the former chief negotiators of peace agreements possess the power to reject any provisions that threaten their power, even if this means exploiting instability to subvert national unity, peace, and democracy.

National Disunity and Insecurity

Endless instability, then, means endless transitioning to peace and national unity. In South Sudan, national unity underscores three general factors: societal consensus, the internalization of normative constraints (or the rule of law), and the fair distribution of public money. The CPA stipulated several measures of South Sudan's national unity, including revenue sharing, a census, self-determination, and the limited reintegration of its armed forces. But the pursuit of these goals also unveiled the brutal means of consolidating political power, including the 2010 elections and 2011 referendum, in which the SPLM intimidated people at the polls. These events also symptomized the relatively short timeline for civic training and preparation, a lack of timely, substantive engagement by the Troika, and the flimsy integration of the SPLA. The CPA was supposed to offer a choice between two forms of national unity: one being the unity of Sudan, the other a new state of South Sudan. Yet Sudanese national unity ultimately proved unattractive for South Sudan's ruling elite, who used their power to unify the South Sudanese around statehood. The problem was that the national unity they had forged remained largely nominal. While declaring independence from the common enemy (or Sudan) had helped unify the South Sudanese, it also disguised the many rifts in South Sudan's politics. National unity, in short, had become increasingly illusionary, since it relied on a self-serving elite to promote it.

This was especially true for the security forces. The SPLA, for instance, was still a nonprofessional army, consisting of a loose-knit network of different militias. By 2010, Kiir had managed to inflate the number of fighters of the SPLA to deter Sudan from disrupting the referendum process. But the many Nuer soldiers who had joined the SPLA were never comfortable in their new roles. Many would end up fighting for the SPLM-IO during South Sudan's civil war. Factionalism and patronage in this respect fueled the conditions of insecurity and distrust that undermined any good faith effort to unify the armed forces, including the Necessary Unified Forces (NUF) stipulated under R-ARCSS. Despite some early, promising results in retraining soldiers at the cantonment sites in Juba, the formation of the NUF has been delayed by a series of logistical problems and a lack of resources at these sites.[9]

Naturally, the most essential ingredient for making the NUF work was interethnic solidarity. For Garang, solidarity was about promoting the

self-determination of the South Sudanese people. This meant recognizing the democratic rights of all Sudanese and ending the bigotry and racism of the "Old Sudan." Garang's goal was to use armed resistance to compel the Government of Sudan (GoS) to recognize the equality of all South Sudanese as a condition of achieving national unity in Sudan. Garang's vision, however, never sat well with the former militant leaders of Anyanya—the first armed resistance movement of the South—and later, the Anyanya II. For these leaders, secession remained the only means of liberating South Sudan from the North's oppression. By the early 1990s, Garang's SPLA had splintered into two factions: the SPLA-Torit and SPLA-Nasir. Riek Machar, one of the leaders of the SPLA-Nasir (and a member of the Nuer ethnic group), had mobilized political support by appealing to the Nuer's secessionist sentiment and initiating a cycle of unrelenting tribal factionalism that would haunt the interim period.

The interim period (2005–2011) saw the expansion of militaristic and monetized patronage networks. To pay for political loyalty of new recruits and subordinates, the ruling elite siphoned off profits from the oil revenue that had begun to flow into the coffers of the Government of Southern Sudan. And with little international oversight, the leaders took what they wanted. The full extent of the corruption would not become clear until 2013 when the International Monetary Fund, the World Bank, and media groups began to investigate the trail of missing money tied to the ruling elite's financial schemes and unsigned contracts. For its part, the GoSS never followed up on its investigations of corruption. Its lackluster efforts, it turned out, had become part of larger strategy to politicize justice.

A Moral Reckoning and the Dilemma of Transitional Justice

Such lackluster efforts involved Kiir's offer of blanket immunity from criminal prosecution and promising higher office (sinecures) to rebel commanders in exchange for (re)joining the SPLM/A. Kiir may have had little choice but to support some of the rebel factions and rogue militias—since imposing discipline on SPLA fighters risked a military coup. However, in tacitly summoning their support to divide the government's main opposition, he also became complicit in perpetrating war crimes (e.g., gang rape and mass killings), for which he has long denied any responsibility, even as he calls on his people to forgive and forget his past abuses.

Amidst such denial, there is the question of whether criminal punishment can ever be meted out when the leaders treat justice as a threat to peace. Opponents of forcefully inserting justice into peace processes (e.g., political leaders and diplomats) claim that when suspected perpetrators are the chief negotiators

8   SOUTH SUDAN'S FATEFUL STRUGGLE

of the peace process, justice mechanisms will limit their willingness to make concessions and to agree on issues. Why would any leader, for instance, agree to establishing a court that will likely investigate and prosecute him or her for war crimes? Justice mechanisms for this reason only serve to disrupt and strain the peace process by discouraging leaders from cooperating.[10] In 2016, for example, Kiir argued that a war crimes court would only open old wounds or worsen grievances and cause more instability. But rather than dismissing the role of justice in the peace process, he seemed to approve a truth commission modeled after the South African Truth and Reconciliation Commission (he would later renege on this promise). The SATRC had granted immunity from criminal prosecution in exchange for a confession of guilt. Kiir thus seemed content to use the truth commission to shield himself from prosecution.[11]

The idea that he would weaponize such a commission underscores the difficult challenge of merging peace with justice. For human rights activists and civil society actors, the coupling of a truth commission and a hybrid war crimes court represents an encompassing and effective process of healing and accountability. Encompassing in this sense reflects how the proposed Hybrid Court for South Sudan is based on a mix of international customary law and customary/tribal law (a recognized source of law in South Sudan's Transitional Constitution). The HCSS is part of a larger project of hybrid justice in which civil society activists are seeking to combine customary and statutory law to advance moral accountability and human rights in South Sudan. The South Sudan Law Society, for example, has implemented a number of programs designed to train tribal chiefs to learn and apply statutory law, which codifies human rights.[12] Its two principal aims are to bridge what it sees as a gap between customary and statutory law in South Sudan and to eliminate the abusive effects of traditional norms in the country (albeit mostly in countryside villages), such as child marriage and child conscription.

The looming question, therefore, is whether justice can be effectively integrated into a framework for long-term peace and security. If the persistent trend of impunity is limiting the transition to a national unity government and stable democracy, then at some point justice will need to be imposed. And yet imposing justice also implies either a willing outside power to enforce justice, or a new government to administer justice. The potential fallout from the latter is that it may stoke grievances and lead to accusations of victor's justice by the targeted perpetrators. Moreover, there is no assurance that the new leaders or empowered victims will not apply justice equally and impartially. The dilemma, then, is that in imposing justice to achieve long-term peace and stability, a foreign force or new domestic leaders may also tend to stoke the grievances that lead to more violence and instability.

One way to work beyond the dilemma is to build a more elaborate system of hybrid justice that expands the holistic scope of the law and for that matter, brings together past, future, and recent efforts to unify the country. This would involve among other things the equal treatment of all people and parties under the law. Whether or not this means subjecting foreign workers or UN peacekeepers to justice, the ultimate goal is to root out the exclusionary practices and grievances that fuel the violence in South Sudan.[13] The idea is that a comprehensive peace agreement also requires a comprehensive moral agreement or reckoning with the past to overcome the consequences of partialized peace (that favors the leaders) and justice. By comprehensive reckoning, I mean justice that is holistic and not singularly about forgiving the leaders and forgetting their crimes, nor recognizing the singular primacy of victims' justice and restoring the rights and needs of victims. It must constitute a collective effort to meet these moral goals: namely, to empower the people and civil society actors to shape the political system, to eliminate harmful customs and discriminatory laws, and to confront the totality of violence that stretches back to colonial times.

Reconstituting Peace and Democracy

The main problem with the CPA was that it failed to produce a stable framework of governance. Some of this had to do with the inability to reach agreement on boundary disputes, which eventually led to an unpleasant divorce between Sudan and South Sudan. Yet the Troika's prevailing goal, it seemed, was to contain the spread of Islamic fundamentalism by promoting democracy and human rights. An important part of that effort was helping to frame the 2005 Interim Constitution, a document containing a progressive list of political and civil rights and principles. However, when the southern leaders assembled to adopt a transitional constitution to replace and revise the Interim Constitution, they agreed to concentrate more power in the executive by removing certain checks on presidential power, that is, by allowing the president to appoint new judges and legislators. It was not so much what they revised but how they did it without consulting the people and civil society groups. Of course there was probably not the time to consult the people, but in relenting to Kiir's demands, they also encouraged [Kiir's] future violations of the Transitional Constitution, violations that would eventually provoke the party infighting that would lead to civil war and force the government to suspend presidential elections.

Despite these violations, many civilians and officials have remained hopeful that a permanent constitution will eventually be adopted. Unlike the Transitional Constitution, a permanent constitution has become a far more concerted attempt

10   SOUTH SUDAN'S FATEFUL STRUGGLE

to include and represent the people. For example, the National Constitutional Review Commission, which was established by Kiir in 2012, and the National Constitution Amendment Commission—a body tasked with drafting a permanent constitution—allowed civil society groups and the people to play a direct role in drafting the permanent constitution. This was clearly an improvement from the drafting process of the Transitional Constitution, which was elite-driven and done in haste. But the question it raised was whether a permanent constitution represented a reliable mandate to protect and enforce the people's rights. A constitution, after all, is only as good as its institutions that enable citizens to seek redress and fair representation. Yet many remained optimistic that a permanent constitution would finally bind the new government to the will of the people.

However, after years of neglect and abuse, many of South Sudan's institutions—including its judiciary and the National Assembly—remain broken. Without proper funding and oversight, a newly restructured government of national unity is bound to meet the same fate. The militarized ruling elite are still likely to make the same rash, impulsive decisions that lead to insecurity and instability, including its decision to stop oil production in 2012, which was prompted by the Government of Sudan's action to increase the fees to transport South Sudan's oil through Sudan to the Red Sea. South Sudan's leaders believed that in punishing Sudan for raising the transport fees, they were carrying out the will of the South Sudanese people. Yet they never stopped to think of the consequences for their people, who they never consulted. When the oil pipelines were finally turned back on, austerity measures were implemented to curb rising inflation and interest rates, leading to more insecurity and ultimately to the outbreak of war.

The civil war eventually created its own constitutional crisis. Not only did the government suspend the activities of NCRC but it justified, in Kiir's view, the violations (and virtual suspension) of the Transitional Constitution to conduct the war. By mid-2014, the United Nations had shifted its focus on nation-building to humanitarian assistance. The United Nations Mission in South Sudan (UNMISS), for example, took on thousands of IDPs and erected eight Protection of Civilians (POC) camps across the country.[14] Investigations of human rights atrocities soon followed. The UN Human Rights Council issued its first detailed report in the spring of 2016, which followed on the heels of the African Union's Commission of Inquiry in South Sudan (AUCISS) report on human rights abuses. South Sudan had quickly become the worst humanitarian crisis in Africa with nearly 2.4 million refugees displaced and over a half of its civilian population left food insecure.

As the ruling elite found new ways to steal public money, there was the nagging question of whether the Troika, United Nations, and regional bodies, such as the African Union and IGAD, were doing enough to help restore peace and

security. For its part, the United States sanctioned individual governmental officials and even discussed invoking the dormant UN Trusteeship (the island of Palau was the last country in 1993 to gain statehood under the UN organ).[15] Yet by freezing the assets and travel of government officials, the United States and the United Nations had finally managed to pressure political leaders to sign the Agreement on the Resolution of the Conflict in South Sudan (ARCSS).[16]

But after a second outbreak of war in 2016, it was clear that sanctions were not enough to keep the parties on track toward peace. Later that year, war fatigue had begun to set in, as regional actors and opposition groups ramped up efforts to renew peace talks. The result was a diverse power sharing agreement, which promised to further pressure Kiir to implement R-ARCSS. However, infighting soon slowed down its implementation.

By August 2022, the RTGoNU was still without a permanent constitution. Having decided to delay presidential elections until 2024, the parties to the RTGoNU resorted to more finger pointing and blaming. The growing instability certainly does not bode well for South Sudan's future. The role of the RTGoNU was to restore hope and stability. Yet the fact that it had failed to meet the deadlines set forth in R-ARCSS may be due to false expectations, or its being asked to do too much in too short a time to achieve a stable national unity government. Whatever the case may be, it's important to understand the relationship between the warlike ruling elite and the failed transitions to peace.

One of my aims in the book is to address how these warlike factors such as militarized patronage and pervasive corruption, created the quasi-permanent conditions of instability and the flawed process of transitioning to peace. Another aim is to show how the ruling elite's politicization of justice reproduces the conditions of violence and subverts a fuller moral reckoning (without political pretense) with past abuses. If transitioning to peace is doomed to fail, then ultimately the challenge is not simply what South Sudan is transitioning to or from, but through what? "If there never was a bureaucracy or a judiciary to fail," as Mahmood Mamdani puts it, then "South Sudan was a failed transition."[17] I shall address the roots of this failing process and analyze the implications of South Sudan's militarized past and the ways in which people and civil society actors have been repressed and excluded from governance and the peace process.

Outline of the Book

South Sudan has a long history of oppression and occupation. Chapter 1 traces the roots of South Sudan's liberation movement to Ottoman occupation of South Sudan, when the Ottomans recruited South Sudanese to fight in a slave army. The chapter goes on to examine the Mahdist state and how it planted the seeds for

12   SOUTH SUDAN'S FATEFUL STRUGGLE

Egyptian and Sudanese nationalism. British colonial rule eventually introduced an elaborate administrative system based on the indirect rule of the local population. This ultimately reinforced the division of Sudan into two regions, or between the North and the South, which would worsen after the independence of Sudan (1956). In fact, Sudanese independence led to a new phase of oppression and discrimination of the South Sudanese by the Sudanese government, which gave rise to armed resistance in the South in the late 1950s. The Anyanya waged a brutal war against the Sudanese government, but it was the moderate wing of the South Sudan resistance movement that would negotiate an end to the first civil war and end up forming an autonomous regional government of South Sudan. I will discuss how the government failed to mend tensions between the North and the South and continued to marginalize the South.

Chapter 2 discusses the events and trends of Sudan's prolonged second civil war. Arguably the most important was the formation of the SPLM and the influence of John Garang. Here I offer an in-depth look at Garang's vision of a New Sudan, and the subsequent split in the SPLM in 1991 between the SPLA-Nasir and the SPLA-Torit, which, as mentioned earlier, led to a South–South war. I then move on to show how tribal factionalism weakened the SPLM and allowed Khartoum to contain the SPLA by allying with southern anti-SPLA forces. By the late 1990s, international policymakers had downplayed the crucial role of ethnic factionalism and treated the cause as a clash between an Islamist authoritarian North and Christian, democratic South. I argue that this position oversimplified the conflict and ultimately downplayed the need for morally redressing the effects of war and for promoting accountability. Finally, I analyze the CPA and its key unresolved issues, including an integrated security force and border disputes.

In Chapter 3, I analyze the transition from autonomy to new statehood during the interim period. In particular, I examine the difficult transition from autonomy to statehood by probing some of the tensions between Garang's New Sudan and secessionism as well as Salva Kiir's role in preserving the unity of the SPLM. I then move on to discuss how the SPLM consolidated its power in the 2010 elections and advanced the referendum process. The SPLM's political domination, as we shall see, excluded civil society actors from the drafting of the Transitional Constitution, which symptomized its lack of preparedness to govern the new state. Poor governance also reflected the pervasive corruption that stemmed from the emergence of patronage networks and the lack of mechanisms to monitor the sudden influx of oil revenue into the region. It also raised the issue of whether the Troika and international donors facilitated the mounting corruption by not assuming a more active and critical role in the development of the southern region.

Chapter 4 discusses the events that led to the outbreak of South Sudan's civil war and the persistence of systemic corruption, that is, Kiir's ability to reallocate

more public money to finance his patronage network and the war. I argue that the pervasive system of corruption helped insulate the leaders from the effects of war, encouraging them to extract rents and resources. In analyzing the ties between South Sudan's war economy and the economy of nonstate rebel militias, I develop the concept of militarized patronage to describe the operations of South Sudan's war economy, the militarization of its oil sector, and the leaders' economic policies. Militarized patronage, I show, reflected the emerging link between kleptocracy and the civil war in which the national government and armed factions came to share economic and personal incentives to fight, that is, to profit and increase the flow of arm supplies. In this way, the informal economy of armed conflict had become increasingly entwined with the national war economy as the government used state assets and resources (e.g., oil production) to pay tribal-based militias to fight their main opposition. To assess this trend, I shall address a series of events, including the false transparency of the oil sector, the leaders' fateful decision to shut off its oil pipelines, and the impact of targeted sanctions imposed by the United States and the United Nations to punish high-ranking government officials.

One of my aims in Chapter 5 is to analyze the scale of human rights abuses and refugee flows since the start of the civil war. In particular, I examine the government's and rebel groups' role in committing these abuses, including child conscription, mass rape, and mass killings, and the issues surrounding South Sudan's harmful cultural customs. I shall also draw on several interviews to offer an in-depth account of the plight of the IDPs at the UN's Protection of Civilians camps. My other aim is to discuss the challenges of implementing a regime of transitional justice that can orchestrate a comprehensive moral reckoning with the past and dissolve the culture of impunity of the ruling elite. Here I discuss the parameters of hybrid justice, such as the HCSS and the Commission of Truth, Reconciliation, and Healing, as well as the political leaders' strategic attempts to curtail transitional justice and to justify their own moral immunity.

In Chapter 6, I examine the events that led up to the signing of R-ARCSS and the dynamics of the power-sharing agreement, including the role of the South Sudan's Opposition Alliance (SSPOA). The aim of R-ARCSS was to incentivize the parties to reach a flexible consensus on issues and to help them overcome their own deep-seated misgivings about issues, which include security and federalism.

My aim in the concluding chapter is to analyze the short and long-term challenges of implementing R-ARCSS, including consensus building, intercommunal violence, party infighting, COVID-19, corruption in the oil market, and demilitarizing society. To meet these challenges and reduce the tensions in RTGoNU, I argue that the parties need to adopt an integrative approach to governing or implementing R-ARCSS, which seeks a concerted

14 SOUTH SUDAN'S FATEFUL STRUGGLE

balance of justice, accountability, peace, and democratic mechanisms. The fact that the national elite continues to repress civil society in the peace process underscores the deep-seated ties of exclusion and governance. In addressing this underlying problem, I shall offer various ideas and strategies regarding what I call an integrative social contract as well as the proper alignment of regional politics with long-term peace.

1

Slave Soldiers, British Colonial Rule, and Armed Resistance

In the late nineteenth century, much of the southern region of what is today Sudan was considered ungovernable hinterland. Britain at this time had occupied the northern region (or Egypt), and treated the natives in southern Sudan as either savages or backward peoples. Its empire had reached new heights and stretched from Southeast Asia and the Middle East to northern parts of Africa. And there were now new "civilization standards" that defined the parameters of the "civilized state," and that gave rise to agreements (e.g., the 1885 Berlin Conference), which allowed it to assert administrative control over its occupied territories in Africa. Colonization had also propelled Britain's superior military technology and the need to draw on this advantage to extract raw materials for its rapidly industrializing economy. Morally, Britain saw itself as the civilizer or savior (of the backward natives), which, in helping to end much of the slave trade, was also bent on modernizing key parts of the region, that is, improving education and roads.

But modernization did not apply to the South; it was largely restricted to the North and its mostly Arab population. Britain's rationale for this was based on the belief that the northern Arabs were better suited to modern development (e.g., civic and specialized education) and more capable of governing their own civil affairs. By treating the South Sudanese as inferior and savage people, they neglected southern Sudan and created severe inequality between northern and southern Sudan. They consequently had little interest in engaging the South Sudanese, ruling first by patrol and then by appointing indigenous rulers or tribal chiefs to administer local affairs. In the end, the British wanted to keep the South Sudanese passive and prevent them from rising up against the North, which also meant discouraging the modernized Arabs in the North from uniting with the less developed South Sudanese. A hands-off policy, as one British official put it, would "ensure that Southern Sudan, by its history and by the accidents of geography, river transport, and so on, must turn more to the North rather than to Uganda and Congo."[1] The strategy therefore was twofold: (1) to make the South more dependent on the North and (2) to isolate the tribal groups from one another while assigning different identities to these groups to promote indirect rule.

South Sudan's Fateful Struggle. Steven C. Roach, Oxford University Press. © Oxford University Press 2023.
DOI: 10.1093/oso/9780190057848.003.0002

16   SOUTH SUDAN'S FATEFUL STRUGGLE

I shall trace the roots of this division to the slavery and slave trade of the Turkiyyah period, before moving on to address Britain's indirect rule in the South and its impact on tribal relations and development, as well as the rise of the southern guerilla movement, the Anyanya, during Sudan's first civil war (1955–1972). Finally, I examine the new autonomous government in the South (1972–1983) and how Khartoum's lack of investment in its institutions and infrastructure created tensions and problems that eventually led to the outbreak of Sudan's second civil war.

Slave Soldiers

In 1821, Muhammad Ali, the Turkish Viceroy of the Ottoman sultan in Istanbul, who had ruled over Egypt since 1805, established control over Sudan, forming the Turco-Egyptian regime. He had pushed southward, using superior firepower to subdue and convert the Arab tribe, Shaiqiya, into an irregular cavalry and tax collectors.[2] From 1821 to 1885, the period known as Turkiyyah, the Ali dynasty ruled over Sudan. During his reign (1805–1848), Ali attempted to modernize both Egypt and Sudan by improving the army, tax collection, and Arabic schools, and by incorporating Western science and the study of medicine into the school curriculum.[3] The new modern bureaucracy improved the management of Sudan and eventually led Ali to break off ties with the Ottoman sultan.

Crucial to Ali's rule was the promotion of law and order. He was able to assemble a vast police force to enforce sharia law and to control the affairs of his dynasty. It was by all accounts an ambitious plan that required more troops. The problem though was that there simply were not enough men to conscript; nor were there men willing to volunteer. Ali Kurshid Pasha, the governor general of Sudan, had to bridge this gap by capturing and enslaving Shilluk and Dinka in the Nuba Mountains and White Nile region. Despite the harsh terrain, he managed to forcibly conscript thousands of local tribesmen into what became a permanent "slave" army intended to protect the locals—many of whom had lacked the means to defend themselves. Slave soldiers were known as al-jihadiyya. They were essentially mercenary fighters who were expected to serve their regiment for life. Yet they were powerless to challenge military leaders. Many, in fact, lacked the necessary discipline and commitment to engage in combat, making them unreliable fighters. The high desertion rates also undermined the regime's capacity to maintain order in the southern region. Still, many others proved to be excellent, well-acclimated fighters. And in exploiting their skills, the Ottoman government loaned the fighters out to other countries with commercial interests in remote parts of the world, including France (under Napoleon III), which

SLAVE SOLDIERS, BRITISH COLONIAL RULE, AND ARMED RESISTANCE   17

sent nearly 500 *jihadiyya* to help Emperor Maximilian I of Mexico to suppress Mexican rebels.[4]

Ali's forces captured the slaves in raids conducted between 1830 and 1836 in southern Sudan. But the invasions came at a heavy human cost. In 1832, nearly 1,500 of his 6,000 men force were killed during the expedition to Jabal Ataka. Still Pasha found other ways to increase his army. He hired poachers and their privately armed trading companies operating in the lawless hinterlands of the Blue Nile, Nuba Mountains, and Bahr al Ghazal, to conscript more slaves. He also began imposing a tax on the local people and even required the tribal chiefs to surrender one of their own people as a slave. In time, the policies would help sustain the slave army and the desire of the *jihadiyya* to fight throughout much of the mid-nineteenth century.

Despite their prevalence, however, little is actually known of the *jihadiyya*. It is unclear just how many *jihadiyya* existed at any one time during the year. Estimates range from 5,000 to 9,000.[5] Their roles also tended to vary from regiment to regiment. When they were not fighting or preparing for battle, the *jihadiyya* were forced into menial labor, putting the army at increased risk. The suffering made them eager to fight, but also less loyal and reliable. The question of why the Ottomans would rely on these fighters was never clear. As it turned out, they had become indispensable, dispensable fighters.[6]

During much of the Turkiyyah period, the slave trade increased to meet the rising demand for ivory. The rising demand for slave labor in turn fueled a growing Arab merchant class[7] that profited from the transport of heavy ivory downstream (along the Nile) to the Red Sea.[8] As Richard Gray observed, "it was estimated that about ten to twelve thousand slaves were annually imported into Egypt; a Frenchman was reported to be shipping whole boatloads down the Nile."[9] It also led Abbas Pasha (1849–1853) and Mohamed Said Pasha Said (1854–1863) to conscript more slave soldiers, which increased the size of their armies from 18,000 to 27,000 men. The British reacted to the increase by extending its trade routes in Ottoman Egypt and Sudan. The Ottoman rulers, however, sought to play down the need for resistance to Britain's growing influence. Arakil Bey al-Armani, who was appointed by Christian Armenians to serve as Governor of Khartoum and Sennar, called for toleration of all Christians. The move helped ease political tensions between the Ottomans and the British, while also offending many Muslims. By the 1860s, Armani had appointed several European Christians to high offices in Sudan and ultimately introduced Christianity to many non-Muslim Africans in Sudan.

After Ismail Pasha (1863–1879) succeeded Armani, there was a renewed effort to abolish slavery. Ismail had modernized Egypt and Sudan by constructing new railroads, river steamers, telegraph networks, and a versatile (modern) army. His modernization plan was based on streamlining service and delivery

18 SOUTH SUDAN'S FATEFUL STRUGGLE

through specialized labor and efficient production. And it soon rendered slavery inefficient,[10] making the *jihadiyya* increasingly dispensable and burdensome. Nonetheless, Ismail's openness to change was a welcome trend that appeared to stem largely from his Sufist beliefs or mystical and gnostic devotion to life and the inspiration this devotion created to incorporate Christian customs into Islam. But it also placed him at odds with Salafism, the traditional religious clergy of Turco-Egyptian administration that adhered to a strict orthodox interpretation of Islam and treated such incorporation as an act of heresy. Sufism would eventually help drive the expansion of the Ottoman Empire in the mid-nineteenth century.

However, in tolerating native customs, Ismail was able to better control local affairs and to collaborate more closely with Western states to bring an end to the slave trade. In 1874, he appointed Charles Gordon as Governor of Equatoria to help accomplish this moral task. Gordon had served as British Ambassador to Sudan and became well versed in the ways of Sudanese life. He was convinced that in inspiring the natives to convert to Christianity, he was doing God's work. But he was neither a righteous proselytizer nor bigot. In fact, he was one of the few British officials who insisted on protecting the rights and needs of the natives while openly encouraging them to abandon their animism, the belief in the spiritual presence of animate objects. As a strong supporter of the Anti-Slavery Society—an evangelical Christian group stationed in London—he had dedicated his life to ending slavery.

Much of Gordon's work was inspired by the earlier efforts of the Roman Catholic missionaries to spread Christianity to South Sudan. Having arrived in Sudan in 1842, the missionaries set up hospitals and schools to aid the sick. By the late 1850s, the Catholic Church had established its first mission in Gondokoro and expanded its system of schools. But after several missionaries died from sicknesses, Pope Pius IX replaced the order with Franciscans, and in 1864, closed down the mission. It would take another 30 years before the Catholic Church returned to Sudan. In the meantime, evangelicals from the Presbyterian and Anglican churches would begin to pour into Sudan, determined to civilize and save the souls of the "savages."

The spread of Christianity and British rule spurred a growing Islamic revival in the Sudan in the early 1880s. This was inspired by Muhammad Ahmad bin Abdullah (later Muhammed al-Mahdi), a Muslim cleric and Dongalawi Sufi, who advocated for a renewal of the Islamic faith in Sudan. Ahmad stressed unity and spiritual purity—tenets that attracted Muslims who had grown disenchanted with Salafism's orthodox school of thought. Ahmad's jihadist movement—which many have considered as the inspiration for Sudan's nationalist movement—drew together native fighters to defend Sudan's Muslim faith from foreign infidels. Ahmad would eventually declare himself as the "al-Mahdi"

(The redeemer of faith) and announce to Sudanese leaders in northern Sudan of the "Expected Mahdi."[11] In early 1882, the Mahdi's army scored its greatest victory: it defeated a 7,100 British force in the city of Al Ubayyid and captured the towns of Sheikan and Darfur.

But his early successes barely rankled the British. Britain, it seemed, was more concerned with France's penetration into Ethiopia and the threat this posed to its trade route from Egypt to India. To outflank France, Britain made the decision to occupy Egypt in the summer of 1882, a decision based on the financial instability of Egypt and the recent mutiny by Egyptian troops that left several British soldiers dead. Britain had managed to position itself against both the Mahdi and France to launch an expedition to drive out the Mahdi from Sudan. The force was headed by Colonel William Hicks, a retired officer from the Indian army who tried to assure officials that the soldiers were prepared to fight. However, the fighters were in fact ill-equipped and lacked the necessary discipline to hold back the Mahdi's army. In November 1883, Mahdist forces easily defeated Hick's army at Shaykan, a city located just south of El Obeid. The defeat forced Britain to reinforce their military presence in the region and to take further control over the economic affairs of the Egyptian government.

To bolster its economic influence over the region, Britain sent in several financial advisors to privatize the economy and to open up Egypt's markets. Politically, the advisors recommended that the Sudanese be granted autonomy or self-government. They reasoned that Britain could better maintain its trade routes by allowing the appointed leaders to peacefully administer local affairs. The problem, however, was that Britain confronted an overzealous force that was capable of overwhelming its better trained force. In early 1884, Britain ordered Gordon to withdraw his troops from its southern garrisons. Later that year, the Mahdi arrived at the town of Omdurman, where he set up his headquarters. Britain meanwhile attempted to shore up its forces in Khartoum to force the Mahdi to act. Fortunately for the Mahdi, the dry season had left parts of the Nile exposed, which allowed his forces to traverse the exposed ground and to attack the walls of Khartoum. In the early hours of January 26, 1885, Mahdist forces destroyed the British/Egyptian garrison, killing Gordon and reducing much of Khartoum to rubble.

The Mahdi then proceeded to erect a new state, the Mahdiyya (Mahdist State), a theocracy based on sharia law and the Mahdi's own precepts. Although the Mahdi died six months later, the new Mahdist state by this time had become self-functioning. Administered by a circle of clerics, it extended as far west as Darfur, and stretched from Kassala in the east to the Sudd in the South. It also introduced centralized rule but remained fractured and unable to control the periphery in the east and along its southern borders, where there was a large non-Muslim population. In order to maintain stability along the periphery, Abdallahi

20 SOUTH SUDAN'S FATEFUL STRUGGLE

ibn Muhammad, the new Khalifa (and successor to the Mahdi), increased the state's military power. But the action soon backfired when several non-Muslims actively resisted the troops. The protests weakened the Khalifa, who began to look for a regional ally (such as Ethiopia) to protect the regime against foreign attacks. After he failed to secure one, he made the rash decision to invade Egypt in 1898.

The British, however, were ready this time. Along with Egyptian troops, they quickly overran the Mahdist forces in the North and began to head south towards the Sudan, marking the beginning of the end of the Mahdist state. Britain, which had initially treated the Mahdist state as a buffer against the regional influence of French and Belgium, could no longer depend on it to hold off the French and Belgians. It was simply too fragile and unstable. Besides, Britain had rapidly improved its logistics and military superiority, which put it in a position to overwhelm the Mahdist army. Vengeance still motivated the British, to be sure. But it was not a central driving factor. Rather, it was Britain's fear that Mahdist rule threatened to cut off key access points of its trade route to parts of Africa and Asia.[12]

Still, as vulnerable as the Mahdist state was, it had managed for a time to keep the British at bay, which had become a source of pride for Islamists and future Sudanese and Egyptian nationalists.[13] Mahdist rule was also instrumental in reinforcing Britain's racist attitudes of the negro South. The Arabs of course were of lighter skin, members of the Ottoman civilization, which the British treated as peripheral or semi-civilized.[14] To be fully civilized in this case was to meet so-called "civilization standards." Not surprisingly, only European states—which formed the "Family of Nations"—were deemed as civilized states.[15] This was not to say that Arab Muslims remained incapable of forming their own civilized state, but rather that more time and guidance by Western countries was needed to achieve this full-fledged status.[16] The British, like other European countries, then, were convinced that they had a moral responsibility, even a sanctified right, to develop uncivilized peoples by forcibly educating them about British civil law, manners, values, and beliefs. Yet it was a self-proclaimed responsibility that also informed British racial and moral superiority and that worked in conjunction with British civic imperialism to justify colonialization.

The Berlin Conference (1885) provided the legal framework for this dual process. It was organized by Otto Von Bismarck and attended by 14 European powers (including Britain), and instituted a so-called spheres of influence that was designed to advance Europe's economic interests and essentially eliminate all forms of self-governance and self-determination of the African peoples. In stripping the African peoples of their naturalized rights, the 14 powers had agreed to their self-declared right to rule on behalf of the African people. In some cases, such rule was interpreted as an unfettered tool to exploit and abuse the

local population. For example, in the Free State of the Congo, which Leopold II, the ruler of Belgium, had established, it became a license to torture and kill the native peoples.[17] The legalized abuse stemmed from the self-serving nature of the legal framework, which had enabled European countries to profit from their extended sphere of influence in many parts of Africa, often at a great human cost to the African peoples. The General Act of the agreement, for instance, stipulated the conditions for annexing lands and expanding trade on the African continent, while also obligating all signatories to end slavery and the slave trade. But in according the European countries a special responsibility to govern the African peoples, the agreement drew up unclear legal boundaries, which only served to reinforce the Europeans' self-proclaimed control over these peoples' political destiny.

Under the principle of effective occupation, for example, all European countries acquired rights to govern an area through prearranged treaties.[18] Yet there were no clear guidelines about how European countries would administer local affairs, or whether, for instance, direct administration was needed. That of course was left up to the colonizing country. In Britain's case, administrative policy came to symptomize the benign neglect of the population living in the southern region of Sudan. The primary goal of annexation, as mentioned earlier, was to provide a buffer against Belgium's and France's threat to its economic influence in the region. However, when this geopolitical threat waned in the 1890s, Britain undertook a far more systematic effort to administer colonial rule over the less-developed Arabs in the North and the natives in the South.

A crucial moral pillar of its colonial rule was the so-called civilizing process. As Norbert Elias explains of the process: "it reflected how individuals learned to impose their own virtues through the interdependent and immanent regularities of society and self-restraint."[19] "The denser the web of interdependence becomes," he wrote, "the larger the social spaces over which this network extends and which become integrated into functional or institutional units—the more threatened is the social existence of the individual who gives way to spontaneous impulses and emotions."[20] Britain's social advantage in this respect reflected the growing influence of Christian evangelicalism in the region. Their religious mission of civilizing the uncivilized involved teaching the natives to read the Bible in English and making them familiar with Western (or British) customs. It effectively forced the natives to renounce their traditional customs, which ultimately helped to shore up Britain's economic and political control over the region.

The civilizing mission, it turned out, was good for business. For Cecile Rhodes, the British mining pioneer, this meant engineering the "Cape to Cairo" railway which would link South and East Africa and suppress any native revolts that could obstruct this trade route. In this respect, Britain's defeat of the Mahdist state was as much a commercial as it was a long-term geopolitical victory. The

22 SOUTH SUDAN'S FATEFUL STRUGGLE

final venture began in 1895, when Horatio Kitchener was put in charge of the Anglo-Egyptian Nile Expeditionary Force consisting of approximately 25,600 troops. British troops made up a third of the force, which used large steamers to travel the Nile while receiving the bulk of its supplies by rail.[21] When the force finally reached the outskirts of Omdurman in September 1898, it used its superior military equipment to rout the Mahdi and to reclaim Sudan.[22]

The decisive victory provided crucial momentum for the British to move further up the Nile. Belgium a feared the growing British threat, and consequently entered into alliances with the Aazande prince, Raf I, and the Feroge tribal chief. Belgium was hoping to advance its interests in the Bahr al Ghazal watershed, but it failed in the end to achieve any lasting gains.[23] Meanwhile, further down the river, the British ran into a French force led by Jean Baptiste Marchand, who had advanced up the Upper Nile region to declare the area around Fashoda a French protectorate (the area lied directly south of the Mahdist-controlled area of Sudan). Kitchener's 1,500-man army had by now moved upstream to battle the Mahdi's army. This caught the French off-guard and immediately raised the political stakes for France, which entered into heated negotiations with the British to resolve the crisis. But after a standoff in which both sides laid claim to the area, the French eventually backed down, fearing that war with Britain would undermine its ability to counter German aggression in other parts of Africa. The two countries would never again threaten the other with war. And Britain would eventually succeed in driving out the French from the Nile Basin to take full control of Sudan.

Pacification and Chiefdom

Having faced down its competitors, Britain entered into an agreement with Egypt to exercise shared control of the region. The 1899 Anglo-Egyptian Condominium represented a hybrid framework of governance that ended Britain's military rule and provided the legal basis for its continued military occupation of Egypt and colonial rule in the region. Yet at its core, it remained an unequal partnership between Britain and Egypt. Britain, in fact, still maintained de facto control over the affairs of Egypt and Sudan, while Egypt was limited to administering local government. Under these terms, Britain still retained the right to rule by conquest—a right that effectively entitled it to impose military rule (where needed) to resolve local disputes and to pacify the local population. Specifically, the Condominium stipulated that "the supreme military and civil command in Sudan shall be vested in one officer, termed the Governor-General of Sudan. He shall be appointed by Khedival Decree on the recommendation of Her Britannic Majesty's Government and shall be removed only by Khedival

SLAVE SOLDIERS, BRITISH COLONIAL RULE, AND ARMED RESISTANCE   23

Decree with the consent of Her Britannic Majesty's Government."[24] Britain, in other words, possessed veto power over most of Egypt's decision-making and administrative affairs. This was clearly not the civic constraint Egypt had bargained for, despite Britain's pledges to carry out its duties of civil administration.[25]

Britain's veto power was a key feature of its colonial rule. By retaining its monopoly over state violence, it could still use its military superiority to govern. Unlike Muhammad Ali's vision of a unified Egyptian regime spanning the upper Nile (or Egypt and Sudan), Britain's plan for unified rule relied on military strategies and tactics to govern the people and to uphold law and order, particularly during the early years of the Condominium (1899–1920). It was a plan based on three aims: (1) to project fear in the local population of its military presence, (2) to subjugate Egyptian authority to British rule, and (3) to keep the country divided politically so that it could govern through its military power, that is, separating religious groups geopolitically. Britain thus hoped to govern and control unrest by modernizing and pacifying the population.

The idea was to eventually transition Sudan from military to civic rule. But this also required cooperation by the Egyptians and a fair distribution of resources. Britain struggled to meet both conditions. In fact, inequality worsened in these early years, as Britain chose to invest more in the North than in the South. This had as much to do with its preference for modernizing the North as it did with its racial bias against the negroes in the South. The South Sudanese in their view were more intractable and ill-equipped to lead. What this view overlooked, however, was the South Sudanese's collective self-determination. Indeed, the South Sudanese had already liberated themselves from Mahdist rule, long before the arrival of the British forces. Moreover, they never treated the Anglo-Egyptian army as liberators. Most South Sudanese, in fact, saw the Anglo-Egyptian army as foreign invaders—an external force that would never look after and represent their interests. It was little wonder, then, that Britain focused most, if not all, its energies on investing in the North's educational and legal system (i.e., civil procedure, health system, and infrastructure) in much the same way it did in British India. For unlike the primitive, pagan Africans in the South, the Arabs, in the minds of British officials, were largely civilized and exuded civic restraint. Having migrated to Sudan from Egypt, the Arabs had engaged in commerce and formed a middle-class identity in the early modern period. Arabic, by this time, had become the language of commerce and power and allowed the Arabs to assert their customs over the negro natives in South Sudan. The Arabs were also slaves as well as slaveowners, something that the British downplayed by treating the Arabs as a homogeneous people who were superior to the black natives in the South. The British in this sense had learned, as Mahmood Mamdani argues, to distinguish between settler (the Arabs) and native (negro southerners) to justify self-governance in accordance with civil and procedural law.[26] The Arabs in

24 SOUTH SUDAN'S FATEFUL STRUGGLE

this case were expected to show restraint as administrators of civil law in the North, while the tribal chiefs were counted on to support British administrators through the application of customary law in the South.[27] Civil law was, in short, regarded as a more advanced form of law than customary law, which was based on tribal custom. The British believed that administering it could extend their civic influence and discourage Egyptian resistance, even though such civic control ensured the second-class citizenship of the Egyptians.

In the South, such civic control was largely absent. Here, pacification was the prevailing policy that enabled the British to impose their will on tribal groups by appointing a provincial governor whose authority relied on military patrols (comprised principally of Egyptian troops) to govern the South. The government by patrol collected taxes on the exchange of goods, such as animals and transport, and enforced the law against slavery and the slave trade. In 1902, the first garrisons of the Anglo-Egyptian army were responsible for patrolling vast swaths of land with little or no infrastructure. Most of the commerce was conducted on the Nile, which required vessels to be cleaned regularly for debris and sediment. The patrols' main task was to protect British and Egyptian vessels against attacks to ensure the flow of goods. Given the vast stretches of land, the British left the administration of local affairs largely to the tribal leaders, who acted as the sole authority and could at any time of crisis, call on the patrols for assistance. In this way, the British depended on the tribal chiefs' legitimacy—which derived from their roles as judges of tribal laws and their longstanding authority to resolve conflicts involving cattle ownership, marriage, and land disputes.

Still, the relationship between tribal leaders and patrols remained fraught. Many tribal authorities opposed Britain's government by patrol. The Shilluks, for instance, had their own system of hierarchical government and were able to expand their kingdom in the Upper Nile, while the Azande occupied large swaths of the hinterland.[28] For them, government by patrol was always about the British maintaining an imposing presence in the region to keep the diverse number of ethnic groups in check. As the largest two groups, the Nuer and Dinka made up nearly 50 percent of the population and consisted of numerous subclans that in the case of the Nuer, included Jikany, Lou, and Nyuong. By engaging these and other tribal groups in the region on a strictly limited basis, the administrative patrols represented Britain's profound detachment from its colonialized, tribal subjects.

"Tribe," it should be noted, referred to the static and primordial qualities of a group unfit to govern itself democratically. Tribes could neither evolve nor compete for resources like civilized peoples, but merely survived off the land.[29] The concept emerged from a series of academic studies on native behavior and custom in the first half of the twentieth century, which used tropes and binary terms to analyze the behavior of ethnic communities (i.e., docile and not docile).

Edward Evans-Prichard, the British anthropologist, concluded that the Nuer's egalitarian traits and resistance to centralized rule made them less fit to rule than their Dinka competitors. The Lou Nuer, it turned out, were especially resistant to patrols and British indirect rule. The British interpreted this as a weakness, or as a stubborn unwillingness to learn and behave properly, even though the trait reflected their ability to scatter and flee quickly into the bush. Naturally, the British feared that legitimizing customary beliefs would only make them appear weak and that this would possibly limit their ability to pacify the population. So instead of cultivating relations with the tribes, they adopted divisive strategies for playing one tribe off of another.[30] They had in effect weaponized tribal identity by casting negative light on tribal strengths. For them, the Nuer's resistance and egalitarian trait revealed an irrational impulsiveness, while the Dinka's docility was seen as a developed disposition. Through this inverted binary logic, they had learned to maintain tribal (dis-)order.

But the overt prejudice underlying government by patrol also introduced practical problems of managing the population. First, the patrols provoked deep resentment among the villagers, not only because of restrictions placed on their way of life, but also for unfairly aiding enemy tribes. In fact, the resentment concerning such brutal mistreatment spurred revenge attacks, with one of the first and more notorious attacks occurring in 1902, when Myang Mathiang, the leader of the Agar Dinka, attacked government soldiers for restricting their assistance to the Dinka, The Shab-e Field force was eventually sent in to hunt down Mathiang, but in their pursuit of Mathiang, it burned down homes, killed several hundred villagers, and stole hundreds of cattle. In another case, the patrols failed to stop cattle raiding and interethnic violence. When the Murle, for example, attacked the Bor Dinka in 1906, the "Beir Patrol" was sent in to restore order. Yet, instead of bringing peace and security to the area, it killed the Murle drum-chief, spurring the Murle to carry out revenge attacks against the government in 1909–1910.[31]

Second, Britain's land policy, which established new provincial boundaries and districts to settle land disputes between ethnic groups, failed to stem the interethnic violence caused by cattle raiding, particularly among the Murle and Bor Dinka in the Bahr al Ghazal area. This not only undermined expectations of non-partisan rule but also limited enforcement in the area.[32] To make matters worse, the patrols often failed to operate as a neutral force, or refrain from entering into alliances with favored ethnic groups. Some Dinka chiefs tended to see the patrols as allies whose military support was crucial for defending against attacks by the Nuer, Shilluk, and Murle. However, this was more the exception than norm. A majority of tribes distrusted and despised the patrols, which over the years, had indiscriminately killed innocent victims, burned down homes and villages, and forcibly removed the chief and other tribal authorities who

26 SOUTH SUDAN'S FATEFUL STRUGGLE

had failed to carry out their administrative duties, that is, paying taxes. Not surprisingly, there were frequent violent uprisings in southern villages patrolled by British troops. The Aklab Dinka, for example, killed 3,000 policemen in October 1919, leading to the wholesale destruction of villages, the taking of cattle, and the patrols' capture of the leader of the resistance, Kon Anok.[33]

Third, pacification provoked the leaders to engage in immoral and negligent behavior. Britain's policy of rewarding loyalty encouraged some tribal leaders to summon British patrols to defend against outside attacks and internal resistance.[34] The chiefs then used the patrols to bolster their authority and to divert attention away from their corruption (e.g., stealing). Rather than instilling a sense of law and order, the patrols had demoralized and destabilized many tribal communities.

Finally, the patrols' presence did little to root out what was left of the *jihadiyya* and other informal networks of slavery and slave trading. If anything, their cruel attacks had created the conditions for more lawlessness, violence, and enslavement. This was due in large part to the lack of manpower and expertise to administer order. The patrols therefore had to rely on divisive and inhumane tactics to project fear and maintain order in the South—which only made the tribes more violent and warlike. Yet this was the price of Britain's disengaged and militaristic rule in the South and its dictatorial modernization of the North, where organized resistance would eventually emerge to threaten its colonial rule and global hegemony.

The Challenge of Indirect Rule

In 1919, Britain, along with 31 other countries, negotiated the terms of the League of Nations, including its mandate to transfer former Ottoman Empire lands to one of the four allied powers, namely, Britain, France, Italy, and the United States. The mandate system represented a pragmatic attempt to civilize and develop the local population through democratic self-rule and cultural empowerment. To make it work, though, League officials needed the local population to cooperate with its demands for political and land reform. Yet in some mandated areas and colonies, the local population had already begun to resist their rulers. At the negotiations of the League of Nations, for instance, Britain faced increasing resistance by a vocal Wafd Party delegation. Led by the Saad Zaghlul, a charismatic visionary of Egyptian nationalism, the Wafd Party consisted of Egyptian nationalists who had been inspired by the Ottoman sultan's declaration of *jihad* against English speaking countries—a Fatwa issued on February 1, 1914. The party demanded an end to British rule in Egypt and called for Egyptian independence from Britain. By May 1919, their calls

to action had led to mass demonstrations on the streets of Cairo, resulting in approximately 800 deaths and the creation of the Milner Commission to resolve the crisis.[35] The commission recommended that Britain relinquish the protectorate and enter into a treaty with Egypt. But after the British Parliament failed to reach consensus on the treaty, Lord Alenby, the High Commissioner, unilaterally declared Egypt's independence on February 28, 1922 and officially recognized the new Kingdom of Egypt. The Egyptians were still allowed to run their affairs on a national level, but their liberation from British influence was by no means complete. Britain still exercised control over the Suez Canal Zone and other ports where they maintained a small military force that provided protection of foreigners. In addition, the Egyptian military was not allowed to exercise jurisdiction over Sudan.[36]

Britain focused most of its attention on governing Sudan. It now worked more closely with Sudanese authorities—who had established the Sudan Defense Forces (SDF)—to tighten its control over the South. By 1922, it adopted a stricter version of the "Closed District Ordinance" to shore up its rule in South Sudan. The Closed District Ordinance was meant to curtail the spread of Islam and Arabic and, through the teachings of Christian missionaries, to promote the use of English in schools. For Christian missionaries, it was now easier to enter southern Sudan. Their increasing numbers would eventually create what turned out to be a new fault line: the Tenth Parallel dividing Islam and Christianity in Sudan and restricting foreign influences.[37] The Tenth Parallel was the ignominious, geographic marker of Britain's willful neglect of South Sudan and its people.[38] Although Christian missionaries could enter the South freely, they were restricted from migrating to northern Sudan.

The restriction was part of Britain's plan to govern Sudan as two separate entities: one that was Arabic and practiced Islam; the other that was English speaking and mostly Christianized. Just as it had done in Egypt in the early twentieth century, Britain devoted more of its resources to modernizing the North at the expense of the South. The modernization plan, however, ended up fueling nationalist sentiment in the mostly Arab North by inspiring more northern Sudanese intellectuals to express kinship with their liberated Arab brethren and nationalists in Egypt. The northern Sudanese nationalists began to work with Egyptian nationalists to resist British rule and to carve out a new Sudanese nationalist identity. At the same time, the vast majority of South Sudanese were never brought into this nationalist movement. They were effectively excluded from Sudanese nationalism and remained divided among themselves, afflicted by what some called a 'Southern identity complex' that described how they had learned to internalize their oppression and backwardness.[39] Many South Sudanese simply refused to take part in any nationalist movement, or to participate in the British-controlled Sudanese government.

28   SOUTH SUDAN'S FATEFUL STRUGGLE

By 1923, the northern Sudanese had organized their own anticolonial resistance movement. Calling it the "White Flag League," it was founded by the southern military officers, Lieutenant Ali Abdullatif and Abdulah Khalil, who called for Sudanese independence from Britain as well as unity with Egypt. Under the command of First Lieutenant Abdul Fadil Alma, the League hatched its plan for an insurrection in early 1924. But after the British learned about the plan, they quickly put an end to it by blowing up the garrison where the White Flag soldiers were stationed. Despite this setback, the White Flag League had raised awareness of the oppression of British colonial rule in Sudan and had managed to justify the need to reestablish ties with the newly independent, client state of Egypt. Their members had effectively drawn on their training in British universities to wage their struggle against the British and their colonized pawns. In *Beyond a Boundary*, C. L. R. James wrote that "Reactionaries would hold up the English as models far above us. [But] the incipient nationalists armed themselves with bombs for debunking. In all the drumming and fifing done to England, I could distinguish no order."[40] Anticolonialism was thus a movement borne from the collective awareness of ending colonial oppression. Yet in the South, the people were simply too undeveloped and disorganized to resist such oppression.

Britain's idea all along was to keep the South Sudanese permanently divided against themselves and by extension, against the northern Arabs. As such, their plan was to prevent the South Sudanese from uniting with the North and rising up against the British. It was essential for the British, then, to keep the South unequal and undeveloped if it wished to suppress nationalist sentiment in the South. Their "southern policy," for example, suggested that the British greatly feared the South's development. However, this raised the question of whether the British were in fact better off underdeveloping the South by turning it into a neglected Christianized region to counter the North. The South Sudanese, after all, shared little affinity with the mostly Muslim North and for that reason, were unlikely to join the Sudanese nationalists to resist British oppression. As Ann Mosely Lesch writes, the British had adopted a "policy that would have made sense if it had led to the separation of the South from the North. . . . turning it into an independent state or attaching it to a neighboring African country."[41] Britain, however, was content to create two permanent, irreconcilable entities: a modernized North with a national identity rooted in the Islamic nation; and a southern identity divided along tribal lines and weighed down by an inferiority complex.

In the end, Britain's divisive approach created deep-seated southern grievances against the North. To make matters worse, the Sudanese nationalists showed few signs of sympathizing with the southerners. If anything, their distrust and disrespect of the South Sudanese had fueled further resentment in the South Sudanese toward the northern Sudanese. It could also be argued that the British derived

SLAVE SOLDIERS, BRITISH COLONIAL RULE, AND ARMED RESISTANCE   29

little strategic advantage from dividing the two Sudans. In the eyes of British Lord Cromer and Governor-General Sir Reginal Wingate, the policy not only failed to offer a strategic buffer against Islamic political forces but increased the social gap between the largely Muslim North and Christian South. In its attempts to suppress anticolonial nationalist resistance, Britain had managed to create the conditions for two nationalist uprisings.

The Southern Policy

Britain therefore needed a more flexible policy to maintain order. One way it did this was to broaden the mission and reach of the Anglo-Egyptian army. The newly established SDF, for example, led to the appointment of Sudanese officers and soldiers, and created an officer academy located in Omdurman, a town in Sudan.[42] The majority of Sudanese officers came from the North, but some were recruited from the South.[43] The SDF battalion consisted of four major army corps: The Eastern Arab Corps in Kasala, the Western Arab Corps in Darfur, the Camel Corps in Kordofan, and the Equatoria Corps or Southern Corps that oversaw three southern provinces. Many of the South Sudanese soldiers would end up serving in the Equatoria Corps, which helped reinforce indigenous rule in the South. The new SDF became an instrumental part of "The Southern Policy" in which the British sought to promote indirect rule.

Britain's Southern Policy was the vision of Harold MacMichael, a colonial administrator. His 1930 memorandum on "The Southern Policy" assured natives that the Governors and District Chiefs (DCs) would assume a less invasive role in the administration of local affairs, and that the tribal authorities would in turn be entrusted with greater power to administer their local affairs. The memorandum stated that "the policy of the Government in the Southern Sudan was to build up a series of self-contained racial and tribal units with structure and organization based, to whatever extent, on the customs requirements of equity and good government of indigenous customs, tribal usage, and beliefs."[44] MacMichael assumed that all the ethnic groups in Sudan came from three groups: Negro, Hamitic Berber, and Arab. The plan was to show the evolution of division among these groups into separate groups in order to understand the truth of racial relations in Sudan. On a practical level, MacMichael wanted a new system to administer land rights, one that could lay the procedures for local officials to uphold the rights. The chiefs would have the final say on disputes, even though their authority would remain subordinate to the British.

To carry out the Southern Policy, the British used the census to classify the indigenous groups. The 1929 census, for instance, inserted "tribe" into categories

30   SOUTH SUDAN'S FATEFUL STRUGGLE

of "groups of tribes" and "races" and required members to identify their native tribe.[45] British officials used these categories to justify the number of administrative units. The result, however, was the creation of more administrative units than actual tribes. As Mahmood Mamdani points out:

> What happened was that colonial officials created new administrative divisions and it was these, not any native practice, that constituted tribes. When residents were asked to name their tribe, they named their native authority. Residents deemed native understood that it was through tribe and tribe alone that they legitimately organize to make demands from the native state.[46]

Under indirect rule, the chiefs were expected to maintain order. Some British officials were concerned about the lack of oversight over the chiefs, including MacMichael himself, who feared that they would abuse their authority by oppressing their people and attacking other tribes in an attempt to gain favor with their people. His concern was that the British had no actual way to prevent a rogue chief from potentially destabilizing intertribal relations. Still, MacMichael believed that such destabilization was unlikely, given that the British controlled intertribal relations and that the native peoples feared British authority more than their own. More importantly, governing through chiefly power provided an important advantage for the British: a secular means of countering the extremism of Islamic nationalist movements. Under its Southern Policy, Britain was able to isolate native groups by installing systems of governance that could keep them apart.

Yet with little oversight of these systems, the chiefs ended up ignoring the rules and regulations and depending more on customary law to settle disputes. They were becoming, in effect, more insulated from the tribal communities that they had communicated with over many years. Tribal authorities soon found themselves in an increasingly difficult predicament. While Britain's Southern Policy had empowered them, it also undermined their ability to settle their disputes with other tribal communities. The fact was that only the British possessed the resources to settle these disputes. Accordingly, the chiefs confronted a reluctant hegemon, a power unwilling to promote intergroup solidarity. A fine line thus emerged between inter-group and intra-group conflict. Toeing it meant patching differences among the sub-clans while not inciting other ethnic groups. The Nilotic Dinka and Nuer, for instance, increasingly relied on largely ceremonial chiefs to work across the "segmentary lineages" (the tribal division of kin groups) and intercommunal disputes. Calling on British forces was always an option of last resort for tribal leaders.

Britain's neglect of the region meant that other actors had to play a more direct and concerted role in addressing the personal grievances (of tribal members

against their leaders) that threatened intratribal stability. Christian missionaries took up this role by establishing several small biblical schools to educate the South Sudanese. They did so under what was called "The Sphere System," which required missionaries to educate natives peoples in certain areas of the southern region. It was a system that not surprisingly lacked public scrutiny. In fact, only two inspectors of education had been assigned to oversee missionary work and to assist evangelicals' and Catholic missionaries' efforts to convert the natives. The underfunded and understaffed system reflected Britain's half-hearted plan to educate the native population and to supplant native customs, beliefs, and language.[47] With few resources devoted to public schooling, public education lagged far behind private schooling, leaving a vast majority of South Sudanese illiterate and unable to write in English.

By 1939, the public-private gap in education prompted Christopher Cox, the Governor-General, to require Catholics and Protestants to operate with more public transparency.[48] Pressure thus mounted on British authorities to secularize education and to begin constructing more primary public schools in the South in hopes of integrating the educational system into one administrative unit in Bar al Ghazal and Equatoria. By now, the education gap between the North and South had widened. The British government had invested nearly five times more in the schools in the North than in the South. In addition, it had yet to establish a single government school in the South. In fact, only 2,700 boys and 635 girls attended secondary school in 1939; just 2,020 boys were enrolled at intermediate school.[49]

The question, however, was why the lackluster effort to educate the native population of South Sudan? Was it not in Britain's geopolitical interest to "civilize" the South Sudanese by educating them? Why had the British renounced such a fundamental duty to develop the native population? In the minds of many British officials, the South Sudanese were simply too savage to benefit from British assistance. MacMichael and George Stewart Symes, the Governor-General of Sudan, considered southerners as either untamed, or part of what Symes called "monkeydom." There was, one could argue, a dark side of British decency, that is, a sensibility grounded in kindness and moderation, which had caused the British to detach themselves even further from the South Sudanese. The British, it turned out, did not wish to bring themselves to the level of primitive tribes by recognizing the intrinsic value of their "tribal lore . . . handicrafts . . . native music, animal husbandry."[50]

By the late 1930s, one could see the handwriting on the wall. "The South," as Robert Collins writes, "had largely disappeared as an instrument of Native Administration, not by any fiat issued by Khartoum, but from the realities on the ground that relentlessly undermined it."[51] Britain for its part never felt guilty about neglecting the South. The natives after all were either too lazy or

32   SOUTH SUDAN'S FATEFUL STRUGGLE

inherently incapable of development. But after Symes was replaced by Sir Hubert Huddleston in 1940, the South would enter into an even darker period of near complete isolation. The Great Depression and World War II had caused Britain to redistribute more of its resources to the North, leaving South Sudan with no public secondary school; only a few primary schools that predominantly focused on tribal lore and the rules of good character. So great was the redistribution that British officials began to favor a new policy of forcibly integrating the South with the North rather than dividing them for strategic reasons. As Sir James Robertson, the British Civil Secretary, declared in 1947: "It has begun to be clear, I think, that the Southern Sudan, by its history and by the accidents of geography, river transport, and so on, must turn more to the North rather than to Uganda and Congo."[52]

These new policy considerations reflected the emerging international focus on decolonization after World War II. The newly created UN General Assembly took up the issue of decolonization in 1947. The question was whether to recognize a colonized people's right to self-determination.[53] Could, in other words, self-determination be considered a universal right of all oppressed colonized peoples? It was a question that pitted Soviet bloc states in the UN General Assembly—that hoped to adopt a collective right of self-determination— against Western countries which, fearing the implications of colonial unrest, had tried to formulate the concept as an individual human right. As this UN initiative unfolded, officials assembled in Juba to discuss self-rule in the South. Here they managed to agree on the creation of a new Sudanese national parliament with district councils, but were unable to reach consensus on a measure to unite the administrative elite and the tribal chiefs in the South. The talks eventually provided a framework for two successive five-year plans (1947–1951, 1951–1956) that sought to develop the region and to close the social equality gap between the South and the North. The first five-year plan, for example, created the funds to establish the South's first secondary school in Rumbek and more elementary schools for boys and girls. Missionary schools, however, still outnumbered government-sponsored elementary schools, which seemed to explain the increasing conversion rate of the South Sudanese to Christianity.[54] They remained important largely because of their role in detribalizing society and instilling humility and compassion. The British had counted on them to discourage any South Sudanese from joining the northern nationalists to resist British rule. In this way, they remained an important tool for neutralizing resistance against their tribal leaders.

But in reality, there was little the British could do to repress Sudanese nationalist sentiment. By the late 1940s, Sudanese nationalists had emerged into a well-organized movement that influenced the affairs of the Sudanese government run

by the Sudanese and the British. The Sudanese state's primary goal at this time was addressing Britain's refusal to discuss Sudanese sovereignty or self-government within the Condominium. To work toward the goal, it had consciously aligned itself with the Egyptian government, in particular with its demands to remove all remaining British troops stationed in Egypt and to gain full control over Sudan, where the Sudanese nationalists hoped to work with the Egyptian government to win its full-fledged sovereignty. The demands stemmed from the shortcomings of the Anglo-Egyptian Treaty of 1936, which required the British to withdraw almost all British troops from Egypt, except for the Suez Canal Zone where 10,000 soldiers remained. Moreover, the treaty made no reference to Egyptian sovereignty in Sudan—a point not lost on the Sudanese who demanded more democratic self-rule.

The Sudan Legislative Assembly held its first elections in 1948 and formed an Executive Council consisting of seven Sudanese ministers (out of a total of 12). But some of the Egyptian parties objected to the arrangement, insisting that the Assembly was illegitimate; the objectors included the Independent Front, the Socialist Republican Party, and the Ummah Party. The dispute soon led several Sudanese legislators and a British High Court judge to draw up a Statute of Self-Government, which was submitted to the Assembly in May 1952 and eventually confirmed by the British government. More importantly, it finally allowed the Sudanese government to determine how to govern its own affairs with minimal British influence.

The Egyptian government though refused to take up the Sudan question. It insisted that it was entitled to rule over Sudan, a position not shared by much of the public. Many suspected that King Farouk was behind the decision—all in a secretive effort to do the bidding of the British. Eventually, the protestors took to the streets to voice their anger of the government's decision. And in July 1952, the Free Officers Movement, led by Egyptian generals and officers, including Abdul Nasser and Anwar Sadat, staged a coup d'etat against the Egyptian government—finally freeing Egypt of British control (via the 1936 Treaty). The military officers' coup brought to power a new government that called for social justice and forced King Farouk to abdicate his throne. As one of its first actions, it took up the Sudan question by making the self-government agreement more acceptable to all parties.[55] By October, the new Egyptian government entered into negotiations with the Sudanese Independent Front (or independents), the Socialist Republican Party, and the Liberal Party, and brought the unionists into the National Unionist Party (NUP), which had earlier opposed a forced union between the Sudanese and Egyptian governments. Accordingly, they made sure that a new plan would be acceptable to all Sudanese people, and that Britain would not be able to fix the status quo via the Self-Government Act.

34 SOUTH SUDAN'S FATEFUL STRUGGLE

Still, there was the issue of how to preempt Britain's ability to decide the terms of the Statute of Self-Government.[56] One of these terms concerned the inclusion of the Governor-General's special responsibilities of managing the affairs pursuant to the statute. The fear was that Britain would use its administrative power to continue to divide the South and North of Sudan in order to justify its military occupation of the area. Yet the Egyptian government outmaneuvered Britain by addressing the former Egyptian government's grievances stemming from the 1936 treaty and Condominium agreement. The grievances involved the Sudanese government's limited sovereign power and the role of King Farouk, who had maintained cordial relations with Britain in exchange for Britain's providing him protection, should his reign be threatened.[57] But the King's support of Fascism had severely soured his relations with Britain, which failed to come to his aid during the revolutionary coup.

In November 1952, the amendments to the new constitution were placed in the Egyptian Note, a document that officially recognized the Sudanese government as a sovereign entity. Rather than contesting such recognition and delaying negotiations, Britain accepted the amendments in January 1953. A month later, the Anglo-Egyptian Agreement was signed, creating a new legislature and laying the groundwork for the withdrawal of British and Egyptian troops (per the recommendation granted under the Note). The agreement also rescinded parts of the 1952 Constitution that included the office of British Governor General. Sudan's political parties now had three years in which to implement a plan for self-government. And once the British withdrew their forces, as the agreement stipulated, "the Sudanese Armed Forces: should be entrusted with keeping security and public order, and the Governor-General should have no authority over these forces."[58]

In the South, the British had to reassess its legal and political commitments as it prepared to leave Sudan. In particular, it faced the issue of whether the safeguards of self-rule were still needed to protect the South Sudanese, that is, restrictions on the number of southern members in the Legislative Assembly. British officials consulted with South Sudanese intellectuals and political leaders about continued safeguards for their people. Many South Sudanese leaders remained skeptical of the agreement and the new Sudanese government's commitment to develop the South. But in having suffered so long under British colonial rule, the South Sudanese eventually decided to support the Anglo-Egyptian Agreement (and its clause of Sudanese self-determination) and to reject any need for further British safeguards.

The agreement marked an uncertain turning point in the history of South Sudan. British colonial rule had officially ended in the South; however, the South remained severely undeveloped after years of neglect by the British. Moreover, the agreement provided few assurances that the new Sudanese government

would be inclusive or undertake new measures to improve the plight of the South Sudanese. In reflecting on South Sudan's future at this historical juncture, Robert Collins concluded,

> No one in 1954 could undo the introduction of Christianity and English into the South. No one in 1954 could wave the magic wand of economic development to transform the South into a cornucopia of productivity. But in 1954, by heeding the warnings from southern members of the NUP in parliament, by taking into account aspirations, not simply civil service exams, by demonstrating the unity of the nation and honoring lavish election promises, by including all of its participants, North and South, the government could have taken a decisive step unimpeded by the weight of history, elevated by the optimism of a new beginning for Sudan, and within the abilities of men untrammeled by any cosmic forces beyond their control, to include the southern Sudanese in the administration of the new nation.[59]

The agreement also triggered a final wave of Sudanization. In 1954, the Sudanization committee replaced British and Egyptian army and civil service personnel with Sudanese officers. That same year, Sudan held its first parliamentary elections, with the NUP winning a majority of the seats and Isma'il al-Azhari becoming the first prime minister. Al Azhari of course faced many challenges. Perhaps the most crucial was what to do about the South Sudanese' demands for autonomous governance. The Southern Liberal Party, for example, called for expanded autonomy of three districts controlled by the South Sudanese. Although it celebrated the end of condominium politics and the official separation of secular government and missionary schools, it remained wary of the new Sudanese government. It had already begun to strategize against the government by pressing for the union of Sudanese and Egyptian governments, which it hoped would establish a buffer between a potentially hostile northern government and the South Sudanese. Its main fear was that a soon-to-be independent Sudanese government would use its power to crack down on the Christianized South.

In August 1955, their fears were finally realized. Northern soldiers stormed the Armory in the southern town of Torit, after learning that some of the Equatoria Corps were planning to kill northern soldiers. The attack triggered an uprising among southern soldiers, policemen, prison guards, and civilians, who killed 261 northern soldiers and 75 southerners.[60] After it restored order, the Sudanese government detained hundreds of prisoners and summarily executed 120 of the mutineers. Khartoum's harsh retribution was designed to suppress the movement. However, it ended up creating deep-seated grievances in the South Sudanese. The South Sudanese government had proved that it could be just as cruel and inhumane as its predecessor. The violent event had neither

36   SOUTH SUDAN'S FATEFUL STRUGGLE

suppressed nor purged the South of its rebellious elements. Rather, it stood for a new cause to unite against and resist the North and became a seminal point in the South's struggle for national self-determination against the North. Although there were few capable political leaders to mobilize southern armed resistance, the Torit Massacre had sown the seeds of a militancy that would profoundly shape the politics in the South. Yet it would take another eight years before any cohesive armed struggle for national self-determination emerged in the South. Until then, the southern political parties—which had settled on a federalist solution for the South—would have to contend with a state government riven by ideological differences.

Sudan meanwhile officially declared its independence from Britain and Egypt on December 19, 1955, just four months after the Torit Massacre.[61] The event marked a brief period of collective rejoicing among northerners and southerners who together had finally driven out their common enemy. But it would also expose the deep ideological rifts in Sudanese society and between Sudanese and South Sudanese society. After a contentious period of campaigning, Ismail al-Azhan was elected as first Prime Minister of Sudan. Within months, he would confront the perils of ruling a country divided by Islam and Christian principles. Al-Azhan's first challenge was setting forth an agenda that balanced secular and religious aspirational goals. However, it was his support for secular politics that angered the *Khatmiyya*, a radical Sufi order that used its ties to the government to weaken al-Azhan's standing in his NUP majority party and the People's Democratic Party (PDP). In the South, meanwhile, al-Azhan faced increasing pressure by southern politicians to address the severe economic inequality and underrepresentation of the South Sudanese. The newly formed Southern Sudanese Federalist Party (SSFP), for instance, which had won 40 seats in the new parliament, pressed al-Azhan to consider measures that devolved more power to the southern districts.

But the SSFP's federalist push was largely ignored amidst the rising demands for integrating Sudan. The SSFP still had to convince many South Sudanese to trust a government that continued to see itself as an Arab state (or state within one Arab nation). As Abdal-Rahmen al Mahdi, a leading Sudanese politician, declared, "The Sudan is an integral part of the Arab world and as such must accept the leadership of the two Islamic religious leaders of the Sudan, anybody dissenting from this view must quit from the bureaucracy and security sector; increased racial and religious persecution by state institutions; and gross disparities in economic development will only persist."[62] Al Azhan was eventually succeeded by Abdulah Khalil who pressed even harder for an Arab state that threatened the cultural heritage of the South. But Khartoum grossly miscalculated the mood in the South, where support for autonomy was now competing with the rising demand for southern independence. The more that

Rebellion and Autonomy in the South

By 1958, corruption and factionalism inside the national parliament produced widespread discontent within Sudan. With resentment against Khartoum running high, two senior officers, Ibrahim Abboud and Aba Ahmad Abd al-Wahab led a successful coup against the coalition government in November 1958. They subsequently established a Supreme Council of Armed Forces to govern Sudan, with Abboud eventually emerging as the sole leader. But Abboud's military regime failed to stabilize Sudan. Having undermined the transition to civilian rule, it adopted a southern policy that restricted movement among locals and foreign missionaries seeking to enter Sudan. By 1963, Abboud had suspended the parliament and prevented southerners from lodging complaints against the Sudanese government. Like the British, he had come increasingly to rely on tribal chiefs and customary law to block local government reforms designed to reduce the literacy gap between the North and the South. In effect, Khartoum had become an extension of the former Condominium regime: banning political activities considered as threatening to the Sudanese government, detaining suspected rebels, and restricting the movement of civilians in South Sudan, particularly in Torit, where the government maintained a comparable system of intelligence to monitor the population. Under the new regime, surveillance monitoring increased, producing an increasing number of "outlaws" in the South.[63] I will therefore analyze the Sudanese government's oppressive tactics by chronicling the rise of the South's armed resistance movement and by showing how its predation, lawlessness, and lack of discipline played out during Sudan's first civil war.

More than any other factor, Khartoum's repressive policies helped fuel armed resistance in the South. Many of the fighters who took part in the mutiny (or were suspected to have done so) and who fled to the bush, began to communicate with those captured and released from prison by the government as well as political exiles, the former southern politicians and civil service employees/servants. All of them accepted violence as the sole means of getting the government to take them seriously. As the leading proponents for independence. Joseph Oduho, Saturnino Lahure, and William Deng, drew on their political expertise to form the South African Closed District National Union (SACDNU) in February 1962 and to jockey for international support that included modest amounts of funding from US religious organizations.[64] International support was crucial to

38 SOUTH SUDAN'S FATEFUL STRUGGLE

maintaining and legitimizing their secessionist campaign. And their hope was to create an expansive and reliable support network.

However, many key actors were unwilling to publicly support their cause. This included the neighboring countries, the Organization of African Unity (OAU)[65] and the United Nations, which, while sympathetic to the Southerners' opposition to Islamicization, continued to support the Sudanese government. For them, the principle of sovereignty was at stake and the Sudanese state was still too young a sovereign member of the United Nations to be abandoned. State sovereignty, and not justice (or the moral cause of a rebel group), in other words, was the determining principle of state and international order. International organizations had a duty to protect their members—especially when their sovereignty was threatened.[66] It was true that Sudan may have been a young country that had finally freed itself of British colonialism, but this was not, as some have suggested, the main reason for siding with the Sudanese state.[67] The new OAU and UN had a duty to support prima facie the sovereignty of its new members and to uphold the duty of noninterference among its members, that is, not to recognize secessionist groups. To ignore this duty risked violating the UN Charter and international law. In a letter to the OAU, the leaders of the southern resistance movement put the matter in the following terms: "The origins of "Southern Sudan's Contract between the Northerners and Southerners was, from the outset, a bloody contract . . . between forces of domination on the one hand and those struggling against their subjugation on the other."[68]

However, the outside politicians still lacked economic support. As educated, skilled political leaders, they obviously did not wish to seize booty or impose border taxes. But their options were limited. And the fact that they lacked military training made it increasingly difficult to conduct military operations. Their only choice was to work more closely with and to listen to the trained military soldiers who could conduct the logistics of their military operations. The leaders with military training included Joseph Lagu, Severino Fuli, George Muras, and George Kwani. Together, with the outside politicians, they met in Kenya in 1963 to discuss the formation of a militarized rebel group. They agreed to call the movement the Sudan Pan-African Freedom Fighters (SPAFF), but soon settled on the more popular name of Anyanya (which literally means snake venom in the Madi language), whose motto was: "It is better to die than to live a slave of the greedy Arabs."[69]

The Anyanya quickly grew in popularity, which placed increasing pressure on the SANU. This caused the SANU to split into a domestic faction and a radical foreign wing. William Deng led the moderate SANU-William wing that called for autonomy, while Lahure and Oduho emerged as the leaders of the radical wing that had broken away from Deng. Together with Aggrey Jaden, they formed an armed secessionist group, the Azania Liberation Front (ALF), named after

the Greek Azania. In 1967, the ALF established what amounted to a shadow government, the National Transitional Government of South Sudan (NTGSS).[70] Gordon Muortat Mayen, Aggrey Jaden and Joseph Lagu would eventually replace Muortat as the leaders of Anyanya in 1965 to form the Southern Sudan Liberation Movement, the political wing of Anyanya in charge of directing the military movement against Khartoum.

Militarily, though, the Anyanya faced a growing shortage of resources and military supplies. It lacked, for instance, high-grade weapons, ammunition, equipment, provisions, rear bases, transportation, and communication lines to carry out its operational tasks. By the late 1960s, conditions had worsened considerably. "The group," as Øystein Rolandsen and Nicki Kindersly explain, "had to live off the land within a largely subsistence economy, and their limited capacity to control, coordinate, and command Anyanya groups offered local rebel leaders few incentives to cede authority to their rivals."[71] Both the SAF and the Anyanya employed measures to test the loyalty of local civilians. In early 1965, for example, the local government in Torit adopted "loyalty" identification cards and forced tribal chiefs to issue pass permits to designate newcomers to the town. This would eventually pave the way for "peace villages," in which the Torit government arrested civilians and relocated them to administrative towns or peace villages. Meanwhile, the Anyanya rebels, after taking control of parts of Torit, closed-down schools and turned the schools into barracks. In the end, loyalty came down to which side succeeded most in protecting the local civilians from predatory cattle raiding.

The two warring sides thus continued to engage one another in a vicious cycle of violence. The attacks involved a range of abuses, including abduction, forced appearance, and the torture of suspected collaborators with the enemy. In some cases, the Anyanya rebels were reported to have cut off the ears of suspected collaborators.[72] This naturally took a heavy toll on the civilian population, which had come to fear and distrust both sides. Increasingly, the people became skeptical of the Anyanya's commitment to justice and freedom as well as its ability to counter the surveillance tactics of the Sudanese government. The Anyanya's predatory tactics, it is worth noting, would eventually anticipate the SPLM/A's abuses in the 1990s and its later use of brute force to govern South Sudan.

By the late 1960s, poor military logistics had led to increasing competition and factionalism inside the group. Lagu, however, was determined to fix the problem by establishing ties with Israel, which had been looking for ways to pressure its Arab neighbors after the Six-Day War in 1967, where it had launched a preemptive strike against its Arab neighbors (including Sudan) to extend its borders and occupy parts of the West Bank. For Israel, the Anyanya represented a potentially important counterweight to the Sudanese government. So, in 1969, it agreed to ship Lagu's Anyanya clandestine military supplies, and shipments,

40 SOUTH SUDAN'S FATEFUL STRUGGLE

which were channeled through Uganda to a base in Owinkkabul, located near Nimule, a southern town lying close to the Uganda border. Lagu then distributed arms shipments to his Anyanya commanders and in return for the supplies, the commanders pledged their loyalty to him. Lagu even had a surplus of supplies to train his own personal military force. For Israel, a better equipped Anyanya constituted a strategic opportunity to destabilize Sudan and to punish it and Egypt for signing the Khartoum Declaration, which had required each signatory to pledge "no peace with Israel."[73] The United States and the United Nations, however, were critical of Israel's strategic objectives. They feared more than anything that its support of the Anyanya would embolden the Islamic hardliners in Khartoum and potentially undermine the fragile democratic regime of Ismail al-Azhari. Whether or not this was true, it was clear that a stark line remained between secular and Islamic rule, particularly between the communists and Islamic nationalists.

In May 1969, ideological tensions led Jaafar Muhammed Nimeiri, a military officer, to oust Azhari in a coup d'état that brought his Sudanese Socialist Union to power. Nimeiri promptly appointed himself as Prime Minister. Just three months later, the leaders of the Sudanese Communist Party carried out a failed coup against Nimeiri and were executed. The event prompted Nimeiri to abandon the Soviet Union (but not his socialist goals) and to enter into an alliance with the United States. Nimeiri then proceeded to nationalize the economy and to sideline Islamist forces before opening up channels of communication with the Anyanya. In the meantime, Lagu had managed to establish the South Sudan Liberation Movement (SSLM) in an effort to encourage solidarity within the Anyanya. To bring together the Anyanya, the SSLM adopted a pragmatic approach calling for compromise and consultation, especially on the question of South Sudan's self-determination. In the summer of 1971, Lagu held a conference to announce that the SSLM was united in its support of negotiations with the government, even though he had yet to notify any of the small militant groups comprising the Anyanya.

At the All African Conference of Churches, Khartoum and the SSLM reached an agreement on the cessation of conflict and soon began talks on a peace agreement in Addis Ababa, where Abel Alier represented the Sudanese government and Ezboni Mondiri, the SSLM delegation. Burgess Carr, the Secretary General of the All African Conference of Churches, and Emperor Haile Selassie, Ethiopia's monarch, mediated the talks. Their main task was to get the two sides to find common ground on the issue of self-rule for the southern region. But they faced two key obstacles: (1) the Anyanya's splinter groups that continued to demand independence and (2) getting the South Sudanese to trust Nimeiri who, through his support of Pan-Africanism (or Arab national unity), had marginalized the South Sudanese by excluding non-Arabs. Lagu, for his part,

had to convince the Anyanya members that self-rule was indeed in their interest, and that it constituted the most realistic means of achieving self-determination and promoting development. It would not be an easy task. He knew that Nimeiri would never accept secession.

So Lagu sped up negotiations to pressure the discontents to accept autonomy. The strategy soon paid off. The two sides signed the Addis Ababa Agreement which granted self-rule to the southern region, dissolved the three separate regions Al-Istiwā'iyyah (Equatoria), Baḥr al Ghazāl, and A'ālī al-Nīl (Upper Nile), and established a regional legislature to rule the affairs of the Southern Sudan Autonomous Region (SSAR). The parties also agreed to integrate the Anyanya soldiers into the national army and the police forces stationed in the region by consenting that "the recruitment and integration of citizens from the Southern region shall be determined by a Joint Military Commission taking into account the need for initial separate deployment of troops with a view to achieve a smooth integration into the national force."[74] The commission would be responsible for the creation of Southern Command that would consist of 6,000 soldiers from the North and 6,000 former Anyanya soldiers who would have to be retrained.[75] It was by no means a perfect arrangement. The South Sudanese, after all, had to make a major concession on its demand for independence. But for many this was the price to pay for peace.

Lagu in the meantime devoted much of his time selling or championing the autonomy promised by the agreement. Not long after the peace agreement was signed, he stated that "we took up arms and we fought for equality . . . we do no condemn the Arabs, our fight is for an African identity—as distinct from Arab."[76] As the new Major General of the Southern Command, Lagu had managed to bring an end to the civil war. But it came at a high price. To overcome the Anyanya's objections, he had to rush the agreement, forcing him to rely almost exclusively on his own discretion. The decision to not consult the Southerners on the terms of the agreement left many southerners feeling not only marginalized but understandably suspicious of the agreement and the regional institutions of Southern Sudan. This was hardly the way to build peace in a region where war had destroyed 60 concrete bridges and nearly 500 culverts, decimated the cash crops, left nearly a third of the roads in the region impassable, and forced the two secondary schools to migrate to the North.[77] With infant mortality rates at their highest levels since Sudanese independence, the South Sudanese had to find a way to survive. Rebuilding the economy would naturally entail an enormous investment by the Sudanese government and other foreign entities—a commitment that the government was simply not in a position to fulfill. Nimeiri still faced stiff opposition by the hardline Islamists like Hassan al-Turabi, who saw the Addis Ababa Accord as a sellout and flawed approach for resolving the problem of South Sudan.

42 SOUTH SUDAN'S FATEFUL STRUGGLE

The transition to regional autonomy, then, was anything but certain. Lagu's failure to consult the South Sudanese people, the unreasonable expectations of integrating Anyanya fighters, and the scheming Sudanese government pointed to a deeply encumbered transitional process of building peace and administering effective self- governance. South Sudan was still too divided and devastated by the civil war to govern its own affairs. The fact that it never engaged in any collective reckoning with the war through a formal process of reconciliation and healing for instance, suggested that the South Sudanese were mentally and psychologically unprepared to transition to stable regional governance. South Sudan in the end was driven by fatigue to settle on autonomy. But being tired of war was never sufficient to start a transitional process. It merely exposed the need for collective, public trust in the local politicians' ability to revitalize, develop, and govern the economy.

Regional Autonomy and the Reversion to War

Public trust depends on upholding the rules and laws in a transparent manner and governing by consensus and constraint. On one level, the Addis Ababa Accord offered a promising framework for meeting these conditions. The framework, in fact, consisted of an autonomous Southern Regional Government (SRG), with a prime minister appointed by the Regional Assembly that was based in Juba and a High Executive Council (HEC) comprised of ministers and regional president appointed by the President of the Regional Assembly. The SRG created basic bureaucratic and judicial structures of governance, assisted over one million Southerners return to their homeland, and held a successful election for the regional assembly members in October 1973. But over time the political environment became increasingly fractious, as Abel Alier and Joseph Lagu vied for control of the High Executive Council (with Alier winning the vote). Khartoum, for its part, governed with the acquiescence of Southern leaders, which only widened the sectarian divisions amongst the South Sudanese, particularly the Equatorians, the Dinka, Nuer, and other cattle-raising ethnic groups, and revealed what I suggested above as the deep-seated cleavages caused by years of war and neglect.

The SRG was divided between anti and pro-Khartoum forces. The "outsiders" were those who fought for the Anyanya or took up arms to fight against the Sudanese government. The "insiders" meanwhile were the moderates who had remained loyal to Khartoum by working as government soldiers and civil servants in the Sudanese government. Nimeiri naturally preferred the insiders, who were more educated and cooperative. In fact, he appointed many to office and counted on them, in turn, to run the affairs in the southern region, including education,

tax collection, and the judiciary.[78] But in taking sides, he also marginalized the outsiders and stoked secessionist sentiment of many Anyanya holdouts, that is, those unwilling to integrate into the Sudanese Armed Forces (SAF).

The cleavage between insiders and outsiders determined many of the conflicts inside the SRG. One of these concerned the official language of the region. The compromise reached under the Addis Ababa Agreement was that Arabic would serve as the official language "for the Sudan and English as the principal language for the Southern region."[79] But the Southern delegation continued to demand that English serve as the official language of the South. For them, Arabic was a primary fuel of Northern Sudanese nationalism and a source of grievance for those still committed to the independence of the Southern region. Beyond this, it was taught in the majority of schools in the South to train and examine army officers. Teaching in Arabic soon led to debate in the SRG, resulting in a bill that proposed to make English the language of instruction at the primary and secondary schools. The bill, however, failed to pass, leaving pro-Khartoum insiders such as Alier, convinced that "this generation will leave school knowing Arabic which is a rich and civilized language."[80]

Lagu came under increasing scrutiny by SRG members. Benjamin Bol, a former member of the HEC, accused Lagu of stealing nearly 2.5 million dollars from government coffers.[81] Lagu had appointed several outsiders to regional government positions that paid generously. Yet many assembly members refused to work and comply with these pro-Nimeiri official. In 1980, their growing dismay led them to dissolve the regional parliament and appoint Peter Gatwok as interim leader of the regional assembly, until elections could be held later that year. This, however, did not stop Nimeiri's interventions of the southern region, which had stirred up deep resentment among southern politicians who saw them as last-ditch efforts to hold onto power in the face of mounting pressure. The increasingly volatile relationship between Khartoum and the SRG threatened to further destabilize the SRG. And Lagu appeared powerless to resolve the matter. If he opted for deeper autonomy, the action would require a three-quarters vote in the National Assembly as well as a southern referendum that addressed the freedom of religion and the African identity of Sudan's national character. At this point, there was simply too much discord in the SRG to reach a concerted consensus on the issue of expanded autonomy.

To make matters worse, many Anyanya insurgents had not integrated into the National Army as hoped. The plan was of course to reintegrate them into the Southern Command over a five-year period. But the years of war had hardened the Anyanya fighters' political attitudes. Many were simply unwilling to serve in regimented army battalions stationed throughout the South. As Abel Alier put it: "[The Anyanya] were fighting for independence against the 'Arabs' until the Agreement came and took them by surprise. It was not the type of

44   SOUTH SUDAN'S FATEFUL STRUGGLE

arrangement the ordinary Anyanya had expected . . . to be in one army with their long-standing enemy."[82] A majority of Anyanya rebels thus chose not to integrate. Instead, they elected to reorganize into armed factions that would later coalesce into the Anyanya II.[83] By the mid-1970s, the Anyanya had attacked military installations and government buildings in the North. Unsurprisingly, they still enjoyed wide support from both civilians and southern officials who had grown frustrated with Nimeiri and his shifting policies that had fractured the South and widened the gap between insiders and outsiders.

Nowhere was this more evident than with the proposal to build a canal to the east of the Sudd, in the vast network of verdant swamps of the White Nile. Sir William Gastin, a preeminent hydrologist had already proposed a canal for the area, after making three trips to the Nile basin from 1899 to 1903. In his "Report on the Basis of the Upper Nile," 1904, he concluded that nearly 60 percent of the waters in the Sudd were lost to evaporation and transpiration.[84] Egypt and Sudan eventually drew up plans for the Jonglei Canal Project in 1958, extending from the mouth of Sebat river to the town of Malakal. The project, which began construction in 1978, was expected to develop the South by freeing up more grazing land and offering a more direct, alternative route around the Sudd. This, in turn, would facilitate the delivery of goods, which for many insiders, promised to generate additional revenue to fund other projects.[85]

But outsiders and many civilians saw it differently. For them, it was yet another scheme orchestrated by the Sudanese government to exploit the South. While draining parts of the Sudd was expected to create more arable land, it also figured to eliminate (dry up) the amount of grazing land and hurt cattle herders by diverting much needed water away from South Sudan to downstream riparian countries. In fact, Egypt expected to boost its water supply by an estimated 5 to 7 percent. Because of these dubious benefits, the canal failed to elicit the support of many South Sudanese, who considered it a top-down project that would not improve primary schools, nor provide the needed material resources to reduce cattle raiding and interethnic strife in the South. Nimeiri ultimately dismissed these concerns about the project's trickle-down effect in the Southern region and proceeded with the project. Eventually the project was stopped in 1984 after the SPLA fired a missile on the French company constructing it, leaving nearly 240 kilometers of the 360 kilometers of the canal unbuilt.[86]

Nimeiri also managed to infuriate the South Sudanese further with his decision to take control of the oil fields in the South. Chevron had discovered oil in Bentiu, in 1978. Shortly thereafter, it announced that a pipeline line would run from this region to the Port of Sudan. The announcement triggered demonstrations in the South where protesters demanded that the oil be transported through Kenya to Mombasa.[87] Rather than appeasing the demonstrations, Nimeiri replaced southern soldiers stationed in Bentiu with northern officers. The decision was

met with immediate anger and consternation by South Sudanese officials, who accused Nimeiri of violating the Addis Ababa Agreement, which had called for an integrated army. The Southern Regional Assembly soon responded by approving a bill that condemned the government's action and Chevron, which had started construction on an oil refinery in Kosti in March 1981.[88] Many assembly members of the SRG openly chastised Chevron for taking sides with the government on such a controversial issue. Chevron though refused to talk with southern officials, who by now, suspected collusion between Chevron and Khartoum. In April 1981, Anyanya rebel fighters repeatedly attacked the refinery, forcing Chevon to withdraw from Sudan altogether.

Nimeiri was coming under increasing economic and political pressure to address the violence in the South. He soon devised a plan to incorporate various areas in the South where much of the oil had been discovered, including the Helig area and parts of the Upper Nile, and to seize control of the rights in these areas to extract the oil. As expected, the plan triggered stiff southern resistance, eventually forcing Nimeiri to shelve the plan. But by mid-1983, northern officers had assumed many high-level posts in the South, which allowed more southern units to be rapidly redeployed to the North and to heighten tensions. In May 1983, rebel fighters led by John Garang finally mutinied in Battalion 105 in Bor and formed the SPLA. Nimeiri responded by dissolving the Southern Regional Assembly on June 5 and by imposing sharia law on the largely Christian South. The second civil war had finally started.

Conclusion

The outbreak of war in 1983 effectively dissolved the Addis Ababa Agreement. For many, however, this was the product of the flaws in the agreement itself, including the absence of any checks and balances to govern relations (and conflicts) between the central and local government. Nimeiri had managed to use southern regional autonomy to control and manage the population. His many policy shifts would eventually earn him the nickname, "the chameleon" and allow him to survive politically by balancing support of the southerners' cause against the hardline Islamists in Khartoum, who had advocated for Islamicizing the South. Nimeiri in effect did whatever he could to survive politically, which created problems he could not overcome. For the South Sudanese, the 11 years of southern regional autonomy brought some political benefits and a much-needed reprieve from war; however, it ultimately exposed a divisiveness and lack of political discipline that Khartoum was able to manipulate for political gain. And yet, Khartoum's intrusiveness and the limits of the Addis Ababa Agreement tell only part of the story of the South failed autonomous rule. There was also the

46 SOUTH SUDAN'S FATEFUL STRUGGLE

failure to promote accountability and inclusion and the ruling elites' growing ability to deflect responsibility for their own problems, simply by blaming the corrupt policies of Khartoum.

This should not minimize the importance of Khartoum's divisive tactics. Khartoum, after all, had become more of an extension than an actual break from British colonial rule. In fact, the many years of indirect rule and neglect had reinforced the North's perception of the southerners' inferiority. British colonial rule left a complicated legacy in this respect. Having inspired Sudanese nationalism and modernized the North, it left the new Sudanese state government with a southern population that could no longer be ruled externally or from a distance. The South Sudanese resistance movement cut across multiple ethnic lines and lacked the military restraint to counter the divisive tactics of the enemy. Both factors presaged a difficult future of transitioning to peaceful rule and democracy. Underdevelopment, in short, introduced conditions that made it increasingly difficult to unite as an oppressed national community. And while the British had managed to divide Sudan along religious lines, it was the Sudanese Islamic rulers, who, in seeking to impose their laws and customs on the South Sudanese, had fractured the Anyanya and limited its influence. The ever-militant Anyanya was, in the end, forced to put down its arms and accept autonomy. It had never showed a concerted willingness to compel their more pragmatic rulers to end social inequality and to adopt a democratic vision of self-determination and liberation. That would come later.

2

The Divided Movement and a Framework for Peace

After the outbreak of the Sudan's second civil war in 1983, some of the Anyanya II rebels joined the SPLA; however, others, including several senior members, refused to take part. The conflict between the Anyanya's senior members and SPLA leaders called attention to the simmering dispute between secession and autonomy and over national unity. The Anyanya II rebels rejected autonomy and advocated for an independent South Sudan. Garang and the SPLA, by contrast, called for an armed revolution to unify and democratize the Sudanese state. Their aim was to revolutionize the state by ending its racial oppression of the South and closing the inequality gap between the South and the North. For them, the South's national question was an integral part of the "New Sudan."

Garang's "New Sudan" was an ambitious plan to unify all Sudanese minorities and tribes into one Sudanese nation. The idea was to use armed rebellion to change fundamentally how the Sudanese state governed and set (its racist) policy. But many Anyanya II fighters believed that it ignored the unchanging reality of Khartoum's desire to meddle in the South's affairs. The only realistic course was to create an independent state to prevent the Government of Sudan from using its power to divide and oppress the South. Such concern reflected a deeply held secessionist sentiment shared by many South Sudanese. Yet the formation of the SPLM/A represented something new: a more organized, armed rebellion with a far more ambitious goal of liberating all oppressed minorities. This, it turned out, convinced enough former Anyanya fighters to pledge their loyalty to Garang and his vision of a democratic, socialist nation-state.

However, the rise of factionalism inside the SPLM/A exposed many contradictory effects of its armed struggle. Rather than unifying soldiers around a common cause of ending Khartoum's racism, armed struggle led to abuses that divided the SPLM/A along tribal and ideological lines. The strict militarism that Garang had counted on to impose order on SPLA ranks became a source of grievance among some of his commanders, who saw it as a betrayal of the democratic ideals he was advocating. The result was a dramatic split in the SPLM/A into two main factions that organized largely along Dinka and Nuer lines and held competing visions of national unity: one that advocated independence; the

---

South Sudan's Fateful Struggle. Steven C. Roach, Oxford University Press. © Oxford University Press 2023.
DOI: 10.1093/oso/9780190057848.003.0003

48   SOUTH SUDAN'S FATEFUL STRUGGLE

other unity with a democratic Sudan. The split would lead some factions to align with Khartoum to fight Garang's SPLA.

By the 1990s, factionalism created a South–South conflict that diminished the centrality of factors that drove the North–South axis. The problem, though, was that international leaders and policymakers clung to the influence of the North–South axis of conflict by focusing almost exclusively on the clash between the authoritarian, Islamist North and the Christian South. This position, I argue, oversimplified the conflict by downplaying the core, destabilizing effects of factionalism. The result was the tendency to downplay and ignore the moral accountability and reconciliation that could redress the brutal effects of war. In the end, the CPA reflected a flawed framework, since it failed to link this source of insecurity and instability with the practical issues of building peace (e.g., border disputes and wealth sharing). What this suggested was that many of the unattended effects of Sudan's second civil war, such as profiteering and clientelist politics, fueled the need for a militarism to expand the patronage networks. In this chapter, I'll first discuss Garang's New Sudan and how factionalism in the SPLM/A emerged from the intersection of secessionism and ethnic identity politics to politicize deep-seated grievances. I'll then move on to address the strategic rationale of powerful states and organizations to bring an end to the war.

The SPLA and Its Vision

After years of manipulating the SRG in the summer of 1983. Nimeiri effectively reincorporated three districts in the South into the Government of Sudan, ending nearly 11 years of autonomy. To placate the Islamists, he consequently implemented the notorious "September Laws" that instituted sharia appeals courts with their harsh punitive codes (e.g., stoning, flogging, hanging, and the amputation of limbs). The measures, in his view, were needed to eliminate southern resistance, particularly in the military. But many southerners in the Southern Command—especially those sent to the North—simply refused to fight for the Sudanese Armed Forces. This included Kerubino Kuanyin Bol and William Nyuong Bany, who claimed Nimeiri's measures violated the Addis Ababa Agreement, particularly the rule that no southern soldier would be stationed in the North. Bol, it turned out, had already hatched a plan to start a rebellion inside Battalion 105.

But a government informant tipped off the plan to government authorities.[1] Nimeiri responded by sending in additional forces to the city of Bor to reinforce the SAF Battalion 84, which consisted of 500 Sudanese soldiers. Kerubino's aim was to take over Battalion 105 and place it under the control of the Anyanya II guerrillas.[2] He had initially received support from Garang, who at the time, was a

colonel in the Southern Command and secretly working behind the scenes with the mutineers. When the mutineers failed to execute Kerubino's plan and fled to the Ethiopia, Garang took an alternative route out of Bor and eventually joined the leaders of the Adura Camp to establish the SPLA on May 16, 1983, which soon elected Garang as its new leader.[3]

Although a majority of former military and political leaders of South Sudan supported Garang, he faced stiff opposition by several former Anyanya II leaders, including Samuel Gai Tut and Akwon Atem, who were considered the old guard of the Anyanya. Both insisted that Garang lacked the military training and experience needed to lead the SPLM/A and that their own seniority and past military experience entitled them to lead the armed force. Kerubino Bol and Nyuon Bany, who had withheld their support for Garang, were less skeptical and soon pledged loyalty to him. But Tut and Atem and other senior Anyanya II officials refused to join the SPLM/A and instead remained with the Anyanya II.[4]

The SPLM/A received the bulk of its logistical support from Menjistu Halie Mariam, the communist leader of Ethiopia (1977–1991). In the SPLM/A, Menjistu saw a potential ally in his efforts to defeat the Islamists in Khartoum and to set up a new secular, socialist Sudanese state. Garang knew this and worked with the Ethiopian government, which provided him and his troops a safe haven. Menjistu in turn remained true to Garang by supporting his efforts to impose discipline within Garang's own ranks, which included his decision to detain and arrest Arik Thon Arok who had openly challenged Garang.[5] For some, Menjistu assumed too much influence over the SPLM/A's affairs, even though he provided no direct financial support of the movement—perhaps as a way of keeping up the appearance of neutrality toward the Government of Sudan.

By July 1983, the SPLM had released its manifesto calling for a "united, democratic and secular Sudan."[6] It pledged its commitment to national diversity and democratization and to end social inequality in the South, declaring that "its intentions of bringing all current guerrilla units in the southern Sudan under one united, integrated liberation army which was not organized along tribal lines"[7] It thus downplayed ethnic divisions and stressed the comradery and loyalty of its army regiments consisting of Dinka, Nuer, Shilluk, Azande, and Murle.[8] The primary goal was to wage an armed struggle to achieve a democratic "New Sudan" that would replace the racist "Old Sudan."

The Man and His Vision

Garang possessed a charisma and mix of military and academic that past South Sudanese leaders had lacked. He was born on June 23, 1945, and as the sixth oldest in a family of 10, was an inquisitive and disciplined child. By the age of

50   SOUTH SUDAN'S FATEFUL STRUGGLE

17, he had joined the Anyanya I rebellion, whose leaders quickly recognized his prowess and urged him to develop his skills further. He eventually moved to Nyeri, Kenya in 1962, where he taught high school, before moving on to attend the University of Dar es Salaam in Tanzania for his undergraduate studies. At Dar es Salaam, he studied the laws and dynamics of colonial oppression and British colonialism and befriended Yoweri Museveni, the future leader of Uganda. Together the two founded "The University Students African Revolution Front," a student organization with a revolutionary agenda based on Marxist-Leninist principles of class equality and oppression. Like so many future African leaders, the two were inspired by Leopold Senghor's negritude and Aimé Césaire's and Frantz Fanon's writings on black identity. Both Césaire and Fanon shared the idea that black African identity was largely what the white race made of it. African negroes, in other words, had learned to experience and understand their place in the world through the ideas and perspectives of Westerners.[9] The more they sought to understand their place in society, the more they became beholden to Western ideas.

In *The Wretched of the Earth*, Fanon argued that the colonial world had dehumanized African natives and instilled black natives with inferior self-images. The only means of overcoming this inferiority complex was through a collective armed struggle that synthesized violence and native cultural identity.[10] Because colonialism was an inherently violent system, the anticolonial resistance movement needed to carry out the absolute means of violence to achieve true liberation and what Fanon called a "new humanism." Fanon embraced the notion of authenticity to describe the native national culture and the possibilities of transcending the colonial state. Garang, by comparison, appealed to national cultural unity (of all ethnic and tribal groups in Sudan) to overcome the bigotry and racism of the Sudanese state. The idea was that the "Old Sudan" was still "looking for its soul and spirit, and for its true identity," and that its "unviable unity" reflected the unrealized potential of representing all groups equally.[11]

In essence, Garang was a third-world, democratic socialist. He knew that African culture lied at the core of social change, but he was determined to study the scientific laws of the capitalist, colonial state. One of his early guides was Walter Rodney, a widely recognized scholar in the emerging field of African neocolonial studies.[12] In *How Europe Undeveloped Africa*, Rodney contended that the West had exploited Africans and their material and natural resources, depriving them of the training and resources needed to develop their national economies, that is, an adequate standard of living and the social opportunities to govern and develop their economies.[13] Underdevelopment described the shortage of capital to invest in the neocolonial state economy and to meet development goals (e.g., infrastructure). The gap reflected the low industrial production levels and standards of living in developing countries. Rodney theorized

that the underdevelopment of the economy was the result of the overpricing of inputs and continued dependence on developed countries. This helped convince Garang that Sudanese officials were underdeveloping the South by employing practices designed to oppress and exclude the South Sudanese.

In his PhD dissertation, "Identifying, Selecting, and Implementing Rural Development Strategies for Socio-Economic Development in the Jonglei Projects Area in the Southern Region, Sudan," he analyzed Sudan's extractive policies and politics in southern Sudan.[14] In particular, he studied the effects of low crop yield, flooding, and limited irrigation, and formulated strategies for remedying these effects.[15] In the case of the proposed Jonglei project—which we discussed in Chapter 1—he devised a dual strategy of improving crop rotation and water reallocation to increase local crop yields. The strategy was intended to remedy the severe mismanagement and unfair distribution of water resources in the undeveloped Jonglei region, where the government had failed to meet the basic needs of the South Sudanese.[16] It is worth noting that in allowing more water to flow downstream, the Sudanese government sought to distribute a greater share of the water to the northern region of Sudan and to Egypt. It was precisely this sort of unequal treatment that would later anticipate many of the future challenges of the Nile Basin Initiative (NBI)—a joint partnership of nine riparian countries established in 1999 to provide a new set of mechanisms for distributing the Nile's waters fairly and equally.[17]

Garang's dissertation research was based largely on Marxist-Leninist principles of class exploitation, surplus value, and class inequality But the work also departed from Marxism by abandoning Marx's teleological theory of class revolution, which held that class revolution would dissolve the bourgeois state's oppressive mechanisms (i.e., private property) and national culture. Unlike other revolutionary third-world thinkers, Garang had come to believe fervently in armed struggle to achieve the national unity and of all peoples and classes in a new, inclusive democratic state. His idea stemmed in part from his Christian animist faith—or his understanding of the vital ways and customs of Sudan's Indigenous peoples—and revealed a deep cultural and social tension between his New Sudan and the Marxsist-Leninist tenet of the dissolution of national culture.[18]

Still, there were strong similarities between Marx and Garang on the national question. Garang, for instance, believed that South Sudan was historically backward and too undeveloped economically to transition to statehood. Yet to dissolve the important role of culture in unifying the national state was not the answer to resolving the South's problems. Rather, it was to preserve tribal and national culture in the New Sudan to help anchor a new national identity of Sudan. Ending severe poverty in the South was therefore central to an evolving democratic Sudan that would take time, patience, resolve, and new strategies.

52   SOUTH SUDAN'S FATEFUL STRUGGLE

It was this evolutionary perspective that ultimately displaced the radical elements of his revolutionary mission and underscored his pragmatic vision of armed struggle to end social inequality and racial bigotry. However, for Garang, it was essential to understand that war itself was not destroying the nation of Sudan. As he put it in a 2005 speech delivered at the United Nations, "no one grows old in war.... Let us therefore become Sudan, what is wrong with that?"[19] The New Sudan, he believed, would emerge from war to become a nation in which Arabs and Africans alike learned to take pride in their common struggle and descent. No one tribe or nationality therefore should ever be allowed to dominate another and create division. In his view, "The Sectarian and Religious Bigotry that dominated the political scene since independence ... failed to allow a balanced development for all the regions to be struck."[20] To secede from Sudan, as the Anyanya II secessionists demanded, amounted to a lost opportunity to achieve true national unity.

For Garang, then, the fundamental question was liberation from what? If armed rebellion leads to permanent separation from those who share a common descent, then it also becomes an obstacle to creating national unity for all Sudanese. For armed rebellion to achieve such unity, it had to engage and transform the underlying conditions of its disunity and insecurity, that is, corruption and authoritarianism. The problem with secessionism was that it offered few guarantees for lasting national unity and national security, especially if there was a shortage of resources. National unity would dissolve if the movement became detached from the unjust social and historical circumstances that shaped the struggle. Garang had managed to anticipate the inherently unstable condition of violent secessionism, especially when unattended grievances caused secession to merge with tribal identity politics. But the looming question was whether armed struggle could eliminate the corrupt rule of Khartoum. After all, it was the racism and corruption of the Sudanese state that drove the leaders' desire to meddle in and divide the South. As long as this meddlesomeness paid off in terms of dividing the SPLM/A, there seemed little hope for a new Sudan.

Militias, Militaristic Tensions

Garang of course knew this and assembled a diverse army to meet the challenge. He was aware that the majority of SPLA fighters were Dinka and wanted to reassure all his soldiers that the SPLA remained one unit—united by the desire to end Khartoum's corruption and racism. "The SPLA is your army," he told the soldiers at a gathering in Bor, "when it does something wrong, the civilian will have the room to ask: why is our army doing this wrong thing? That is the work

and nature of the SPLM: to create this relationship such that there is the right of everyone to ask questions."[21] But there was only so much that his pep talks could do to maintain solidarity. The right he spoke of required mechanisms to redress soldiers' grievances and to maintain morale, mechanisms that were either absent or too undeveloped to be effective. As a result, there were few clear-cut rules and procedures for carrying out tasks and assignments (and allowing challenges to wrongful commands or orders, for instance), which left much of the authority and discretionary power concentrated at the top, and made communication among the top and low-level commanders difficult.

Poor communication created considerable uncertainty regarding the proper execution of duties. If there were grievances among the soldiers, for instance, they could at least hope to resolve them with their own commander. However, for the commanders, the only formal outlet of redress was Garang. It was not difficult therefore to see how Garang`s Dinka background had emerged as a source of suspicion among some SPLA fighters. Given that his own authority remained paramount, any failure to share power could be interpreted as an unwanted projection of cultural pride and the basis of discrimination.

To maintain cohesion, then, the SPLA leaders needed to stay focused on the common enemy, that is, Khartoum. The Sudanese government, after all, had long discriminated against the South Sudanese. And in joining forces with some southern rebels, it soon found a way to manipulate the simmering tensions inside the SPLM/A: by offering assistance to the ethnic factions that felt disrespected by the majority tribe, the Dinka. In some cases, the Sudanese Armed Forces were able to appeal directly to the tribal grievances of the SPLA fighters to conduct its counter-resistance campaign against the SPLA. The campaign involved the mobilization of various tribal militias, including the Nuer, the Misseriya, the Rizaiqat Baqqars, and the Murahlin militias in the South Kordofan and Darfur areas. This in turn forced Garang to recruit more South Sudanese soldiers to counterattack the SAF. But the increased fighting soon led to economic shortages and to more civilian casualties, particularly in Bahr al Ghazal and Equatoria, where the SPLA counted on civilian support. Garang was consequently forced to levy taxes on the people devastated by the fighting in order to pay for more supplies. In a speech delivered at Bor, he tried to reassure the people that the SPLA fighters were simply trying to improve their lives.

And we can't just say it, we have to do it such that people can see it. If we collected money from people, we will definitely build schools and if we don't, the youth will ask, where is that school of ours? And where is our road that was to be built? The place where the civilians will be asking these words, the strong voice that they will be talking, is what we have called the SPLM, such that it will be their government. . . . Before you came here, this place was just a forest/

54 SOUTH SUDAN'S FATEFUL STRUGGLE

bush, and there was nothing here as you know . . . everything can go on slowly, move slowly as you have done it before in your training. It starts with hand-to-hand combat, followed by combat skills, basic rifle marksmanship and weapons training.[22]

On the battlefield, Garang scored a series of victories in Western Equatoria. In 1986, he seized control of a wide swath of territory in Sudan, stretching from Western Equatoria to the Blue Nile region. He had managed to consolidate power through an informal chain of command that allowed the SPLA commanders to make decisions without his direct approval (although each was expected to consult Garang before making key decisions). However, because of the lack of rules and mechanisms, there was little transparency and oversight to monitor relations between the SPLA leaders and civilians. Indeed, as the SPLA seized more land, it saw more opportunities to tax the goods crossing the borders it controlled and to collect booty on stolen cattle in the newly controlled areas. There was simply too little time and desire to create more mechanisms inside the SPLA command structure. Besides, Khartoum was equally, if not more, ruthless in its treatment of civilians during the war. Arab militias known as the Beggara, had already aligned with the People's Defense Force (PDF), a unit of the Sudanese Army, to capture land and people in the Bahr al Ghazal; many of the captured soldiers were turned into slave laborers. Yet they were little match for an impassioned SPLA, which had cornered these militias in 1987 to gain control over wide tracts of newly acquired territory.[23] One of the SPLA's first actions was to free the slave laborers and offer them the opportunity to voluntarily join their ranks. As the SPLM/A grew in size and became more intrepid, Khartoum was left to choose between increasing or abandoning its support of these militias. It eventually settled on the former.

The Sudanese government meanwhile faced increasing economic and social turmoil caused by widespread starvation, high inflation rates, rising unemployment, and diminishing wages in the cities.[24] Its decision to finance massive irrigation projects with borrowed capital intended to boost agricultural output increased the external debt to nearly a billion US dollars—a figure that exceeded its yearly gross national product.[25] Throughout the countryside, falling standards of living rapidly increased migration into the overcrowded cities. In the Bahr al Ghazal and Equatorial regions, for instance, starvation threatened millions of civilians. After taking several months to declare a famine, Nimeiri eventually forced thousands of rural migrants to relocate to agricultural areas in a campaign known as *Kasha*.[26] The campaign followed his recommitment to Islam (he was born a Muslim), in which he imposed sharia law on the South Sudanese people (i.e., sharia appeals courts that imposed harsh, punitive measures, such as stoning, flogging, hanging, and the amputation of limbs).[27] Many civilians

who protested the imposition—including activists and moderate Muslims in the North such as Mohamed Taha, a prominent engineer—were consequently detained and then executed after brief trials. Meanwhile, in the South, people filled the streets to protest the Islamic edicts.

By April 1985, Nimeiri's rule stood at the precipice. Thousands of workers had taken to the streets in Khartoum to protest the worsening economic conditions. High-ranking officials eventually ousted him from office and established a transitional government with Sadig al Mahdi as the newly appointed leader. Mahdi quickly vowed to rescind the sharia codes in the South, but broke his promise after he rejected in December 1988, a Democratic Unionist Party peace plan with the SPLM/A, which would have suspended the codes and created a shared power arrangement with the SPLM/A. The decision would prove fateful. Just four months later, Colonel Omar Hassan al-Bashir staged yet another coup d'etat that ousted Mahdi and brought to power the Revolutionary Command Council of National Salvation—a military government that quickly banned trade unions and nonreligious organizations.[28]

The SPLA and Factionalism

The Revolutionary Command Council of National Salvation ushered in a new era of Islamic governance, spearheaded by the National Islamic Front (NIF).[29] As the leader of the NIF, Dr. Hassan al-Turabi sought to turn Sudan into an Islamic state. He had hoped to use the conflict between the Arab North and non-Arab South to summon economic and political support from Libya and Egypt.[30] But he and Bashir would soon be outmaneuvered by the SPLM/A, which continued to seize more land from the national government.

The SPLM/A leaders knew what to expect from the SAF. Many of them, it turned out, had already served in the SAF and possessed an intimate knowledge of the SAF's logistics and tactics, which had changed little since their desertion from the SAF. Many also identified themselves as Christians as well as members of tribal communities. But despite this strategic advantage and religious difference, the SPLM/A faced its own enemy from within: the commanders' increasing competition and criticism of Garang. Much of this stemmed from the loose chain of command structure discussed earlier, which allowed commanders to make decisions, sometimes without Garang's direct approval (each however was expected to consult Garang before making key decisions). As mentioned earlier, because of poor communication, there was little way to monitor the commanders' ability to administer the newly won areas. The commanders, in effect, were encouraged to cover up their poor decisions and human rights abuses while also reflexively assigning blame to Khartoum.

56 SOUTH SUDAN'S FATEFUL STRUGGLE

The problem was that Khartoum's deceptiveness also reinforced the need for a strong and forceful leader to keep the SPLM/A unified. That person of course was Garang himself. Garang was not just a forceful leader: he was also charismatic and self-confident and knew how to command the loyalty of his troops. Over time, however, it was this very self confidence that made him more militaristic and created distance between him and those commanders who felt deprived of a voice in decision making. By failing to include many of his commanders on important decisions, Garang had begun to work against the movement's democratic goals. As the two most vocal critics, Riek Machar, a Nuer commander, and Lam Akol, a Shilluk commander, were among the first (commanders) to publicly criticize Garang's policies.

In 1989, they announced that Garang had turned the SPLM/A into a dictatorship that failed to consult its high-ranking officials and that disrespected their opinions and views. For Machar and Akol, Garang's authoritarianism had lowered morale and rendered him unaccountable for his actions, especially in regards to human rights atrocities. Garang, in their view, was out of touch with the South Sudanese people's growing determination to be independent from Sudan. His continued rejection of secession not only underestimated the South Sudanese people's will to break free from Sudan's oppression but also curtailed their energy to fight the common enemy.

Machar and Akol's public criticism reflected their growing ambition to control the SPLM/A.[31] To their credit, both possessed the skills to carry out their demands. Like Garang, they were among the few commanders who had earned a PhD; both were articulate, well-educated, and confident with proven military records. And both drew on their military and intellectual prowess to score impressive, strategic victories during the civil war. Machar, for instance, had managed to erect a bulwark against Sudan's forces in the Western part of the Upper Nile region. The victory had arguably increased his determination to outmaneuver Garang, even though Garang still enjoyed strong support by his Dinka base and had proved himself an adroit politician by playing off the United States and Ethiopia to condemn the NIF. Nevertheless, Machar and Akol were convinced that they could oust Garang from power.

It was a risky prospect, however. For both Machar and Akol could be accused of committing human rights abuses and showing an indifference to the needs of civilians and SPLA soldiers. Machar's ambition, as Sharon Hutchinson put it, "remained amiss and sought to undermine, if not destroy any mediating structure standing between him and local troops, including when necessary, bonds of kinship."[32] In pressing for a new SPLM/A platform, Machar and Akol had come to believe in their own righteousness. Whatever misdeeds they committed were the result of Garang's failed leadership. The point of course was to show how

Garang's militaristic rule had betrayed the need for accountability and the democratic structure of the SPLM/A.

Despite the public attacks, Garang remained confident and defiant. His rationale for strong military rule inside the SPLM/A was to maintain an effective army to curtail Khartoum's ability to exploit the SPLM/A's weaknesses. In this way, Akol's and Machar's attacks were only providing the ammunition for Khartoum to divide the SPLM/A and to divert attention away from the enemy's vices—including its corruption, bigotry, and racism. Garang thus saw his militaristic policies as a necessary safeguard against the exploitative and destabilizing effects of these vices.

By early 1991, Garang's other major challenge was maintaining his foreign allies. The most essential was the Mengistu regime, which by now, had become increasingly unstable. For Akol, Machar, and Gordon Kong Chol, however, this seemed to be the opportunity they had been waiting for: to attack Garang's alliance with an unpopular Mengistu, while also currying favor with the West that had long opposed Menjistu. The strategy seemed to work, at least initially. Garang's undying loyalty to Menjistu made him look tone deaf to the democratic forces sweeping across East Africa in the early 1990s. More importantly, Garang missed the opportunity to engage with the Ethiopian People's Revolutionary Democratic Front (EPRDF), whose victory seemed inevitable at the time. But despite their animosity of Menjistu, the major powers continued to support Garang. Akol, Machar, and Chol, who expected the United States to support their democratic cause, had overlooked a key dimension of US foreign policy: its unstated priority of supporting authoritarian rulers to safeguard its interests overseas. The United States clung to an intransigent Garang precisely because of his proven ability to pressure and counter the Islamic fundamentalism of the Sudanese government.

Still, Garang's intransigence remained disconcerting. He had failed to adopt a new policy for maintaining control over major cities, and routinely ignored the advice of his commanders. Machar, Akol, and Chol were convinced that Garang had privileged Dinka interests inside the SPLM. Garang tried to downplay this tribal issue, but for many Nuer, his Dinka identity had become indelibly tied to his authoritarian rule. In particular, it showed the extent to which he had used Dinka majority rule to discriminate along tribal lines. What it suggested was that tribal bias had long shaped the decisions of the SPLM/A and caused some of the most brutal incidents of violence. For instance, in 1985, the SPLA attacked the civilians belonging to the Jikany-Nuer, an ethnic group living in a small village located near the Sudanese and Ethiopian shared border. The violent conflict started after a Jikany-Nuer villager killed an SPLA soldier in retaliation for killing one of their tribal members over a dispute involving food. The SPLA, in

turn, retaliated and massacred several hundred villagers. Although Garang and the Nuer commanders eventually forgave one another for the incident, many Nuer continued to hold festering grievances against Garang.

On August 28, 1991, Machar, Akol, and Chol finally acted on these grievances by officially announcing their declaration to remove Garang in a radio address broadcasted by the BBC. The announcement opened with harsh words for Garang, stating that "His megalomania and misguided policies alienated many and marginalized a wide cross section of members and potential members of the Movement. Garang was leading the Movement to doom."[33] The declaration stressed the need for rejuvenating the SPLM/A and ending human rights abuses (i.e., treating refugees and civilians humanely and abiding by the Geneva Conventions). Machar, Akol, and Chol also called on the Anyanya II fighters and government soldiers to join what would eventually become known as SPLA-Nasir. The founders of SPLA-Nasir wanted

> to assure all friends of the Movement that there is no split whatsoever. Whatever noises being made against the change are nothing more than a storm in a teacup and have no foundation on the ground. Like any other dictators, John Garang has surrounded himself with a coterie of opportunists, simpletons and flatterers. It will take him and them some time to realize that their dream world is at an end.[34]

Many Anyanya II members and government soldiers backed the declaration, hoping that it would lead to a collective uprising against Garang. Instead, it created an official split in the SPLA between the Nasir group and Garang's SPLA-Torit or Mainstream. Garang, for his part, was anxious to stamp out the revolt, dispatching William Nyuon Bany to march along the Jonglei canal to the Upper Nile—the only area where the Nasir group had managed to mobilize an army. The SPLA-Nasir meanwhile began to run low on supplies and lacked the logistical support to fight Garang's army. After considering their options, they chose to accept support from the Sudanese government, while at the same time attempting to maintain an antigovernment stance. With Khartoum's backing, then, Machar's army attacked the Dinka in the Bor region (Jonglei) in November 1991, killing an estimated 2,000 civilians.

Machar was quick to deny any involvement in what came to be known as the Bor massacre. But this did little to curtail the mounting suspicion of his role in the massacre. His suspected involvement caused him to lose credibility on one of the central pledges stated in the Nasir declaration: to protect the human rights of the South Sudanese. As he saw his support in the southern region erode, he and his Nasir faction turned to Khartoum, signing an agreement with the GoS

in Frankfurt, Germany. The text, however, left out the Nasir faction's demand for secession, which for many, amounted to a sell-out to Khartoum.

The agreement provided an important advantage for the GoS: it allowed the SAF to move more freely through Nasir-held territory and as such to regain some of the land it had lost to the SPLA, including parts of Jonglei and East Equatoria. After some of the Nuer commanders formed their own factions (such as William Nyuon Bany in September 1992 and Kerubino Kuanivan Bol in November 1993), other militias joined the Nasir faction to form a single movement known as the SPLA-Unified.[35] Garang's SPLA-Torit in the meantime reaffirmed its goals and saw the people's faith in its leadership restored. By the end of 1993, Garang was seen as the one leader genuinely committed to defeating the GoS and its rebel allies in the southern resistance movement. This had a profound effect on the perceived legitimacy of the SPLA-United and caused Machar to become more militaristic in an attempt to hold the movement together. Indeed, Machar found himself in a difficult position of having to fight with limited ammunition and arms supplies. Seeing his support network shrink around him, he had become increasingly isolated within his movement and leery of his own associates. This culminated in late 1993 in the dismissal of Akol, his deputy commander, who had criticized his decisions and actions.

Garang managed to capitalize on Machar's perceived treachery by strengthening his military ties to the neighboring state leaders that opposed the GoS. Yoweri Museveni, the President of Uganda and long-time friend of Garang, provided Garang with military assistance to contain the SAF, while also offsetting Mobuto's support of Khartoum and Nuer splinter groups.[36] However, the fighting intensified between the SPLA-United and the SPLA-Torit, resulting in more civilian casualties and human rights abuses. Humanitarian workers found it increasingly difficult to reach the wounded and the countless, starving victims. Eventually, the two warring sides were accused of using humanitarian aid to make up for shortages among their own ranks. Reflecting on these events, Donald Petterson, the former Ambassador to Sudan, wrote that

> I saw Garang in Uganda, on the night of February 28. I found him to be as inflexible as Riek on the question of putting aside their differences in order to end the fighting. Fighting the enemy, whether the government or another rebel faction, took precedence, and neither Garang nor Riek saw anything wrong with taking relief food meant for starving civilians and using it to feed soldiers and officials.[37]

Garang's and Machar's exploits amounted to mutual collateral damage. Both, it seemed, were willing to deflect responsibility for their abuses by accusing the

60   SOUTH SUDAN'S FATEFUL STRUGGLE

other of abuse or singling out Khartoum's meddlesome role in the conflict. The GoS, it turned out, was Garang's best shield against accountability, particularly given its adversarial relationship to the United States and neighboring countries. Yet Garang needed additional allies, including the government of Ethiopia led by the EPRDF. The Ethiopian government had already closed down SPLA camps and forced many SPLA fighters to return to South Sudan. The most immediate effect, wrote Douglas Johnson, was "the SPLA's loss of protected bases and secular supply lines, . . . and its highly effective radio station."[38] Furthermore, the Ethiopian government had allied itself with the GoS and turned over many sensitive SPLA files to the GoS, which later shared these files with its allies, including the SPLM-United, which hoped to use the information to move faster against Garang's SPLA.

But by the mid-1990s, both Machar and Garang were accused of committing wide-scale human rights abuses. In a subsequent interview in 2004 on *Hardtalk*, a BBC news show, Garang was asked if he bore any responsibility for the reported atrocities (e.g., torture and summary executions of civilians and fighters as well as the forced conscription of children) in April 1993. Garang denied the allegations and instead blamed the Sudanese government,[39] insisting that "When it has been investigated . . . It will show that Khartoum's corruption is the cause of the suffering of 2 million people."

To be fair to Garang, Khartoum had become the Nasir faction's principal supplier of arms. He was thus fighting two enemies at the same time, and in trying to counteract them, had allegedly resorted to torturing civilians suspected of colluding with the Nasir faction. The abuses, though, loomed large over Garang and eventually caused him to lose outside support and to impose a food tax on the people to replenish supplies.

Machar and Akol meanwhile counted on more fighters to defect from Garang's SPLA-Torit. However, many stayed loyal while others returned from the bush or other rebel groups. The great exodus from Garang's SPLA-Torit had failed to materialize. And Machar and Akol now faced their own challenges of defeating Garang, which included the lack of trust stemming from the collusion with the enemy and violating core principles of the Nasir declaration (e.g., human rights).[40] Both factors had strained much of their credibility on the issue of secession. How could one reasonably press for independence when the enemy from whom you were trying to secede was aiding your struggle? If nothing else, the contradiction created uncertainty about Machar's and Akol's ambitions and even seemed to turn Machar into a public double agent (persona non grata with the South Sudanese) who was doing the GoS's political bidding. The Nasir faction's secessionist agenda, in short, had become increasingly tenuous, especially as the Sudanese government sought to strengthen its ties with Hassan al-Turabi to sponsor terrorism.

In Machar, therefore, the GoS had found someone willing to pressure and destabilize Garang's SPLA-Torit. But Machar's treachery led more members of the Nuer community to oppose him. Many Nuer leaders, in fact, chose to migrate back to the SPLA-Torit. This was a heavy price to pay. And it was never entirely clear what Machar hoped to achieve by collaborating with the Government of Sudan. Was it simply an attempt to outmaneuver Garang, his chief rival? And if so, how did he expect to advance the South's self-determination when his main support came from the entity that was either likely to reject such a demand or force him to accept the limited terms of autonomy? The uncertainty cut directly to Machar's reckless pursuit of power, which left him cornered within his own party, the SPPM, desperate to resurrect his agenda of an independent South Sudan.

In late 1994, he created his own splinter movement, the Southern Sudan Independence Movement (SSIM), hoping that his Nuer soldiers and other Nuer youth would join the movement. But by now, he had lost almost all credibility as a leader of the Nuer people, many of whom refused to join or support the SSIM. His duplicity ultimately led other Nuer to form their own splinter groups to fight Garang's SPLA-Torit. The fighting between these groups and the SPLA-Torit resulted in the indiscriminate killing of countless civilians and the alienation of much of the civilian population in Nuer communities, which had now turned to the Nuer White Army—a loose band of volunteer fighters from Nuer communities (mostly Lou Nuer) for protection. Having emerged from the 1991 split of the SPLA, the White Army had helped protect the Nuer communities against the marauding militias that often threatened their lives and cattle. Yet it was for all intents and purposes a last line of defense of Nuer communities—far from the well-trained armed force that could replace the SPLA-United and take up the call for democratic accountability and human rights protection.

The SPLA-United, in fact, had grown increasingly fractious. Akol had formed his own faction of the SPLA-United in Tonga, which consequently forced the SPLA-United to change its name to the SSIM.[41] Machar, for his part, expelled Kerubino from the SSIM for having entered into an agreement with the GoS on behalf of the SSIM. In an effort to broaden the SSIM's appeal, Machar held high-level talks with Mohamed Salih, Sudan's Vice President, and agreed to the 1996 Peace Charter (1996), which called for peace and the unification of Sudan.[42] The plan was to steer the rebel factions in a new direction and allow the government to become a more compelling alternative to Garang's SPLA-Torit liberation. Yet Machar's decision to sign the Peace Charter placed him once again in the untenable position of making peace with the enemy from whom he was still trying to secede. Few inside the SPLM/A actually saw this as a good faith effort to make peace with the enemy; many ridiculed it as an unconditional surrender to Khartoum's authoritarianism.[43]

62 SOUTH SUDAN'S FATEFUL STRUGGLE

As it turned out, the Dinka and Nuer people were not as ignorant as Machar assumed. They knew about the limits of entering a pact with an adversary that had exploited them for many years. Still, Machar forged ahead. And on April 21, 1997, he and the leaders of the NIF—as well as various Nuer-based rebel forces—signed the Khartoum Peace Agreement (KPA). The rebel groups included the SSIM, the Union of Sudan African Parties led by Samuel Bol, the Sudan People's Liberation Movement headed by Kerubino Bol, and the Equatoria Defense Force. Machar seemed convinced that this was the only way to secure independence from Khartoum. But Garang's SPLA-Torit, which saw the move as treacherous, rejected the agreement outright. Khartoum now sought to outflank Garang by rejecting all his counterproposals, a move that led to a stalemate in negotiations to end the hostilities, particularly in the Bahr al Ghazal region.[44] Garang, though, eventually relented and agreed to sign the KPA.

The agreement contained provisions that would later be incorporated (and adjusted) into the CPA. Among these were a five-year period of rebuilding and recovery from the civil war, the promotion of the freedom of religion and movement, and a federal agreement that would pave the way for independence. For his cooperation, Machar was named the Commander-in-Chief of the newly formed South Sudan Defense Force and President of the Southern Sudan Coordinating Council. He was now committed to working directly with Khartoum to defeat Garang and achieve independence from Khartoum. But the problem was that Khartoum was never fully on board with secession. Machar either did not want to believe this or he simply failed to appreciate the depth of Khartoum's angst with independence and the South Sudanese people's displeasure with his own alliance with Khartoum. The KPA, in the end, underscored his growing detachment from the Nuer community, which never expected Khartoum to faithfully carry out the terms of the agreement.[45]

In 1998, there was growing disenchantment with the Nuer elites' war on the south, or South–South war.[46] Deep divisions within the Western Nuer community forced individual Nuer to take refuge with the SPLA-Torit. Many, in fact, chose to defect to the SPLA instead of joining one of the growing numbers of splinter groups in the South, which included the SSDF-2 in Juba, the SSDF-Friendly to the SPLA, and the SSDF-United. The government welcomed the plurality as a sign of the South's growing diversity (of opinion) and the Nuer community's determination to contest the SPLA-Torit's hegemony. But in reality, factionalism reflected the violent clashes that tore at the social fabric of the Nuer community and forced more Western Nuer to seek refuge with the SPLA-Torit.

The increasing violence prompted religious and tribal leaders to call for reconciliation and healing and to ultimately adopt the Nuer West Bank Peace and Reconciliation Process held in Wunlit, Bahr al Ghazal in February 1999. The conference was sponsored by the New Sudan Council of Churches and attended

by the leaders of the SPLA-Torit, the SSDF-United, church officials, tribal chiefs and several Dinka from Rumbek (e.g., Tonj and Yirol), Western Nuer, and civil society leaders. The Wunlit Dinka-Nuer covenant called for a permanent cease fire, amnesty, and the freedom of movement.[47] However, neither Garang nor Machar attended the conference. Garang instead had Salva Kiir, his deputy, participate on his behalf, while Machar remained in Khartoum. Machar and Western Nuer would eventually meet in the town of Waat in December 1999 to discuss the Covenant as well as strategies to reunite the community. The Nuer leaders agreed to abandon all ties with the Government of Sudan and pledged to make the South Sudan Liberation Movement independent of both the GoS and the SPLA-Torit.

The Wunlit conference had helped heal and unify much of the (Western) Nuer community. Yet its limited reach also raised the issue of how to broaden the reckoning process to include the ties between the SPLM/A and SSLM. How would a broader reckoning process enable the South Sudanese leaders to work together to further resist and ultimately govern the affairs of the South Sudanese people? As the starting point of the South's healing process, the Wunlit Conference remained important, and as Luka Biong Deng argues, "contributed to the unification of the different factions, which subsequently strengthened the position of the SPLM/A when signing the CPA."[48] Deng found that Khartoum's invasive and divisive role—and not factionalism itself—remained the greatest threat to the South Sudanese people's way of life. In other words, it was primarily this invasiveness, and not the factional leaders, that had led to the politicization of tribal identity. What was critical to understand of Wunlit, Deng concluded, was that it led to an understanding of "increased common threats. . . . and cooperation and motivation to pool their resources effectively by forming extended households and taking care of the victims of the civil war."[49] Wunlit had helped build the social capital that the civil war had destroyed, that is, the trust and social bonds needed to hold together the assemblage of tribal communities.

However, critics argued that the conference was ultimately a flawed attempt to achieve peace through local justice. The fact that the conference was not fully inclusive—it did not include other ethnic groups such as the Murle, the Shilluk and the Azande but focused almost entirely on Dinka and Nuer relations—reflected its limited scope. It thus failed to redress the many grievances that had caused the SPLM/A to splinter, including those of the Dinka from the 1991 Bor massacre. All of this raised the question of how a locally driven moral solution could resolve what was essentially a political problem of divided, tribal loyalty. The Wunlit conference seemed at best a good faith effort to work toward this solution at the national level. It was still too localized or rooted in customary law to produce a national reckoning process of healing and accountability in South Sudan. Customary law was limited in scope and applied to the rule

64   SOUTH SUDAN'S FATEFUL STRUGGLE

of tribal customs and local disputes involving the theft of livestock, marriage, and so forth. It did not address the conflicts between state and society and accountability for atrocities. Wunlit "[a]s a pragmatic process," writes Mahmood Mamdani, "papered over deep divisions opened up by 1991. . . . The 'reconciliation' that followed was driven by short-term considerations and was unable to avert the disaster in 2013."[50] Yet Wunlit did point to the important prospect of combining customary and statutory law to address the conflicts between state and society. I shall address this potential role in Chapter 5, where I discuss civil society's efforts to train the chiefs in statutory law and to revise existing law which has curtailed their discretionary power at the communal level. Here it's important to stress the stark division between the Sudanese state and South Sudanese society and the fact that customary law remained at the bottom rung of a hierarchical arrangement of justice—designed by the British in the early twentieth century—which isolated its broader impact on society.

Wunlit in this sense failed to bolster Machar's cause. Machar still had to convince the Nuer people that collaboration with Khartoum was a necessary tradeoff to achieve independence for South Sudan. This meant that he had to rely on Khartoum to carry out its commitment to the KPA. But by late 2000, Khartoum began to back away from its commitment, leaving Machar powerless to negotiate. When the GoS failed to implement a referendum on self-determination for South Sudan, Machar had no choice but to cut off all ties to Khartoum in early 2001, making him persona non grata in the southern movement. Taban Gai, one of his closest, loyal contacts, eventually chose to leave the SPDF to rejoin the SPLA. Gai declared that, "We have seen our disunity benefiting only the Khartoum government which has been using it to kill us more. And now with the revenue of oil they have become more intransigent."[51] Gai's own admission of guilt over his collusion was followed by Machar's rejoining the SPLA. Ever the tactician, Machar had managed to open up a channel of communication with Garang to convince Garang to take him back in. For Garang, Machar's action marked an opportunity to reunify the SPLA under his leadership and to work toward the larger goal of national unity. Justin Yac, an SPLA official, summed it up best:

> During apartheid in South Africa there were a lot of atrocities committed by whites against blacks and blacks against whites but then there was reconciliation . . . All of us are guilty of one thing or other.

Yac though seemed to overlook a key difference between the two movements: namely, the moral and political leadership of Nelson Mandela (Madiba) and Desmond Tutu. Yet, the comparison was apt in the sense that reconciliation figured to end the ethnic and racial divide within the country.

THE DIVIDED MOVEMENT   65

When the SPDF reunited with the SPLA on May 28, 2001, it officially ended nearly 11 years of Nuer and Dinka disunity.[52]

Perhaps more important, SPLM/A reunification cut off a key source of Khartoum's influence and motivated more alienated Nuer fighters to join the SPLA. In marking an official end to the South-South war, the reunification of Nuer and Dinka allowed the Intergovernmental Authority on Development (IGAD) to refocus on the North-South war and on ending the stalemate between the Islamic North and Christian South. IGAD, which had mediated the NCP and SPLM/A conflict, and whose members included Djibouti, Ethiopia, Eritrea, Kenya, Somalia, Sudan, and Uganda, was a Western-funded organization that in 1995, had expanded its mandate on development to include peace and security.[53] At its seventh session meeting held in July 1999, it adopted measures that included an invigorated secretariat and newly empowered envoys from Eritrea, Ethiopia, and Uganda.[54] The Libya-Egypt Initiative, for instance, managed to bring both the GoS and the SPLM/A to the table to agree to a permanent ceasefire. The United States by this time had already expanded its economic ties with the SPLM/A through a carrot and stick approach intended to induce Sudan to cooperate with IGAD. It offered nearly $3 million in logistical support to the SPLM/A and pressured Khartoum by threatening to keep Sudan on its terrorist list.

The growing alliance with the SPLA had as much to do with counterpressuring the government of Sudan as it did with the United States' desire to promote Garang, the liberal reformer. The United States, in fact, expected Garang to temper his socialist ideology and in the process, embrace political liberalism. The idea was, as John Young points out, to turn Garang into a liberal democrat and "encourage him to abandon any orthodox Marxist-Leninist principles such as class warfare, imperialism, and the dissolution of private property."[55] The fact that Garang was never a hardened communist ideologue made this goal feasible. Yet it also casted new light on his pragmatic skills and goals of securing economic support from the Ethiopia's Derg and Eastern European countries. The United States—the champion of liberal democracy—now provided essential economic and political support to the SPLA, despite Garang's reported human rights abuses. It was support that further solidified Garang's role as a unifier of the South and an ally in pressuring Khartoum.

Making Peace

A combination of factors, then, created a favorable environment for brokering a ceasefire and a peace process. First, the SPLA's unification decreased Bashir's political leverage over the movement. The emergence of a much less

influential Sudan People's Defense Force (SPDF), led by Paulino Matip, meant that Khartoum essentially lost its ability to divide and subvert the SPLM/A. Second, the peace process offered the NCP an opportunity to end a costly war that had accounted for nearly 15 percent of the government's gross domestic product in 2000. Moreover, given the economic sanctions levied against the Sudanese government for its support of terrorism, the NCP feared that a prolonged war would lead to increased sanctions. It was also unclear if Sudan could continue to depend on oil revenue alone to finance the war. The sharp drop in oil prices had increased its public debt and left it cash-strapped.[56] Third, while a reunited SPLM/A could never defeat the SAF, the SPLA's victories in the Eastern Equatoria and Bahr al Ghazal convinced the SAF that it could not win the war. As Garang would later state, "There are no shortcuts to peace."[57]

As the United States secured ties with the SPLM/A, its relations with Sudan remained fraught with uncertainty. After the attacks on the Nairobi and Dar es Salaam Embassies in 1998, the United States launched cruise missiles into Sudan that destroyed Sudan's pharmaceutical plant, Al-Shifa. The attacks were meant to punish Sudan for its alleged involvement in the terrorist attacks on the Embassies. But it came at a time when President Bill Clinton was facing impeachment and needed, it seemed, an event to distract the public's attention. The Clinton administration claimed to have evidence that proved that the factory was attempting to produce the VX nerve gas, and that revealed the ties between the Sudanese government and Iran and Bin Laden (who despite being driven out of the Sudan, continued to own a firm in the country). Meanwhile, the owners of the factory and the Sudanese government insisted that they were only making medicine.

Eventually, the United States conceded that while their evidence was faulty, it was insufficient to rule out the factory's role.[58] The owners of the factory then decided to sue the US government, only to have their suit dismissed in a US appeals court on the grounds that the court could not take up a case involving the political question doctrine.[59] When it was later revealed that the factory was likely used to manufacture medicines for the United Nations, Turabi and Bashir became incensed, calling the bombing a terrorist attack that would only help produce more terrorists.[60]

This, however, did little to alleviate the pressure on the Sudanese government. In November 1999, the United States signed a bill authorizing the release of economic and military aid to the SPLA. None of the assistance was classified as humanitarian, which was surprising, given the scope of the humanitarian crisis. But by now, the United States' main strategy in Sudan was to counter the threat posed by political Islam to democracy and human rights.[61] And this meant investing in Garang's SPLM/A in order to bring the civil war to an end and to build a peaceful, democratic Sudanese nation-state.

The United States saw the war in largely binary terms, between a Christian democratic South and an Islamic North. In championing Garang as a liberal reformer, the "Circle" or "Friends of South Sudan," a group that included the UN Envoy Susan Rice, John Prendergast, the founder of the Enough Project, and Ted Dagne, treated Garang as the savior of the South Sudanese people and a future state ruler. There was apparently little consideration given to South Sudan's undeveloped institutions, Garang's alleged human rights abuses, the tension between Garang's New Sudan and the South's secessionist sentiment, and the SPLM/A's factionalism that had divided the organization along tribal lines.[62] The "Circle's" strategy essentially ignored Nuer concerns about Garang's authoritarianism and his refusal to share power. For them, Garang had succeeded in reigning in the opportunists who sought to divide the SPLM/A, while at the same time maintaining a barrier against Bashir in the South. The "Circle," in short, succeeded in casting Garang as the protagonist of peace, a leader committed to US values in the region and the best hope of establishing a new democratic state. But in so doing, they also oversimplified the conflict and diminished the need for an internal reckoning (of the SPLM/A with South Sudanese society) with past abuses.

Another issue of the United States' support of Garang was whether it could count on Garang to fulfill his role as savior. Would he see the difference between his militaristic past and the soft approach needed to realize his New Sudan vision? The United States seemed to think so. But Garang's liberal democratic qualities hinged on something else: the appeal of his democratic vision to South Sudanese, and not just the United States. The reality was that Garang's New Sudan vision enjoyed limited appeal, since it assumed that Khartoum would someday accede to it. Few expected Garang's New Sudan to produce Sudanese national unity and a national unity more compelling than South Sudanese national unity. The fact was that Hassan al-Turabi remained a powerful influence within the NIF, despite the heightening tensions between him and Bashir, which stemmed from [Turabi's] alleged ties to a 1995 assassination attempt on Hosni Mubarak, the former Egyptian President. This meant that Khartoum and Juba remained deeply divided on basic social issues.[63] There were simply too many social and psychological barriers to realizing the New Sudan.

The United States also oversimplified the nature of the conflict. A large contingency of US leaders preferred to see the struggle in biblical terms, or principally between Islamic Muslims in the North and Christians in the South. Spurred by evangelical preachers like Franklin Graham, the son of Billy Graham and spiritual advisor to President George W. Bush, the United States saw its higher mission in terms of bringing peace to the region where Islam had become a "wicked religion."[64] It was a mission of course that enjoyed a long history, starting with the Christian evangelicals' efforts in the nineteenth century. Now it was part of large

68 SOUTH SUDAN'S FATEFUL STRUGGLE

network of actors seeking to promote peace in the region, where US evangelical Christians had joined forces with secular NGOs, for example, Save the Children and the Anti-Defamation League, to redress the violence and human suffering.

In September 2001, President Bush bolstered the mission by appointing former US Senator John Danforth, a former Christian Evangelical minister himself, as US Special Envoy to Sudan. Danforth was sent to Sudan in response to the Sudan's attack on the South, which had resulted in numerous civilian deaths. His overarching objective was to open up moral dialogue between the two sides that had expressed a desire for peace. One of his early objectives was to get both the SPLM/A and NCP to recognize their role in the perpetration of human rights atrocities and then bring both sides in line with international human rights norms. But its implementation depended largely on the ability and willingness of IGAD to mediate the dispute between both warring sides. This had become a source of considerable grievance for the NCP, since IGAD seemed to be an appendage of Western influence. Furthermore, the measures appeared to target the NCP by focusing on its human rights violations.[65] The NCP responded by calling attention to the SPLM/A's ties with the rebels in Darfur, the Western region of Sudan. Then, somewhat unexpectedly, it sent a force to the Nuba Mountains in January 2002 to drive out the rebels.

The move forced Senator Danforth, who had intended to visit the area, to fly directly to Khartoum, where he spoke out against Sudan's blatant violation of the measures.[66] Danforth would eventually submit his report (the Danforth Report) to President George W. Bush on April 26, 2002, which confirmed a ceasefire in the Nuba Mountains. The report outlined several confidence-building measures, including: (1) facilitating and allowing the delivery of humanitarian aid to reach its intended target in the Nuba Mountains, the Central Equatoria, and Bahr al Ghazal regions; (2) allowing for temporary cessations of conflict in the regions where the authorities could conduct humanitarian assessments; (3) bringing an end to slavery; and (4) ceasing with aerial bombardment of the civilian population.[67] It also stressed the SPLM/A's and NCP's desire to end the conflict and called on the United States to collaborate with other countries to establish a permanent ceasefire.[68] In many ways, the report forced the United States to prioritize the protection of religious and cultural freedoms and revenue sharing, but not the complex dynamics of party factionalism (and its tribal dimension), including the role of Khartoum. The United States had adopted a narrative in which a unified SPLM/A stood for democracy and peace and the theocratic Sudan represented a threat to the United States' national interests.[69]

Sudan in this respect had become a pariah state due to its support of terrorists overseas. Although it condemned the 9-11 attacks on the World Trade Center and Pentagon, it was also a strong critic of the US invasion of Afghanistan in November 2001. In fact, it had ended up indirectly supporting al-Qaeda by not

condemning the Taliban-controlled state that harbored al-Qaeda fighters. The Bush administration responded by imposing more sanctions on Sudan, a decision that followed the US House of Representatives' adoption of the Sudan Peace Act, which denied Sudan's access to oil revenue that was being allocated for military purposes. Still, the United States' big-stick approach proved too controversial for other countries to support. In their view, the United States was seeking to apply a financial law to an international situation.[70]

By early 2003, Bashir openly supported Hamas and other terrorist organizations. And rather than punishing Sudan, the United States adopted a different approach: to incentivize it to stop its support of terrorism. Colin Powell, the US Secretary of State, pledged to drop Sudan from the United States' list of terrorist states and to drop all sanctions, if it agreed to cooperate with the United States' demands. It is difficult to know if Powell's demands compelled the NCP to drop its support of terrorists. But by now, Bashir feared the consequences of the US global campaign against political Islam (i.e., the invasion of Afghanistan made Bashir believe that Sudan could be next). The NCP had a stark choice, then: either continue resisting the United States' growing influence in South Sudan or agree to reconcile its differences with the SPLM/A and with the newly formed Troika comprising the United States, the United Kingdom, and Norway.

The Comprehensive Peace Agreement

The Government of Sudan chose the latter. In June 2002, it met with SPLM/A leaders in Machakos, Kenya to begin the first phase of negotiations on a draft framework agreement on governance, self-determination, elections, a consensus on wealth and power sharing, border dispute resolution, and democratization.[71] The Machakos Protocols included commitments by both sides to adopt a six-year period for implementing the agreement, a referendum on self-determination, and separating church and state. This had come after both sides agreed to make key concessions on administering Islamic law or sharia in the North and a referendum on self-determination. The GoS ultimately agreed to exempt sharia in the South, and the SPLM, in turn, was willing to allow the GoS to enforce sharia in the North.[72] The SPLM initially wanted a short transition period of either two to four years, but the GoS insisted on a 10-year timeline. Eventually, both sides agreed to a six-year period and a referendum on self-determination that would be held at the end of the six-year period. For the SPLM, extending the interim period was needed to give unity a chance. However, for the GoS, the referendum meant losing the southern region and considerable access to material resources. As a result, the government wanted further assurances and specific commitments to wealth and power sharing.

70 SOUTH SUDAN'S FATEFUL STRUGGLE

These would come in subsequent meetings held in February 2003 in Karen, Kenya, where the parties discussed the new terms of wealth sharing. Yet with the Troika acting as observers of the talks, the two sides could not agree on a specific percentage of shared oil revenue. The issue was whether the two sides needed a successful formula of "equitable" power to work out their differences—a formula that would allow both warring sides to interpret and justify their claims to wealth sharing. For the SPLM, leveling the playing field was not simply about dividing their shares evenly, but also compensating the South Sudanese for the oppression that had left the educational system and economic sector severely undeveloped in relation to the North. The SPLM wanted the cost of reparations factored into the final percentage share of natural resources. It was wary about surrendering too much of its natural resources to the North.

Still, the considerable wealth gap between the North and South managed to impede the consensus based on the working formula. This ultimately limited IGAD's mediation efforts and led to the Troika's more active role in shaping the peace process. Their first and perhaps most controversial action was designating Garang and Ali Osman Taha, the Vice President of Sudan, as the sole lead negotiators of the SPLM delegation and the GoS, respectively. What it demonstrated was an ability to control a process in which they determined the parameters, or how and which issues were prioritized and negotiated. Their primary goal was to make the negotiating process more efficient and at the same time, pressure both sides to reach agreement on key issues, including a framework for a new structure of government. But streamlining the peace process was a risky move, since it meant that if the negotiations failed there would be no higher authority to which to appeal.[73] With no apparent democratic procedure to hold these two principals to account for their decisions, the Troika had to rely on these leaders' stature to suppress the political internal strife within their own parties.

And yet to allow the talks to become bogged down in debate only risked further delays and a loss of credibility. The fact that there was no discussion of democratic institutional building and moral accountability for human rights atrocities suggested that the Troika had already settled on a streamlined approach to reaching peace.[74] This meant steering clear of any divisive issues that could complicate and delay the talks. It also contradicted earlier condemnations of and recommendations for ending the violence. Both the United States and the United Nations, for instance, condemned the scorched-earth tactics and aerial bombing launched by the GoS (for its military support of the Janjaweed's refusal to provide better access to relief workers). In June 2004, Colin Powell became the first US Secretary of State to visit the devastated areas in nearly two decades—where he called on the international community to act promptly to end the violence. At the same time, the US Senate, in an unprecedented move to declare

the Darfur situation a genocide, approved a resolution that called on the Bush administration to "impose targeted means, including visa bans and the freezing of assets, against officials and other individuals of the Government of Sudan."[75]

Another issue concerned the cessation of fighting in areas with disputed boundaries. The CPA consisted of two protocols on three disputed areas: The *Protocol on the Resolution of Conflict in Southern Kordofan and Blue Nile States* (2004); and the *Protocol on the Resolution of Conflict in the Abyei Area* (2004). Each protocol contained the rules and procedures for resolving these disputes concerning land. But Khartoum's continued support of anti-SPLM/A forces (e.g., the SPLA-North and the SSDF) impeded and ultimately thwarted any binding agreement. In addition, the SPLA's attacks on the SAF in Torit further dampened interest in implementing the protocols, while also highlighting the seeming irreconcilable claims of both warring sides to the areas under dispute.

The SPLM wanted Abyei, the Blue Nile, and Nuba Mountains to be designated as three areas and as such, to hold separate referendums to determine their status. However, the GoS rejected the idea, suspecting that a referendum on South Sudan would enable all three areas to be absorbed by a new state of South Sudan. Should this happen, the GoS would lose all rights to oil in these areas. As a result, a stalemate in negotiations ensued, which the United States eventually broke when Senator Danforth encouraged both sides to agree on Abyei's special administrative status. Under this tentative agreement, Abyei would be administered by the presidency; its borders determined by the Abyei Borders Commission. A referendum would be held later in the future to settle the claims of the Ngok Dinka and the Misseriya, an Arab-based tribe living in the area.

The commission submitted their final report in July 2005. But Khartoum quickly rejected it. Their main concern was that the commission had based their findings on only twentieth and twenty-first century sources rather than early historical sources that would alter the conclusions of the commission. Khartoum's rejection was also based on its concern with the potential loss of oil rights related to the conflict between its land-use right and the Misseriya, whose secondary rights to resources complicated the GoS's claims. Yet the experts of the commission found that the border stipulated by the Abyei Protocol should "bisect" in this area of overlapping secondary rights.[76] Douglas Johnson, an appointed member of the commission, believed that the GoS had no intention of agreeing to this recommendation, since it knew that Misseriya leadership would reject it (which they did). "Khartoum," he writes, "continued a policy of surreptitious annexation by encouraging the settlement of Misseriya in the former Dinka territory, while impeding the return of the displaced Ngok Dinka."[77] This soon led to renewed violence in the areas, and eventually to the consent by the SPLM/A and the GoS to have the UN Permanent Court of Administration resolve the matter in 2008.

72   SOUTH SUDAN'S FATEFUL STRUGGLE

Abyei's contested boundaries highlighted the complex issues of regional security. The most difficult concerned the integration of security forces. The GoS had demanded one integral force, or the reintegration of the SPLA into the SAF. The SPLM rejected this demand and successfully pressured Khartoum to agree to the SPLA's continued existence. In its defense, Garang had reasoned that the SPLM/A was the only player in the South capable of implementing the CPA. The SPLM/A also insisted that the SAF withdraw its troops from the southern region in order to prevent the GoS from meddling in its affairs. This meant recruiting well-trained leaders and officials to run the affairs of the new government pursuant to the Interim Constitution and the CPA.

In late 2003, the two sides still had not reached agreement on many key issues, including wealth sharing. President Bush repeatedly telephoned Garang and Bashir to encourage them to work out their differences and to sign the CPA. The two finally agreed to resolve two key issues: (1) maintaining the SPLA as a fighting force, and (2) specifying the amounts or percentages of wealth sharing (e.g., oil revenue). They also agreed, after months of trying to work out a formula of equitable power, to an equal share of rights to oil and access to water. The North would receive 50 percent of oil revenue; the Southern region, 48 percent; and the surrounding regions and states, 2 percent.[78] An Oil Revenue Stabilization Account would oversee the distribution of profits, and the terms of the agreement on wealth sharing would apply to all areas with the exception of Abyei.

Bashir eventually agreed to both conditions. But infighting within the SPLM/A led to a lengthy impasse between the two warring sides in late 2004. Neither was willing speak to the other. The impasse soon forced the UN Security Council to hold a special meeting in Nairobi in November 2004, in which it issued an ultimatum: that unless they resolved their differences and signed the agreement, they would face severe repercussions by the end of 2004.[79] On December 31, 2004, the two warring sides signed the Permanent Ceasefire and Security Arrangement, which required both to participate in the Disarmament, Demobilization, and Reintegration (DDR) program. The program applied to only the SAF and SPLA and outlawed all other militias, which were forced to disband and reintegrate into either the SAF or SPLA.[80] It also created a National DDR Coordination Council to separate the DDR process in the South and North; a joint DDR Council would administer the DDR program in the three areas. By late 2005, an Interim DDR program was created to enhance the capacity building of DDR institutions, to reintegrate former soldiers, and to train personnel. The Interim DDR was tasked with identifying the needs of groups, or so-called Special Needs Groups that included elderly and disabled fighters and women and conscripted children. By 2007, a National Strategic Plan for the DDR had been established; nearly 130,000 people from the North and South participated in the plan. The DDR would thus

remain a bright spot of national security during the interim period, providing a stable and reliable mechanism of reintegration.

The GoS thus wanted a united national army. But the SPLM rejected its demand to disband the SPLA and to reintegrate its soldiers into the SAF. The representatives for the SPLM insisted that the SPLA still provided the security needed to implement the terms of the CPA. The GoS eventually relented, agreeing to withdraw its troops from the southern region, even though it still expected the SPLA to be converted into a national force (if unity, not secession, succeeded). Bashir, in the end, failed to secure the favorable concessions he had hoped to achieve.

Despite the concessions, international policymakers were losing patience, frustrated with the lagging pace of negotiations. They eventually pressured the two sides to accept the terms of the CPA. And on January 9, 2005, the two warring sides signed the CPA, bringing an official end to one of the bloodiest, protracted civil wars and creating the Government of Southern Sudan (GoSS)—with Garang appointed as its President (and the Vice President of the GoS)—and an Interim Constitution of Southern Sudan.[81]

The Interim Constitution stipulated the rules, principles, and structure for governing Southern Sudan. It was drafted by Western law firms and legal institutions such as the Max Planck Institute, which had consulted the Troika and European Union, respectively. Not surprisingly, it featured an extensive list of political, civil, economic, and cultural rights and democratic rules. But there were few mechanisms to enforce these rights and to prosecute the violators of human rights. Moreover, protecting the regional leaders and civilians against Sudan's encroachments was no longer the key issue. Rather, it was ensuring the development of regional institutions to protect the rights of the South Sudanese people. Despite the emphasis on human rights protections, such as religious and cultural freedoms, it soon became apparent that the Interim Constitution was not the binding agreement that many assumed. The sudden influx of oil revenue and the shared feeling that Sudan would somehow renege on its commitments and return the country to war, seemed to eclipse the constitution's influence. In short, the CPA, in failing to address the accountability of leaders for past abuses, had nurtured (albeit unintentionally) a culture of impunity, in which personal entitlement to power undermined the very spirit of the constitution and its normative constraints.[82]

The issue, then, was not simply whether the CPA failed or was flawed, but how negotiators expected to succeed in the long term when there was no actual reckoning with the past violence and rights abuses. To succeed in this respect, the parties to the agreement had to address the root cause of party factionalism and the violent intersections of secessionism and tribal identity politics. However, the Troika decided to prioritize the religious binaries of the conflict to suit

74 SOUTH SUDAN'S FATEFUL STRUGGLE

their national interests of countering terrorism and promoting liberal democracy. And while the imposition of sharia had helped ignite the war, the South Sudanese had grown tired of it—and the violence stemming from tribal identity politics. They of course still feared the Islamists in the North, but their principal concern, it could be argued, was the intertribal violence and party factionalism. The question therefore was how the SPLM/A could liberate itself from the debilitating effects of factionalism and end the North's oppression of the South.

To its credit, the CPA did liberate the South Sudanese from much of the oppression by the North. In providing a detailed road map for peace between the South and North, it allowed the GoS to retain 75 percent control of the two chambers of parliament, the SPLM 70 percent of the seats in the transitional parliament.[83] The hope was that as the SPLM evolved as a political entity, it would come to downplay its dependence on a strong military force and seek to integrate its forces into the SAF. But the reality was that the SPLM/A remained a largely divided movement, with a military force made up of loosely connected militias. As long as it remained a nonprofessional unit, Sudan had to settle on working with and partly absorbing rogue/rebel militias into its forces.

An Uncertain Legacy

Garang's immediate task as the new President of the GoSS and Vice President of the GoS, was to provide for the basic needs of the South Sudanese people. "For the last 21 years," he said in a National Public Radio interview in 2005, "I have been looking for guns and bullets to fight war."[84] His wish now was to go from guns to a new market for producing agricultural goods that, in his view, would prevent Sudan from "becoming chauvinistic and fascist." The United States and international officials saw him as a liberal democrat whose social pragmatism offered the best hope for promoting human rights and democracy in the region. For Garang the post-CPA era presented an opportunity to advance this agenda and ultimately to test his vision of a New Sudan.

However, on July 30, 2005, after visiting Khartoum where crowds numbered in the millions had welcomed his return. Garang was killed when his helicopter crashed in bad weather near the border of Sudan and Uganda. Many suspected foul play and took to the streets to protest the government. Riots broke out in Juba and other areas of Sudan, even as SPLM/A leaders urged the people to show restraint. In in her eulogy of Garang, Rebecca De Mabior, Garang's wife, called on the South Sudanese to set aside their grievances and recognize her husband's singular achievement of negotiating the CPA and bringing peace and autonomy to the region.[85] Although her words were meant to reassure the South Sudanese of their future, they also raised the issue of Garang's legacy: whether

he had prepared the South Sudanese leaders to accept and implement his New Sudan, a vision he had hoped would suture past wounds and divisions. Garang had proved to be a skilled and charismatic leader who was deified by many of his people and regarded by them as the "Moses" of the South Sudanese. Yet it was never clear if his deification had produced a concerted commitment to carry out his New Sudan vision, or if it had diminished the secessionist sentiment of his Dinka commanders. He clearly had loyal commanders, which included Salva Kiir, arguably his most loyal lieutenant. Kiir lacked Garang's charisma and education, but made up for these shortcomings with a discerning intelligence, a sharp attention to detail, and an impressive memory.

Garang's untimely death ultimately left a void in South Sudan's politics and the post-CPA process. It was never clear if his charisma and influence would help the SPLM/A transition to a new democratic state, given his own autocratic tendencies as military commander. No one of course will know. We can only speculate on whether Garang's communicative skills and sense of commitment to the CPA (as the leader and sole negotiator) would have prevented some of the pitfalls of the interim period, such as the failure to resolve border disputes and the misappropriation of billions of dollars in oil revenue. Or if he would have advocated consistently for human rights protections and civil society, especially given his denial of rights abuses and scorched-earth tactics that contributed to the starvation of countless civilians. Whatever Garang's legacy may be, South Sudan's problems remain deep-seated and complex—the result of years of neglect, which left it largely unprepared to govern its affairs and to confront the past.

Conclusion

The SPLM/A emerged as a promising armed resistance movement with an ambitious vision of transforming the country into a democratic, multiethnic state. Despite its success on the field of battle, its mission was afflicted by a combination of unruly personal ambition and tribal politics. In 1991 this culminated in a rebellion that split the SPLM/A into two factions—and led Machar to form an alliance with Khartoum to counteract Garang's SPLA-Torit. The alliance between Machar and Khartoum divided the Nuer community and increased the violence in much of the Nuer community. The Wunlit Conference offered some relief and even reconciliation for the Nuer, but it was hardly sufficient to heal the wounds caused by the war.

Although Garang managed to reunite much of the SPLM/A in 2001, there was little time (and perhaps interest) to put together a more comprehensive process of moral reckoning with past abuses and grievances. The SPLM/A had to negotiate peace with Khartoum and put together a complex framework for sharing

resources. The two sides, as we saw, remained divided on many issues (e.g., security), which led to delays and significant international pressure to sign the agreement. Yet Garang was able to draw on his skills to work out many differences with the other side, which made his death and failure to orchestrate some reckoning all the more tragic.

The CPA of course was supposed to offer a long-term framework for resolving border disputes and any conflict over resource sharing. But many of these issues would remain unresolved, even with international arbitration. In many ways, then, the CPA seemed more like a process of patching old wounds than actual healing. The parties to the CPA never in this sense put an end to the South-South war; they merely paused this war and ended the North-South war.

In the end, the Troika, was never concerned with healing per se, since it was more important to stop the violence. It had become involved in the region in order to seize control of the narrative of bringing peace to Sudan, which meant linking peace and democracy with countering terrorism and providing humanitarian protection to the Christian southerners being persecuted by the Islamic North. In short, the Troika extruded factors like democratic and moral accountability for human rights abuses and doomed, as we shall see in the next chapter, South Sudan's ability and willingness to transition to functional statehood.

3

The Troubled Transition

The interim period saw South Sudan eventually transition to new statehood. And unlike its first autonomous arrangement (1972–1983), the Government of Sudan accepted the outcome. The difference this time was the international pressure on Bashir and the SPLM/A's consolidation of power. Both seemed to compel Bashir to accept the results of the 2010 general elections and the subsequent 2011 referendum. The eventual outcome, though, also followed a lengthy period in which the SPLM/A and NCP had tried to make unity attractive for Sudanese citizens and concerned international players.

But making unity attractive was difficult and for some, unrealistic. It had the unfortunate effect, as some have noted, of becoming a "straight jacket that made it difficult for involved parties to plan the transition to an independent South Sudan."[1] Furthermore, Garang's death had led to a growing ambivalence toward Sudanese national unity. Fewer SPLM/A leaders and civilians believed that a democratic, multiethnic state of Sudan could be achieved, especially given Khartoum's past duplicity. And yet to opt for secession, the SPLM/A leaders also had to make such a demand attractive and necessary. Attractive in this case referred to the political and military preparedness of the South Sudanese leaders, and meant selling secession as a peaceful way to assert control over South Sudan's political destiny as a new democratic state. Necessary, by comparison, reflected the ability of the SPLM/A to frame secession not as a choice but as an earned collective right of the South Sudanese to be free from northern oppression. In merging the two, then, the SPLM/A sought to champion its political and military power.

Secession in effect became the SPLM/A's solution to national liberation. Yet there were still issues about the ruling elite's preparedness and ability to govern a new state. If secession, for instance, was largely an instrument to gain political domination over the people, then what mechanisms would be put into place to check the effects of SPLM domination, such as corruption, lack of transparency, and accountability? Much of this depended on the SPLM's own willingness and civic training to implement such mechanisms. But it was unclear if the key international actors such as the Troika, would be willing to offer the services for such training and oversight. For many, the Troika had in many ways facilitated corruption by not effectively monitoring the GoSS's affairs, that is, the flow of oil wealth and democratic institutional building. To address these issues, therefore,

South Sudan's Fateful Struggle. Steven C. Roach, Oxford University Press. © Oxford University Press 2023.
DOI: 10.1093/oso/9780190057848.003.0004

SOUTH SUDAN'S FATEFUL STRUGGLE

I shall discuss Kiir's role in the consolidation of the SPLM's power and the events and forces that shaped corruption and led to the adoption of the Transitional Constitution.

A Change of Guard

After Garang died in July 2005, Kiir, the second in command to Garang, had to take over for a man who many deified as the "Moses" of the South Sudanese people. It was a tough act to follow, but Kiir had developed a close working relationship with Garang and had learned about the SPLA's logistics. Like Garang, Kiir was a Dinka who had ambitious plans for liberating South Sudan from Sudan.[2] In 1967, at the age of 16, he joined the Anyanya and served under Joseph Lagu (Kiir would later appoint Lagu to serve as his advisor) as a low-ranking officer. For the next several years, he remained an active member of the Anyanya II, and in 1983, joined other Anyanya II members to establish the SPLA. He would turn out to be one of Garang's most trusted loyal advisors on issues such as self-determination. At the Machakos talks, for instance, he helped draft the terms of self-determination of a united Sudan, while advising Garang on other security issues. Even after Garang's death, he spoke in support of a "New Sudan," stating, "Well, we agreed in the Comprehensive Peace Agreement, that we work for the unity of Sudan. And so, according to the Machakos Protocol, unity of our country is the priority of the two parties in the agreement. And so, it doesn't cross our mind that secession is the first objective of the SPLM."[3]

Still, Kiir's support for making unity attractive remained strained. In October 2007, the SPLM pulled out of the Government of National Unity to condemn what it saw as the NCP's unwillingness to demarcate the official borders of the southern region. The GoS, it seemed, wanted to prevent officials from administering the census, even though it was needed to register voters and hold elections in the South. It feared that it would give the SPLM an important advantage in the upcoming national elections. But in the end, it was international pressure that eventually compelled it to hold the census.

Kiir's main challenge at this early stage of the interim period was appeasing Bashir's intransigence and the large international donors' concern that secession would destabilize the Sudanese government. In 2005, for instance, the International Criminal Court had opened an investigation into Bashir's ties to the violence in the Darfur region. Bashir was also unwilling to compromise on the boundaries of South Kordofan and Abyei areas of South Sudan. In light of Bashir's continued intransigence, it was becoming clear that the Old Sudan was not ready to yield to the New Sudan. Kiir, though, sought to articulate his own vision of the New Sudan.

The vision of bringing about radical and fundamental change in the Sudan is based on the correct and visionary definition of the central problem of Sudan as embedded in the concept of "Old Sudan", which is characterized by racism, religious intolerance, instability, and wars. The New Sudan is a Sudan, which is based on what unites and not on what divides, a Sudan which lives in peace within itself and its neighbors, and with the rest of humanity, and a Sudan which is united by the voluntary and free will of its people and achieved through the exercise of self-determination.[4]

For Kiir, the New Sudan remained an integral part of the SPLM/A's mission. Ever loyal to Garang, even in death, he clung to the idea that South Sudan's struggle for self-determination was ultimately about unifying the nation of Sudan. Publicly, he was still trying to make unity attractive, even though he distrusted Bashir and did not rule out secession. He had, it appeared, effectively learned to privately hedge his bets on secession by watching Bashir's weakening power play out. Bashir's subsequent 2009 arrest warrant for genocide by the ICC, for example, had largely isolated him diplomatically.[5] Bashir responded by aggressively condemning the warrant and encouraging his followers to protest the ICC which he labeled as an imperialist tool of the West.[6] He then ordered additional troops to Darfur to drive out the humanitarian workers in the region (e.g., Doctors without Borders). His growing hostility caused some US diplomats such as Andrew Natsios, the US Special Envoy to Sudan, to accuse the ICC of over meddling in the peace process.[7]

Whether the ICC's meddlesome role was to blame, Bashir's hostile actions had clearly made unity less attractive for the SPLM and international donors. Moreover, even though the CPA did not address the situation in Darfur, Kiir could still use it to stress Bashir's lawlessness and poor leadership.[8] Indeed, in a 2006 meeting with President George W. Bush, he insisted that "the people in Darfur will still be looking forward . . . to peace . . . It is a joint mission that we have taken upon ourselves. . . . that we have to bring peace to the Darfur the way that we have brought peace to Southern Sudan."[9] Kiir naturally wanted more international support for the SPLM's efforts to reintegrate the SPLA. He knew, for instance, that such support would earn him the good will of the international community, which he hoped to use to advance the South Sudanese' self-determination and regional security.

Loyalty and Reconciliation

Another challenge facing Kiir was the reintegration of the armed forces, in particular, the incorporation of rebellious factions such as the Other Armed

80 SOUTH SUDAN'S FATEFUL STRUGGLE

Groups (OAG) and the Southern Sudan Defense Forces (SSDF), which were not party to the CPA. The SSDF, for example, consisted of nearly 50,000 troops and represented perhaps the largest, most immediate threat to the SPLA. Unsurprisingly, the SPLM/A looked to reach an understanding with these factions. It soon opened talks with the rebels, and in January 2006, signed the Juba Declaration, which established a framework for reintegrating the militia forces into the SPLA (not including the SSDF).[10] Kiir meanwhile decided to appoint Matip, the former commander of the SSDF, as the deputy commander of the SPLA.[11]

The declaration created the Ministry of Defense and led to the appointment of Dominic Dim Deng as the first Minister of Defense. It also helped weaken the ties between the SSDF and the SAF by undermining the SAF's ability (via the SSDF) to pressure the SPLA in areas such as the Upper Nile. As important as the Juba Declaration was to the GoSS's security, there were still tensions between the SPLM/A and the rogue militia commanders who had refused to sign the declaration. Rather than negotiating within the framework, Kiir adopted his own plan to entice the rebel leaders to rejoin the SPLA. Known as the "Big Tent strategy," the plan promised defectors immunity from prosecution as well as a position or sinecure in the government. By incentivizing the defectors to return to the SPLA, Kiir hoped to reduce the risks of imposing more discipline on his own security forces and to avert any more defections. He was seemingly aware that soldiers stood to earn higher bonuses in a rogue militia. What he was offering the defectors, then, was the chance to enter into illicit contracts and to use oil rents to offset these higher bonuses. But was it enough to keep the military officers on the side of the government's security forces? For Kiir, it seemed the only way to outcompete the militia leaders, who had come to treat armed rebellion as a way of life or occupation.[12] And yet in promising higher office as an alternative to this warring occupation, he was also effectively rewarding rebellious behavior and incentivizing other officers to rebel.

Kiir's strategy was not just contradictory. It also contributed to the bloated military budget. By 2011, the military and police sectors accounted for nearly 70 percent of the total annual budget, with an estimated 745 generals on the payroll.[13] Kiir haddoubled the defense budget in 2011, leading to an increase in average salary of a soldier from $175 to $225 per month.[14] The $225 was nearly double that of the soldier serving in the SAF.[15] This naturally provided Kiir with a much-needed economic advantage in recruiting troops, which may have helped deter Bashir from meddling further in the GoSS's affairs. Still, the regional government's bloated budget reflected the woeful neglect of investment in the region's infrastructure and institution building. For a government with the largest public expenditure per capita, this was a serious cause for concern.

Divided Loyalties and a Fractured National Identity

Perhaps the most vexing issue during the interim period was whether making unity attractive would ever resolve the South Sudanese national question. The SPLM/A seemed content to try to make unity attractive in the early stages. The problem was that the GoSS's unfettered access to oil revenue during the interim period had caused more government leaders and officials to extract rents and siphon off oil profits. As the ruling elite became wealthier and more assertive, they also grew increasingly detached from the will of the people and less interested in promoting their rights and basic needs. This raised the difficult question of how the South Sudanese people could come together to determine the course of their political fate.

The CPA, as mentioned in Chapter 2, officially provided the South Sudanese with the choice of either remaining part of Sudan or seceding from it. Unity, for some, would force them to settle their differences with the Sudanese government; Sudan in turn would protect the rights, freedoms, and needs of all Sudanese. The initial idea therefore was to prioritize unity, or make it the preferred option, since the overall political stakes were lower for working toward unity. But making unity attractive also meant sacrificing resources, that is, giving up some military power to achieve an integrated security force and trusting the other side to carry out its obligations. It turned out that neither side was willing to concede too much in this regard, especially if it meant giving up some of their sovereignty. For the SPLM, the more burdensome unity was, the more attractive secession became. Unlike unity, secession had more to do with making independence necessary. Here the issue was whether the other parties would give up on making unity attractive and see secession as a necessary, inevitable option. Bashir naturally feared secession more than unity, since he stood to lose a great deal more than the SPLM if the South seceded (i.e., the ownership of the very resources needed to control the South). And yet making unity attractive ultimately meant recognizing the equality of the South Sudanese whom many Northerners still disrespected and disparaged.

All of this placed Bashir in a difficult predicament. For while he had to appease international authorities—who had shown support for secession—to receive economic assistance, he also had to placate his base of Islamic hardliners who were solidly opposed to secession. In the first few years of the interim period (2005–2008), he had managed to walk a fine line by focusing nationalist anger on other issues, such as his opposition to the ICC. But by 2008, implementing the CPA's targets (e.g., revenue sharing) had taken a toll on the NCP and SPLM/A. The two parties found themselves increasingly at odds with one another as they dealt with mounting international pressure and internal dissension. For the SPLM, making unity attractive was never enough to make secession necessary, since many

82   SOUTH SUDAN'S FATEFUL STRUGGLE

hardliners inside the NCP still regarded it as a threat to Sudan's sovereignty, especially given their long-held, albeit worn goal of assimilating southerners into an Islamic state. To make secession seem necessary, the SPLM also had to enhance its legitimacy through elections and to convince Sudan to settle peacefully on secession. This meant raising the stakes of returning to war, which neither side of course wanted.

Another factor at work was monetized patronage. The ruling elite in the South had used their easy access to oil revenue and clientelist networks to accrue large sums of personal wealth and power. The system of corruption stemmed from the GoSS's share of resources and represented a dual system of corruption in Sudan—one in the South and the other in the North. The ruling elites in the South thus needed a permanent governing framework within which to grow and sustain the system. This naturally made statehood increasingly appealing. By 2008, it was hard to ignore the negative impact of the oil money flowing into the South. Indeed, the influx of money had created a new social class in Juba, where many large houses had begun to appear on the outskirts of the city, along with shiny new SUVs that filled the streets. The patrons had also indulged in the accepted practice of polygamy in South Sudan to build extensive kinship networks, which, in one case, consisted of nearly 60 children. For some, the inflow of material wealth had come at an increasing social cost: namely, the eroded value of tribal customs, which had led more youth to abandon their tribal customs and rituals (i.e., many of the young Nuer males, who had moved to Juba, refused to undergo an initiation rite of marking their foreheads). Still, it was never clear if monetization was having a pacifying effect on ethnic and tribal groups.[16] As much as monetized patronage diminished the appeal of tribal culture during the late interim period, it also underscored the enduring nature of tribal customs that informed identity, belonging, and communal order. In the case of the Dinka, as Mohamed Salih observed, "the role of elders is what counterbalances the aggressive and military orientation of the youth."[17] Monetized patronage, in this sense, described the growing ties between political power and tribal identity as well as the instrumental value of tribal identity for South Sudan's corrupt, ruling elite.

Endemic Corruption

The interim period was also a period that, despite international interest and the millions of dollars in donations, lacked financial and regulatory controls. Transitioning from a predatory economy to one with enforceable rules had proved elusive. For the most part, the United States and other major donors did little to change the predatory nature of this informal economy. The trouble was that many of the commanders and soldiers who had fought during the civil war

THE TROUBLED TRANSITION   83

treated the new wealth as a reward for their past service. As such, they felt entitled to take what they could—a sentiment shared by many career fighters who had willfully resorted to stealing public money. Nonetheless, among the billions of dollars in oil revenue collected from 2005 to 2006, at least a billion was discovered missing. When the regional parliament summoned Arthur Akuien Chol, former Minister of Finance and Economic Planning, to address certain purchases— including one involving vehicles bought at inflated price—Chol tried to deflect blame onto Machar who he claimed had approved the purchase. Machar denied any such wrongdoing and even joked about the need only to "take a million."[18] All told, the leaders and government officials stole an estimated 30 percent of the revenue collected during the first three years of the GoSS; the rest went almost exclusively to Juba to finance the lavish lifestyles of the ruling elite.[19]

Corruption seemed to be pervasive. And yet there was little way to verify it. Just prior to his death, Garang reflected on its erosive effect on the liberation movement. "There is no meaning of revolution," he wrote, "unless it makes our people happy . . . unless the barest of things are not available to people, then the people will drive us into the sea."[20] Kiir also shared this sentiment in a 2006 speech where he stated that, "Many of our friends died to achieve these objectives. Yet, once we got to power, we forgot what we fought for and began to enrich ourselves at the expense of our people."[21] To make matters worse, Sudan's second civil war had destroyed much of its infrastructure and economy. And there was no quick fix or incentive to properly allocate the large lump sums of money now pouring into the region. The GoSS essentially paid lip service to any suggestions for a restricted fund to channel oil revenue for public spending from which southern elites would not be allowed to withdraw for personal reasons. Hilde Johnson, the Former Minister of International Development of Norway and Head of UNMISS, recounted raising such a prospect with Kiir:

> I pointed to other African countries where petroleum had become a curse rather than a blessing, and where corruption was undermining development and destroying fragile institutions. The SPLM/A and its leaders were at great risk of developing the same bad habits. I told the chairman, unless the process was checked at the outset, it was crucial to establish a mechanism of control and oversight, making corruption more difficult, otherwise it would destroy everything they had fought for.[22]

But the GoSS leaders never took her advice. Nor did they feel the need for greater transparency.

The lack of oversight and accounting systems had created the conditions for stealing more and issuing contracts that could not be traced or monitored. In short, there was no independent system to confirm the delivery of services and transactions and to redress cases of mismanagement.

84   SOUTH SUDAN'S FATEFUL STRUGGLE

Perhaps the most notorious case of mismanagement was the Dura Saga. From 2005 to 2006, the GoSS issued several contracts to buy sorghum, a grain known locally as Dura. The contracts involved building new food storage houses to address the recurring food shortages. But many of these companies, as it turned out, never received any money. An estimated 1 million, for instance, was never transferred to this contract, and it was widely believed that government officials had siphoned off the money. Numerous companies had accepted contracts for work they were unable to deliver. Yet the figures were never reported by the government, nor could the Auditor General gain access to relevant information. In fact, it was not until 2013 that World Bank auditors determined that 290 companies were paid without ever signing a contract and that 150 companies had been grossly overpaid.[23] In response to the allegations, the national government announced the formation of a government panel to investigate the scandal. John Luk Jok, the Minister of Legal Affairs at the time, headed the government committee and concluded that nearly 1 million of sorghum failed to reach the state governments ahead of a projected famine in 2008.

The Dura scandal exposed what many had feared: a longstanding pattern of government corruption. From 2008 to 2011, the GoSS had allotted nearly 1.7 million dollars for road construction; only 75 miles of road had been paved by 2011.[24] International authorities appeared to be oblivious to the extent of corruption. They were more concerned with meeting human development goals— such as decreasing the infant mortality rate and the region's high illiteracy rate. International donors at this time committed nearly 1.2 billion dollars, which accounted for 80 percent of its investment in basic needs (or human development) in South Sudan.[25] Nearly 40 percent of this aid was developed on a bilateral basis; the rest came from pooled funds established by multilateral agencies. In 2010, for instance, the United States was the largest source of outside economic assistance, donating nearly 411,000,000 dollars, well ahead of the United Kingdom and Norway.[26] None of this aid directly supported the GoSS budget; again it was primarily aimed at meeting basic needs.[27]

The biggest source of corruption was oil revenue. GoSS officials controlled the allocation of oil revenue but channeled the payments or rents (a portion of the nation's income that come from producing resources) into personal accounts. Under the Wealth Sharing Agreement (WSA), the GoSS received 50 percent of oil revenue. However, the WSA failed to ensure transparency in the oil sector, where there were few mechanisms to monitor expenditures. Still, it was not just oil rents that drove corruption. The GoSS also used its authority to make land deals with foreign investors.[28] In fact, it leased nearly 5 percent of all its land holdings to foreign investors, which resulted in the displacement of tribal communities. The investors were obligated to compensate local communities under the 2009 Land Act, but paid very little into social services of the affected communities. In many cases, there were no signed contracts to verify the terms of the deals.

The mounting corruption did not go undetected for long, however. In 2009, Kiir eventually adopted the Anti-Corruption Commission Act to investigate officials accused of corruption. That year, the commission opened up several investigations, but only six cases of corruption were filed with the Ministry of Justice. None were adjudicated. Ultimately, there were no actual trials, which left many to wonder about what happened to much of the money. The commission only managed to recover 60 million dollars, a fraction of the 4 billion that was believed stolen during the interim period.[29]

The adoption in 2011 of the Audit Chamber Act, which created the National Audit Chamber and Office of the Auditor General, was equally ineffective. The act stipulated that the Auditor General "carry out his/her duties impartially to prosecute corruption crimes."[30] At the time, the Auditor General, who was appointed by Kiir, seemed like a promising mechanism to combat corruption. But like others charged to investigate past crimes, his office lacked the resources to carry out its duties. It seemed clear that neither Kiir nor other leaders had any actual intention of making these judicial bodies functional. And yet, by adopting them, they appeared to confirm the SPLM/A's commitment to judicial fairness and accountability. Both were crucial for winning elections, mobilizing support for a new referendum, and convincing stakeholders that it was prepared to govern a new state.

The March to Independence

On July 8, 2008, the GoS and SPLM officials agreed on a mixed electoral system based on majoritarian and proportional representation. Yet gathering the necessary data and securing cooperation of the parties on a census proved difficult. Disputes arose. The SPLM, for example, contended that the census should include all returning IDPs, and that it would withhold its commitment to the process until it did. Preliminary results had indicated that the total population of Southern Sudan was 3.8 million, but South Sudanese officials insisted that the actual number was much higher. On May 12, 2009, the final results of the census were released, putting Sudan's total population at 39,154,490, with 8,260,490 residing in the South.[31]

By the fall of 2009, officials had announced that the elections would take place on April 12, 2010. This marked nearly a one-year delay from the CPA's stated target of July 2009, and there was concern that holding the elections during the rainy season (summer)—when some of the roads become impassable—would negatively affect campaigning. As the ruling party of the GoSS, the SPLM, however, was determined to tighten its grip on power. In November 2009, it began to clamp down on the opposition that still supported unity. Rather than discussing its merits and shortcomings, it turned the issue of unity into a loyalty test.

86 SOUTH SUDAN'S FATEFUL STRUGGLE

Supporters of unity were treated as disloyal sympathizers of the Sudanese government. The SPLM/A also portrayed the tribal and ethnic conflicts in the countryside as a threat to the integrity of the elections, and then used this to clamp down on tribal conflicts to appear like the party that could maintain order and stability. When it was not trying to redirect attention from its own weaknesses, it resorted to more overtly repressive tactics. During registration (November to December 2009), there were reports of arbitrary arrests and detentions of civilians who had been critical of the SPLM and debated the need for secession versus unity. The abuse eventually carried over into the campaigning period—from January to April—when many members of opposing parties were restricted access to the media.[32] Moreover, the SPLM did not stop with party opposition. It also began arbitrarily arresting journalists who had written stories on sensitive issues involving the SPLM/A. This included a journalist in Torit who had been detained by security officials in January 2010 for having written an article on corruption. The arrest, as it turned out, was part of the SPLM/A's wide-scale effort to instill fear in the population, particularly in journalists and the opposition,[33] in order to secure a majority of votes—or more than 50 percent that was required to avoid a run-off—and to demonstrate its strength and popularity in relation to the NCP, even if it meant compromising the integrity of the elections.[34]

Unsurprisingly, the SPLM scored a sweeping victory. Kiir won nearly 93 percent of the overall vote while Lam Akol, the leader of the SPLM-Democratic Change (established in 2009), received 7 percent. The SPLM also won 160 of the 170 seats in the Southern Sudanese legislature.[35] There of course were many accusations of irregularities in the election process. But after the Carter Center issued its final report, which concluded that the election largely met international standards (Carter himself stated that he was satisfied enough with the elections to support the election results), the accusations were easily dismissed. The SPLM and other parties could finally turn their attention to the referendum process and to the transition to statehood.[36]

For the SPLM, the election victory had become a mandate for independence. And yet it was unclear whether such a mandate truly expressed the will of the people and their democratic aspirations. The political scientists Lotje De Vries and Mareike Schomerus write that "while independence was presented as the ultimate fulfilment of self-determination in South Sudan, this narrow interpretation of the concept has deepened the democratic deficit and created a political environment that favored the SPLM."[37] The fact that elections were held so close to the referendum date—only months apart—meant that there was little time to debate and discuss the issue of the referendum, including how to transition to statehood. The SPLM turned this into an opportunity to further solidify its status as the dominant political party which could best liberate the people from Khartoum's oppression. As DeVries and Schomerus claim, this "resulted

THE TROUBLED TRANSITION   87

in blind faith in the forces of change and freedom, which acted as a damper on the political processes of debate, opposition and non-violent dissent . . . Falling into line with the SPLM/A . . . became synonymous with being a good southern Sudanese."[38] With its wide margin of victory in the 2010 elections, the SPLM had effectively addressed that question on its own terms, and not in consultation with civil society or foreign actors. At the same time, the Troika showed little interest in discussing the issue of statehood; it accepted the electoral results at face value and focused almost exclusively on the technicalities concerning the elections and referendum processes. The SPLM/A had thus made independence a fait accompli and unity both unattractive and unnecessary. So sweeping was its perceived mandate that it had convinced Bashir to accept and support the referendum process.

Still, the SPLM remained wary of Bashir. The GoS, after all, stood to lose the most from the secession of South Sudan, including control of several oil production facilities. Kiir's plan therefore was to project the appearance of unity of the SPLA and make secession more compelling. However, by the fall of 2010, it was becoming increasingly uncertain whether the commission overseeing the referendum process could effectively monitor the vote. Both the SPLM and NCP still needed to resolve disputes concerning who could and could not vote. Beyond this, the ongoing border disputes related to the agreements on Abyei and South Kordofan made Bashir increasingly uneasy about the outcome of the referendum, particularly the loss of Sudan's ownership of the oil that lied under the ground in these areas. The SPLM meanwhile continued to plan for this expected outcome by using its electoral victory to lead, organize, and coordinate efforts to address the unresolved issues of the transition to statehood with various South Sudanese parties.

In mid-October 2010, it held the All South Sudanese Political Parties Conference (ASSPPC). Here, the goal was to reach consensus on the parameters and conditions of holding the referendum and transitioning to statehood. Representatives from twenty different parties, along with civil society and faith-based groups, attended the conference to promote "a free, fair, transparent and peaceful referendum."[39] The parties discussed the broad parameters of a Transitional Constitution that would replace the 2005 Interim Constitution of Southern Sudan. After four days of discussions and meetings, the parties agreed on four broad resolutions regarding statehood or the condition of "yes" to the referendum.

First, they agreed on a transitional period that would begin on July 9, 2011 and last until a period agreed upon by all parties. Second, because Kiir was currently serving as President of the GoSS and won a majority of votes in the 2010 elections, it was determined that he would assume the Presidency of the Republic of South Sudan during the transitional phase or until presidential elections were held in 2015. Third, the parties unanimously agreed that the new Government of South

88   SOUTH SUDAN'S FATEFUL STRUGGLE

Sudan would schedule elections for the Constituent Assembly, which would then review and vote on a permanent constitution. In the case of a 'yes' vote on the referendum, the government would establish a Constitutional Review Commission (CRC) tasked with reviewing the terms of the 2005 Interim Constitution and drafting the Transitional Constitution. Lastly, agreement was reached on holding an all-party National Constitutional Conference to determine the parameters of a permanent constitution and to set up General Elections at the end of the transitional period to elect the representatives of the new Constituent Assembly.[40] By adopting these four resolutions, the parties to the ASSPPC paved the way for a vote on independence.

The referendum vote was held on January 9, 2011.[41] Over 99 percent of the population attended, with 97.3 percent of the eligible voters voting "yes" on independence. In Juba, a jubilant celebration broke out on the streets, with many South Sudanese waving the South Sudanese flag. Nearly all IGAD countries had come out in support of secession, with the exception of Egypt, which still supported Sudan's decision to make unity attractive. What had once been regarded as a distant outcome had become reality: the GoSS had peacefully seceded from the North. But now came the hard part: implementing a constitution that would transition it to statehood.

Compromises and Constitutional Control

The Transitional Constitution revised the 2005 Interim Constitution of Southern Sudan (ICISS) and stipulated the new terms of South Sudan's sovereignty. The Interim Constitution had provided a constitutional framework for the GoSS, but it was a subsidiary part of the Interim National Constitution of Sudan that encompassed two governing systems. The ICISS and the National Interim Constitution of the Sudan thus represented two separate systems of government. But now, South Sudan's constitution needed changes to function separately from Sudan's constitution, changes that included the new powers of the executive and the other branches of government, including the judiciary and the legislature.

In January 2011, South Sudanese officials formed a technical review committee to begin drafting the Transitional Constitution. However, the committee's mandate was largely restricted to addressing the legality of revisions to the 2005 constitution. When it finally completed its work in April 2011, it failed to recommend a timeline for adopting the permanent constitution. For some, this was a calculated move by SPLM members to avoid making any substantive amendments that would force it to decentralize the government's authority. But it raised issues regarding the relationship between customary law—which constituted a source of law in the Transitional Constitution—and statutory law, which codified the civil and political rights of all civilians. These were issues that

many hoped could be resolved by a future permanent constitution. For now, though, it was agreed that the number of amendments needed to be restricted to streamline the process.

Yet it soon became clear that the ICISS required more than simply a couple of amendments or technical fixes to function properly. For the SPLM leaders who dominated the process, it was important to keep the focus on these technical issues, since it allowed them to circumvent more substantive issues, such as the official length of term for the President and the limitation of executive power. Moreover, in excluding civil society groups from participating at the meetings, they had eliminated a key source of political pressure. The Transitional Constitution ended up concentrating more power in the executive office and made the issue of federalism or decentralized governance moot. Not only did it allow the executive to enjoy a disproportionate share of revenue to budget operations, but it also left local authorities with little discretion to address the needs of the people. In addition, the President could remove the governors of the state and dissolve state assemblies,[42] and, in times of crises, reserved the unrestricted power to declare an emergency. Given that there were few procedures in place to determine how the President would administer these emergency powers, it was unclear as to how or to what degree he (or she) would exercise them. The President was in effect free to administer such power with little or no oversight.

Critics feared the consequences of such executive privilege. They saw it, for instance, as a power grab, a ruse for the President to maintain and tighten his grip on power.[43] Most expected the permanent constitution to resolve this issue, along with establishing a more inclusive and democratic federalist system. Yet the question was when? There was still considerable uncertainty about the national government's commitment to laying the groundwork for its adoption. It had, for example, adopted the Political Inclusion Act in 2012, but this was largely to appease international actors—including the European Union and the United Nations—which had already begun to pressure the government to be more inclusive and transparent. Moreover, the act seemed flawed since it left the definition of political inclusion undefined and vague regarding who should be included.

A more promising development was the creation of the National Constitutional Review Commission, whose immediate task was to revise the Transitional Constitution. Chaired by John Luk Jok, the Legal Affairs Minister, the commission consisted of twenty committee members appointed by Kiir, nineteen of whom were from the SPLM.[44] But soon after its formation, critics accused Kiir of SPLM party privilege or underrepresentation. Pressure from the other South Sudanese parties eventually prompted Kiir to add 14 members from other parties, but only after he decided to add 17 more members belonging to the SPLM.[45] The commission in its first year faced many daunting tasks, which included addressing the constitutionality of the people's grazing rights and stipulating the mechanisms to resolve disputes regarding these rights.

90 SOUTH SUDAN'S FATEFUL STRUGGLE

The majority of SPLM members on the commission dismissed the need for mechanisms of conflict prevention, with the exception of Article 149, which called for a mechanism of demobilization, disarmament, and reintegration.[46]

The commission, however, did manage to adopt one amendment concerning the President's power to dismiss and appoint a new vice president. Many insisted that the Vice President should be allowed to succeed the President and serve out his term in the event of incapacity or resignation. Machar, for one, insisted that the Vice President should automatically succeed the President in the event of incapacity or resignation. On other issues such as equal representation, civil society, and women's groups pressed for stronger affirmative action provisions. They had criticized Kiir for restricting the participation of women's groups and ignoring their demands for special representation for victims of gender-based violence. Kiir largely dismissed the criticism, insisting that it was not in keeping with the ideals that the SPLM/A had fought for, including unity and equality. He apparently had more pressing issues on his mind, as South Sudan prepared to start the operations of its new state in July 2011.

Border Issues

The most pressing issue concerned the ongoing border disputes in Abyei, South Kordofan, and Upper Blue Nile regions. The referendum on South Sudan's secession was supposed to coincide with a referendum on Abyei, which would determine whether the area belonged to Sudan or South Sudan. But the vote on Abyei's political fate was postponed after the South objected that the Misseriya could not be counted as citizens due to their nomadic existence of crossing in and out of the area. This followed a tortuous process of implementing the Abyei Protocol of the CPA, which had established Abyei as an administered area and created the Abyei Commission to demarcate the boundaries.

In 2007, the ABC issued its proposed ruling for demarcating the boundaries. Yet the National Congress quickly rejected its so-called binding proposal. Clashes erupted between the SAF and SPLM forces in Abyei and its oil fields—the economic prize of this small area—displacing nearly 25,000 civilians.[47] The mounting casualties eventually convinced both sides to agree to a suspension of hostilities by having the dispute settled by the Abyei Arbitration Tribunal, a subsidiary court of the Permanent Court of International Arbitration. In July 2009, the AAT issued its ruling, recommending that both sides commit themselves to peace. It concluded that the Abyei Boundary Commission exceeded its mandate and that the proposed new boundaries placed most of the oil field outside of Abyei.

After postponing the vote, the Sudanese government promptly rejected the Abyei Referendum Act as a dispute settlement mechanism for resolving the disputes. In February 2011, the Sudanese government and its allies began

to attack villages in Abyei. By May 2011, following a reported ambush by the SPLA on the northern army, the SAF invaded and occupied Abyei. The violent clashes between the Northern and Southern armies displaced more than 100,000 Ngor Dinka and created a crisis that placed the peace process on the "precipice of war."[48] Khartoum may have simply been demonstrating their military might and technical advantage in order to buttress their claim to the region.[49] The UN Security Council assured both parties that the conflict would not obstruct nor delay the July 9 implementation of South Sudan's statehood. In June, it unanimously approved the deployment of a 4,200-member Ethiopian peacekeeping force, the UN Interim Security Force for Abyei (UNISFA).[50]

National elections in the meantime had failed to legitimize the governorships in South Kordofan, which bordered Abyei and the Blue Nile. Instead, they stoked tensions between joint forces and leaders running the civilian government in both states. In South Kordofan, the Sudanese government postponed state elections until April 2011. And in the Blue Nile, Malik Agar, who was once an SPLA commander and close confident of Garang, won the state governorship by defeating Farah Ibrahim Mohamed Al-Aggar, his NCP rival, by nearly nine thousand votes.[51] Agar's victory was a bitter pill to swallow for Bashir, who still considered him an insurgent and who, after weeks of waiting for Bashir to confirm the result, elected to become the leader of the SPLM's northern faction, the SPLM-North. As the new leader of the SPLM-N, he pressed for further democratic autonomy within Sudan. But by September, Bashir had deposed Agar—a move that alienated many of the civilians who had supported Agar.

Like Abyei, the conflict in South Kordofan ended in stalemate. The SPLM-N and the GoS eventually reached a political solution and agreed to hold elections in June 2011. Ahmad Muhammad Arun—now an indicted war criminal by the International Criminal Court—was elected governor. The SPLM-N, though, contested the result, accusing Khartoum of rigging the elections. Fighting soon broke out between the SPLM-N and SAF, which then spilled over into the Nuba Mountains area of the Blue Nile state. Although the conflict was closely tied to the war in Darfur (the SPLM-N assisted the rebels in Darfur), the United Nations, balked at demands for delaying the July 11 implementation of South Sudan's statehood. On July 11, President Obama recognized South Sudan as a new state—the fifty-fourth state of Africa and one hundred and ninety-third member of the United Nations. But as monumental as the event was, it did little to stem the conflict, or reduce the scale of human rights atrocities perpetrated by all sides, including the displacement of hundreds of millions of civilians.[52] The African Union High-Level Implementation Panel (AUHIP) eventually issued its own proposal for new boundaries in September 2012, which, as we shall in Chapter 4, failed to resolve the border dispute.

The seemingly endless border disputes in Abyei and South Kordofan highlighted the stark differences between South Sudan and Sudan. Both sides

92 SOUTH SUDAN'S FATEFUL STRUGGLE

tried to hold onto whatever land they could to shore up their sovereignty, especially given that the disputed land involved oil rights. While Bashir had to defend his country's right to preserve its national wealth, the SPLM had to demonstrate that it was unified, that it could stand up to Sudan. Having consolidated its power in the national elections and the referendum process, it also seemed to believe that new statehood could provide the needed leverage to resolve these disputes. Still, wealth sharing in these three cases and in general, would prove far more intractable than expected.

Conclusion

International donors had poured millions of dollars into Southern Sudan in hopes of making a difference in the country's future. But in doing so they had also unwittingly helped buttress a ruling elite inside the SPLM that used the elections and the referendum process to consolidate its power. Self-determination came to represent a fettered right, which, stripped of its democratic character, revealed a self-(inflicted) willingness of the ruling elite to control the political destiny of the country. The SPLM leaders, therefore, were free to impose their authority on the people, but were ultimately unprepared to govern the country. There were simply too many factors shaping this outcome, including a relatively short interim period, the Troika's political pressure, fear of factionalism, and Bashir's antics. Yet together, they had managed to hem the SPLM into a position of advocating a new nation that it was ill-prepared to govern effectively.

In the end, the CPA remained a flawed framework for solving South Sudan's national question. Its ambitious objectives exceeded the grasp of its mechanisms and the parties involved. The reality was that neither side was prepared to apply the terms of the peace agreement. Indeed, the problem was not that New Sudan had natively counted on the backing and sacrifices by Bashir, nor that Garang's premature death caused the SPLM to revert back to secession or not make any effort to make unity attractive, but rather, that the absence of any moral reckoning would allow grievances to fester, and insecurity within the SPLM, to dictate a rash response. The question, then, was whether South Sudan was ever truly prepared to transition effectively to a new state, and with the help of international actors, learn to govern by constraint and the rule of law. The answer of course would depend on its willingness to reckon meaningfully with the past abuses that had so profoundly shaped its political destiny and had led to false expectations for ending wide-scale corruption, party factionalism, the effects of the clientelist politics rooted in the predatory war practices of the past, and promoting accountability.

4

Kleptocracy and Its Warring Contents

After fighting broke out in the presidential quarters on December 15, 2013, Salva Kiir's SPLA began attacking Nuer officials and civilians. The bloody assault left hundreds dead—many on the streets of Juba—and forced countless Nuer to flee the city and to seek refuge inside the UN compound. Within weeks, the SPLM had formally split into two principal groups, the SPLM-Government and SPLM-IO, and Ethiopian troops were sent into Juba to assist government forces. By early 2014, the war had killed thousands of civilians and forced many international donors and international organizations to focus almost exclusively on their humanitarian operations. The question on many people's minds was how a ruling elite, which enjoyed access to an extensive supply of oil revenue as well as wide-scale international support, could resort to war. Many pointed to South Sudan's fateful decision to shut off its oil pipelines in 2012, which eventually led to austerity measures and party infighting.[1]

But the outbreak of civil war was the product of many factors, including monetized patronage, armed factionalism, and rampant corruption. Together these factors had destabilized the country and increased armed conflict by rebel factions, depriving the state of the necessary resources for building the country's infrastructure and institutions. Armed conflict, in fact, reflected a larger trend of Africa's endless wars in which nonstate armed groups fought to extract resources and rents from the government and international donors. Kiir in this case had no choice but to appease or work with many of the rebel factions, since the rebel leaders profited from armed conflict and paid their soldiers higher wages than SPLA soldiers. If Kiir tried to impose more discipline on its armed forces, he risked a coup.

The civil war, then, revealed what Jason Stearns writes was "a patchwork of patronage networks linking government officials to militias and local power brokers—all of them using violence to bolster their status and obtain resources."[2] These networks were not simply monetized in terms of paid loyalty to subordinates, but also heavily militarized. Militarized patronage refers to the rulers' instinctual and methodical use of militarism (and its features of strict discipline, order, and training) to expand these networks. Militarism in this sense was integral to patronage and the extreme violence in South Sudan. Over time, I argue, it helped shape and was shaped in turn by the country's kleptocracy and civil war in which the national government and armed factions came to share

South Sudan's Fateful Struggle. Steven C. Roach, Oxford University Press. © Oxford University Press 2023.
DOI: 10.1093/oso/9780190057848.003.0005

94 SOUTH SUDAN'S FATEFUL STRUGGLE

economic and personal incentives to fight, that is, to profiteer and increase the flow of arm supplies. In this way, the informal economy of armed conflict had become increasingly entwined with the national war economy, as the government used state assets and resources (e.g., oil production) to pay tribal-based militias (e.g., Padang Dinka) to fight their main opposition. The conjoined economies, in short, reflected the militarization of the oil sector.

I shall analyze this trend by examining the historical and cultural dynamics of militarized patronage, showing how militarism facilitated the rise of kleptocratic behavior in South Sudan. I then move on to discuss the system of corruption and the nontransparency of the oil sector and the leaders' fateful decision to shut off its oil pipelines. Drawing on the resource curse literature, I size up the structural factors of corruption and the various ways that the national government used its power over the national budget to extract more rent and resources.[3] Here I show how, despite the massive curtailment of oil revenue, government authorities still managed to profit from the war. Finally, I assess the impact of targeted sanctions imposed by the United States and the United Nations on high-ranking governmental officials.

The Warlike State

A war economy can either be destructive or productive. When it is productive, it reflects the state's ability to shift from the manufacturing and production of service and consumer goods to producing more war supplies (i.e., the United States during World War II). But this tends to be the exception. Most war economies are in fact destructive and self-depleting. In some cases, they can justify nation-building but cost trillions of dollars to finance (and increase the national debt of the sponsoring country). In Afghanistan, for instance, much of the money earmarked for nation-building went into the pockets of the corrupt leaders; bribes in this case became a common and accepted means of financing the transactions of government services.

The United States invested far less in South Sudan and essentially stopped funding the government altogether when the civil war broke out. The GRSS thus lacked the resources to increase the production of military supplies and began to rely on local militias to secure control of land and to fight the SPLM-IO in the Upper Nile and Jonglei states. Its protracted civil war led to a significant reduction in oil production, which drained the economy of much-needed money to finance the basic needs of the people and public goods. South Sudan's war economy was in part based on the use of government assets and resources to pay tribal-based rogue militias to fight the opposition. For these militias, money also came from the seizure of booty and the control of land that allowed them to buy

small arms and extract resources and rents from local government to conduct their activities.

Some of the armed factions eventually joined forces with the SPLM-IO to oppose the government. This tug of war struggle took root in the 1990s, when mounting discontent with Garang's militarism split the movement to spawn the series of militia rebellions that would threaten the GoSS and the GRSS. Although the CPA officially ended the civil war, armed conflict continued in the countryside, leading to a growing influx of small arms into South Sudan and other African countries (e.g., Chad, The DRC, Rwanda). The trend was spurred in part by economic liberalization in Africa during the 1980s, when privatization and deregulation forced many African countries to adopt austerity measures to increase their efficiency on investment in the country. By shifting money away from the social sector, privatization led to increasing unemployment among the youth and a growing pool of young poor men to recruit. Money from oil smuggling also helped fund illicit activities and businesses and enable rebel factions to finance their operations. As their numbers proliferated, the rural peasants, who had been marginalized by international investment in the agricultural sector, joined the armed factions.[4] In South Sudan, the SPLA and rebel leaders, as mentioned in Chapter 2, collected booty and border taxes to pay their fighters. But this did little to stymie the lucrative market for rebellion; the SSDF, for instance, never stopped fighting the SPLA or the GoSS. The profitability of fighting meant that a rebel factional leader such as Matip, could pay his soldiers higher bonuses, especially given that war presented opportunities to collect more booty and to extract resources and rents. Kiir, as we saw in Chapter 4, tried to entice rebel leaders to return to the SPLM by promising immunity and higher office. Yet because these rebel factions did not directly threaten the major cities, there was neither the will nor resources to defeat them in the countryside.

The endless armed conflict in the countryside defined a new type of war on the African continent. As Jeffrey Gettlemen put it, armed conflicts "exhibited a predatory style of warfare in Africa where combatants don't have an ideology. . . . and want only cash, guns and a license to rampage."[5] Armed conflicts in Africa were no longer about secession and liberation that had sustained the all-out civil wars of the 1980s.[6] They had become primarily about bargaining economically and profiteering. By the late 1990s, their numbers had rapidly increased across the African continent to destabilize more African states. However, they failed to pose a direct threat to national governments. In fact, these new wars were never about taking over governments or instigating prolonged civil war. As Stearns writes, "Gone are the days of bloody, all out civil wars . . . African has entered an age of grinding low level conflicts and instability."[7] Endless armed conflicts symptomized the limits of power in terms of what the corrupt national government could do to impose law and order on the countryside. In effect, they had

96 SOUTH SUDAN'S FATEFUL STRUGGLE

created their own permanent subnational economy driven by illicit activities and the struggle to seize land and control over the flow of goods and services. As Paul Collier argues in *Wars, Guns, and Votes,* the spoils of war had led to parallel economies in which smuggling goods and looting enemy supplies had equipped insurgents with political motives to continue warring at whatever cost.[8]

In South Sudan, then, there was an uneasy coupling of this nonstate informal war economy and the government's war economy. This unlikely enmeshment reflected the complementary incentives for waging violence and war. The national government, with its war chest or stated-owned oil assets, was able to employ rebel factions to conduct its war operations in remote places. The rebel factions in turn used the money to extend their illicit activities, or warring business, with little regard for the basic rights of civilians.[9] War was thus integral to the working relationship between the government and these groups, and in reinforcing their persistent predatory behavior, made peacebuilding an elusive objective. More than anything, keeping the peace and peacebuilding exposed the troubling gap between this gnawing reality of war and the peace process. For while the national government was unable to stop the rebel groups from disrupting the peace process—or enforcing complete compliance with the cessation of hostilities agreement—it could still use them (and their recruitment of soldiers from the SPLM-IO, for instance) to weaken their legitimate political opposition.

Another dynamic of South Sudan's war economy was the militarization of its ruling elite. Much of this could be traced to Sudan's second civil war, particularly to Garang's militaristic authority that helped stoke rebellion inside the SPLM/A. Militarism played a central role in party and state governance by determining how South Sudan's leaders exercised political power more through military prowess than political compromise and consensus building. Indeed, the ruling elite—especially those who had been officers during the second civil war in Sudan—relied almost exclusively on their military skills and status to gain political power. Patronage, as we shall see, became a vehicle for such militarism. It allowed the officers to command the soldier loyalty they had lost during the war and to rule with a sense of self-entitlement that made them feel immune from public scrutiny. Because some expected the war to return during the interim period, they of course took what they could get.

For the Sentry Project—an initiative started by John Prendergast and George Clooney, the actor, the taking of South Sudan's wealth exposed wide-scale corruption and the need for more public scrutiny of the national elite. The organization reported an intricate and extensive trail of missing money dating back to the interim period, including paid expenses for an overextended stay at one of Juba's five-star hotels (i.e., a case that involved a stay of 12 years).[10] One of the most notorious examples of graft was Wara Wara Investment, a shell company created by

Seed Ahmed Hussein, otherwise known as the "Al-Cardinal."[11] Paul Malong, the former military chief of staff, had funneled millions of dollars into the company to become a principal shareholder of the company. In 2016, he made off with nearly the 2 million dollars and fled to Kenya.[12]

Malong's theft was perhaps the most notorious incident of corruption. Like so many other military elite, Malong had depended on the loyalty of paid army personnel and soldiers, and exploited his government position and military clout to extract rent and resources. He had essentially become a head patron to former military subordinates, someone who competed for political power in what Alex de Waal writes is a "political marketplace," or governance based on monetized patronage.

> In advanced political marketplace governance systems, the conduct of political business as exchange is the central feature, and the prices of the commodities of cooperation, and allegiance are determined by supply and demand. . . . Real politics is the bargaining and coercion that constitutes these transactions.[13]

In South Sudan's political marketplace, there are no fixed rules to regulate the supply and demand. Much of this is due to the fact that South Sudan's political elites were already accustomed to an unregulated system of governance dating back to the second civil war in Sudan, when SPLA commanders regularly seized booty and collected border taxes to pay for multiple dowries.[14] The war, in fact, saw a dramatic rise in the value of dowries, with some fetching as much as 30,000 US dollars in cattle and cash. The accumulation of wealth also encouraged wealthy males to marry multiple wives—as many as 15 wives in one case—to expand their kinship networks. The commanders also lavished soldiers and military subordinates with gifts. With the increasing expenditures came a growing class of intermediaries, a class with the means to protect and conduct the secretive transactions between the commander and seller of goods. The intermediaries charged commission rates that inflated the prices of SUVs and new mansions that began to appear on the outskirts of Juba. "The accruing wealth," writes Clemence Pinaud, "resulted in the creation of a new military aristocracy . . . and allowed the SPLA to become a space for resource accumulation by its commanders, who used their newly acquired wealth to expand their immediate kinship networks."[15] One might quibble about the term aristocracy here, since it implies the acquisition of old wealth and qualification to rule. The South Sudanese military commanders failed to meet both criteria, having acquired the bulk of their wealth through the black market. Perhaps a more appropriate term to describe their false social status is a "ruling social racket" that was focused on extracting rent to invest in their illegal schemes. But given how the commanders used their military influence, it was not simply monetization that

directly informed the meaning of patronage per se. Rather it was a militarism in which military training and status played a key role in their ability to compete and bargain on the political marketplace.

Another way of distinguishing militarized patronage from other forms of patronage is to understand how the SPLM failed to develop into a formal, governing political body. With few independent, regulatory mechanisms the political and military elite essentially took what they wanted. And yet the more they took, the more they felt entitled to the money. The South Sudanese scholar, Peter Adwok Nyaba, pointed to this primal need in the 1990s, when he argued that there never was a distinct boundary between the SPLM and SPLM; that too many of the rulers and soldiers remained "militarized subjects." The problem, he wrote, was that "the inculcation of distinct military discipline and the requirement of instantaneous obedience and indoctrination to the cult-like enforcements were more like objects than subjects of liberation."[16] The SPLM/A's prevailing instinct was to actively suppress any dissent that might lead to public scrutiny of its governing authority. Indeed, these former military rulers needed not just obedient soldiers but a third party or intermediary to conduct their transactions and illicit activities. This illicit arrangement in turn reinforced a sense of false privilege, since it allowed them to display their wealth without having to account for such wealth. The dynamic played out on a daily basis in South Sudan's black market. As Patrick Riruyo, a USAID analyst, explained to me, "There was no way the elites can buy a new land cruiser on their government salary; but none really care about the costs of their borrowed political power."[17] To appreciate this is to realize that no government official can actually buy a new car in South Sudan. All goods need to be imported from neighboring countries, such as Kenya. This naturally drives up the transactional costs, as intermediaries—who control the transactions—seek to raise the retail price by as much as 60 percent. Thus, a car that fetches $50,000 on the open market in Kenya would typically sell for $80,000 on South Sudan's black market. Almost all of the $30,000 goes directly to the intermediary overseeing the transaction.

The black-market rate and the official rate constitute a system of parallel exchange rates. The elites have routinely manipulated the official rate to increase the value of their assets and to help pay others inside their network for their loyalty. Monetizing political loyalty in this way is "never a one-off transaction," as Riyuyo explained, "it's always recurring, sometimes involving monthly or yearly payments."[18] The ruling elite and rebel leaders, then, have used their money to recruit paid subordinates and soldiers into their militias. In expanding their patronage networks, they have bolstered their forces and dispersed the nation-state loyalty needed to build an integrated military force. For some, militarizing patronage has caused national identity to fracture along tribal lines and led the ruling elite to place their personal interests above the nation.

Window Dressing Transparency

In his first and only meeting with Kiir at the White House in the summer of 2011, President Obama asked Kiir to discuss his vision of South Sudan. But instead of directly responding to the question, Kiir grew silent, before turning to his advisors to provide an answer.[19] For those in the room, it was discomfiting and even strange to see a leader of a country defer to his advisers to articulate the country's vision. To make matters worse, when Kiir was asked about his support of the SPLM-N, he denied that the SPLM-N was operating in Sudan, despite US intelligence that clearly indicated otherwise. Kiir had clearly been caught in a lie; his relations with the Obama administration would remain icy for the next five years.

Still, Kiir was determined to show the government's commitment to transparency in the oil sector. In the following year, he proposed and passed a series of rules and regulations for allocating oil revenue. The 2012 Petroleum Act and Petroleum Revenue Management Bill (PRMB) were among the most sweeping regulations adopted to promote national development. The Petroleum Act, for instance, stipulated the principles of transparency and distribution of profits, and was eventually incorporated into the Transitional Constitution. It declared that "The People of South Sudan shall benefit equitably from the revenue derived from petroleum," and that "the value of petroleum resources shall be maximized and its value shall be converted into lasting benefit for current future generations."[20] It also provided that any information can be withheld if "it contains property data" or "information sensitive company data." It is unclear what constituted sensitive data and whether such data could be deemed sensitive enough to be withheld from public scrutiny. And yet such secrecy could also redound to the leaders' advantage and justify the withholding of information about oil revenue.

The Petroleum Act, which worked in conjunction with the Petroleum Revenue Management Agreement, stipulated the creation of a national resource fund (NRF) for protecting natural resources. The agreement consisted of two components: the Petroleum Revenue Account that comprised 75 percent of petroleum revenue, and the Petroleum Revenue Savings funds.[21] The former was set up to channel revenue into accounts that NGOs and citizens could monitor, which included the Oil Revenue Stabilization Account and the Future Generations Funds. Both were designed to defray the difference between actual money accrued on a quarterly basis and the benchmark price on the world market (a price determined by world indexes of the price of oil). It was then decided that when the sale of oil exceeded benchmark rates, the excess revenue could be transferred into the Future Generation Funds—a source of revenue for the state and its citizens. But there was still the practical issue of how

to transfer the money so that it could promote the welfare of the people. How, in other words, would the government set up the account to ensure the proper transfer into what some demanded as "a trusted special account. . . . or simply a segregated account held by the treasury."[22] The Bank of South Sudan was still too small to manage such an account. So, officials agreed to set up an account under the government treasury. As Joseph Bell and Teresa Faria put it, "building a permanent fund requires the restriction of current expenditures to a level below oil revenues, at least during the initial period of production."[23] The plan, then, was to make the fund accessible in five years. When activated, the money could be withdrawn at a minimum rate of 10 percent of the total fund to finance capital investments "deemed" to benefit future generations and to foster long-term growth.[24] The fund would also promote local accountability by addressing the political and social grievances of communities living near the oil fields.[25]

In 2012, Kiir also established the South Transparency Initiative. Officials hailed it as "the gold standard of for openness and transparency on issues of oil extraction."[26] Yet within months, it led to a polarizing debate on the need for transparency in the National Assembly. As it turned out, the assembly had voted in favor of restricting the public's access to oil contracts, reasoning that the people lacked the knowledge to exercise control over the contracts. Critics roundly criticized the vote for violating the spirit of the Petroleum Act, which had called for legislative oversight through the publication of reports. They insisted that the legislature had a duty to be pragmatic and realistic in the delivery and service of the revenue, and that the assembly members simply did not trust the people's judgment on one of the country's most vital issues of national development. The assembly, after all, was set up to pass laws based on the deliberation and input of the citizens. By keeping the people out of the loop, the assembly was essentially failing to represent its constituents. It seemed that there was no longer "any meaning," wrote Emma Vickers, "in providing citizens with information if they can't use it to hold their leaders to account."[27] But this trust deficit was not simply a reflection of societal ills, such as the high illiteracy rates. It also reflected something more perverse: namely, that the assembly members could be bribed on public goods issues in which the people had a vested right to know.

The Sudd Institute, a prominent think tank located in Juba, published several detailed reports on and recommendations for promoting accountability in the oil sector. Its 2012 *Blueprint for Prosperity Report*, for instance, called for a single fund to simplify and streamline the rules regarding oversight. It also proposed creating new institutional bodies, including an Audit Chamber, to monitor the oil sector, as well as publishing regular, detailed production and financial data of all oil sector contracts to ensure that all new deals were negotiated or signed within an open and competitive process. Ultimately, the goal was "to improve civil society with enough technical and political support to provide a robust

check on how contracts and revenue are managed."[28] Kiir, for his part, did not comment on the proposed new rules and regulations for monitoring oil revenue. As was his custom, he preferred to remain silent on such public debates and civil society's efforts to bring transparency to the oil sector.

Creating the Curse

With money flowing into the new state government's coffers and international donors funding much of the basic needs of the South Sudanese people, South Sudan's future development seemed promising. But its endemic corruption and mismanagement thwarted these plans and exposed a recklessness that steered the country increasingly to war, leading Pagan Amum, the former SPLM General Secretary, to state that "It's only a curse when you are stupid!"[29] Some have even used the notion of "liberation curse" to explain the national affliction with self-enrichment and the country's authoritarianism.[30] The resource curse, by comparison, describes the ill-effects of poor government and decision-making. In South Sudan's case, it offers a compelling theory to understand the country's instability and the expanding patchwork of patronage networks that helped lead the country into war.

The root feature of the resource course is the state's poor and wasteful allocation of resources. Michael Ross, a political scientist, argues that governments receive massive profit windfalls from the sale of oil that tend to outstrip the public consumption of profits.[31] In turn, the acquisition of massive state assets or rents creates excess revenue that state elites siphon off and place into personal accounts. The siphoned-off revenue invariably means less money to fund public goods projects and confusing balance sheets that "make it difficult to establish transparency."[32] Accordingly, with little or no functioning "tax bureaucracy," there is no reliable way to hold the elites accountable for extracting rents. Nigeria, for instance, saw much of the profit from its oil revenue go directly to the personal accounts of the leaders, including Osanjo Abache, the former President of Nigeria, who reportedly siphoned off 3 billion dollars of oil revenue.[33] Yet the lack of public accountability, as Terry Karl claims, "is an integral part of the calculation of rulers to retain their political support by distributing petrodollars to their friends, allies, and social support bases."[34]

The fact that oil revenue accounts for roughly 98 percent of the annual budget and nearly 64 percent of South Sudan's Gross National Product means that South Sudan depends heavily on oil to finance its public projects.[35] The "Dutch Disease" describes how such heavy reliance on oil can lead to a decline in other sectors of the economy by inflating the value of the country's currency and making the other sectors less competitive. In order to manage such inflationary effects in

102 SOUTH SUDAN'S FATEFUL STRUGGLE

South Sudan, the ruling elite have tried to stabilize the official exchange rate by keeping the SSP pegged to the value of dollar. In December 2015, the national government decided to float the South Sudanese pound, resulting in a tenfold increase in the SSP official rate. Inflation soon spiraled out of control, diminished the worth of domestic holdings of banks and large companies, and depleted the national reserve holdings of US dollars. Many companies consequently had to borrow more in South Sudanese Pounds to offset the costs of paying the debt—including South Sudan's biggest producer of beer, the White Bull company.

South Sudan's mismanagement was largely a product of economic liberalization. Speculation and deregulation had the contradictory of effect of buoying South Sudan's informal economy and its lax controls. The UN Panel of Experts in South Sudan found that the "degree of informality that limits meaningful controls and oversight . . . reflects how the Treasury and the Ministry of Finance have been effectively privatized."[36] Private trading of the oil, for instance, ended up diverting money away from public investment infrastructure. Nowhere was this more evident than in the GRSS's practice of preselling its oil to other countries. When the government pre-sells its oil, it receives advance payment for the oil on the promise to deliver it in the future, typically within months. The oil companies in turn receive a discount on the oil and end up charging a substantial rate of interest on the prepaid oil. The revenue is then collected ahead of production, making it difficult to oversee and monitor a vast amount of the government's purchases. Although South Sudan's crude oil has become more competitive on the global market, as more traders pre-purchase its oil on the open market,[37] the practice has failed to increase returns and profit. In fact, it has saddled the national government with debt.

Another problem is the secretive manner of procurement that has made it difficult to ascertain the competitiveness of the prices listed in the contracts. The fact that the procurement of goods and services often exceeds the actual profits of the sector means that some of the contracts were underreported. The company "Lou for Trading," for example, was a contract worth nearly $540 million dollars, but it exceeded, as the Panel of Experts on South Sudan found, "the entire budget for goods and services."[38] Because of the sheer size of the contract, it was nearly impossible to verify the delivery of public services. The likely conclusion reached by many was that it was broken down into different pieces and delivered to informal services—for instance for the purchase of SUVs for government officials. But it was impossible to be sure.

The speculative contracts in the oil sector have nonetheless led to the loss of millions of dollars—money that could have been invested in infrastructure. And the United States, despite its active role in peace talks, has had little stake in South Sudan's oil sector. In the early 1980s, it spent large sums of money to form a large consortium. However, it began to curtail its investment in the mid-1980s, after

fighting between the SPLA and the Sudanese government in the southern region led to attacks on Chevron's oil facilities. Chevron had asked for more security from the Sudanese government, but the government failed to keep the facilities safe from future attacks.[39] By 1990, the United States officially pulled out of Sudan's oil market, leaving it with no vital economic interests in the state. China and other oil producers would eventually form Dar Petroleum, the major oil conglomerate, which comprises the majority of oil shares held by South Sudan, including the China National Petroleum Corporation (CNPC), or Sinopec, and the Malaysian state-owned Petronas. Together, these two corporations hold nearly 55 percent of the total shares; the remainder is held by SSTO, a private oil firm based in Egypt. Much of the balance of shares belongs to the Nile Petroleum Corporation (Nilepet), South Sudan's state-owned oil enterprise, with facilities concentrated in three designated areas called blocks.[40] Nilepet though lacks the technological expertise, resources, and economies of scale to achieve efficient returns on their investment like these larger national companies. In fact, the foreign-owned oil companies typically use their advanced technological capacity and economies of scale to negotiate a majority share and return on profits. As a result, Nilepet's production levels depend in large part on the technological inputs produced by these other companies, which amounts to yet another added cost of producing its oil.

As South Sudan's largest state-owned industry, Nilepet has also helped provide a key source of war financing. Yet after independence, it also faced the challenge of exporting the oil. As a landlocked country, South Sudan had to rely on Sudan to transport the crude oil to ports where it could be refined and eventually shipped. This left it particularly vulnerable to Sudan, which determined the price of transporting the oil.

The Fateful Decision

The challenge required both countries to work together in exporting the oil, even though both still mistrusted one another. Kiir and other South Sudanese leaders resented the fact that Khartoum controlled parts of its oil production, even as it benefited from its ties with the oil company, Total. The resentment underscored years of frustration with Sudan's corrupt elite, which had conducted "off-the-book" deals with oil traders that enabled it to avoid sharing revenues with the GRSS.[41] The money from these deals then went into secret currency accounts that placed the GRSS's exchange reserves (in liquid assets) at great risk, while also limiting the GRSS's access to Production Sharing Agreements (PSAs) between the government and operating companies. PSAs, which are long-term contracts between the government and oil company or another government, stipulate the

amount of money each party will receive from the extraction of oil. Under a PSA, the oil company assumes the risk of exploring and producing the oil but shares a certain amount of the profit with government. Shortly after declaring independence in 2011, South Sudan entered into a PSA with virtually all the major oil companies.[42] However, none yielded any positive results, and in 2013, the outbreak of war drastically curtailed the prewar production of nearly 400,000 barrels per day to 175,000 barrels per day.[43] Since 2015, the South Sudanese government has made it its mission to return to prewar levels by signing more PSAs to extract more of its unexplored oil, including its six-year agreement signed with South Africa to explore and extract oil from Block B in the Jonglei state.[44]

For South Sudan, then, Sudan was now a rival state bent on cheating and outcompeting South Sudan for oil profits. For a realist thinker of international relations, it was a situation in which both competing states were aggressively seeking to maximize their interests at the expense of the other.[45] Both were acting out of fear and seeking to compel the other side to act. With their relationship fraught with tension, the South Sudanese leaders began entertaining in late 2011, the nuclear option of shutting off the flow of oil to Sudan. The idea came after the NCP began to unilaterally tax the oil sent to its refineries, a clear violation of the CPA. Sudan still felt entitled to some of South Sudan's oil, largely because there was no final agreement between Sudan and South Sudan regarding the terms for transporting the oil. Sudan's parliament eventually approved a resolution that increased the fees for transporting South Sudanese oil to $35. Typical user fees ranged from 10 cents to $3.50, which meant that Sudan was being overcharged.[46] The GoS retaliated by refusing to pay the transit fees. Khartoum consequently began to siphon off 815 million dollars to compensate for the loss in transit fees, stealing in effect much of South Sudan's oil.

As tensions grew between the two countries, some SPLM leaders, which included Pagan Amum, were convinced that a shutdown of the oil pipelines would weaken Sudan and allow South Sudan to take control of its political destiny by reclaiming some of Sudan's oil. Amum was certain that South Sudan had enough resources to outlast Sudan, which at that time, depended more on oil for its everyday operations than South Sudan. Machar also agreed with this assessment. In late 2011, he announced the South Sudanese government's plan to build a 2,000-kilometer pipeline that would run through Kenya and Ethiopia to the Gulf of Aden. Machar—who would oversee the plan—indicated that it would take roughly 12 months to complete. But this also underestimated the time it would take to complete the project through mountainous terrain in Ethiopia, which was expected to lead to engineering challenges and operational delays.[47] Unsurprisingly, few took the proposed project seriously, including the Sudanese officials who refused to relent on their exorbitant demands.

In late January 2012, the African Union High-Level Implementation Panel organized a special summit meeting in Addis Ababa to settle the countries differences and to reach agreement on the terms of oil production. Menes Zenawi, the Prime Minster of Ethiopia, mediated the talks that were attended by Mwai Kibaki, the President of Kenya, and Thabo Mbeki, the President of South Africa and Chair of the AUHIP. On January 27, after hours of negotiations, Kiir stated that he needed more time to think about the terms of the agreement.[48] He was concerned that shutting off the oil pipelines would destabilize the country and eliminate a cashflow that had helped finance his personal security. But later that evening, in defiance of Kiir, Amum unilaterally announced that the government would shut down its oil pipelines, effectively rescinding the negotiated agreement with a lower transit fee (that Bashir had agreed to). In his view, shutting down the oil pipelines would not only end up hurting Sudan's economy the most, but was in the best interests of the South Sudanese people, even though he had not consulted citizens and other branches of government on the decision.

The shutdown ended up hurting both sides, and eventually forced Kiir to impose harsh austerity measures, such as cutting many services. To make up for the shortfall, the government had to borrow an estimated $4.5 million and spend nearly $2 billion of its reserves.[49] It was never quite clear how officials had negotiated most of the loans, or even where the money was spent. Many suspected that the government had benefited financially from the loans. Austerity, however, led to still more political restrictions. Kiir closed South Sudan's borders with Sudan and cut off trading with Sudan and its neighbors. The decision provoked a harsh response by critics. The Secretary General of South Sudan's Chamber of Commerce, for example, stated that "it is not for the interests of the common citizens and the interests of the business people that these borders should be closed."[50] Closing its borders meant that those holding a passport would be effectively denied entry, leading thousands of South Sudanese citizens to become stranded in Sudan.

By the summer of 2012, the inflation rate had risen 80 percent in the country and the South Sudanese pound had lost a third of its value against the US dollar on the black market. Severe food shortages became widespread, causing nearly 40 percent of the civilian population to become food insecure.[51] Moreover, powerful donor states and UN agencies began to reassess their investment in the country's development, including the construction of start-up roads. In 2011 alone, the United States had pledged approximately 400 million dollars to improve health and educational services. By the summer of 2014, that number had declined sharply, as the US Department of State and the US Agency for International Development (USAID) shifted much of its development aid to emergency humanitarian assistance.[52]

106 SOUTH SUDAN'S FATEFUL STRUGGLE

With tensions running high and the two countries losing billions of dollars in oil revenue, the two sides finally agreed to meet in Addis Ababa in September 2012, where they signed a cooperation agreement that set the transit fee at $8.40 on the crude oil transferred from Helig to the port of Sudan, and required South Sudan to pay Khartoum 3.08 billion dollars to compensate for nearly three quarters of lost oil production.[53] In addition, both sides agreed to withdraw their troops at least six miles from their borders and to reduce military training within a fourteen-mile buffer zone. Although they discussed the issue of the SPLM-N in South Kordofan and the Blue Nile, no plan was put into place to disband the group. The terms of the agreement were virtually identical to the one Kiir had rejected in January. However, after months of severe economic hardship and declining rates of oil revenue, Kiir had to settle on a deal.

In April 2012, South Sudan finally reopened its oil pipelines. To mark the event, Kiir met Bashir in Juba on April 13 to discuss the implementation of the agreement. The two leaders appeared jovial in public, pledging to address key land issues, particularly the border dispute in Abyei, where officials had decided to form a joint administration and to hold a referendum to resolve the area's status. As such, the two leaders left in place the contested, de facto administrative structures established under the June 2011 UN Agreement on Temporary Arrangements for the Administration and Security of the Abyei Area.[54] One of these structures included South Sudan's administrative control over the oil field in the northern part of Abyei where the Ngok Dinka resided. Another involved the reduction of SAF troops in the area around the Diffra oil fields, or the southernmost part where many nomadic Misseriya roamed. The Abyei area was vital to both sides' interests, but it was also rife with ethnic tensions arising from land ownership. Kiir's poor handling of the shutdown only helped worsen tensions between Sudan and South Sudan.

It took several months to return to pre–shut down levels of oil production. In halting production, the shutdown caused much of the machinery to go unused or to lie in desuetude. Extensive repairs were needed to make them functional. Kiir had to draw on the country's oil reserves to cover essential repair costs and make the delivery system effective for investing in the basic infrastructure.[55] In July 2013, Stephen Dhieu Dau, the National Minister of Petroleum and Mining, declared that "the first priority is to deliver the necessary services to the community of the oil-producing areas such as clean drinking water, healthcare centers, schools, and road networks."[56] Within months, the oil money began to flow into the national coffers, with many urging the national government to sign the Petroleum Revenue Management Bill. When I asked Dhieu at the Rainbow Hotel in Juba in early August 2013 about the new cabinet's decision to sign the bill into law (it had already been passed b the National Assembly), he indicated with a slight grin "that it was the natural thing to do."[57]

But it felt like a hollow pledge. Perhaps because only a year earlier, it was leaked that billions in oil revenue had been stolen from state coffers during the interim period. It was not clear who had leaked the information, but in a public letter sent to all government officials, Kiir asked governmental officials to give back the money they had stolen during the interim period, a sum that amounted to nearly 4 million dollars. The announcement seemed to alleviate concerns of the powerful state donors and UN agencies. Yet it led to heated debate inside the National Legislative Assembly, where legislators who had supported Kiir's initiative fended off critics who accused Kiir of misdeeds and using the announcement to divert attention away from his own malfeasance. Kiir never responded publicly to the criticism, nor did he open up a formal investigation into the matter. Ultimately, only a small fraction of the money was returned voluntarily. Still, the leak, as Hilde Johnson writes, led to a "growing willingness to go public with what they knew, primarily to undermine other factions."[58] Corruption in effect had become a tool the different political factions used to attack other factions.

Exploiting Crisis and the War

In the summer of 2013, infighting in the SPLM/A came to a head. Vice President Machar publicly declared his intention to run against Kiir in 2015 and then openly criticized Kiir's handling of corruption inside the SPLM and the service delivery of goods. In late July, Kiir issued a decree forming a new Cabinet and reducing the number of cabinet ministers from 14 to 10. In the process, he dismissed 10 ministers and high-ranking officials, including Machar, and other ministers, most notably, Pagan Amum. A week after making his decision, Kiir stated that he "removed the former Vice President because he decided to go astray." He added that Machar had "used the public media to discredit the government in which he was a party before the international community," and that "This was an act of disrespect and [shows an] intention to hurt the image of this country."[59] Machar later accused Kiir of not consulting party members and respecting the opinion of his cabinets, before warning him not to remove any more party leaders who disagreed with him.

Meanwhile, many South Sudanese officials and citizens remained guardedly optimistic. Some even welcomed the decree as an opportunity "to re-energize the SPLM" with the appointment of qualified officials "or technocrats" and "to make room for a new start,"[60] while others saw it as chance to "Obamatize" politics in the country by saying "yes, we can" to ending tribal politics.[61] Yet behind the scenes, the infighting got worse. By the fall of 2013, Kiir threatened to delay the upcoming SPLM convention—which would set the rules for the 2015 presidential election—and extend more controversial amnesties to woo back rebel

108   SOUTH SUDAN'S FATEFUL STRUGGLE

leaders such as David Yau Yau who, as mentioned earlier, was attacking government forces and civilians in Eastern Jonglei.[62]

The feud between Kiir and Machar reached a feverish pitch in the fall of 2013 after Machar sided with Khartoum and publicly supported its demands for the SPLM to cut off all ties to the SPLM-N. By this time, Sudan had threatened to shut down its oil pipeline connecting South Sudan with the port at the Red Sea, unless SPLM leaders withdrew their support of the SPLM-N rebels who continued to attack SAF troops in the Upper Blue Nile and South Kordofan. In a move reminiscent of his earlier collaboration with the Sudanese government in the 1990s, Machar even led a delegation to Khartoum to pressure the GoS to accept Sudan's demand. Khartoum later dropped its threat, fearing that another shutdown would cause permanent damage to both countries' economies. This effectively isolated Machar politically while raising suspicion about his ulterior motives to seize control of the national government.

In the weeks after Kiir sacked Machar, Kiir threatened to replace more SPLM officials. To show his further resolve, he officially announced his plan to run for the Presidency in November, a move that provoked anger given that he had made earlier promises to step down after four years. Kiir had decided that because of his support for Khartoum, Machar was no longer trustworthy. Machar's move had also convinced more South Sudanese to mobilize support for Kiir. The Rescue the President group, for instance, which consisted of several military commanders, senior elders, and Dinka civilians, openly pledged their support for Kiir. This only seemed to embolden Kiir, who had become increasingly wary of a possible coup d'etat. At the same time, unconfirmed reports indicated that the government was storing up armed supplies in the event of an assault.

On December 15 someone attempted to break into the presidential armory. The officer in charge of the armory (a Nuer) shot and killed his deputy—a Dinka who had refused to open the armory. It was never entirely clear why the Nuer commander insisted on entering the armory. Was he intending to steal arms or was it simply a misunderstanding? Either way, Kiir declared that the opposition had mounted a coup. Rumors quickly spread that troops loyal to Machar had deliberately attacked government forces. The government reacted by killing thousands of civilians in Juba—almost all of them Nuer. The brutal campaign of ethnic cleansing forced thousands of Nuer to flee the city and take refuge in the UN compound located on the outskirts of Juba. Tut Gatlak Tut, who worked for a Norwegian NGO, recounted how government soldiers had gone from street corner to street corner searching for Nuer and "chasing Nuer like me all the way to the compound."[63] He had managed to reach the compound by foot, Tut was one of thousands of internally displaced peoples in Juba, which made it difficult to verify the identities of all IDPs. In some cases, Dinka fighters were allowed

to enter into the camps and to attack Nuer. The government in effect had managed to use its power to dehumanize the Nuer as traitors. It was as Mahmood Mamdani put it, "tribalism in its consummate form."[64]

After word got out that innocent Nuer were being targeted and killed, the Nuer community retaliated. Peter Gadet, an SPLA commander, led the mutiny by inspiring the spontaneous reemergence of the White Army in Bentiu, which then attacked and killed Dinka civilians and army guards. Within days, the numbers of White Army fighters swelled to 50,000 and attacked and killed civilians and army forces. Having overwhelmed government forces in Bentiu, the White Army fighters headed south to Juba, where they threatened Kiir's government, and prompted President Yoweri Museveni, the leader of Uganda, to send several thousands of Ugandan troops into Juba to assist Kiir.

Museveni's intervention saved Kiir's regime from collapse. For Museveni, this meant propping up an ally to counter Khartoum's influence and to defend the regional interests of the United States and the United Kingdom, which provided him billions of dollars in military aid annually. For Kiir, it was an opportunity to reimpose his political power over the budget and to shore up his personal security. Naturally, the question was how the war would affect his power, or his ability to maintain his patronage network? But with war, nothing is ever certain.

Crisis Mismanagement

The civil war, it turned out, had created a spillover effect of corruption. In January 2014, President Kiir decreed the formation of the Crisis Management Committee, which consisted of 27 government officials.[65] In Kiir's view, the CMC was a way of regaining the upper hand in the crisis and promoting awareness of the national government's position. As such, it was tasked with addressing and mitigating the social, economic, political, and diplomatic effects of the conflict and raising awareness among the population and regional and international actors of the government version of events. It was headed by James Wani Igga, the Vice President, and operated outside the purview of the Ministry of Finance, which would typically administer the finances of such a committee.[66]

But instead of managing the crisis, the CMC Secretariat and Bank of Sudan provided cash payments to government officials, military generals, ministers, and businessmen. No attempt was made to gain the approval of the Ministry of Finance and Economic Planning, leading to inconsistences with the Public Financial Management and Accountability Act that regulated the Ministry's actions.[67] Not only did the national government fail to stop the malfeasance, it also benefitted from the CMC. The largest payments ultimately went to the National Security Services and the Office of the President. Obuto Mamur Mate,

110   SOUTH SUDAN'S FATEFUL STRUGGLE

for instance, received nearly 5 million SSP through an account with the Bank of South Sudan.[68]

So pervasive was the corruption of the CMC that many people began to call it the "Corruption Management Committee." Of the 446 million SSP disbursed to the committee, only 84 million SSP could be traced or accounted for. The remaining 362 million was used to pay for lavish hotel stays in Juba—even while the hotel occupants lived in well-built homes in Juba. Moreover, no justification was given for the purported cash payments made to individuals. It was not until 2017 that the full scale of the CMC's corruption was made public. The CMC of course was supposed to alleviate the effects of the crisis, but instead, it worsened them and the people's suffering by profiteering from the civil war.

Militarizing the Oil Sector

There was also no auditing system to deter political leaders from rent-seeking. As early as 2014, the SPLA-Government forces secured the oil blocks in the Unity and Upper Nile states and used the revenue to carry out attacks on the SPLA-IO forces in the area. Nilepet's delivery of 251 barrels of diesel oil to military forces in the Upper Nile, for instance, had helped finance the operations of the Padang militia, an ethnic Dinka group loyal to President Kiir.[69] Militarizing the oil sector produced millions of dollars for the government, and it was the result of two factors. First, as discussed in Chapter 3, the SPLA remained a largely nonprofessionalized force united by a loose network of militia units. These militia units were largely organized along ethnic tribal lines and consisted of fighters belonging to different tribal groups. Yet the lack of cohesion meant that the government could be more flexible in supporting the Padang militia, which had pledged to fight the SPLA-IO rebels.

Second, the National Security Service—an agency of the central government—had by now secretly infiltrated oil production operations and used the funds to invest in the operation of their own activities. By 2015, the NSS had become one of South Sudan's most powerful government agencies. A UN report found that the NSS had received substantial amount of money from the Office of the President. From 2018 to 2019, for instance, the President's office allocated 4,681,364,253 South Sudanese Pounds to the NSS.[70] As the Panel of Experts in South Sudan would later put it, "The NSS has not only pursued a number of independent commercial revenue streams but also liberated it from financial dependence on the government."[71] As the major source of external revenue, then, Nilepet maintained close ties to the NSS. The NSS Director Lt. Akol Koor Kuc, for example, held a position on the board of Nilepet, while many Nilepet shareholders remained active agents of the NSS. Lt. Kur in fact commanded the

"Inside Tiger" and the "Outside Tiger," two killing squads responsible for the killings of journalists, civil society activists, and other critics of the government.

Another report published by the Sentry concluded that the NSS had used "oil revenue for a wide range of security expenses while skirting oversight and circumventing normal revenue collection and procurement procedures."[72] The report was notable not just for its detailed reporting but also because of the extensive global media attention it had attracted.[73] The global attention also forced the GRSS to respond to the findings. Ateny Wek, the spokesman for the government, insisted that "South Sudan is not looking for guns now, South Sudan is at peace. I don't know why the Sentry is putting out wrong stories against South Sudan."[74] It was impossible to verify this statement, since there was no accurate way to track the sale of arms or to determine its provenance. But the flow of arms had become an increasing concern for many regional neighbors, such as Uganda, which feared that the arms they shipped to South Sudan could fall into the hands of the rebels. Their concern stemmed from a 2014 incident in which the United States and EU member countries (including Slovakia and Bulgaria) had exported small arms and ammunition to Uganda. But instead of using the guns, Museveni's government secretly shipped them to the GRSS. This, however, violated key provisions of the EU arms embargoes. To make matters worse, the Slovakian government claimed that it was unaware of the destination of the shipments, even though it was Slovakia's clientelist network that made it possible for offshore companies to act as intermediaries of supplies to South Sudan— including a Seychellois company that brokered the export of ammunition from Romania through the Slovak Republic to Uganda.[75]

The 2014 incident revealed the many secret supply lines of arms sales, lines that allowed the national government to escape the punishing effects of sanctions, while also using its ownership of Nilepet to finance the war. The war had thus created new, albeit limited opportunities to loot the country. For the United States, United Nations, and African Union, it had become clear that more had to be done if they were to wield a more pointed, financial stick to stop the abuses and the war.

Stopping Corruption through Sanctions

That stick, it would turn out, would involve both state and individual targeted sanctions. Washington policymakers and many human rights activists welcomed the sanctions against the political leaders. But others demanded more action. Testifying before a US committee that was tasked with addressing the effects of the war in South Sudan, Prendergast insisted that the country was a "hijacked state," and that US leaders had to do more to enforce existing sanctions.[76]

112 SOUTH SUDAN'S FATEFUL STRUGGLE

President Obama had already signed an Executive Order on April 7, 2014, which declared an asset freeze and travel bans on any individual found to have committed gross human violations and threatened peace and security.[77] The order also established South Sudan Sanctions Program, which the US Department of the Treasury was responsible for administering. Within a few months, the United States had imposed asset freezes and travel sanctions on rebel officials and lower-ranking Sudanese officials of Kiir's regime. The sanctions—which did not target Kiir or Machar—were intended to send a signal to these leaders that Washington would no longer tolerate their corruption and abuses. The United States soon took its case to the United Nations, where it began drafting a UNSC resolution that called for further sanctions on individuals who threatened peace in South Sudan. When South Sudan learned of its plan, they sent a high-level delegation—led by Barnaba Marial Benjamin, the foreign minister (who carried a letter written by Kiir stating that sanction would only hamper dialogue and peace talks)—to Washington in December 2014 to pressure the Obama administration to reconsider the resolution.[78] But the United States remained unpersuaded.

In March 2015, the UNSC met to discuss and vote on the resolution. Although Russia and China voiced concern about the punitive approach—that it would hinder the peace process—the resolution passed.[79] By early July, the Security Council Committee, which was in charge of implementing UNSC 2206, declared travel bans and asset freezes on six individuals, including SPLA major generals Simon Gatwech Dual and James Koang Chuol.[80] The following year it would impose further travel bans that were later renewed under a new resolution that established the Panel of Experts on South Sudan.

All the success, though, raised the important question of whether the United States' and United Nation's coercive approach was working. Although its immediate impact was difficult to gauge, that is, the leaders seemed to be getting around its worst effects, it was clear that it had brought considerable pressure on the South Sudanese leaders. More importantly, it seemed to offer IGAD a critical tool for pressuring the leaders to come to the table. By August 2015, IGAD announced that the warring parties had agreed to sign the Agreement on the Resolution of Conflict in South Sudan (ARCSS). Kiir remained cool towards the deal, even suggesting it had been imposed by foreign governments. After the 2015 peace deal fell apart in the summer of 2016, the United States and United Kingdom proposed a revised Security Council resolution that would go a step further than the earlier round of sanctions. This time, the two countries were asking the UN Security Council to impose an arms embargo on the country, thus raising the stakes for the Security Council. Angola, for instance, quickly objected to the resolution, insisting that more time was needed to work out the details. Russia meanwhile maintained that it would only aggravate the situation by increasing political tensions in the country. After several more rounds

of meetings, the Security Council eventually rejected the proposed resolution on December 23, 2016, when Angola, China, Egypt, Japan, Malaysia, Russia, and Senegal abstained, leaving the resolution one vote short of the needed majority for passage.[81] The abstaining members shared the concern that Kiir had already made efforts to make peace, which included the South Sudan National Dialogue and early efforts to revitalize the (national) DDR in order to reduce the amount of existing weapons in the hands of civilians.[82] As Petr Ilichev, the Russian Deputy to the United Nations, put it, "Sound peace in South Sudan will not be brought about by a security council arms embargo, but rather by targeted measures to disarm civilians as well as demobilize and reintegrate combatants."[83] But it was impossible to ignore the destructive influence of small arms, especially illegal ones, and how this had already hampered efforts to institute effective national and UN-administered DDR programs.

In fact, more and more illegal arms had continued to flow into South Sudan. By May 2017, a UN special commission reported that arms from the Ukraine were flowing into South Sudan. The panel traced two L-39 jets to a Ukrainian company, which were then sent to Gulu, Uganda, before being flown to the Juba International Airport. The commission also received several reports that Egypt had been sending weapons to South Sudan, along with the Democratic Republic of the Congo.[84] All of this pointed to the elusive nature of such arms and to the idea supported by China and Russia: that sanctions were failing to stop the flow of arms into South Sudan. For these two countries maintaining the status quo was still the best way to promote stability and direct investment in the country. China, for example, had already invested large sums of money in the infrastructure, that is, the new airport terminal in Juba and new roads linking Juba with Bentiu and other cities in South Sudan. It had, for instance, contributed 700 troops to serve in UNMISS and appointed Major General Chaoying Yang to replace the Kenyan major commander of UNMISS.[85] With these commitments, China had hoped to gain a major foothold in the country's economy by supporting the status quo leadership.

But it was precisely its tacit support of the corrupt national elite that had deepened skepticism of its economic investment in the country. The fact that sanctions targeted the individual corrupt leaders, and not the South Sudanese economy, made China's position even more tenuous. In the minds of the South Sudanese people, targeted sanctions had boosted their hope for sustainable peace, the rule of law, and democracy. Still, it took the United Nations and United States several years before finally imposing sanctions on the top leaders, or in this case, the Vice President, Taban Gai, in January 2020. Perhaps they had lost interest or were simply reluctant to lose China's and Russia's support? Either way, they faced a difficult predicament: impose sanctions on the top leaders or risk retaliation or the refusal by the leaders to cooperate with their demands.

114   SOUTH SUDAN'S FATEFUL STRUGGLE

If the sanctions imposed on Taban Gai were any indication, it was not that the United Nations, European Union, and the United States were willing to take that risk, but rather that the threat of sanctions was finally striking at what mattered most: their personal political power.

Conclusion

Independence was supposed to free the South Sudanese people from Sudan's oppression and to enable them to develop their own democratic state. But in reality, it did neither. Instead, it created a new state apparatus of corruption and patronage, a neopatrimonial state based on the leaders' ability and willingness to use their power over the budget to gain political and economic advantage. Kiir naturally became the chief patron of the state because of his influence over the national budget. Liberation's curse in this sense seemed to reflect South Sudan's deep-seated affliction with corruption.

The country had already doomed itself by militarizing and monetizing its patronage system. In practical terms, this meant that any steep and sustained drop in the global price of oil would invariably force the leaders to instinctively resort to the threat violence to preserve their political power. The leaders of course still needed to legitimize these threats by paying off their loyalists/subordinates and leaving just enough to invest in public goods. Yet the new kleptocratic state they created was not only unstable and extractive but opportunizing at every turn, even in times of war.

The system of corruption, in short, had become an intricate web of informal networks of patronage that had produced perverse incentives to exercise power. It thus formed formidable barriers to inclusion, transparency, and accountability and showed how the national war economy stemmed in part from the economics of armed factionalism. The civil war ended any illusion that South Sudan had overcome the destructive effects of factionalism. In sowing its own uncertainty, militarized patronage had resulted in a nonprofessional army and the politicization of tribal identity. South Sudan's civil war made the country even more dependent on outside aid and the status quo. Whether or not sanctions worked, they raised the issue of whether accountability could ever be achieved by force alone.

5

Impunity, Human Rights, and the Struggle for Justice

On July 11, 2016, nearly 100 government soldiers forced their way into the Terrain Hotel compound—which sits on the outskirts of Juba—and killed a local journalist, gang-raped the women, and tortured hotel residents with mock executions. The owner of the hotel had pleaded with UN peacekeepers to intervene, but the peacekeepers never left their UN compound located just a half mile from the hotel.[1] The situation was simply too dangerous since it risked placing UN troops in harm's way.

A month before the hotel incident, Salva Kiir's troops had attacked SPLM/A-IO forces in the Guedele sector of Juba, shattering the fragile peace process and leaving the city and its people severely traumatized. Tension still filled the streets when my colleague and I arrived a month later. We tried walking from Juba City to the Paradise Hotel (which we had done in December 2015 when we last visited); however, we were soon assaulted by a man on a *boda boda* (a cargo bike), who tried to grab my backpack. This was before an open-air truck filled with government troops had pulled up alongside us, just as we arrived at the hotel. With our blood racing, we began to wonder why we had come to South Sudan and whether we would be able to conduct any research (e.g., interviews).

Juba still felt like a war zone to us. And the people were angry and frustrated at their leaders for returning the country to war. Many wanted them to take responsibility for the violence and to be held to account for the bloodshed. But this also required the leaders to relax their grip on power and to approve the Hybrid Court for South Sudan (HCSS), which was part of the Agreement on the Resolution of the Conflict in South Sudan (ARCSS). The leaders of course knew that the political stakes of holding trials were high—that they could be imprisoned for life. So they learned to walk a fine line between maintaining international support during and after the war and approving the HCSS, hoping to somehow convince people that the HCSS would destabilize the country and that the Commission for Truth, Reconciliation, and Healing (CTRH) would be the best opportunity to promote peace and national unity.

It was all part of a larger strategy to temporize on the need for justice to resolve the country's problems and to create more uncertainty about the prospects of victims' justice. In *Neither Settler Nor Native*, Mahmood Mamdani argues that

South Sudan's Fateful Struggle. Steven C. Roach, Oxford University Press. © Oxford University Press 2023.
DOI: 10.1093/oso/9780190057848.003.0006

116 SOUTH SUDAN'S FATEFUL STRUGGLE

there is no assurance that even the victims-turned leaders will exercise power any differently from their predecessors who had repressed them. For him, justice becomes a way for those in power to punish and exact revenge in the name of accountability. As he puts it, "Transitional justice normalizes violence by calling it criminal while giving the political system the opportunity to justify and empower itself by meting out punishment."[2] Criminal justice is ultimately about making "the history of the violence go away," and forgetting how it was produced in the first place (i.e., colonialism).

Punishing the criminals, in his view, does not uproot the violence; it merley patches up old wounds. The real task lies in understanding how to make justice more inclusive or more encompassing of the will and public conscience of the people. But how does one begin to do this when that very will remains divided and aggrieved by those administering the (in)justice? It's a question that involves brokering a peace process that has long excluded the people and enabled the leaders to politicize justice.[3]

The project of hybrid justice in South Sudan, I argue, is a crucial attempt to address this challenge of inclusive justice. Yet it remains one piece of a much larger puzzle of breaking the cycle of violence in South Sudan. My aim in this chapter is to address this puzzle by examining the human rights abuses in South Sudan and the efforts to implement a regime of transitional justice that can embody a comprehensive moral reckoning with the past. I conclude that the ruling elites have managed to fracture such a reckoning process by politicizing justice and repressing civil society—the one agent capable of reconciling justice with peace.

The Culture of Impunity

Pursuing justice is always a strategic enterprise. Even international courts, which rely on cooperation to administer criminal justice, must devise strategies to pressure state authorities to surrender criminals to the court. When those criminals are the very state authorities negotiating the terms of peace, the state learns to counter-strategize justice by using resources to block investigations and prosecutions. In South Sudan, impunity for human rights violations reflects a long-standing pattern of government neglect, which has played out against the backdrop of unrelenting war, ethnic violence, and strategic international intervention. As we saw earlier in Chapter 2, there was never a moral reckoning in South Sudan, since past international leaders and policymakers failed to prioritize or take seriously the issue of moral accountability. The Comprehensive Peace Agreement (CPA) championed conflict resolution, constitutionalism, and democracy, but essentially ignored the causes of human rights abuses and their part in transitioning the country from war to long-term peace. Their part of course

was to get the warring parties to internalize human rights norms by tackling the abuses and by learning to uphold the rights of victims.

But this never occurred in South Sudan. In fact, the opposite has come true. South Sudan's political leaders have learned to externalize human rights protection by assigning their causes to outside factors and enemy actors, that is, the Sudanese state and other factions. Denial in this sense enables them to rationalize human rights abuses and to blame their people, the media, and civil society groups for the country's problems and their own misdeeds. This is how they have learned to weaponize fear and project their own power at the expense of human rights protections. What ultimately drives this denial is a sense of impunity—a false assurance that they will never be held morally responsible for their abuses. The leaders' political strategy is to either limit or efface any liability for their misdeeds.

The principal foil to this strategy is civil society activism. Civil society leaders in South Sudan are trained to raise public awareness of not only the leaders' misdeeds but also the people's awareness of their rights. But their capacity is ultimately determined by the resources to fight the government's repression of the people's rights. This is why in a resource-deprived country such as South Sudan, so many civil society and media leaders have become the target of government repression, including Peter Biar Ajak, a Cambridge University–trained economist. As one of the most vocal critics of the government, Ajak has published numerous articles and has held interviews criticizing the government's lack of transparency. Ajak's credentials are impressive. He is the founding Director of Strategic Analyses and Research and leader of the South Sudan Young Leaders Forum (SSYLF) formed in early 2018.[4] He had learned to overcome extreme adversity as a refugee by fleeing war and starvation in the Sudan. In 2001, he arrived in the United States and graduated from the University of Pennsylvania and Harvard University, before moving on to Cambridge University's PhD program in economics and becoming a World Bank consultant and economic analyst of Sudan and other African countries.

By the late 2000s, Ajak had become a vocal member of the South Sudanese diaspora.[5] After South Sudan gained its independence in 2011, he and other members of South Sudan's diaspora were eager to help build the country's institutions.[6] But the ruling national elite never warmed to the diaspora's overtures. In fact, the state still distrusted them after a near majority of diaspora members voted in favor of unity.[7] Nonetheless, Ajak (a member of the Nuer tribe) elected to stay in South Sudan to raise awareness of the government's lack of transparency. It was a decision that would prove fateful.

On July 28, 2016, Ajak was detained at the Juba International Airport by the NSS while en route to Aweil, a city in Northern Bahr al Ghazal, to commemorate the release of former child soldiers conscripted by the SPLA during Sudan's

118 SOUTH SUDAN'S FATEFUL STRUGGLE

second civil war. The NSS took Ajak to their headquarters for interrogation, then placed him at the "Blue House"—a prison in the Jebel sector of Juba—where he was denied access to legal counsel during the first six weeks of imprisonment. On September 7, 2018, nearly two years later, the government finally charged him with treason and later sabotage, insurgency, and weapons possession stemming from an alleged attempt to stage an uprising in October 2018 at the "Blue House." But the trial never took place, and Ajak was finally released in late 2019 due to mounting international pressure on the government to release him.[8]

A month after his release, I ran into Ajak on my way to interview NGO officials. Looking gaunt, he mentioned that he was glad to be free and had no definite plans to leave South Sudan. But with NSS guards monitoring his every movement, he eventually returned to the United States where he wrote about his ordeal and urged foreign leaders to take action against the government.[9] In a *Washington Post* op-ed, for example, he condemned the corruption of the government and criticized the lack of political will to further pressure the national government. Ajak of course knew that that national government could be successfully pressured. As a high-profile prisoner, he had become a political liability for the national government, which still needed to maintain good relations with its international donors.

The NSS would release more high-profile political prisoners in 2019, including Colonel Joseph Bakosoro, former state governor of Western Equatoria and leader of the National Movement for Change, whom I met on the outskirts of Juba in January 2020. Bakosoro exuded an air of confidence and eventually opened up about his experience in the "Blue House" where he had been detained on trumped-up charges. He made it clear from the outset that he was a political prisoner, but that his status as a former state government official had earned him privileges that kept him from being severely tortured. Over time he had learned to use his privilege to shield others from torture. He told me how he claimed responsibility for a cell phone that had been smuggled into the prison and belonged to his cell mate. "That probably saved his life," he said with a grin.[10] I then asked about his and the country's trauma caused by the war. "Trauma," he said in a staid voice, "had entered the blood and veins of every person because of the SPLM's inability to govern." And no amount of Christian faith, he suggested, could heal the wounds of war, let alone bring about meaningful redemption. "The Bible," as he put it, "would never be enough to govern." What he meant by this was that the government had come to expect immunity from all sources of higher authority, and that invoking God's name to promote peace and hope was simply another way of diverting attention from its corruption. But this ruse also, he suggested, had to be turned into an instrument to pressure the leaders to reconcile or settle their ethnic differences and to promote inclusivity. Inclusive governance was what Bakosoro had longed for—as far back as 2012, when he dissolved the NMC

IMPUNITY, HUMAN RIGHTS, AND THE STRUGGLE FOR JUSTICE 119

and rejoined the SPLM, hoping that the national government would speed up its efforts to implement the Revitalized Agreement on the Resolution of Conflict in South Sudan (as we shall see in Chapter 7).

Still. the war, as Bakosoro put it, had created a "tsunami of uncertainty" about SPLM leadership. For him, the SPLM had misled the people because they themselves lacked the civic training to protect human rights and to encourage open dialogue. The question, then, was whether there was a role for justice when the leaders could use their power of office to thwart legal accountability, and when so many state leaders could threaten others with impunity. How does one dissolve a culture impunity whose dynamic of denial and victimization extrudes guilt and moral responsibility to embrace self-entitlement and self-enrichment? For Bakosoro, the issue was how to get rid of the leaders' recklessness and their ability to politicize ethnic hostilities, but in truth, it pointed to the far more difficult task of isolating the guilt of the leaders from the tribal and national community. In short, to criminalize state leaders—which is still a relatively new and challenged international norm—is also to remove the obstacles blocking the unification of the state and nation. In the view of many civil society leaders in South Sudan, the nation was never allowed to shape the state. Rather, the state was used by the leaders to shape and oppress the nation. The state's culture of impunity, in other words, had eclipsed the national culture based on equality, freedom, and human dignity.

The challenge therefore was to erect a state that could embody this national culture. This meant creating national unity and eliminating exclusion and underrepresentation. But South Sudan's colonial past and its history of violence offered a difficult lesson. Its nation-state was an illusionary and harmful idea, a situation "in which," as Mamdani writes, "the nationalist dream was imposed on the reality of colonially imposed fragmentation leading to new rounds of national building and ethnic cleansing."[11] The idea of course is that the nation has to be liberated from colonial violence in order to achieve unity and to restore the dignity of the colonized. For Frantz Fanon, this meant putting violence into motion, that is, using it against the enemy (colonizers) to achieve national liberation.

The enemy who analyzes the forces of the insurrection, who delves deeper and deeper into the study of that global adversary, the colonized subject, identifies the ideological weakness and spiritual inability of certain segments of the population. The enemy discovers alongside a well- organized and disciplined insurrectionary front line, a human mass whose commitment is constantly threatened by the addictive cycle of physiological poverty, humiliation, and irresponsibility. The enemy will use the mass even if it costs a fortune. He will create spontaneity by force of the bayonet and exemplary punishment. . . . The

120 SOUTH SUDAN'S FATEFUL STRUGGLE

leader of the insurrection watches as the nation literally keels over. Whole tribes are transformed into Harkis and armed with the latest weapons, set off on the warpath to invade the rival tribe, labeled as nationalist for the occasion. Unanimity in combat so rich in combat and so grandiose during the initial hours of the insurrection is at a crucial turning point. The proletariat education of the masses is now recognized as an historical necessity.[12]

Educating the masses, in other words, was a national necessity for carrying out an armed insurrection. For Fanon, the colonial leaders and their national subordinates (i.e., the national bourgeoisie) remained unwilling to engage the natives, who they considered as savages lacking any capacity for ethics. The colonizers only knew how to divide and to dehumanize the natives. For the revolutionary leaders to overcome the petrified system of colonialism, they had to mobilize the entire oppressed population. In South Sudan, as we saw in Chapter 1, the years of willful neglect by the British ended up dehumanizing the southern Sudanese, leaving deep-seated remnants of division and distrust. The SPLM/A, to its credit, saw Sudanese rule as a remnant of British colonial rule, but in the end, introjected this and other remnants of colonial violence by politicizing tribal identity and disengaging from the people.

Which returns us to Garang's vision of unifying southern masses through a democratic and multiethnic ethnic Sudanese state. Did Garang recognize the absolute necessity of educating the masses of their rights through democratic participation? And was such education the key to reshaping these political realities of South Sudan's colonial past? As I argued in Chapter 2, Garang's New Sudan seemed to overestimate the good will and faith of Sudanese leaders and the bad faith of South Sudan's national elite—namely their denial of the possibility of the people's emancipation as well as their moral accountability to the people. What was missing in South Sudan's struggle for national liberation was the moral necessity of confronting such bad faith. South Sudan's corrupt elite had learned to monopolize the use of fear to defuse the need for criminal accountability and to brutalize the population. Fear, in effect, had become a tool rather than a moral end in the struggle for self-determination.

The end in this case was moral accountability. And like the moral deterrent effect, it assumes that leaders can be morally persuaded against resorting to brute violence by internalizing the fear of punishment. But in a culture of impunity, the rational calculations of power are hardly, if ever, based on moral considerations. There is no way, in short, for ethics, morality, and the rule of law to reliably constrain the use of violence; the culture of impunity simply feeds off uncertainty and the irrationality to create cyclical violence and grave injustices.

In his nonfictional novel *What Is the What*, Dave Eggers captures this irrational cycle of violence during the 1990s. Speaking through the first voice

IMPUNITY, HUMAN RIGHTS, AND THE STRUGGLE FOR JUSTICE 121

account of Ajak, a young, lost boy caught up in the second Sudanese civil war, and trapped by a sense of persecution, he writes:

> The UN workers had begun to assemble barriers, six feet tall and arranged like hallways. The fences would ensure that we would walk single file on our way to be counted only once. Even those among us, the younger Sudanese primarily, who were not so worried until then, became gravely concerned when the fences went up. It was a malevolent-looking thing, that maze of fencing orange and opaque. Soon even the best educated among us brought into the suspicion that this was a plan to eliminate the Dinka. Most of the Sudanese my age had learned of the Holocaust, and were convinced that this was a plan much like that used to eliminate the Jews in Germany and Poland. I was dubious of the growing paranoia, but Gop was a believer. As rational a man he was, he had a long memory for injustices visited upon the people of Sudan.[13]

All the long-term suffering experienced during war accumulates over time. And very slowly, it erodes the rational capacity to make sense of this suffering. Paranoia seeps through the cracks of rationality and into the minds of people, blurring in this case the distinction between the UN's humanitarian mission and Khartoum's ruthless strategies. The outside world becomes increasingly uncertain and triggers in the person the tendency to retreat to or affirm one's tribal identity. At the same time, the retreat does not cause the violence but symptomizes the politicization of tribal identity. Violence, in other words, becomes a matter of the political survival of the tribal community. The moral purpose of deterrence is not a solution for ending violence but a rational effort to make the violence go away. The objective can't simply be to replace the culture of impunity with one of punishment that downplays the value of healing and restoration, but a holistic, national plan for reconciliation in which all political leaders learn to finally face the truth. Yet, the long history of paying lip service to human rights norms, as we shall see, shows just how the ruling elite have made this idea hopelessly elusive.

The Human Rights Gap

South Sudan's Transitional Constitution revised the structure of government and reestablished the progressive list of human rights of the 2005 Interim Constitution. It held that "every person has the inherent right to life, dignity and the integrity of his or her person which shall be protected by law; no one shall be arbitrarily deprived of his or her lie."[14] Still, the outbreak of war in 2013 was followed by mass scale violence and gross human rights abuses. Within a couple

122 SOUTH SUDAN'S FATEFUL STRUGGLE

of years, the United Nations, African Union, and international human rights NGOs had issued reports on the scale of human rights atrocities in the country. The United Nations Human Rights Council, for example, found that the national government and rebel forces maintained indirect ties with rogue militias that carried out gang rape, torture, child conscription, and mass killings.[15] And in their 2020 report, the UN Human Rights Commission reached the conclusion that "the norm has become increased securitization of state institutions that sow fear and terror in an environment in which citizens are deprived of their fundamental human rights, and where torture, intimidation, and enforced disappearance have become the norm."

Given the scale of violations, it was easy to forget that South Sudan had created its own human rights commission, the South Sudan Human Rights Commission (SSHCR). Kiir established it in 2011 to uphold the human rights listed in the Transitional Constitution and to bring transparency to the investigation of these violations. Articles 145 through 157 of the Transitional Constitution, for instance, required officials to monitor compliance with the Constitution's Bill of Rights and to "investigate, on its own initiative, or on a complaint made by any person or group of persons, against any violation of human rights and fundamental freedoms." The SSHRC was also set up to be neutral, or to operate independently of the government, while serving as a voice of human rights activists and the people. In fact, it's mission was to "defend the people's human rights and fundamental freedoms against all forms of abuse and violation. . . . while monitoring compliance of all levels of government with international and regional human rights treaties and conventions ratified by the Republic of South Sudan."[16] Machar, who as Vice President and the former director of the SPLM/A, initiated discussion and dialogue on the principles that would guide the SSHCR and announced that the SSHCR would help "to incorporate human rights into the SPLM/A."[17] But in doing so, he expressed caution about its prospects, admitting that "reaching common understanding on human rights would be a challenge."[18]

As late as 2014, the SSHRC continued to issue reports critical of the government's activities, including a March 2014 report condemning the government's suppression of the media and the hundreds of people killed in the streets by government forces and the White Army.[19] Machar responded to the report by insisting the SPLM-IO—and its ties to the White Army that carried out the attacks on Dinka civilians in Bor and other towns north of Juba—was justified in carrying out the attacks against an oppressive and authoritarian government. As he saw it, because the government had aggressively attacked the Nuer people, the SPLM-IO's violent resistance amounted to self-defense. Of course, he was right to blame the government's brutal suppression of the White Army officials, which had led to nearly 600 reported deaths from December 2013 to

January 2014. However, the White Army was also responsible for the slaughter of thousands of innocent Dinka civilians. Had it not been for Yoweri Museveni, who sent in reinforcements to stop the White Army, the White Army would have likely defeated the government's forces.

The March 2014 SSHRC report also concluded that both sides were at fault for the conflict and that, in politicizing tribal identity, they threatened to escalate the conflict into ethnic cleansing. "It is this ethnic dimension of the conflict," the report stated, "which is most worrying and if not resolved could lead to a national calamity with genocide—a possibility given the fact that both the Nuer and Dinka are large groups with heavy armed militias."[20] It was a remarkable conclusion to reach given that the commission was just two years old. Yet the violence struck at the very core mission of the SSHRC. The problem was getting the national government to cooperate with the SSHRC and to stop suppressing the media's role in exposing the government's abuses. But by mid-2014, the government had already taken steps to curtail the SSHRC's mission by preventing it from "visiting police jails, prisons and related facilities with a view to assessing and inspecting conditions of the inmates and making recommendations to the relevant authority" and expressing an "opinion or present advice to government organs on any issue related to human rights and fundamental freedoms."[21]

Despite its many promises to abide by the SSHRC's rulings, the government essentially ignored the 2014 report. The SSHRC had in fact become a growing political liability. And in further limiting the SSHRC's operations, it imposed drastic budget cuts on the commission, which reduced its resources to fulfill its caseload and to carry out credible, impartial investigations of human rights abuses, particularly those committed by the government and military officials. In a matter of weeks, Kiir had managed to delegitimize its authority and cast aside any negative reports of its human rights violations. He had stopped short of dissolving it, since doing so would have brought unwanted international attention. Instead, he weaponized the SSHRC by forcing it to investigate its political enemies or the SPLM-IO's human rights violations. The SSHRC, in effect, was doing the government's political bidding.

SSHRC officials—all of whom had been appointed by Kiir—found themselves in an increasingly delicate situation. They knew the consequences of investigating government officials, but they also realized their limits in targeting the principal violators. The only way of easing the predicament was to open up more investigations of the rebels. Anything less would lead to further budget cuts. Given the deteriorating state of human rights in South Sudan, it fell increasingly to international organizations, regional bodies, and NGOs to monitor the government's human rights abuses. What they soon uncovered were the many root causes of human rights violations, including the serious harm caused by tribal customs and norms.

124 SOUTH SUDAN'S FATEFUL STRUGGLE

Conscripting Children

Perhaps the most controversial issue was the violation of a child's rights, in particular child conscription. Over the years, the abuse had attracted increasing international attention; however, in South Sudan, it seemed to underscore an unnerving ambivalence about the rights of children during war. In December 2015, I asked several students at Juba University if they supported child conscription during and after war. Most expressed their concern that banning it would do little to stop commanders from employing it to accrue unfair political advantages. The reality was that child conscription remained entwined with the predatory nature of war in South Sudan. Like other African countries, including Somalia, Sudan, the Central African Republic, and the Democratic Republic of Congo, South Sudan had seen spikes in child conscription during war, despite pledges to recognize the basic rights of children. War seemed to trigger a brutal impulse in which children lost any rights and became tradeable and, in some cases, expendable commodities.

In Yambio and Bentiu, the abuse of children was especially severe. An estimated 15,000 children, mostly between the ages of 14 to 16, were forcibly recruited to fight on behalf of the forces operating in these and other areas—from 2013 to 2016.[22] Many were forced out of school, then taken to camps; others were abducted at gun point. For those fortunate enough to escape conscription, there were few opportunities to play an active role in society. War had clearly worsened the abuse of children and called into question the government's obligations of upholding the rights of the child. South Sudan joined the Convention on the Rights of the Child in 2012, and its Transitional Constitution contained conditions that brought it into conformity with the convention's principles. These included the child's right "(a) to life, survival and development . . . (c) to know and be cared for by his or her parents or legal guardian; (d) not to be subjected to exploitative practices or be abused."[23] But the dire conditions in 2012 had reduced the government's compliance with the convention. Severe malnourishment and starvation, for instance, left many children exceedingly vulnerable, which in turn helped overshadow the progress made during the interwar period when the GRSS and the United Nations undertook a joint initiative to improve the conditions for children. The Child Protection Unit, for example, worked feverishly to provide food assistance to children to address malnourishment, while the UN-based DDR program drew on its resources to reintegrate formerly conscripted children into society.

Still, the progress proved short-lived. The outbreak of war in late 2013 forced the SPLA-IO rebels to search aggressively for new child recruits, particularly in the towns of Malakal and Bentiu. The children who resisted or were not conscripted, were either killed or tortured. Others were maimed by gunfire

in areas such as Western Bahr al Ghazal and Central Equatoria.[24] Some were even reported to be deliberately fired upon at close range while fleeing SPLA-government forces. In one incident children were abducted at gun point and, as Human Rights Watch found, were "sometimes thrown into battle just a day or two later."[25] Incidences like these became increasingly common as the newly conscripted children were forced to don uniforms and receive training; some were even paid salaries on an irregular basis. The commanders' primary motivation of course was to beef up the military capacity of their tribal communities that found themselves under siege. Child conscription in their view was about protecting their tribal community. Whatever abuse it represented—whether this was to the individual child or in a larger sense, mortgaging away the country's future by undermining production of skilled workers in the future—it was seen as necessary for preserving the community and for boosting the number of troops in their militias. Child conscription, in short, stemmed from a series of combustible factors, including predatory war and patronage.

Yet it was also the abusive nature of some tribal customs, such as child marriage, that enabled the abuse and attracted the attention of international donors. Child marriage has meant that girls as young as 12 years old can be forced into marriage. The father and mother of the girls forced into marriage are often compelled to give them up to the highest bidder (i.e., with the largest dowry).[26] Severe poverty and familial honor make it almost impossible for the girl to say no or escape. In some cases, the dowry represents the line between survival and death, but in most cases, it is ultimately about preserving the family's honor. The girl's resistance invariably risks harming or dishonoring the family, particularly the family elders. A 2013 Human Rights Watch Report found that "girls who try to resist early and forced marriages may suffer brutal consequences at the hands of their families. . . . In other cases, they were held captive and even murdered by their families."[27] In South Sudan, then, the groom, not the bride, pays the dowry. This means that girls are essentially auctioned off to the highest bidder who works with the consenting family members to arrange the marriage. If there is more than one bidder, the family selects the highest dowry, which can fetch up to $20,000 in cattle and cash or both. In such an arrangement, the girl not only has little choice in who she marries but is expected to exercise little. if any, power in the household. This is to ensure that the husband remains the primary breadwinner or so-called "true protector" of the woman in the house. And yet it is precisely this protector status that entitles him to treat his wife as he sees fit, or to abuse her mentally by denying her access to an education. To make matters worse, divorce is often strictly forbidden, especially in the villages where the family risks losing money and honor—even if the husband is accused of raping the wife whose parents are typically reluctant to challenge for fear of losing the dowry money. Child marriage, then, reflects a vicious cycle of violence, which

NGOs, donor agencies, civil society groups have sought to break by raising awareness of gender-based violence.

The violence against children testifies to a troubling gap in the law. Neither the Transitional Constitution nor the penal code recognizes marital rape, as customary law remains one of the sources of law recognized in the Transitional Constitution. One strategy of ending the harm is to reconcile customary law with statute law in order to allow the chiefs more discretionary power to protect the girl from abuse, or in this case, from being forcibly removed from school due to pregnancy. Another is to continue expanding the legal basis of women's rights in South Sudan. The GoSS's 2008 Child Act, for example, was one of the first attempts to recognize the right of the child to a primary education.[28] It came at a time when women were beginning to find a voice in government, that is, organized protests against gender inequality, by assuming a visible and public role in the discussions and meetings concerning the drafting of and amendments to a new permanent constitution. To his credit, Kiir appointed several women to ministerial government posts in the summer of 2013 to replace the ministers sacked by him in the summer of 2013.

The idea of course was to further delegitimize all harmful customs. Not long after independence, many women's groups began to pressure the government to reform marriage laws by first regulating the price of dowries and then ending the bidding process that drove up the price. In addition, they demanded that the government incorporate a provision in the draft of the permanent constitution, requiring that a man and women be at least 18 to qualify for marriage.[29] Neither the Transitional Constitution nor 2009 Penal Statute on Local Government stipulate any specific marriage age. Yet, as of the writing of this book, no agreement had been reached on a proper threshold age for marriage in the draft of the permanent constitution, even though approximately 52 percent of married women in South Sudan remain under the age of 18. The lack of progress eventually led the United Nations Children's Fund (UNICEF), in 2017, to work with the national government on the National Strategic Action Ban to ban child marriage by 2030.[30] The plan sought to promote positive social norms through dialogue and surveys. But the war's devasting effects on villages and towns worked against these aims.

In the city of Malakal, for example, the war left many severely traumatized. In one case, the fighting directly targeted women at the Malakal hospital where in February 2014, rebel forces kidnapped eight women--who would never be seen again.[31] The attack was one of a series of assaults carried out by the warring sides against the civilian population. When I visited Malakal in January 2020, I spoke with Joseph Mijack, the Minister of Gender and Social Welfare. The Ministry of Gender and Social Welfare was housed in one of many government buildings riddled with bullet holes on its exterior walls. Inside, the hallways were empty,

the floors coated with a thick film of dirt. Mijack told me that that the challenge of redressing gender violence was "getting all the women to voluntarily come to the center of town to speak about their grievances."[32] The problem, he explained, was that the town still lacked an adequate police force to ensure their protection.

In driving through the middle of Malakal, it was hard to believe that it was once a bustling city. The town had seen some of the most intense fighting and brutal treatment of civilians of the civil war, which forced almost all the inhabitants to flee to the neighboring UN compound. Government forces had also driven the Shilluk—a proud ethnic group that had occupied the area for thousands of years and even established a kingdom—out of the city and to the other side (the western bank) of the White Nile. This was after a Shilluk-based opposition group, the Shilluk Agwelek, attacked Dinka militias as well as Shilluk civilians for supporting opposition forces. All the fighting had decimated many parts of the town and left the airport terminal building pockmarked with bullet holes. When I arrived at the airport, there were still no security officials to check my papers. The dirt road connecting the airport to the town center (and the UN compound in the opposite direction) ran through an area where rows of thatched roof, wood frame houses had been razed (Photo 5.1). The only traces of them were the scorched metal chairs that still stood and the metal poles that had once supported the houses. I was told that thousands of innocent civilians lost their lives here, killed by government and rebel forces. A once densely populated area was now a ghostly crime scene.

In the town's center, I spoke with James Aguer, Secretary General of the Upper Nile State, who tried to assure me that Malakal was on the mend, despite the challenges of rebuilding the city. "Only UNICEF and a few nongovernmental organizations," he said, "were helping to rebuild the houses and officials have estimated nearly 50,000 homes had been destroyed."[33] That seemed a very conservative estimate after observing the countless number of razed houses (100,000 homes was more reasonable). Whatever the number, a vast majority of the inhabitants who had fled the violence had found refuge at the Protection of Civilians (PoC) camp inside the UN compound (Photo 5.2), which sat 10 miles outside of the city. Aguer's task was to encourage the IDPs living inside the camp to come back and visit the town, hoping that they might begin to feel safer there.

The task was complicated by a number of factors, however. First, the internally displaced people were still too traumatized by the war to willingly seek help, and because of the shortage of counseling services, many could not be treated. Second, the government still needed to find a way to get the SSPDF officers, who now occupied the standing houses that were once occupied by some of the refugees, to leave these homes to encourage their rightful inhabitants to return from the PoC camp (Photo 5.3). The problem was that the SSPDF still provided most of the security to the town. Moreover, there was no local law or rules to

Photo 5.1 Remnants of a razed village just outside of the center of Malakal.

Photo 5.2 The Protection of Civilians Camp in the UN Compound in Malakal.

force them to leave. Many officers therefore seemed content to stay, as if they were entitled to live there.

Finally, there was the disparity in service between the UN PoC camp and the city. The PoC camp was outfitted with roads, shops, informal restaurants (or eating places), educational facilities, and a beefed-up UN Security force for protecting the IDPs from any future attack (Photo 5.4). The camp was literally a small city. In fact, it was almost as large as the core district of Malakal and

Photo 5.3 The center of the UN PoC camp in Malakal.

Photo 5.4 Shopkeeper at the UN PoC camp in Malakal.

comprised nearly a third of the compound. As one might expect, the disparity between the PoC camp and town did little to encourage the PoC IDPs to return to the city. The decent conditions of the PoC camp had essentially created an economic and psychological incentive to stay. For the IDPs to leave, they needed to be further assured that the fighting had ended, and that there was an effective, reliable force to police the city.

Another reason for staying at the PoC camp was that the IDPs enjoyed quick and relatively easy access to the many NGOs and international agencies located

130 SOUTH SUDAN'S FATEFUL STRUGGLE

in the compound's eastern end. This was important since the UNDEP and various NGOs offered what local government agencies lacked, namely, funds to provide proper training of caseworkers to counsel woman and to treat the symptoms of gender-based violence. The International Medical Corporation (IMC) is one of the NGOs that was performing some of the most interesting work to meet the basic needs of the displaced people. The IMC had developed a program in which company officers subsidized $120 to the women victimized by violence. The money could be used by the woman to conduct household planning including the purchase of goods and the means to file a report if the husband misused the money. Gertrude Callaway, the Director of the IMC at the Malakal Compound, said that "the results of the program were largely positive and had enhanced communication and dialogue between the husband and wife."[34] She also pointed out that "to get rid of gender-based violence, you need to show that women are worthy of making important choices about money spent, but that there are no guarantees." Like so many NGO officials I spoke to at the compound, the shared feeling was that the NGOs had become the only reliable source of assistance. With local governments cash strapped, it was largely up to the NGOs and civil society actors to bridge the financial gap between local and national government. Still, there was a problem with taking on such a responsibility. As Kari Oyen, a Director at Norwegian Church Aid, pointed out, "too much money is thrown at local CSOs without fully evaluating them." The NCA was working with South Sudan Churches Council (SSCC) to improve sanitation in villages and to curb gender-based violence.[35] The NCA's relationship with the SSCC was complicated since its organization's goals did not always support the Church's mission, that is, with regards to abortion. Yet it was a common problem for most CSOs which found it difficult to coordinate their activities with the SSCC to redress the people's suffering.

Despite the high rates of gender-based violence (especially in the countryside), women's advocacy groups in South Sudan pressured legislators to address a key source of the abuse: underrepresentation. In 2013, the women's caucus in the National Assembly drafted and passed a national bill calling for women to make up at least 35 percent of government workers and officials. Although the provision was not binding, it did call attention to the need for improved access to education for girls and more female lawyers, judges, chiefs, and mayors. It had also helped create more opportunities for women to serve in higher office, Judith Ruben, for example, was the first female mayor of Yambio, whose main concern was the paucity of female judges and resources to reduce gender-based violence. "There is simply no way to eradicate GBV with one functioning county court," she insisted.[36] The civil war has devastated much of Yambio's infrastructure and institutions, and forced it to rely on a UN Mobile High Court (a provisional court) and customary law judges to investigate and prosecute

most cases involving gender-based violence. An even more telling fact was that a vast majority of incidents of gender-based violence never get investigated or prosecuted at the county level. Most remain at the customary court level, where the paramount and sub-chiefs oversee a crumbling system of justice wrought by the civil war. Edward Yaki, a subchief at Yambio, said that the civil war left many in despair and much more inclined toward violence: "It made it difficult to preside over cases since many had become more disrespectful of us," he told me.[37] Yaki was expressing a shared concern held by many sub- and paramount chiefs: that psychological trauma led more youth to carry guns and to wantonly ignore the chiefs' judgments. Yaki also wanted me to know that he had experienced the violence first-hand, having witnessed the Lord's Resistance Army, which had crossed into the DRC border, butcher his cousin and uncle. Then he told me that the problem was that "we really need written statutes" to administer justice. It was a striking thing to hear from a chief, since customary law was based an oral tradition that had long upheld the authority of the chiefs. But now that law was being fundamentally challenged by the effects of the civil war, that is, high rates of unemployment, alcoholism, and trauma. In short, the war had created a gap between customary and statutory law, which the chiefs wanted to fill by learning how to apply written law. The problem though was that many were simply ill-equipped to do this, much less able to address the underlying causes of crime rates (e.g., domestic violence). These were problems best handled by psychologists, not chiefs.

The judges had also seen their people leave the villages to flee the violence. Many of the IDPs included women between the ages of 18 and 59 and children from 5 to 11 years old, who had found refuge in the PoC camps where UN workers (Photo 5.5), not the chiefs, addressed their trauma.[38] While the PoC camps helped restore some of the normalcy of their lives, the war caused them to distrust authority, including that of the chiefs—some of whom maintained relations with the leaders of militia groups- and officials from the United Nations, which in some cases failed to prevent warring parties from entering the compound. In 2016, for instance, government forces attacked the UN compound in Malakal, killing 26 refugees and leaving many IDPs severely traumatized. Unable to fully trust the United Nations, local government officials, and the chiefs, many turned to the Churches (and NGOs) for counseling and healing. In order to meet the demand, the Episcopal Church of Malakal—which stands on the outskirts of Malakal—created several open-air bible teachings. As I sat in one of those chairs, Daniel Makier, the Church's pastor, told me in a soft, upbeat tone of voice, that "many people in town and the camps have lost all faith; our duty is to restore their faith in God and help them with their lives."[39] In doing so, the Church has offered spiritual healing and raised their hopes for lasting peace. Yet it is a hope that remains fragile. "There are just too many layers of distrust," said Makier, "that we

Photo 5.5 A young IDP boy at the UN PoC camp in Malakal

have to work with here in Malakal," He also pointed out that the church simply lacked the resources to provide retraining and professional counseling, and that if the local and national leaders were really serious about rebuilding the lives of the staggering number of IDPs, they would adopt an integrated healing process.

In 2019 alone, an estimated 1.67 million people had been internally displaced and 189,000 remained under protection at PoC sites.[40] Add to this the nearly 2.23 million South Sudanese people who have fled the country seeking refuge into the neighboring countries of the Democratic Republic of Congo, Ethiopia, Kenya, Sudan, and Uganda, and one gets a sense of the scale of the problem and how it has created regional instability.[41] Approximately 300,000 of

IMPUNITY, HUMAN RIGHTS, AND THE STRUGGLE FOR JUSTICE   133

the refugees ended up at the Kukuma refugee camp in Kenya—another 700,000 fled to northern Uganda. Despite the favorable conditions, security in these camps remained lax.[42] With tensions remaining high among the different ethnic groups, officials also had to deal with the specter of ethnic violence in the camps. For example, the Bidi Bid camp in Uganda, which was set up in August 2016, took in nearly 200,000 refugees, most of whom came from smaller ethnic groups from the Yei region in South Sudan. Many of these refugees faced retribution by Dinka militias that had penetrated the camps' borders and accused them of collaborating with Machar's forces. In one case, a father was macheted to death in front of his family members.[43]

These brazen attacks became a regular occurrence, and many suspected that Kiir's government was somehow involved. Whether or not this was true, the perception of his involvement had dampened the refugees' desire to repatriate to South Sudan, or leave their camp in Uganda, where they enjoyed adequate food and water. Additionally, the GRSS had not started rebuilding houses destroyed during the war, or even offer sanitary living conditions. Of the nearly 200,000 who did return to Juba, many found themselves homeless or without shelter.[44] There were also few opportunities to work in Juba. Unemployment of the youth (15–25) stood at 20 percent in 2020, and there was little money to finance local state/government initiatives, such as youth sporting camps. The feeling in and around Juba was that the national government simply did not care about its people, and that it was content to lean on NGOs and UN assistance as well as donations from powerful countries and private organizations to meet the basic needs of its people. Although the civil war had traumatized the people (and even its leaders), it had also made the people grow increasingly tired of the status quo. By 2016, civil society actors had begun to convert this fatigue into positive energy through critical engagement with the cultural arts and media, that is, graffiti and radio shows addressing themes of trauma and courage, while also working to promote support of the HCSS and truth commission. The political leaders, in short, were facing an increasingly vocal civil society. It seemed only a matter of time before their brutal roles were further scrutinized and investigated.

Truth and Consequences

The strategy, then, was to divert attention away from their roles by impugning criminal justice and repressing their people. They had by now learned to abide by a "rule by law," not the rule of law.[45] The "rule by law" describes a condition in which the law serves the interests of the political elites and their capacity to legitimize their authority through fear and threats. By stripping the law of its autonomy and impartiality, government leaders had become the patrons of a

system designed to obviate the rule of law. The rule by law thus reflects the many debilitating effects of the civil war on the justice system. Judges, for instance, had become overwhelmed with cases; there simply were not enough to handle even the worst cases.[46] In fact, an estimated 120 judges presided over all the cases in court.[47] There were also troubling variations in legal training of South Sudanese judges, which led judges to possess divergent views of the relationship of statutory law to customary law. Raimondo Geri Legge, a former high court judge, pointed out that despite adopting a progressive constitution, South Sudan's justice system has remained unstable and incoherent because of the inconsistencies in maintaining precedent and the existence of what he called the "repugnant norms of child marriage and conscription."[48] The civil war, he argued, had produced the fear and violent behavior that engendered a "space for these repugnant norms and further inconsistency in the law where it should not exist."[49]

Legge, it turned out, was forced out of the judiciary. He had returned to the University of Juba's law school—which sits just outside the main campus of Juba—to teach (as associate professor). It offered some escape from the governmental pressures. But after the passage of the NSS Act in 2014, NSS officials began to actively monitor the university, in some cases, dressing up as students to keep track of any critical voices of the national government. On the main campus, the NSS stepped up its efforts to suppress free speech on campus by arresting Dr. Leonzio Angole Onek, the former Dean of the College of Applied and Industrial Sciences at the University of Juba. He was detained and accused of supporting the rebels in October 2015, even though no formal charges were filed.[50] After spending nearly five months in solitary confinement, he was finally released. Five years later, on February 11, 2020, government soldiers placed Taban Lo Liyong, a Juba University professor, in the back of a truck and detained him for several weeks. According to government officials, his essay on the war had threatened to incite an "ethnic war" and rebellion against the state. Yet the government was never able to provide any evidence that his essay had incited an ethnic rebellion. Liyong, in fact, was never charged with an actual crime and was eventually released.[51] The national government offered no reason, and in the end, it became clear that they were merely trying to silence their critics.

The trouble, though, was that Kiir was also de facto chancellor of Juba University. While the role was largely symbolic, it meant that there was no clear line between the university's autonomy and government power. Kiir, in effect, could restrict free and academic speech in order to try to bring academics in line with the government position on the war. What is more, under the NSS Act, the NSS could arbitrarily detain any judge, lawyer, Bar Association member, civil society worker, reporter or academic. The powers of the NSS clearly posed a serious threat to the peace process. "Such powers," as the UN Panel of Experts would later conclude, "are the desire of the National Security Service to retain them

beyond the peace agreement, pose a significant threat to the implementation of the agreement and, by extension, to the peace, security and stability of South Sudan."[52]

Kiir's disingenuous justice strategy, in short, was to promise a lot and deliver little. When he did deliver, there were often further exceptions made. In many cases, files went missing, which prevented any appeal by the victims.[53] The prevention of such appeals was apparently one way of imposing the law to uphold his rule.

Subverting the Rule of Law

The rule by law describes how leaders use the law to advance their political interests and to exploit their hold on power. But it is precisely this hold on power that becomes increasingly precarious as the ruling elite in South Sudan subvert the legal system, stripping it of its independence (or impartiality). By stripping, I mean divesting it of the resources needed to function properly and to train the legal professionals, including attorneys, paralegals, administrators, and former judges. With only 200 attorneys to represent the people on criminal and civil matters, many areas of the country have continued to operate with little or no legal counsel to service the needs of the people.[54] In Malakal, for instance, there were only two lawyers to file the mountains of complaints by the citizens. The fighting had destroyed much of the town's infrastructure. This included the heavily damaged building that once housed the High Court.[55] It stood directly across the street from the county courthouse, where Aviel Nyong, the only sitting county judge, hears several cases each day. As the only sitting county judge in Malakal, Judge Nyong presides over all the cases that make it to court. On the day I visited him several people stood outside the courthouse waiting to have their cases heard by him. Nyong had previously worked as a legal expert for a human rights NGO, before being appointed county judge in 2018. He was passionate and well-versed in the law, but the heavy workload had taken a toll on him. He mentioned that his biggest concern was "the vast disparity between statute and customary law," which had led to a flood of cases involving gender-based violence that the customary courts simply could not handle. "Women are acutely aware of their bodies and the body of human rights under the Transitional Constitution," he said. But, he added "there is nowhere for them to turn at the customary law level, which is where we come in."[56]

The same faint despair could be felt in Western Equatoria. In the city of Yambio, where eight of the county's 10 courts—as well as the High Court—had been destroyed during the civil war, the justice system was barley operable. The remaining two county courts were overloaded with cases, and the UN Mobile

136 SOUTH SUDAN'S FATEFUL STRUGGLE

High Court had only managed to handle a scant number of cases before it was disbanded in late 2019.[57] The war had exacerbated what was already a lack of national government funding for the court system, which left thousands deprived of their rights and needs. "The statutory court system in South Sudan," the Human Rights Council concluded, "continued to suffer from a trust deficit among citizens."[58] What the trust deficit meant was an erosion of faith in the rule of law at the statutory level. And it suggested that in over-relying on statute law to administer justice, officials had overlooked the role of customary law in restoring such trust.[59]

With statute law, it should be noted, the legislature enacts the written codes or rights and, in most cases, the executive must approve the codes. Statute law in this respect constitutes a uniform set of codes and rights for the county and national courts. During the interim period, the Government of Southern Sudan adopted a series of acts to structure the judiciary, including the Judiciary Act (2008), the Code of Civil Procedure Act (2007), the Code of Criminal Procedure Act of 2008, and eventually the Transitional Constitution (2011). At the top of the hierarchy of statutory courts is the national Supreme Court. Below this is the Court of Appeals and High Court at the regional level, followed by the High Court at the state level, and three classes of county courts, that is, first and second magistrate and Payam courts. Establishing the statutory court system in this way amounted to a systematic effort to modernize the legal justice system for the sake of transitioning to statehood and working beyond the limits of customary law (i.e., its unwritten system of rules and varied procedures).

Britain, as mentioned in Chapter 1, had established customary law in the early twentieth century in South Sudan to administer its policy of indirect rule. Now that very source of law needed to be reformed in relation to statutory courts. So the GoSS adopted The Local Government Act (LGA) of 2009, which recognized the codification of customary law (that would later be incorporated into the Transitional Constitution) and stripped it of many of its vital functions, including its original jurisdiction over criminal matters. The LGA also restructured customary law by establishing three local levels of the lower judiciary: the paramount chief (County), head chief (Payam), and executive chief (Boma). The paramount chief could only hear a criminal case administered by the statutory government courts if it was referred by these courts to the customary court and if it was supervised by the county commissioner. The essential idea of the new judiciary system, then, was to provide a uniform set of substantive procedures for administering law on the national, regional, state, and county levels. By subordinating customary law courts to the statutory courts, the LGA had sought to minimize the influence of customary law and to move more of the country's population to a formal, written set of codes. As a result, the chiefs saw much of their discretionary power and legitimacy diminished. Yet for the vast majority

IMPUNITY, HUMAN RIGHTS, AND THE STRUGGLE FOR JUSTICE   137

of South Sudanese living in the countryside—who still depended on and trusted customary courts to settle disputes over property, petty theft, and marriage—this only served to further marginalize them within the justice system. Not only were the county courts still too expensive for them, but the damage done to these courts had rendered many inoperable.

Government neglect of the judicial system was thus the norm. And it was fueled by two principal factors: (1) the failure to invest in the new county courts; and (2) the executive body's interference in the courts' affairs, which had eroded the autonomy and independent discretionary power of national and regional state level courts. Both had the effect of renewing interest in customary courts, however: not simply because the customary court sustained less damage than the county courts during South Sudan's civil war, but because the marginalization of customary law was tied to efforts to counter the effects of government neglect. Revitalization in this sense was a project based on a core idea: that reconciling the desirable local customs with human rights statutes was the most inclusive and legitimate way to restore the rule of law and to eliminate the "repugnant" norms and customs that violate human rights statutes.

The goal was therefore not to replace customary law with statutory law, but to make these two sources more interactive and mutually reinforcing. This meant educating the chiefs and sub-chiefs on statute law (and its human rights provisions) and equipping them with the skills needed to communicate with county judges. Farouk Ismail, the Program Director at the South Sudan Law Society—which has spear-headed much of the work on this project—indicated that the mission is twofold: to educate more women chiefs to help counter the gender-based violence and to engage the elders of the community about the serious harm of local customs. For him, the goal is to reform the LGA, which had barred chiefs from addressing criminal matters and overseeing many types of civil cases involving domestic abuse human rights violations. The LGA, he explained, created "a serious gap between customary and statutory law, the consequences of which South Sudan was still struggling to overcome."[60] As such, it symptomized the growing divisions within South Sudanese society. This of course raised the issue of whether customary law could finally join forces with statutory law to promote peace and justice in South Sudan. Could the two be synergized or hybridized to legitimize state-level institutions and ultimately promote national reconciliation? Hybrid justice had been tried and tested in various African countries, including Sierra Leonne, Rwanda, and South Africa. In South Sudan, there were already encouraging signs of hybridizing justice, including the legal activist network which consisted of former judges, lawyers, paralegal, and academics. The network had succeeded in holding a series of workshops and meetings on the topic of empowering the chiefs. Regarding this topic, the political scientist Rachel Ibreck writes that,

138 SOUTH SUDAN'S FATEFUL STRUGGLE

Unlike civil servants, chiefs live with their communities and had no option but to do so. They presided over customary courts and involved themselves in problems arising from the war and economic crisis, from the proliferation of arms and youth violence to food shortages. In this sense, their actions were guided by a logic of mutual complementary (or equally complementary roles) that was in stark contrast to the extractive politics of the kleptocracy.[61]

The chiefs were no longer regarded as outside servants of the legal system but as the central subjects of legal change. Legal activists thus hoped that in training them to apply statutory law, they could uniformly reduce gender violence and serious harm at the local and state levels.

The hope, in short, was to make the justice system more inclusive and fairer and in the process, pressure the government to take human rights abuses seriously. International pressure, after all, had compelled Kiir to authorize a commission to investigate the massacre that took place in Juba, from December 2013 to March 2014. However, the commission report, which was completed in December 2014, was never officially released to the public. Nor did any ranking official ever pressure Kiir to release it. It was not until 2018 that international pressure finally forced Kiir to hold a military trial of the soldiers responsible for killing a journalist at the Terrain Hotel in 2016 (as mentioned earlier). The military court found 10 soldiers guilty of murder in September 2018, marking the first time the national government had sentenced high-ranking military officials. But as Joan Nyanyuki, Amnesty International's Director of East Africa, cautioned, "Without international pressure and the involvement of the government whose citizens fell victim to the Terrain attack, there would still be not a single record of meaningful prosecution of the countless gut-wrenching human rights violations and crimes against the people of South Sudan."[62] The trial, however, failed to set a precedent for justice. Instead, it became the exception that proved the rule by law. There still was too much to lose by bringing attention to and endorsing criminal justice.

Peace before Justice?

But the question of criminal punishment did not go away. It continued to loom over the peace process and current transitional government. "Why," as one South Sudanese official proclaimed, "would we wish to prosecute ourselves?"[63] After all, as long as the leaders remained in power, they retained the power to shield themselves from prosecution. The issue, then, was how to get the leaders to confront justice when denial serves their political interest? How does one move beyond denial to get to some notion of truth that will be acceptable to all parties

IMPUNITY, HUMAN RIGHTS, AND THE STRUGGLE FOR JUSTICE 139

involved in the peace process? Is it through a truth commission or war crimes court or both? Kiir and other leaders had signed ARCSS and pledged in this case to discuss and address a hybrid war crimes court and a truth commission. Even if they temporized or ignored this pledge, they still had to confront international pressure and the concern shared by international donors for promoting justice. In short, there was no way of avoiding the issue; they had to find a way of balancing their political interests against international and regional demands for implementing a war crimes court.

In 2016, the AU Peace and Security Council mandated that the AU Office of Legal Counsel devise a plan for implementing the HCSS. The African Union Council met with the United Nations and the South Sudan Ministry of Justice and Constitutional Affairs to discuss the Memorandum of Understanding (MoU) and the Statute of the HCSS. After a weeklong discussion, the parties to ARCSS agreed to adopt a war crimes court. However, after South Sudan's Council of Ministers approved the two instruments, Kiir refused to send the bill to the National Assembly for final approval (he never offered an official reason). It was clear that he feared prosecution. Still, to preserve his power, he needed a strategy to silence his critics on the issue of justice. So, he resolved to conflate forgiveness and forgetting in an effort to shift attention away from the victims' grievances to the leaders' guilt. His idea was that in forgiving the leaders' violent actions, the people (the relatives and friends of the victims, in particular) would eventually forget about the violence. Kiir even had a motto for his plan: "peace through forgiveness." And it appeared on the billboards located along Airport Avenue leading into Juba.

Yet to forgive without at least an official historical record of the victims seemed reckless. For people to forget the pain and suffering inflicted on them as victims, they needed some kind of historical account and/or public apology. Kiir wanted people to believe that forgiving with forgetting was in the country's best interest of avoiding further political instability. Immunity thus became a way of getting people to forgive and forget, but it meant accepting that injustice was unavoidable, even a necessary evil. This of course was a high price to pay for peace and there was no assurance that the same evil would not be committed again. The 2015 AUCISS report addressed this issue by concluding that the CPA had created a fundamentally unstable situation when it failed to institute a regime of reparations for past crimes and to promote a "change in culture," or new social relations,[64] stressing mutual participation of international and local judges.[65] That change in culture ultimately meant depoliticizing criminal punishment. In a dissenting opinion, Mamdani, a member of the AUCISS, argued that if criminal punishment was to work, it also had to be meted out equally, that is, among all parties involved, including UN personnel.[66] Otherwise, criminal justice would exclude certain individuals and perpetuate the grievances of victims. It

140 SOUTH SUDAN'S FATEFUL STRUGGLE

was a bold statement, but one that highlighted the growing political stakes of implementing a fair and impartial court or inclusive justice.

Inclusive Justice

In December 2015, I spoke with several officials who voiced strong support for the CTRH, the CTRHC, and the HCSS. At this time, the warring parties had agreed to implement ARCSS and there was evidence of growing public support for the CTRH. In fact, a nationwide survey conducted the same year showed that 81 percent of the respondents supported reparations from the state for survivors of abuses.[67] It was clear that many South Sudanese had warmed to the idea of the HCSS, as long as it did not obstruct the peace process. But even more expressed support for a truth commission to promote national healing. What was less clear though was the support for both, or whether a truth commission was enough to settle longstanding political grievances or prevent future leaders from committing the same crimes. Amid the uncertainty, the ruling elite sought to shape the narrative on transitional justice by driving a wedge into it.

In June 2016, Kiir and Machar co-authored a *New York Times* op-ed article, where they argued against the HCSS, but in support of the truth commission to advance the peace process. They contended that a war crimes court "would destabilize and further divide the country" and potentially reverse the gains of a truth commission (i.e., moral healing and forgiveness).[68] They pointed to the South African Truth and Reconciliation Commission (SATRC) to bolster their case for truth, not trials. The SATRC, it should be noted, had granted amnesty for confession, which despite being controversial, enabled South Africa to transition to a democratic, multicultural state. Kiir suggested that it would do the same for South Sudan. But to suggest this was ultimately misleading. For the moot success of amnesty was due in large part to the leadership of Nelson Mandela and Desmond Tutu, two of the most trusted moral figures on the African continent. Kiir of course was and is no Nelson Mandela, certainly not the same inspirational leader. Moreover, in a bizarre series of events, Machar, who had recently returned to Juba to be sworn in as Vice President in April 2016, insisted that he had no prior knowledge of the essay. After publicly disavowing the article, he then proceeded to declare his support for the HCSS— a move likely intended to score political points with international officials.[69] Whatever their motives may have been, Kiir and Machar seemed to be engaged in a game of one-upmanship.

The two, in fact, remained deeply wary of one another. In July 2016, Kiir would attack Machar's forces stationed in Juba and drive out Machar from the city. The second outbreak of war would once again test the patience of international

IMPUNITY, HUMAN RIGHTS, AND THE STRUGGLE FOR JUSTICE   141

donors and renew outside interest in a war crimes court. But stopping the hostilities had also become the main priority, which made justice an increasingly sensitive topic of reaching agreement on a new peace agreement. By early 2018, implementing a hybrid war crimes court had become a nonstarter issue for the parties involved in the peace talks. No one wished to discuss it, yet no one was willing to give up on it. Kiir, for instance, still had to placate the supporters of the HCSS, including the United States, which had already invested nearly 4.8 million dollars to help design it.

By now the question was whether the African Union would take up the initiative and pressure the leaders to approve the HCSS. Yet instead of acting, the African Union dithered, before eventually deferring to South Sudan's leadership in order to avoid driving a wedge into the peace process. The African Union feared that its actions would create internal pressures on parties and destabilize the peace process. The decision naturally rankled human rights advocates, who had seen the African Union as the best hope for initiating the implementation of a war crimes court. By early 2019, for example, Amnesty International was calling on the African Union's Peace and Security Council to initiate its own ad hoc hybrid war crimes court to overcome Kiir's unwillingness to implement the HCSS. The PSC in this case reserved the power to invoke Article 3 of the PSC Protocol which allowed it to adopt a court as a measure for addressing a breach in peace and security (i.e., similar to UN Security Council resolution 827, which established the International Criminal Tribunal for the former Yugoslavia). The fact that this did not require South Sudan's MoA signature effectively eliminated a key obstacle to merging peace with justice. Still, the African Union was ultimately reluctant to initiate a process that would amount to a new precedent for interfering in the affairs of one if its member countries. Keeping the bar high on unilateral intervention thus continued to take precedence over justice.

It was also difficult to imagine that South Sudan would sign and ratify the Rome Statute of the International Criminal Court, which allows the UN Security Council to refer a situation in a nonstate party like South Sudan, to the Office of the Prosecutor. South Sudan could still sign a declaration accepting the Court's jurisdiction—per Article 12(3) of the Rome Statute—over crimes committed from 2013 to the present.[70] If it did, the ICC could bring much-needed resources to restore the rule of law in South Sudan. But the problem was politics. South Sudan's leaders could still politicize the court in two ways: by resisting cooperation or by using the court to gain legitimacy and power through the prosecution and elimination of their political opponents (although the ICC could always choose to investigate the political leaders that carried out the self-referral). Even if South Sudan agreed to join the ICC, China and Russia would almost certainly block the resolution referring the situation to the ICC, as they did with the UN arms embargo against South Sudan's leaders.[71]

142 SOUTH SUDAN'S FATEFUL STRUGGLE

Another option was the adoption of a UN International Criminal Tribunal for South Sudan. The tribunal promised to target more military officials—and not just the worst of the worst—and to select judges from South Sudan and other areas of Africa. Moreover, the UN Security Council would be in charge of financing/budgeting the court, and its resolution would create a statute enabling the prosecutor to operate independently of the Security Council. The tribunal therefore would provide a much-needed alternative to the HCSS and like the International Criminal Tribunal for Rwanda, would exercise concurrent jurisdiction with the national government. The drawback of course was that the tribunal required a UNSC resolution, and for Russia, China, or the United States to not invoke their veto power to block the court;[72] any of these countries could use their veto to halt the extended funding of the tribunal. Like the ICC, then, power politics could determine who was prosecuted and investigated and thus compromise the impartiality of the ICC.

In its 2015 resolution, for example, the African Union called on its member states to refuse to cooperate with the ICC. This followed a 2011 AU resolution accusing the ICC of engaging in selective justice or bias against African states and not extending its focus to Afghanistan where the United States was active militarily.[73] As such, the resolutions were triggered by the ICC's exclusive focus on African states—the first eight investigations opened up by the OTP targeted African leaders or rebels. After arrest warrants were issued against two sitting African Heads of State—Sudan's President, Omar al-Bashir, and Libya's leader, Muammar Gaddafi (and later Kenya's leader, Uhuru Kenyatta—whose indictment occurred before he took over as President)—the African Union had had enough. It now promised to firmly oppose the ICC's operations in Africa.

The African Union's anti-ICC stance also stressed the need for local solutions to address the causes of violence. An "African solution" suggested that Africans had overlooked their rich history and authentic system of values and customs; that they needed to draw on these values to determine how justice was administered and how they would meet the standards of international justice. The idea was that they had become dependent on foreign legal mechanisms to resolve the violence and abuses, when, in fact, it was this dependence that limited their capacity to overcome such violence. In other words, such intervention(s) failed to engage the historical and cultural conditions of suffering of most Africans. Victims' justice had to speak to the cultural context of the violence in order to address the political grievances that drove the cycle of violence. Otherwise, one was liable to fall into the trap (or the "flip side") of victors' justice, in which the victims become the victors and stoke new political grievances.[74]

The question now is whether South Sudan's victims can ever truly forgive the perpetrators. Every official, leader, and civilian I spoke to in South Sudan had experienced some degree of trauma or felt victimized. Of course, this is one of the reasons that the ruling elite have felt entitled to paint themselves as the victims

of outside interference and violence committed by the other warring side. But such victimization only serves the interests of the ruling elite and ignores the grievances of victims. Ultimately, the issue is whether we can draw a fair line between legitimate and illegitimate victims to justify the actual rights of victims without stoking further grievances and fueling more violence. The only way to know this is to create an inclusive process in which all people and parties are treated equally and justice is based on the rule of law and effectively divorced from political power.

A Comprehensive Reckoning and Upping the Ante

The problem is that Kiir and other leaders continue to deflect attention away from their own role(s) in the process. Granting amnesty has become a prominent way of doing this. Kiir, for example, granted amnesty to several members of the South Sudan National Liberation Movement/Army (SSNLM/A) and later, to hundreds of fighters of the SPLM/A-IO for their role in the July 2016 hostilities in Juba. His aim of course was to make amends and to entice the opposition to end hostilities against the government. Te strategic tactic amounted to soft pledges to promote justice and peace, including his assurance made to Machar in 2018, that he would not lock him up when he returned to Juba for peace talks. The trouble with such amnesties is that they are based on a politics of selective treatment, not inclusive justice. More importantly, they offer little protection against criminal prosecutors who may be inclined to press ahead with determining what they are hiding and excluding.

Politicized justice also betrays many of Kiir's earlier statements about reconciliation, including his speech announcing the launching of the SPLM's election campaign in 2010, when he declared that

> We have suffered tremendously, millions of us and of the millions displaced whilst others seek refuge. We have a lot of pain, some of us unfortunately continue to inflict pain on ourselves. It is my personal call and the SPLM appeal for us to reach one another; let's heal our wounds, let's preach harmony and peaceful coexistence. Let's forgive one another. I want to work on this healing and reconciliation together.[75]

Kiir would later, in his opening remarks at the Dialogue between the SPLM and Southern Political Parties held in Juba on November 8, 2008, insist that "the dialogue recognized various grievances faced by our people and that we . . . open a new page [and] accept ourselves on an equal footing and unite together as citizens of Southern Sudan."[76] Between the time of his speech and the implementation of R-ARCSS, forgiveness seemed to become more politically expedient,

144 SOUTH SUDAN'S FATEFUL STRUGGLE

an instrument meant to deflect accountability and to restrict the scope of transitional justice. Power had corrupted whatever good intentions Kiir may have had prior to statehood.

These early speeches also expose the hidden elements of his strategy of disowning the violence. First, Kiir failed to make mention of "responsibility," and to "forgive and forget." He may not have wished to open past wounds because they would be too painful to confront, but his speech made no reference to the victims or to victims' justice. It is hard not to miss the underlying intent here: to ignore the guilt of the perpetrators. Kiir should only ask for the forgiveness of the people when he is ready to acknowledge his own responsibility for the violence. For this to happen, he needs to link his own victimhood with that of the people, and in a manner where forgiveness is a voluntary and collective act of reconciliation of perpetrator and victim. To selectively forget, as we discussed earlier, is to disengage oneself from the common tendency to blame; it blocks the process of owning up to the violence. One might argue that forgetting as a form of forgiveness makes it possible to achieve a clean slate on the national conscience. But this only seems to beg the question of South Sudan's reckoning with the past, or whether an empty slate can be filled with a shared feeling or genuine collective determination to break the national cycle of violence.

It's a question about changing the political reality in South Sudan. But how are we to move beyond the culture of impunity when the political leaders control the political and moral narrative of justice? For critics, the revitalization of local customary law, or its reintegration with statute law, is a promising start, since it works from the bottom-up to pressure the government to engage the violence (and its effects) and to achieve inclusive justice. The idea again is not simply to assign rights to the individual victims but to recognize how all of society has been victimized. It may be true, as Mamdani points out, that "The scope of traditional justice is limited to community-based conflicts, not conflicts that arise from state-defined constructs. . . and traditional justice has little to say about the relation between state and society, and thus about individual rights," but when traditional law is combined with statute law, we also begin integrating the different experiences of victimhood into a holistic framework of accountability, which links the ruling elite's ownership of the violence with defending and protecting the human rights of all individuals.[77]

Behind Kiir's current strategy of disowning the violence, then, is the separation of the country's security interests from justice. It is a strategy based on the government's dual capacity to keep the country safe from terrorism and to promote economic investment. In April 2019, for example, Kiir hired a US consulting firm, Gainful Solutions, headed by Michael Ranneberger, the former Ambassador to Kenya, and his partner, Soheil Nazari-Kangarlou, to lobby the US government and other organizations to drop support for the HCSS and to

withdraw its targeted sanctions against individual South Sudanese leaders. As Sam Mednick writes, Ranneberger's and Kangarlou's plan was to undertake "political advocacy to persuade the Administration to reverse current sanctions and prevent further sanctions; mobilizing American companies to invest in South Sudan's oil, natural resources, and other sectors; and engaging in advocacy to encourage the Administration to open a military relationship with South Sudan to enhance the fight against terrorism and promote regional stability."[78] In effect, the plan amounted to an ambitious and bold attempt to reverse longstanding US policy in the country. The United States, as mentioned earlier, had remained a supporter of the war crimes court, having pledged millions of US dollars to its set up.

The Trump administration, however, marked a radical shift from prioritizing human rights and the rule of law to stressing security first and foremost. Trump, in fact, began embracing authoritarian leaders who had committed widescale human right abuses. This included Egypt's President Fattah el-Sissi, who drew on this trend and his ties with Trump, to clamp down on human rights and democracy and to champion a hardline approach to fighting terrorism. Kiir naturally saw this as an opportunity to appeal to Trump's authoritarian sympathies and to advance his own anti-terrorism and anti-rule of law approach to justice that could "delay and ultimately block establishment of the hybrid war crimes court envisaged in the R-ARCSS."[79] In Trump, Kiir seemed to find a sympathetic figure—an ally to thwart the mechanisms of accountability.

But Kiir also had to contend with civil society activism, particularly human rights civil society groups in and outside of South Sudan. Amnesty International, for instance, condemned the partnership as yet another attempt to undermine accountability and justice in South Sudan, before proceeding to name and shame Gainful Solutions to pressure it and Kiir's government to rescind the contract. The pressure in the end paid off. Within a couple of weeks after the contract was made public, it was annulled and replaced by a new, less transparent one signed on May 3, 2019 with the same firm, but for an undisclosed amount.[80] Although the new contract rescinded Article 4 containing the war crimes court, its other security provisions remained. It was yet another example of Kiir's attempts to divert attention away from his alleged crimes and ultimately to disown the violence that threatens to undermine the R-TGoNU.

Conclusion: Impugnation or Impunity?

South Sudan has been the scene of extreme violence and some of the most horrific human rights atrocities. Despite efforts to stem the violence, the leaders continued to use brutal and divisive tactics to govern the country during the civil

146 SOUTH SUDAN'S FATEFUL STRUGGLE

war. This helped underscore the pervasive militarism of the leaders and their ability to forcibly conscript children. The leaders had succeeded in imposing a rule by law that depended on the threat of brute violence to suppress their enemies and to repress their people. It was all part of a larger strategy to subvert the rule of law and counter the pressures for accountability of those responsible for the injustices. In the end, it allowed the leaders to disown the violence that has haunted the country's efforts of achieving peace.

Kiir had managed to deflect attention away from the abuses while asking for the people's forgiveness and forgetting of his crimes. His ultimate goal, as we saw, was to shield himself from justice. He even went so far as to hire a US lobbying company to pressure the US government to reverse its targeted sanctions and rescind its support for the war crimes court. Civil society and NGO pressures eventually forced the government to backtrack and sign a new contract that did not block the HCSS. Yet the event was a reminder of the government leaders' will and determination to prevent an honest and meaningful reckoning with the country's past and present violence: a reckoning, as I argued, which needed to reflect every South Sudanese's shared, albeit varying duty to overcome the violence.

Hybrid justice represented one crucial part of this reckoning process. But it was a part that Kiir managed to control or maneuver around by advocating for a truth commission to justify his immunity and to nullify the need for the HCSS. As one might expect, Kiir's grand strategy of immunity drove a wedge between justice and peace and reflected a disconcerting disengagement from the grievances of the victims. And yet to prevent victims' justice from becoming further entwined with victor's justice, it is important to see transitional justice as part of a wider, collective effort to confront the violence that has claimed so many lives and to end South Sudan's culture of impunity and its reflexes of denial.

6

The Revitalized Peace Process and Civil Society's Challenge

On December 17, 2017, the government and rebel forces signed the Cessation of Hostilities Agreement, which ended the major fighting in many areas of South Sudan. It was the first step in transitioning to a revitalized government of transitional unity, and it would involve the participation of several more parties seeking to share power. But several factors delayed the implementation of the peace agreement in September 2018. The Democratic Alliance headed by Thomas Cirillo's National Salvation Front (NAS) still refused to take part, insisting that R-ARCSS did not address the needs of the people. In addition, growing donor fatigue and impatience by the civilian population had left the leaders with few options other than to negotiate peace. There was even talk of a civilian uprising, even though the years of war had fractured relations and left much of the population ill-prepared to carry out such a rebellion. By 2019, the unemployment rate among the youth between the ages of 12–25 hovered around 20 percent, and there was the question of what future lied ahead for the youth, who had taken to crime and were traumatized by years of war.

Revitalizing the peace process raised several other questions. Were the large donors willing to commit themselves to a new round of peace talks with many of the same players? And would the United States seize the opportunity to assert itself in the talks? The United States, after having placed economic sanctions on several government officials, had essentially given up on Kiir, Machar, and other key players. Like so many outside players, they remained skeptical of their commitments to peace. The revitalized peace still did not offer any guarantees that the parties would carry out the agreement; nor did it consist of meaningful consensus-building measures. The fact that there were more players sitting at the negotiating table meant more opportunities to disagree, and more difficulties of working together to implement the key provisions of the peace agreement. In fact, the peace talks that took place from 2018 to 2020 still reflected a fragile consensus, leading the UN Panel of Experts on South Sudan to conclude that. "In practical terms, therefore, the revitalized peace agreement did not emerge from exhaustive multilateral negotiations. . . nor was it a comprehensive commitment

South Sudan's Fateful Struggle. Steven C. Roach, Oxford University Press. © Oxford University Press 2023.
DOI: 10.1093/oso/9780190057848.003.0007

148   SOUTH SUDAN'S FATEFUL STRUGGLE

to reshaping the political process in line with an ambitious text, but a renewed framework for the familiar political bargaining process that has shaped politics and resource allocation in South Sudan since its independence."[1]

Nonetheless, the party leaders had to bargain over a number of pressing issues, including the number of provincial states, territorial boundaries, an integrated security force, a permanent constitution, and legal accountability. The most pressing issue was whether Kiir would rescind his earlier presidential decree that increased the number of states from 10 to 28 (and later, 32). Rescinding the degree meant breaking with his Dinka base of hardline supporters, namely, the Jieng Council of Elders. But, on February 15, 2020, after calling out the Jieng Councils for their inflexibility, Kiir announced that he was annulling the presidential decree of 32 states. It was a concession everyone had waited for, and it quickly paved the way for the signing of the agreement on February 22, 2020, which created the Revitalized Transitional Government of National Unity. But the crucial challenge, I argue, was uncoupling the implementation process from the tribal politics that had doomed the first peace process (2015–2016). For it remained unclear whether the fragile consensus of the parties could support the changes needed to transition to a national unity government.

Accordingly, to revitalize ARCSS and reach agreement on key items such as a unified security force, constitutional reform, and democratic elections, the parties had to overcome their own deep-seated misgivings about issues such as security and federalism. This, however, would also expose the growing uncertainty about the inclusion of civil society actors and the continued dismay with the elite-driven, power sharing agreement.

An Unstable Peace

"Revitalized" may not have been the best term to describe the renewed peace talks. For it suggested that there was a need to reenergize what was clearly from the start a lackluster and doomed peace process in 2015.[2] From the outset, Kiir made it clear that the peace process had been imposed on his government by IGAD. Although Machar may have showed a firmer commitment to the peace process, it was difficult to see how they could settle their differences and gain back the trust needed to integrate their military forces into a unified army. It was a tall order to fill. And in a matter of weeks it would be further complicated by Kiir's controversial measures.

The most critical was expanding the number of provincial states. By decree, Kiir announced that the 10-state structure would be replaced by 28 new states. The decree would go into effect in 30 days and Kiir's rationale was that it decentralized further power to the localities. Decentralization, he reasoned, was

in keeping with the referendum of 2011, in which the government was expected to exercise its authority to promote national unity and peace. "We should therefore abandon," Kiir declared, "the culture of war and embrace culture of peace, co-existence and hard work such [that] you and I together develop our country because our country is a country of opportunities."[3] But the idea of a so-called culture of peace was ultimately an affirmation of South Sudan's rich diversity of tribal groups, an idea Garang used to sell his New Sudan vision. The problem was that Kiir's decree complicated a federal solution by devolving power not along principled, but preferential ethnic lines.

Federalism had long maintained a contentious place in South Sudan's political landscape. The British were among the first to introduce a quasi-federal system. Under their system of indirect rule, as we saw in Chapter 1, much, if not all the decision-making power, was concentrated at the state level. Towns and villages (Boma) were largely cut off from this power source—unable to channel their own limited power to any state body. After Sudanese leaders granted the South its autonomy in 1972, the GoS routinely manipulated its legislative chambers before dissolving its autonomy in 1983. The GoS's decision may have left southerners disillusioned with federalism and autonomy, but for Garang, it confirmed the obstructive role played by corrupt state leaders. The true promise of a federal structure in this respect remained unfulfilled—a stunted vision of national unity. The trouble, though, was trying to couple equality with cultural group representation (and empowerment) when there were so many cultural groups vying for power and needing protection. Garang found himself in a difficult predicament of merging these two contested principles to forge a cohesive national identity out of a volatile mosaic of tribal identities.

Kiir's 2015 presidential decree became a testament to this volatility. By granting Kiir the power to appoint state governors and ministers, the decree allowed the governors to set the new boundaries of the provincial states. Yet it remained unclear how these boundaries would be set according to rules and procedures that were still not accepted by all ethnic groups.[4] The uncertainty raised concern about its constitutionality. SPLA-IO officials, for instance, argued that the Transitional Constitution did not grant the President the authority to draw up new state boundaries, nor to unilaterally appoint the governors. In fact, the President was obligated under the Transitional Constitution to consult the National Assembly. What's more, ARCSS was based on 10 administrative states, which meant that the decree was in violation of the agreement. Kiir's decree also excluded other prior federalist proposals, including the SPLM-IO's 2014 plan that attempted to form 21 new states. In the end, however, one could say that it gave most Dinka politicians what they wanted most: a political advantage in future elections, particularly in areas with oil reserves, such as the Ruweng state. Many thus saw it as a strategy to elevate Dinka rule in many counties with a large

150 SOUTH SUDAN'S FATEFUL STRUGGLE

Nuer and Shilluk populations, such as the Upper Nile.[5] If one was a Nuer, Murle, or Shilluk, it was hard not to treat it as a power grab.

As controversial as the decree was, it did not halt the implementation of ARCSS. The parties to ARCSS agreed to negotiate "outside the box" in regard to the 28 states and to treat Kiir's state decree as a political issue, not a legal one.[6] But after Kiir failed to meet a January 22, 2016 deadline for launching the first phase of reintegrating the armed forces, the peace process slowed to a stalemate. Two months later, Machar postponed his return to Juba to serve as Vice President, fearing that the lack of security (given the low number of SPLM-IO troops to protect him) might jeopardize his life. He demanded that government troops be curtailed, and when Kiir eventually agreed to the demand, Machar returned to Juba.

The Reemergence of Civil War

On April 26, 2016, Machar was officially sworn in as Vice President. The ceremony ushered in the national unity government and Machar's willingness to work with Kiir to implement ARCSS. "The war was vicious," Machar would later explain, "We lost a lot of people in it, and we need to bring our people together so they can unite, reconcile, and heal the wounds . . . As long as there is political will, we can overcome all these challenges."[7] Meanwhile, Kiir took the opportunity to declare that the nation's "strength lies in unity."[8] Notwithstanding the rhetoric, the two sides confronted a political crisis. The national government was not only cash strapped but had strained its relations with IGAD when it detained Aly Vergee, Deputy Chief of Staff at JMEC, in April 2016. Although the national government claimed that it was exercising its sovereign right, it failed to offer any reason for his detention.

Meanwhile, divisions and suspicions persisted in the new transitional unity government. Despite Machar's promising statements, he and his SPLM-IO forces never felt comfortable in their new posts. Much of this had to do with Kiir's unwillingness to accept more of Machar's troops to enter Juba and to rescind the 28-state decree. Neither side was ready to make the necessary sacrifices for implementing ARCSS, including a unified army. There was thus mounting distrust on both sides, as intercommunal violence and fighting among government-backed rebel militias spread throughout the countryside, particularly in Jonglei, parts of Equatoria, and the Upper Nile. By mid-2016, Machar was refusing to send many of his soldiers stationed in the western districts of Guedele and Jebel in Juba to cantonment sites, where they would be retrained and eventually integrated into a unified force. The implementation process had literally come to a halt.

On July 3, 2016, fighting broke out on the streets lining the presidential palace, where Machar and Kiir had been holding a press conference. The bodyguards and security personnel for both men had entered into a skirmish outside the palace, as Kiir and Machar pleaded with them to stop fighting. Eventually, Kiir and Machar were rushed into their cars after some of the fighters approached their cars and began shooting. It was reported that Kiir shielded Machar from the bullets, perhaps to reassure Machar and others that he was not the instigator.[9] Yet it was not enough to reassure Machar who soon fled to his resident barracks. A week later, Kiir gave the order to kill Machar after laying siege to the SPLM-IO's barracks. Machar somehow managed to escape and headed south towards the Democratic Republic of the Congo border. Along the way, he suffered a serious leg injury that required medical attention (his troops carried him on their shoulders during the long stretches of the journey). After he crossed into the DRC, he notified DRC authorities that he was stationed in their county. The DRC, which maintained close ties with the South Sudanese government, told him that he and his troops were not welcome. But before the DRC authorities could apprehend him, the UN extracted Machar and offered to transport him to a country willing to take him in.[10] The problem, however, was that there were no takers. Machar had become persona non grata—a political liability because of his opposition to the national government that still enjoyed regional support by neighboring countries. Both Sudan and Ethiopia ended up denying him entry or asylum. Eventually, South Africa's President Jacob Zuma agreed to take in Machar.

No one knew Machar's next move. Not even Machar himself. Some international officials and regional leaders still recognized Machar as the rightful Vice President of South Sudan, even though Kiir had proceeded to appoint Taban Deng Gai as the new Vice President on July 28, 2016. With Gai in office, South Sudanese authorities turned their attention to apprehending Machar, who they now considered an outlaw. There were calls for Machar to openly renounce violence and to return to Juba as a civilian. However, Machar publicly rejected such calls, insisting that Kiir was the aggressor and that his government would likely arrest and torture him if he voluntarily returned to South Sudan. There were even rumors alleging that he was seeking asylum in South Africa. Machar insisted that he was only seeking short-term medical assistance from his personal physician who happened to reside in South Africa. Whatever his intentions, he needed a strategy to confront Kiir and to stay relevant, while also increasing his appeal as the outsider—the one who could cast negative light on Kiir's authoritarian government.[11]

The outsider status of course suited Machar well. He had, after all, sided with foreign governments and enemies to challenge Garang's authority. But the long trek on foot had also taken a heavy toll on him and his SPLM0-IO forces. He was

152 SOUTH SUDAN'S FATEFUL STRUGGLE

no longer the energetic, inspiring rebel of the past. Kiir's offensive had clearly reduced his military influence and convinced many SPLA-IO troops to defect to other militias or return to civilian life rather than risk fighting with the SPLM-IO in northern Uganda. While the defections from the SPLM-IO weakened Machar militarily and politically, many of the defectors ended up joining non-state militias that further pressured the government.

Paradoxically, Kiir found himself increasingly on the defensive—unable to secure public and regional support. Several countries still refused to recognize Taban Gai as the rightful Vice President and to relinquish their doubts about Kiir's role in instigating the conflict. This included Sudan and Uganda. Sudan, for example, had maintained its support of the South Sudanese government after it had cut much of its assistance to SPLM-N.[12] It then proceeded to reject Machar's request to stay in their country after he had been driven out by Kiir. For them, Machar had become a political liability, a threat to their fragile relations with the South Sudanese government. On the other hand, the economic repercussions of the oil pipeline shut-down had clearly tempered its support. Sudan, in fact, still struggled to make up for the hundreds of millions of dollars in lost oil revenue and remained unwilling to seek common ground for extracting and transporting oil to the Port of Sudan.

By 2017, Kiir's main priority was not to improve the economy but to shore up his army. In May, he changed the SPLA to South Sudan Defense Forces (SSDF), and then changed via a republic order the SSDF to South Sudan People's Defense Forces (SSPDF) in September 2018. By replacing "Sudan" with "South Sudan" and "liberation army" with "Defense Forces," Kiir had reaffirmed South Sudan's sovereignty by distancing its army from the SSDF, which had once been allied with the NIF in Sudan's second civil war. While the name change may have been largely symbolic, it seemed to be a part of larger effort to work beyond divisions and to purge the SSPDF of rogue elements, including Paul Malong, who, as mentioned in Chapter 4, had been tied to a series of corruption schemes in which he had used government money to purchase military equipment (which he never purchased). Kiir's actions finally appeared to signal his willingness to revive peace talks.

But the Joint Monitoring and Evaluation Commission (JMEC) and IGAD, which had taken the initiative to revive ARCSS, faced a daunting task: they had to bring together the many different military factions to the table. To meet this challenge, IGAD's Council of Ministers reappointed the IGAD Special Envoy to South Sudan, Dr. Ismail Wais, whose main task was to revitalize interest in a cessation of hostilities agreement and ARCSS. Wais conducted several prerevitalization stakeholders' consultations, followed by a high-level revitalization forum in Addis Ababa. His effort came at a time when the economic

stakes of war could not be higher. The war had already destroyed much of the machinery and stopped oil production at many facilities, leading to a dramatic decline in oil production, from 440,000 barrels per day in 2013 to just 170,000 in 2017. At the same time, the average crude price in US dollars had jumped by nearly 20 percent and forecasters projected a further rise in oil prices in 2018.[13] With oil revenue accounting for up to 98 percent of its budget, pressure mounted to stop the fighting.

On December 21, 2017, Kiir and opposition parties finally signed the Cessation of Hostilities Agreement.[14] The agreement called on all the parties to cease attacks on one another, to ensure the protection of civil society and media, and for each party to comply with international humanitarian and human rights norms, such as ending child conscription. The parties included the SPLM/A-IO and NAS, which both pledged to stop attacking tribal forces and to abide by humanitarian laws. But the challenge of rebuilding trust and transparency hinged on ending all violations to the agreement. This meant that each party needed to comply with all the terms of the agreement and to publicly acknowledge any violations. Despite IGAD's and the AU's best efforts, and the addition of several new opposition parties, many remained wary of the parties' commitments. The fear was that pouring more funds to enforce these commitments would only increase competition for scarce resources among the parties.

Still, mediators saw an opportunity to control the narrative. With the word "revitalize," they had hoped to counter donor fatigue by underscoring the reenergized commitments of more parties to work together to pressure the government. This was intended to reassure officials that R-ARCSS was not simply a repackaging of ARCSS, that this time the parties would have to be larger in number and more diverse in representing the population. The idea, in short, was that a revitalized agreement for peace would establish the mechanisms for reaching consensus and for preventing any one single party from undermining the overall process In February 2018, the South Sudan Opposition Alliance emerged as the largest alliance of parties, consisting of nine parties that included the Federal Democratic Party (FDP), South Sudan Armed Forces (SSAF), the National Salvation Front (NAS), the National Democratic Movement (NDM), the People's Democratic Movement (PDM), the South Sudan Liberation Movement/Army (SSLMA), the South Sudan National Movement for Change (SSNMC), the South Sudan Patriotic Movement/Army (SSPM/A), the South Sudan United Movement/Army (SSUN/A), the United Democratic Republican Alliance (UDRA), and the SPLA-IO. It was South Sudan's largest and most impressive alliance, which promised greater inclusion but also raised the political stakes for peace.

154   SOUTH SUDAN'S FATEFUL STRUGGLE

A Fractured Peace

Building consensus within the alliance posed a significant challenge. While the parties remained steadfast in their commitment to peace, it was not enough to get them to adhere to good faith principles of cooperation and compromise. Tensions, in fact, mounted in the first year of peace talks and led to major splits within the parties. The first occurred in response to the signing of R-ARCSS, in which four of the parties opposed R-ARCSS and insisted that it did not go far enough in offering assurances of democracy and protecting the people's basic needs and rights. What was supposed to be a uniting event, then, eventually turned out to be a fraught task of working together to advance the peace process and the implementation of a new unity government.

The second major split within the SSOA occurred in November 2015, when eight of the groups forming the SSOA, held their first official elections. Peter Gadet Yak, the leader of the United Democratic Republican Alliance, received 62.5 percent of the vote, while Gabriel Changson, the leader of the Federal Democratic Party, won 37.5 percent.[15] Gadet, who had served as General of the SSDP during the second civil war in Sudan, joined the SPLA in 2006, and went on to serve as military general of the Jonglei state from 2013 to 2015, before finally aligning himself with the SPLM-IO. In 2016, he severed ties with Machar and became Chairman of the Military Command Council of the Federal Democratic Party, which would join the SSOA in 2018.

Despite what seemed to be a fair election, Changson contested the outcome, claiming that the election of Gadet was flawed (i.e., stuffing the ballot boxes) and that Gadet was unfit to lead the SSOA, particularly given his human rights record that had led the EU, for example, to impose sanctions on him in 2014 for his involvement in the 2014 Bentiu massacre.[16] Gadet's support came principally from Lam Akol, who had publicly dismissed Changson's claims. Joseph Bakosoro and his SSNMC, meanwhile, put their weight behind Changson. But one week after the elections, the election council voted to dismiss the contested outcome and to validate the original results. The decision did little to ease the tensions between Changson supporters and those of Gadet. Akol, in fact, never accepted the decision; instead, he accused the government of orchestrating the dismissal in order to sow division within the SSOA.[17] In the meantime. there were reports that alleged Changson had turned the FDP into his own kinship network or family business. This only served to amplify tensions further between the FDP and Gadet's UDRA.

Changson was eventually voted in as the new leader of the SSOA after Gadet died from an apparent heart attack on April 15, 2019. By this time, many of Gadet's party members had defected to the government. And Changson's corruption and divisive personality made it increasingly difficult to reach consensus

within the coalition. In June 2019, after being pressured by numerous opposition leaders to step down as interim leader, Changson resigned, leading Josephine Lagu, the senior leader of the People's Democratic Movement (PDM), to become its new interim leader. Changson's failed leadership had cost the SSOA time to work out key issues concerning security and eventually led Lagu and Akol to announce their support for delaying the pretransitional period in order to work out the details of the integration of the armies and to address the issue of Kiir's presidential state decree.

The decree, it is worth noting, left many of the boundaries of these new states unresolved. In fact, it left the Nuer, Asande, and Shilluk ethnic communities in the minority or underrepresented in many of the states with a new Dinka majority. The decree had thus managed to marginalize every major ethnic group. If Kiir was to bend to the wishes of these groups and revert to the 10-state model that the SSOA was asking, he would have to find a way to placate his Dinka base, notably, the Jieng Council of Elders—a group of hardline Dinka leaders whose rigid views on Dinka power had shaped Kiir's policies. Kiir had justified the 32-state decree on the grounds that it decentralized power to the local level. But the problem was that Kiir's plan of decentralization figured to create more inequality at the local level, by empowering the Dinka elite over other groups in several states.

For the Nuer and Murle the issue was not simply about decentralizing power but whether devolving power could promote equality among ethnic groups. Their fear was that leveling the playing field would not only create more competition for power, but also provide more opportunities for the South Sudanese to participate and shape the affairs of local government. The issue of course remained complex and open-ended. And it seemed that by taking up the issue (by decree), Kiir had essentially ignored a problem that had long occupied a space in South Sudan's political imagination, that is, how to promote fair and equal ethnic representation. It came as little surprise, then, that opposition groups rejected the decree as an arbitrary and illegitimate law.[18]

The Peace Process Parameters

The rescission of the bill had become a central priority of the SSOA in its efforts to challenge the SPLM-government's authority and to shape the integrity of the peace process. In its charter, the SSOA committed itself to "accelerate efforts to restore just and durable peace, democracy, and to preserve human rights and the fundamental democratic rights of our people and a new national unity government."[19] It was especially critical of the government and institutionalized corruption. But in the end, the SSOA remained a fragile coalition, held together by

156   SOUTH SUDAN'S FATEFUL STRUGGLE

a tenuous strand of impassioned opposition to the national government. Kiir of course knew this and sought to use it against the SSOA in order to divide them. The question was whether the SSOA could counter this by building consensus through moral persuasion and reasoned moral constraint as they debated the limits and possibilities of inclusion, equal representation, and democratic and legal accountability.

Sharing power required discursive flexibility to reach agreement. However, there were several factors working against this process. First, the power-sharing arrangement consisted of few dynamic mechanisms for consensus-building, such as a mutual veto. The competitive pressures, factional infighting, and the sheer number of parties made such mechanisms either moot or liable to worsen divisions—where "moderation pays" or there are incentives not to adopt extreme measures.[20] In fact, the veto power of the four vice-presidents invited stalemate or "immobilism" in negotiations—a condition when party elites secure benefits from exerting their "hostile sentiment" toward other parties, causing them to disrespect one another.[21] It also threatened to complicate the transfer power to minority parties by suppressing the desire to devolve power, that is, through constitutional amendments. There was no guarantee that any of the parties would not recklessly abuse their power, especially if it meant pleasing their base or ethnic clientele. What this suggested was that dialogue and deliberation on issues was essentially short circuited; certain issues (e.g., the war crimes court) were simply taken off the slate or treated as nonstarters, since they were too controversial.

Second, power-sharing was an elite process that still excluded civil society actors and grassroots organizations. Some of the parties actually went out of their way to urge IGAD to exclude civil society actors in the peace talks, believing that the national government was using them to disrupt the peace process. Power sharing in this sense turned uneasily on a mutual distrust and caution that seemed to increase pressure on the parties involved. It was thus unclear if civil society participation would necessarily destabilize the process.

Third, power sharing conflicted with the goals of strong regional actors that had exerted undue influence on the peace process. In particular, Sudan and Uganda played a crucial role in creating what came to be known as the Khartoum Declaration, signed by both Kiir and Machar on June 27, 2018 in Khartoum.[22] The declaration called for a permanent ceasefire and committed the parties to the new three-year timeline with the broad parameters on ARCSS. It also allowed Sudan and Uganda to monitor and potentially enforce the peace process with their own armies. Naturally, this led to concern that they were using the process to further their regional geopolitical interests, not to stabilize the peace deal. The fear was that in allowing Sudan and Uganda to provide for the regional security force to oversee security in Juba and to train the army units of national military force, the two countries' interest would conflict and potentially undermine any

chances at success for a peace deal. Uganda, for example, had already used its military forces—still stationed inside the southern borders in the country—to protect the country's businesses and material interests in South Sudan. Bashir meanwhile still expected to increase his share of oil running through Sudan to the Red Sea Port. Both countries therefore seemed uninterested in advancing the democratic mechanisms of ARCSS such as democratic elections and human rights enforcement. It is also important to note that both were members of IGAD, which was responsible monitoring ARCSS via JMEC.[23] Despite these deepening concerns, the Khartoum Declaration ended up creating the momentum needed to frame an agreement.

On September 19, 2018, the participating parties signed the revitalized peace agreement. R-ARCSS committed all parties to an eight-month pretransitional period, in which they were expected to form a transitional government of national unity. But Sudan's and Uganda's influence over the peace agreement remained unclear, leading to fears that the two countries could use their influence to divide and destabilize the peace process. Mahmood Mamdani, for example, wrote that

> South Sudan is on its way to becoming an informal protectorate of Sudan and Uganda. By formally acknowledging them as 'guarantors,' the agreement recognizes their strategic role in determining the future of South Sudan: Ugandan troops are physically present to support Kiir's faction, and Sudan provides critical support to opposition groups, including those led by Machar.[24]

Of course, the only real guarantor of peace was South Sudan itself. Yet to be a guarantor, it would also have to overcome the factionalism of its military forces.

National Security and Non-State Militias

If there was an essential pretransitional task, it was to establish a unified military. Such a task proved burdensome for several reasons. One was overcoming the problematic practice of using the payroll to pursue peace, in which the ruling elite profited from maintaining their own security force. Another was the continuing intercommunal violence in many of the 10 states where fighting was driven by cattle raiding—mostly by the dispossessed youth aligned with militias that relied on the forced conscription of children displaced by the war to carry out their attacks on cattle grazers. Continued child conscription made the task of integration increasingly difficult, since many of the parties, including the government, were apparently engaging in the practice. This naturally made the parties

reluctant to give up a key source of recruitment and means of expanding their militias to show their strength at the negotiating table. In addition, for some militias not party to the agreement, the goal was always to disrupt the peace process.

For Thomas Cirillo's National Salvation Front (NAS)—a loose coalition of militias fighting in Central Equatoria—this meant relying on small arms received from neighboring countries such as Sudan and the DRC, to attack the SSPDF.[25] The NAS had somehow managed to exert their influence by using bows and arrows to fight government forces. The tactic had earned them the nickname "Arrow Rangers."[26] It saw its role as pressuring the parties to restructure the peace process, which it claimed was ill-fated and bound to provide "a governance system which renders services to the people of South Sudan."[27] Cirillo called attention to Kiir's state decree by insisting on a "truly federal system." His ultimate aim, it seemed, was to devitalize the corrupt peace process by creating more insecurity. As such, he hoped to unmask the hypocrisy of the government by provoking a violent reprisal(s) by the SSPDF, which would eventually cast doubt on all the parties' commitment to democracy, human rights, and peaceful government.

His strategy nonetheless forced the national government into a difficult predicament. If it did carry out reprisals it would distract and ultimately derail the peace process. And yet if it did not respond forcefully to the NAS' threat in Central Equatoria, it risked losing credibility in effectively implementing a national unity government. In the end, it elected to respond forcefully.

In 2021, the SSPDF launched a series attacks against the NAS—including a February 2 attack on the village of Selema and later, on Wudabi and Lujulo in the Morobo area of Yei River State on February 8 and 9. NAS officials insisted that the SSPDF killed 13 civilians and looted whole villages, and even alleged that "Kiir's ethnic regime" was engaged in an ethnic cleaning campaign in the region that violated the Cessation of Hostilities Agreement.[28] They called on independent investigators to gather evidence of war crimes perpetrated by the SSPDF, which, in their view, was "punishing civilians for allegedly supporting the NAS or because of their ethnic background."[29] The national government dismissed the allegations and reaffirmed its commitment to defeat the NAS and other rogue militias which continued to pose a threat to national stability and the government.

By late 2019, international observers had noted the culpability of both the NAS and the government. In failing to govern and offer support to local government in various areas, the government had allowed conditions, such as employment and the influx of arms and lawlessness, to worsen and for militias to expand their influence to carry out more violent attacks and bloody reprisals. In its 2020 report, the UN Human Rights Council found that "Localized conflicts countrywide have largely been characterized by the absence of the State and the

REVITALIZING THE PEACE PROCESS   159

rule of law, the proliferation of light and heavy weaponry and the State's failure to establish and encourage a shared national identity."[30] In Jonglei, thousands of displaced youth had risen up and attacked villagers. The violence quickly spilled over into the neighboring administrative areas of Pibor, including the eastern cities of Gumuruk and Manyabol, where the MSN and the International Committee of the Red Cross treated numerous civilians with gunshot wounds. The attackers turned out to be armed youth who had organized their own local militias in Jonglei and trekked into Pibor to attack civilians, forcing many to flee into the bush, including staff workers affiliated with the MSN and the ICRC.[31]

In an effort to stem the violence, the national government initiated a new reckoning with intercommunal violence in the summer of 2020. On July 23, 2020, Kiir formed a committee to address the intercommunal violence plaguing the Jonglei and Warrup region. He appointed the Vice President, James Wani Igga to chair the committee. Wani promised to contain the violence within 21 days, an optimistic forecast by a committee that consisted of several senior officials, including Interior Minister Paul Mayom Akec, but no local chiefs, elders, or officials.[32] The committee coordinated its efforts with the UN, which had become involved in the aftermath of the Likiangole attack. UNMISS, for its part, had maintained a strong presence in the region, which according to one UN official, "has been engaging with community leaders on the ground as well as at the national level to stop the violence since the attacks began in December 2019." UNMISS ended up transporting the members of the Government's High-Level Committee, including Igga, to meet with the groups in Bor to find a solution.

Despite the growing government concern with inter-communal violence, the fighting continued into the summer months. On July 22, 2020, armed groups attacked the village of Likuangole, which lied 30 kilometers north of Pibor, displacing nearly 6,000 civilians living within and near the town.[33] The committee observed this and other incidents, but never consulted the people living in the small villages, where most of the violence occurred. It only focused on the major towns, believing that this would yield solutions. Critics were quick to point out that like previous presidential committees, there was no attempt to investigate any crimes or hold high-level officials to account. Although it constituted good first step of addressing the conflict, it led to nothing concrete in terms of recommendations that addressed the root causes of the conflict, such as a lack of accountability and unemployment among the youth.

Mobilizing Constitutional Sentiment

The looming issue of the peace process, then, was whether power sharing was building consensus on the difficult issues. It was clear that the process was more inclusive this time round. But as Jok Madut Jok writes, "the more inclusive the

160 SOUTH SUDAN'S FATEFUL STRUGGLE

mediators want the peace process to be, the more difficult it is to get the primary contenders to agree and the conflict drags on, with disastrous consequences for the population."[34] Inclusion, of course, can raise difficult issues that cannot be worked out in a timely manner, or within the relatively narrow timeline of R-ARCSS. One such issue involved the amendments for bringing the permanent constitution in line with R-ARCSS. Merging constitution making and peace building had proved divisive and had weakened the fragile consensus of the peace process. The idea, however, was to establish a public contract between the people and government,[35] which could stabilize the expectations for implementing the new government.[36] Treating the constitution as an open contract—especially in deeply divided societies like South Sudan—assumes that the parties' commitments are stable over time and that the political leaders value their commitments. Stability works on the trust we place in institutions to neutralize party bias and to prevent any one party from asserting privilege. Yet in many deeply divided developing countries (and developed countries), warring conditions often lead to disingenuous commitments to peace.

Take the case of Burundi. Here the parties to the peace process incorporated various provisions of the Arusha Agreement (2000) into the 2005 Constitution. The leaders of the dominant executive political party, the Conseil Nacional pour La Defense de la Democratie and the Forces ou le Defense de la Democratie (CCNDD-FDP) amended the two-term limit stipulated in the 2009 Constitution to three terms and created a proportional representation system. But the changes did little to root out corruption and patronage. In fact, they led in 2016 to violent clashes between government forces and street protestors, which destabilized the government and left hundreds of protesters killed.

Although the central purpose of a constitutional amendment is to deepen trust in public law, it often ends up becoming a perilous test of such trust, especially when it is imposed or rushed through.[37] As Allen Wiener points out, when one party unilaterally adopts amendments, it creates a situation that "signals that there is no commitment under the new constitution to address the aspiration of that side through the ordinary political process."[38] Proposing too many amendments in a short period of time can pressurize the parties of power-sharing arrangements. In South Sudan, the National Constitutional Amendment Committee (NCAC) introduced a slew of amendments to the final draft of the permanent constitution, leading to delays in the process. The parties failed to work on a gradualist basis in which to adjust to and internalize the new rules.[39] Rather, the compressed timeline for implementing R-ARCSS led to complications that exposed the gap between the Transitional Constitution and R-ARCSS.

The NCAC's task was to close this gap. In January 2019, Gichira Kabara, the NCAC chairman, submitted the TC Amendment Bill to the Minister of Justice

and Constitutional Affairs. The bill effectively allowed the NCAC to amend former amendments to incorporate them into the Transitional Constitution.[40] The expanded bill also proposed increasing the size of the Transitional Legislative Assembly and putting together a unified armed force. This required additional revisions to an earlier amendment found in the SPLA Act (2009) and the Police Service Act. Still, the SPLM-IO objected to amending the government's federal structure and pointed in this case to the difference between decentralization and devolution to make their case. For them, decentralization was a process of delegating and administering power away from a central location. By delegating power to multiple offices, decentralization reflected an indirect and loosely organized dispersal of power.

Devolution though was different. It constituted the actual transfer of power from the federal government to provinces and local government, and involved more deliberation about how to distribute resources and power equally. The SPLM-IO's federalist approach proposed local (subregional) autonomy to empower local communities economically and to equip local government with the capacity to resolve their problems through a fair share of resources. Kiir's plan seemed to ignore this crucial issue of shared capacity building at the local level, that is, setting the budget and making local policy.

Federalism was just one of many issues addressed by the NCAC in its constitutional bill of 124 articles submitted on February 19, 2020. The bill, in fact, proved far more sweeping than expected. And its comprehensiveness indicated that South Sudan's permanent constitution was flexible enough to direct and coordinate institutions of the country. The NCAC, however, never had the opportunity to respond to the government's objections on federalism. It became inactive in the summer 2021 after the government refused to extend its mandate.

The NCAC did establish an effective working relationship with the NCRC, which was responsible for devising the draft of the permanent constitution. Since its establishment in 2012, the NCRC has had to contend with the disruptive effects of the civil war, including its limited access to many parts of the 10 states. John Natanga, the NCRC Secretary General, explained that the drafting of a permanent constitution was delayed by the shortage of government funds caused by the civil war.[41] The commission also lost its original chairman, Akolda Maan Tier, in December 2015. Tier, who had received his law degree from the University of Khartoum School of Law, helped to draw up the Transitional Constitution. As one of the leading authorities on constitutional and customary law in South Sudan, he stressed "the need to reach out to as many people as possible though biweekly workshops in all the ten states." But after the outbreak of war in July 2016, much of the NCRC's outreach had to be suspended.

When I met with Natanga again in January 2020, he indicated that "R-ARCSS had given the committee new life . . . and that the committee was receiving the

162 SOUTH SUDAN'S FATEFUL STRUGGLE

full support of the government to implement the terms of the new agreement."[42] It should be noted that R-ARCSS sought to reconstitute the NCRC with members representing all parties to R-ARCSS, including its committee consul. In addition, it required the NCRC to present its draft text to the commission to the executive and to "a National Constitutional Conference (NCRC) composed of selected representatives from all levels of administrations and registered institutions as shall be stipulated in the legislation governing the Constitution-making process."[43]

The new rules and mechanisms also underscored the promise of interdialogue and cross-party deliberation. By late 2016, Kiir had formed his National Dialogue Committee, which brought the warring parties together to address the key issues. But the fact that Kiir showed little sign of bending on his presidential state decree made the committee seem more like window dressing than a meaningful attempt at reconciliation. Moreover, the NDC was never Kiir's idea to begin with, but rather, that of Festus Magae, the former President of Botswana and the chair of the JMEC, who, in the fall of 2016, called on the parties (e.g., the SPLM/A in Government, the SPLM/A-IO, the SPLM-FD, and other opposition parties) to create a national dialogue as a means of reaching common ground on issues. It was therefore supposed to be all inclusive. Yet Kiir seemed to treat it as an opportunity to empower his Dinka base, by appointing a majority of SPLM-government Dinka members to its council and by excluding anyone living outside of South Sudan from taking part in the dialogue.

After the opposition accused the committee of bias and allowing the dialogue process to fall outside of the framework of ARCSS, Kiir proceeded to appoint two members from the SPLA-FD—which included Rebecca Machar, the widow of John Garang.[44] His concessions were still not enough to overcome the doubts about the legitimacy of the NDC. The commission continued to lack civil society participation, which IGAD and the Troika, as mentioned earlier, tried to push at the peace talks to little avail.[45] The Troika, for example, declared that CSOs were "the best hope for a sustainable peace process inclusive of ordinary men and women, religious leaders, ethnic minorities, and other excluded groups."[46]

The problem was that civil society also demanded sweeping reforms of the new constitution and the terms of R-ARCSS. Since independence, CSOs had pressed for reforms to which the national government paid lip service. In 2011, the Civil Society Referendum Taskforce had called for several reforms that included (1) zero tolerance for violence as a political means and to ensure that elected governments are upheld; (2) zero tolerance for tribalism, nepotism, and corruption; (3) the protection of the freedom of expression and association and peaceful assembly; and (4) the promotion of transparency, accountability, and inclusivity in the expenditure of public funds. CSOs also pressed for enhanced traditional conflict resolution mechanisms like negotiation, mediation, and dialogue to increase public participation and to promote collective nonviolent

REVITALIZING THE PEACE PROCESS   163

action that included vigils, marches, and street art. The civil war, however, had led to strict controls over CSO activity

In 2014, when the issue of the inclusion of civil society was discussed by the warring parties, the SPLM-IO and government insisted that it would overburden the mediation process with issues that could only be addressed after a potential peace deal was struck. The SPLM-IO even threatened to pull out of the talks if civil society and other opposition groups were allowed a seat at the table.[47] The issue surfaced again in 2018, but this time, international actors insisted that their inclusion was a necessary burden of peacemaking. In their petition sent to IGAD, Oxfam reaffirmed this by stating that

> Local civil society organizations are driving grassroots peace processes and narrowing ethnic divides by bringing communities together to talk, and through unconventional peacebuilding methods like sport and cultural exchanges. They are calling for an end to the conflict through street art and poetry as well as through political processes. They are eyes and ears on the ground, assisting in and monitoring the implementation of the peace agreement. These are the people who know what ensuring peace takes on the ground—they know their stories, and they know their country. They have the fundamental right to have a say in defining peace, and—even more importantly—they are vital to ensuring it lasts.[48]

CSO participation in R-ARCSS also raised concerns about its progressive and ameliorative role. First, its inclusion seemed to favor less the people than the government. The thinking here was that because much of civil society was simply too undeveloped to function independently from the state, they would ultimately become sell outs and pawns of the national government. After all, the government already controlled and restricted many of their activities, which limited their influence and independent voice. Second, the opposition parties did not see the CSOs as dependable allies. In fact, as mentioned earlier, they tended to see them as part of the national government's efforts to fracture the opposition alliance. Officials in the end settled on the inclusion of more opposition parties to offset these concerns with promoting CSO participation in the peace process.

Still, for international actors, CSOs in South Sudan remained the best hope for peace and transforming South Sudanese politics. Rachel Ibreck, for example, argues that many CSO activists in the legal sector had learned to "appreciate the duality of law . . . and the ability to contest it while also affirming as critical means of achieving fairness and justice." For the "lawyers, activists, paralegals, and former judges," she writes, "justice was conceptualized as a long-term project and their role in it as a civic duty . . . and change needed to take place within the justice system and the community."[49] The duality of law is about recognizing

164   SOUTH SUDAN'S FATEFUL STRUGGLE

that there are complementary opposites within the justice system, that is, that the rule by law that we discussed in the prior chapter, cannot stand on its own or exist separately from the rule of law. The rule by law is how abusive political power determines the extent to which political leaders control and apply the law to serve their own interests. Yet if self-serving political power ultimately justifies how the law is or is not applied, then there is little way to show how power can be properly exercised in accordance with the rule of law. The idea is that civil-society organizations perform multiple tasks in promoting peace processes, even if they do not have a seat at the negotiating table. Their ultimate role, it could be said, is to assist the people with coping with the effects of war and in becoming self-sufficient and resourceful. In some cases, this has meant assisting and restoring agricultural crops impacted by the fighting. Simon Buony, the Program Director of Nile Hope, a local NGO, indicated that his organization regularly goes out into the countryside to provide villagers with new, enhanced seeds and methods (i.e., crop rotation) designed to increase their yields.[50]

CSOs have also sought more creative and active ways of assisting the people. For instance, "Anataban" (translated "I am tired") is an arts-based youth campaign started in 2016 in response to the civil war in South Sudan. It uses graffiti, sculpture, and poetry as the basis for discussion of social injustice and accountability. Since 2016, it has produced songs and dances intended to revitalize ordinary citizens tired of the effects of war, that is, being marginalized, disempowered, and abused. Culture and creative arts have in this sense become the vehicle for citizens to overcome their psychological trauma caused by the civil war. The movement's success encompasses the work of international NGOs such as Common Ground—which began operations in South Sudan in 2005—to devise and fund scripted radio programs (radio still reaches the most people in South Sudan). Common Ground runs a weekly radio program that reaches civilians in all 10 states and provides weekly forums for victims to discuss their experiences. The weekly programs routinely address issues, such as peacebuilding, gender-based violence, child conscription, and youth unemployment, and allow listeners to voice their opinion and comments on these issues.

One of Common Grounds' most popular weekly radio programs depicts a woman police officer in her struggle to serve and protect the traumatized people. "The show," according to Kenneth Ganna, the Program Manager of Common Ground, "was special because it allowed women, girls and even men, to identify most with the plight of those trying to uphold peace and order in the streets." "The popularity of the show," he added, "came as a surprise, but it showed just how necessary it was to depict the role of security officials in protecting the basic rights and needs of women." Security in this context has made the ordinary citizen acutely aware of their tribal identity and how it has been (mis)used to fracture national identity. South Sudan's national symbols, including its flag, anthem,

Photo 6.1 A Sign for Peace on a soccer field in Aweil.

and pride in its national sport teams—such as its soccer and basketball team—still inform patriotic sentiment in the country (Photo 6.1). But sports can only go so far in promoting the cohesion of national identity. To secure such sentiment, an integrated security force is also needed.

The Price of Peace and Security

The problem was that tribal identity remained a source of recruitment. The leaders relied on this source to boost the number of troops in their militias. Yet it stood in conflict with their commitment to end child conscription, as they attempted to work toward an integrated armed force. The delays associated with this process stemmed from the parties' fears of insecurity in Juba. For Machar, the fear was personal. He had already been driven out of Juba in July 2016, after he refused to send his troops to the cantonment for retraining; many remained part of a specialized SPLM-IO force that was meant to protect Machar. When R-ARCSS was signed in September 2018, Kiir still failed to offer any guarantee for Machar's safety, and neither IGAD, UNMISS, nor the United States took any measures to resolve the situation. Machar eventually returned in late October

166 SOUTH SUDAN'S FATEFUL STRUGGLE

2018, but only after Kiir ordered the release of his advisor and spokesman for the SPLM-IO.[51] The standoff was yet another reminder of the wariness of revitalizing peace and security in South Sudan.

To diminish the wariness, efforts were made to reintegrate the ex-combatants back into society. For its part, the national government reconstituted its Disarmament, Demilitarization, and Reintegration program in September 2019. Kiir appointed Aysen Aler Jangroor, a former SPLA general who had fought alongside Garang in the 1980s, to head the commission. By January 2020, the R-DDR had managed to reintegrate 3,226 ex-combatants into society, which included financial benefits as well as working closely with families to enable them to accept and take in ex-combatants.[52] But the R-DDR ran up against a similar problem experienced by the CPA's DDR, which was largely focused on reintegrating soldiers from rebel militia forces back into the SPLA. Its officials lacked the skills and resources, that is, psychological counseling, to reinte-grate many of the former child soldiers. The CPA-DDR, as we saw in Chapter 3, retrained and reintegrated a large number of soldiers into the SPLA. Many of them were Nuer who helped to dramatically boost the number of SPLA soldiers, just in time for the vote on the referendum. The problem was that the SPLA remained largely nonprofessionalized and susceptible to the forces of ethnic fac-tionalism. And no amount of imposed discipline could make up for the lack of uniform rules and procedures for engagement. This eventually led the AUCISS to conclude that the unity of Dinka and Nuer soldiers in the SPLA was a façade, and that it risked stoking Dinka concerns that the Nuer would use their mili-tary clout to seize control of the government.[53] For the R-DDR to address this problem, then, it needed more resources to help build the NUF.

However, much of the money was still being used to pay the high salaries of officials, including nearly 700 generals. And it still was not clear how many shadow officers remained on the payroll. The parties to the RTGoNU had agreed to end these wasteful practices. But it soon became apparent that the parties wanted the same thing: more security or their own military power to influence the outcomes of the peace process. They were still, in effect, engaged with "pay-roll peace," which describes the process of placing more recruits on the payroll as a means of offering incentives to negotiate and bargain for peace. The process dated back to the earlier attempts to reintegrate the SPLA at the end of the in-terim period, when the number of army personnel reached 240,000—yet with little way of verifying who was active or not. In the case of the NUF, UKAID concluded that "given the real political incentives at work, immediate loyalty will trump professionalization."[54] Doubts thus remained concerning where sol-dier loyalty lied. Was it in the ethnic community or the nation state; and would the NUF create a place for streamlining that loyalty via rules of procedure and engagement, especially if ethnic identity competed with, rather than trumped

professionalization? Either way, it was difficult to see an underfunded NUF escaping the effects of tribal factionalism.

Still, there were some early, promising signs of the NUF's formation. In early April 2020, it was reported that approximately 78,500 army soldiers had registered at the cantonment sites, and 45,000 had been approved for training.[55] As of the writing of this book, the numbers are still too low to operationalize the NUF. The political parties, it seem, are still the product of a militarized society in which owing guns and mobilizing military power is the primary assurance of preserving one's political power. There is what Mamdani alludes to as the reflexive legitimacy of holding arms. "The political order created under the CPA," he writes, "was not a dictatorship of a single party so much as a dictatorship of all armed groups; it legitimized any group bearing arms."[56] Indeed, several of the political parties continue to maintain a militia, or at least ties to one, to buttress their bargaining power.

Donor Frustration: The US, UN, and Nongovernmental Organizations

This sense of insecurity might explain the gloom and doom in Juba in the weeks leading up the formation of the RTGoNU. In early February 2020, the peace process had reached a tense standstill because of Kiir's unwillingness to rescind the presidential state decree.[57] The February 22 deadline marked the end of a 100-day extension for implementing R-ARCSS. And no one, it seemed, was in the mood to seek another extension, or to be blamed for failing to meet it. By now, many international actors had made their demands clear: they would drop all support for South Sudan. The EU, for example, announced that if an agreement was not worked out, it would review its policies in the country and punish any parties responsible for human rights atrocities. The AU by comparison insisted that it would hold consultations among the C8 (including Algeria, Chad, Nigeria, Rwanda, and South Africa), the guarantors of R-ARCSS, to discuss how to proceed with or without the issue resolved.[58]

The political stakes, then, could not be higher. If the deadline was not met, chaos would ensue. Some of the people spoke of a mass uprising against the corrupt political leaders. Joseph Bakosoro, for example, indicated that failure to meet the February 22 deadline would be a tipping point for the people to take to the streets, where "metal drums containing weapons had already begun to be placed."[59] The call-to-arms message raised an important question: Were the people, who had been oppressed and marginalized for so many years, prepared to carry out such a task? Would a spontaneous uprising convince the leaders to leave or change the status quo system of corruption? Some of the

168   SOUTH SUDAN'S FATEFUL STRUGGLE

biggest skeptics of a people's uprising were not the government officials but civil society advocates. For Lorna Merekaje, the Secretary General of South Sudan Democratic Engagement Monitoring and Observation Program, it was unrealistic to expect, much less support, such a movement, "since it would lack the critical organized mass to produce any desired result." "Too many people," she said, "have remained unaware of their rights or are simply too disengaged to carry out a revolution on a scale like that of the June 3 (2019) protestors in Sudan," which ultimately ousted Omar Hassan Bashir and led to the transitional government's announcement in February 2022 that it would surrender him to the International Criminal Court in The Hague.[60]

The only real alternative was to reform the system and implement R-ARCSS one step at a time. But first, the leaders would have to avoid the impending implosion of the peace process, which is why Kiir, as mentioned at the outset, finally went against the advice of the Jieng Council and agreed to rescind the 32-state solution. The leaders also had to contend with donor fatigue, including how the shift in priority from nation-state building to humanitarian emergency assistance led to the decision by powerful countries such as the United States to drop much of its financial support of the national government. From 2016 to 2020, USAID, for instance, was required to focus more of its strategic programming on local initiatives such as community resilience and civil society engagement. In this way, the United States' disengagement from the national government had helped buoy civil society. Still, it came at a cost, namely, the United States' reduced ability and willingness to influence the peace process. By early January 2020, the United States still had yet to appoint a special envoy to help broker the peace process. With tensions rising in Juba, it finally appointed Stuart Symington, a retired Ambassador, as the special envoy on January 21, 2020.[61]

A week later, the US Treasury Department announced that it would impose sanctions on the Vice President, Taban Deng Gai, the first time a sitting cabinet minister had been targeted. The action sent a clear signal to Kiir: the failure to meet the February 22 deadline would lead to more individual economic punishment. Yet this also raised the question of whether the ramped-up punishment by the Trump administration would have any desired effect. It was easy to forget that Kiir and Machar were once avid supporters of Trump's presidential candidacy in 2016. Machar, in fact, stated that "Trump's lack of knowledge of South Sudan," was to him, "a blessing."[62] But Trump never openly embraced the two like he did Egypt's President, Fattah el-Sisi, and other middle eastern strongmen. Coddling and supporting authoritarian leaders of Sub-Saharan Africa, in short, was never a priority of Trump, who at one time referred to African nations as "shitholes."

For Trump, punishment was not a means of defending the values of democracy and human rights, but a self-justifying end in itself. For example, when he

renewed a 2014 executive order on March 27, 2017—declaring South Sudan a national emergency—he likely saw it as a way of intimidating the national government and teaching the leaders a political lesson. In effect, his coercive threat had become an end-all for resolving South Sudan's problems, including the threat of cutting off all financial support to the country. It seemed like a case of justifying power for its own sake rather than using US values (e.g., human rights and democracy) to shape the peace process in a positive and coherent manner.

Trump's hardline approach also ended up exposing the contradictions of his administration's foreign policy in South Sudan. For example, when Nikki Haley, the former US Ambassador to the UN, traveled to South Sudan in October 2017 to consult the leaders, she seemed uninterested in meeting with civil society leaders. Despite her rhetoric of promoting human rights, she hewed a hardline approach that eventually excluded civil society actors. Unsurprisingly, hostile protests erupted outside the UN compound in response to her failure to meet with any civil society or opposition groups. Haley's strategy was to place all the blame on the leaders. This was made clear in her speech delivered to the UN in April 2017, where she declared that "the famine in South Sudan is man-made . . . and the result of an apparent campaign against the civilian population"[63] Michele Sison, the UN Deputy Ambassador, even went so far as to insist "The famine is not a result of drought, it is the result of leaders more interested in political power and personal gain than in stopping violence"[64] These stern words, though, failed to get the leaders to curb their abuses and comply with US demands. In fact, the leaders decided to increase the access fee for humanitarian workers a hundredfold, from $100 to $10,000.[65]

Trump's strategy in the end remained unpredictable and incoherent. Just one month after the parties to R-ARCSS agreed to a 100-day extension to the peace agreement in October 2019, the Trump administration pulled the US Ambassador, Thomas Hushek, from South Sudan. It stated that Ambassador Hushek needed to return to Washington to be debriefed on issues related to the peace process. But for many, the action signaled Trump's willingness to castigate and disparage his diplomatic officials for the slow pace of the peace process. Hushek, however, would return to South Sudan three weeks later, two months ahead of the start of the formation of the RTGoNU.

Conclusion

The approval of R-ARCSS in February 2020 brought many welcome changes. It gave a voice and bargaining power to more parties, brought pressure to bear on ending the 32-state decree, and appeared to promise a unified armed force. Yet the political stakes of approving a new transitional government of national unity

170 SOUTH SUDAN'S FATEFUL STRUGGLE

could not have been higher, and many feared that, unless resolved, stalemate would lead South Sudan back to civil war and extreme violence in many regions, particularly in the Greater Upper Nile and Ruwek area. Still, without the inclusion of civil society actors, it was difficult to embrace its revitalizing effect, or how the country could come together and hold future peaceful democratic elections.

For its part, the UN Security Council voted to approve extending resolution 2428 on May 30, 2020, which included an arms embargo on South Sudan and targeted individual leaders, and extended the mandate of the UN Panel Experts. There was still the question of whether Trump's hardline policy was effective in pressuring South Sudan's leaders to act. Naturally, there was no way to know, but by early 2020, it was clear that the failure to implement the peace agreement had emerged as perhaps the greatest threat to Kiir's political survival.

In the end, it was unclear how the road to peace and justice would end in South Sudan. For too long, international donors had thrown money at South Sudan and imposed their programmatic ideals on the country, allowing the elites to enrich themselves. Donor fatigue was bound to set in. Yet with the creation of the RTGoNU came the ever-present and precious hope of long-term peace and finally tackling many of the country's underlying challenges.

7

A Transitional Government and the Prospects for Peace and National Unity

In late February 2020, Kiir swore in Machar once again as the first Vice President and declared, "For the people of South Sudan, I want to assure you that we will work together to end your suffering." "This day," he added, "marked the official end of the war and we can declare a new dawn of peace . . . which will never be shaken ever again."[1] The announcement came on the heels of high-level talks and a visit to the Vatican, where Pope Francis kissed Kiir's and Machar's feet, exhorting them to end the human suffering in the country. It's difficult to know just how much the Pope's symbolic gesture influenced Kiir's decision to cancel his presidential state decree, especially given that the Pope was not an active player in the peace talks. Yet it is hard to downplay its part in inspiring Kiir to break the impasse that threatened to return the country to war.

After the parties finally approved the RTGoNU in February 2020, Kiir promptly appointed his new Council of Ministers and set into motion policies for decamping (in Juba) and retraining soldiers to serve in the NUF. But building an integrated national security force, as mentioned in Chapter 6, faced continuing hurdles, which included the availability of resources (e.g., guns and ammunition) to train the troops in their cantonments. To make matters worse, there was a spike in intercommunal fighting in the countryside in mid-2020, primarily in Central Equatoria and in the Jonglei state, where the NAS carried out attacks on government troops and civilians. Such challenges complicated efforts to implement the provisions of R-ARCSS within a three-year period, including holding democratic elections at the end of the transitional period in the spring of 2023 and adopting a permanent constitution in April 2022.

Once again, time had become an issue. Would, for instance, the national government and the parties follow through with their commitments to implement these mechanisms? Or would conditions prevent their implementation and cause further delay? When the parties failed to reach agreement on the Transitional Security Arrangement (TSA)—a mechanism designed to stabilize the country—there was fear that the elections could trigger violence. Although Kiir tried to dampen such fear by insisting that the RTGoNU would meet its

South Sudan's Fateful Struggle. Steven C. Roach, Oxford University Press. © Oxford University Press 2023.
DOI: 10.1093/oso/9780190057848.003.0008

172   SOUTH SUDAN'S FATEFUL STRUGGLE

goal, Machar remained unconvinced, claiming that the country would lack the needed security arrangement to hold fair and safe elections. By August 2022, the parties had announced that elections would be moved back to 2024.

The delay was the latest setback in implementing R-ARCSS. And it was difficult to lay all the blame on the government, which had to tackle COVID-19 by closing the country's borders and borrowing money from the International Monetary Fund and World Bank to offset the drop in value of the South Sudanese pound (SSP) caused by the outbreak. South Sudan, in fact, saw its daily production of oil of 250,000 barrels drop to 180,000, which soon forced it to unlock its gold reserves to address the growing number of food insecure, which reached nearly 6.3 million people in 2020, leaving millions on the brink of starvation.[2]

At the same time, the government confronted growing intercommunal violence in Jonglei and Warrup, which complicated the return of South Sudanese refugees to South Sudan. Making matters worse was the largest locust invasion in the country in the summer of 2020, which devastated much of the agricultural fields in the southeastern region of the country.

Given South Sudan's many challenges of achieving stability and implementing R-ARCSS, the RTGoNU appears to represent yet another failed attempt to transition to democracy and peace. There of course is the issue of meeting a tight timeline, but this is not the main cause of the delay or likely failure. Rather, it is the ever-present threat of violence that continues to disrupt the transition to democracy and long-term peace. Brute governance, as we discussed in Chapter 4, is what allows corruption and militarization to persist. Achieving peace therefore may have less to do with the promises to transition to peace and democracy than with actually transitioning away from the country's brute governance. The latter, in other words, is a precondition for realizing the former. And it raises the question of how the RTGoNU is yet another example of a fractured consensus that reinforces brute governance, and if an integrative approach to governance— which seeks a concerted balance of justice, accountability, peace, and democratic mechanisms—can ever be achieved. The fact that the ruling national elite continues to repress civil society in the peace process indicates the deep and sustained link between exclusion and governance. After addressing many of the challenges underlying this problem, I will offer various ideas and strategies regarding what I call an "integrative social contract," as well as the proper alignment of regional politics with long-term peace.

The Reconstituted Transitional Unity Government

The announcement of the new revitalized transitional unity government on February 22 was met with little rejoicing or celebration. Most people, it seemed,

were relieved to see the parties settle their differences and proceed with forming the transitional government of national unity. In having made a major concession to the other parties, Kiir now had to convince these parties that he was serious about implementing R-ARCSS. He could ill-afford delays that had plagued the implementation of ARCSS, and that allowed tensions to build. But COVID-19 and party infighting, that is, resistance by the SPLM-IO, made the task difficult and burdensome, leaving many to wonder if South Sudan was doomed to repeat the mistakes of its past. The Jieng Council, for instance, declared that corruption was responsible for the "crisis of political leadership," in which both Kiir and Machar could no longer be trusted to implement the peace process.[3] The main challenge, for many, was establishing a consistent pace and rhythm of implementing R-ARCSS.

The first two weeks of the implementation process proved to be fast-paced. It saw Kiir appoint 34 new ministers and 10 deputy ministers, which included Angela Teny (the spouse of Vice President Machar), who was appointed Defense Minister, and Beatrice Wani, Foreign Minister.[4] The early progress convinced David Shearer, the Special Representative to the Secretary General and Head of UNMISS, that Kiir and Machar were putting "their country's interests over their own" and demonstrating that "peace also requires courage."[5] Shearer also stressed the UN's role and announced that UNMISS would devote more resources for investing in the rule of law and mobilizing more peacekeepers. "Our action," he stated, "can push South Sudan further towards sustainable peace; our inaction can also help condemn it to failure."[6]

But many civil society groups remained skeptical. Betty Sunday, the Director of Women's Monthly Forum, was one of the civil society members who briefed the Security Council meeting on March 4. She made it clear that the cabinet and council of ministers still had not met the 35 percent threshold of gender representation stipulated in R-ARCSS. Her biggest concern was that there still was no unifying political vision for peace. "How," she asked, "can we have peace when the government has no political vision of peace to steer us toward justice?" When I talked with her, she mentioned that government torture and killings were so pervasive that the evidence of atrocities had to be sneaked out of the country to neighboring countries where it remained with international lawyers. As a strong proponent of criminal justice, she insisted that injustices and corruption continued to stymie democratic equality.[7]

Her other concern was that political leaders were deliberately delaying the adoption of the permanent constitution (and its codification of minimal threshold of 35 percent representation of women). The leaders' plan, in her view, was to use these delays to delegitimize the process, assuming that a new constitution could be adopted. Whether or not this was true, Kiir remained the linchpin between the RTGoNU and a future GoNU, and the one responsible for

moving South Sudan toward elections and the rule of law. The hope of course was that forward momentum would pressure Kiir to set aside his own misgivings and adopt a permanent constitution within the given timeline, or by April 2022 (which has yet to happen as of the writing of this book in December 2022). Once the permanent constitution replaced the troubled Transitional Constitution, it could finally do what the Transitional Constitution had not: offer an effective checks and balances system and stimulate a collective and individual sense of civic duty among representatives. It would in this respect provide the basis for rules, principles, and norms of governance, linking the will of the people with the democratic pluralism of R-ARCSS.

The process of drafting the permanent constitution involved considerable consultation with the people and mediation by committees. All of this was designed to avert the shortcomings of the Transitional Constitution and to bring it in line with the principles of R-ARCSS. But the effort also involved working out many issues, including the powers of the executive and judiciary, and explicating the terms of a federated structure of government. The NCAC, as discussed in Chapter 6, was in charge of consulting the people on these issues because of its mandate of incorporating R-ARCSS into a Comprehensive Amendment Bill. When it completed its work, it had made changes to 124 amendments and submitted the CAB to the national government. The government responded with its own changes to the bill, which included the deletion of "supremacy" and the insertion of new language that stipulated that elections would be pursuant to the Transitional Constitution.[8] These changes, however, came after the NCAC had completed its work, which meant that the NCAC still needed to reincorporate these changes (it had deemed the exclusion of some of its changes as a violation of its mandate). Complicating its task further was the fact that its mandate was provisional; it was set to expire on February 22, 2022.

The government's decision not to renew its mandate prompted some members of the NCAC to write directly to IGAD to pressure the national government to renew the mandate. But IGAD refused to do so, and in the end, the NCAC was unable to complete its task of reviewing all these changes to the CAB. By the fall of 2021, the national government had made mostly procedural and administrative changes. The slow pace of implementation had also led to growing tensions that threatened the stability of the RTGoNU.

Security Challenges

By early 2021, many former SPLM-IO soldiers had either defected to the SSPDF or formed their own militias to oppose the SPML-IO. Much of the dissension stemmed from Machar's decision in January 2021 to withdraw the nomination of

General Johnson Olony—a Shilluk fighter who defected to the SPLM-IO in 2015 and was later accused by several human rights organizations of perpetrating human rights atrocities—to serve as the Governor of the Nile Upper State. Kiir though expressed his deep concern with Olony, who he considered a "warmonger" and a threat to the RTGoNU. He demanded that Machar sign a written statement that would hold him accountable, should Olony break the truce.[9] Machar rejected Kiir's demand and threatened to withhold all his nominees to local government and state commissions unless Kiir nominated Olony. The conflict soon led to a stalemate that lasted for several weeks. In January 2021, Machar tried to break the impasse by nominating Olony's deputy. whom Kiir preferred and then promptly nominated. Olony was bitterly disappointed and felt betrayed by Machar, who, in his view, had caved in to Kiir's demands.[10] A majority of Nuer agreed, believing Machar's concession amounted to an abandonment of the SPLM-IO's efforts to govern the Upper Nile state. This included several SPLM-IO commanders and fighters, who subsequently defected to the SSPDF, with some electing to form their own splinter groups (e.g., a contingency of Lou Nuer in the Upper Nile region). Marginalized by Machar's decision, they accused him of poor leadership and of selling out to Kiir. The SPLA-IO thus ended up losing entire divisions of their army. In Central Equatoria, for example, the Tafeng Division task force of SPLA -IO, which was under the command of Brigadier General Kennedy Ongie Odong, soon joined Thomas Cirillo's NAS. Commander Ongie roundly criticized Machar by claiming that "we are not working for self-interest, we are sacrificing for the population and future generations and we want development, not destruction."[11] Indeed, the growing perception among most Nuer was that Machar was simply too self-interested to lead the Nuer people; that most of his decisions were made for personal reasons and not for welfare of the Nuer people.

Kiir also used government resources to further weaken Machar. By offering economic and political incentives to SPLM-IO fighters to join the SSPDF, he had contributed to a growing exodus of SPLA-IO fighters. Kiir paid any SPLM-IO commander and/or fighter to defect to the SSPDF. The monetary incentives included increases in salary, revenue increases, and added security personnel to administer the resources of acquired land. Kiir's monetary strategy was designed to divide the SPLA-IO. For example, in Central Equatoria, Major General Lukojo, a former SPLA-IO commander, exercised control over an area that stretched from Central Equatoria to Uganda, and where he traded in teak and mahogany and collected tax revenue. The national government was reportedly able to bribe the SPLM-IO warlord by offering him increased control over land in exchange for loyalty to the government. The additional income and tax revenue enabled him to self-finance much of his military operations and to attack SPLM-IO forces to secure more control over the territory.[12] Kiir's proxy attacks had thus managed to

176 SOUTH SUDAN'S FATEFUL STRUGGLE

diminish the influence of the SPLM-IO. His critics, though, were quick to point out that the attacks violated the Cessation of Hostilities Agreement by enabling the hostilities of defecting commanders.

Kiir was also criticized for failing to address the abuses of the NSS. Since the signing of R-ARCSS in 2018, the NSS had come under increasing scrutiny. There were more calls for holding NSS leaders accountable for human rights abuses. As pressure mounted, Lieutenant General Kuc, the head of International Security Bureau of the NSS, announced in January 2020 the creation of a commission to investigate these abuses and the repression of civil society groups. The commission was tasked with carrying out the procedure in the 2015 National Security Act, which required an investigation of the alleged abuses by NSS officials and to mete out punishment where needed. But Kuc never carried out his task. In fact, he brazenly carried out more arbitrary arrests and detentions of journalists and activists.[13]

Another issue was whether the national government could effectively disarm militants and former fighters (now civilians). With a largely ineffective national DDR, it had to rely on its armed forces to disarm former militants. This in turn created uncertainty and confusion about the government's ability to secure cooperation by the former fighters. For instance, in the Warrap state—which consists of a majority of Dinka and is the birthplace of President Kiir—the SSPDF attempted to disarm a group of civilians in the town of Tonj.[14] But the group refused to turn over their arms at a local market. When bystanders joined them, fighting erupted between the civilians and the soldiers, killing nearly 130 people, including 85 civilians and 45 soldiers. By the summer of 2021, intercommunal violence in the Jonglei state had spilled over into the Pibor Administrative Area, one of the newly established administrative areas under the RTGoNU's control.[15] In this case, the national government was simply unwilling or too poorly equipped and cash-strapped to contain, much less reduce, the violence. It was yet another reminder that Kiir lacked the resources to counter the factionalism within and outside the RTGoNU. His inability to resolve such conflicts only deepened concern with the slow pace of implementation of R-ARCSS.

Kiir's Slow Hand

In fact, it took Kiir nearly four months to appoint state governors and ministers. And it wasn't until June 2020 that he finally appointed state governors for eight of the ten states and chief administrators for the Pibor, Ruweng, and Abyei areas. Although the SPOA and SPLM/A-IO had waited for Kiir to act, they eventually announced their own appointees for state governor in the Jonglei and the Upper Nile State. Under R-ARCSS, both parties were entitled to appoint one governor

A TRANSITIONAL GOVERNMENT 177

in each of these states. However, Kiir reserved the power to reject any appointee who did not meet the standard of good conduct, which for the most part, meant no reports of human rights atrocities or convictions for corruption or both. Few had expected Kiir to invoke such power given the fragility of the RTGoNU and the pervasiveness of human rights atrocities that seemed to implicate many of the leaders. So when Kiir finally did invoke the rule to reject Machar's first appointee, Johnson Olony, for human rights abuses, it not only delayed the appointment in the Greater Upper Nile state but also led to accusations that he was seeking to deflect attention away from his own culpability of human rights violations.

Kiir thus found himself in a difficult predicament. To keep the implementation process on track, he also had to make choices that slowed its pace. The expectation for the RTGoNU was that it would be fair and all inclusive, and that traditionally marginalized sectors of the population would finally be able to shape governmental affairs. Yet among the 10 appointees to state governor, only one was a woman. Kiir had clearly failed to meet the 35 percent threshold for female representation mandated by R-ARCSS. For his opponents, this amounted to a clear-cut violation of R-ARCSS; they demanded that he reconsider his decision.[16]

But Kiir never did. The 10 appointments remained in place, which for many was an apparent sign that Kiir wanted to avoid any further delays and restore stability to the entire country. Augustino Ting Mayai, an analyst at the Sudd Institute, stressed that "the lead priority for the new governors is restoring security at state and subnational levels."[17] However, Kiir's decision to reject Olony only seemed to stoke tensions between the government and the SPLM-IO. The issue this raised was whether Kiir was justified in using his position of strength to reject a warmonger, or if he was simply appeasing international concerns while also appealing to his political base. Even if he saw a political opportunity to divide and weaken the SPLM-IO (and Machar by extension), it was difficult to see what he would gain from the move, especially since it would lead more militias to potentially oppose the RTGoNU. The only way to deal with the issue was to appoint more government officials in accordance with R-ARCSS procedure.

By late February 2021, Kiir had managed to appoint state ministers and county commissioners in five of the 10 states, including the Upper Nile, Warrap, Unity, Central Equatoria, and Northern Bahr al Ghazal.[18] Although the government was still behind schedule, the appointments were seen as progress. Three months later, Kiir dissolved the National Assembly in order to reconstitute the Transitional National Legislative Assembly. He appointed James Wani Igga to serve as the Speaker of the Assembly and the R-TNLA, which had increased its number of seats from 400 to 550 members. Under R-ARCSS, the SPLM-Government was allotted 332 members, the SPLM-IO 128, the South Sudan Opposition Alliance 50, the former detainees 10 members, and other political parties 30.[19] Reconstituting the TNLA was crucial to implementing a permanent

178   SOUTH SUDAN'S FATEFUL STRUGGLE

constitution. But adopting it ultimately depended on integrating the security forces.

A Unified Army

The formation of the Necessary Unified Forces (NUF) was intended to take place before the official approval of the TGoNU. Yet there were problems from the start, which included persistent rogue militia attacks on the government and insufficient funding of the cantonment and training sites. All of this led to increased food insecurity and diminished morale among the rank-and-file soldiers. There were also reports of garrisoned soldiers deserting the camps. The DDR process, which was supposed to support the NUF, had also been hampered by accusations of bias toward Dinka soldiers. The government eventually issued a public statement to affirm its commitment to the NUF, declaring that "the central priority is indicating the steps of the unity government, which included the deployment and cantonment of the NUF, improving its training facilities, and establishing central command structure for training and operating the force."[20]

Kiir then decreed the formation of the National Transitional Committee in February 2020, in order to better manage security arrangements. Together with the Ministry of Finance and Planning, the NTC promised to allocate $68.7 million for improving security arrangements.[21] Yet it was never clear just how much of the money had reached its targets. With much of the money earmarked for specific projects—including food and water at the cantonment sites, training the soldiers, and the accommodation of 485 delegates involved in the implementation of the security arrangement—it was difficult to track the money and verify the committee's information. The UN Panel of Experts, for instance, was only able to confirm that "the committee had paid $259,000 of a reported 10 million-dollar hotel bill, leading the hotel management to threaten eviction of the delegates."[22] There was, in short, a large amount of money that could not be accounted for, which amounted to lost resources for the NUF.

To alleviate the problem, Kiir made what was mostly a cosmetic change in April 2021, when he appointed General Santino Deng Wol as the new head of the SSPDF. Kiir's spokesman, Ateny Wek, attempted to play down the move as merely a reshuffling of military leadership. But supporters of Olony saw a double standard being applied to government appointees. Like Olony, Wol had committed atrocities in the Upper Nile state, which were equally, if not more, abhorrent than those committed by Otony (crimes ranging from torching civilians alive to mass rape). Kiir in this case seemed to apply a different standard when it came to justifying his own high-level appointments. In many ways, this complemented his underhanded efforts to diminish his opposition, including

his monetary policy of encouraging soldiers to defect. Although Kiir had managed to bolster the chain of command at the cantonment sites—where many of the soldiers were from the SPLM-IO—he had also paid lip service to the mutual restraint needed to hold together the delicate consensus of the RTGoNU.

There was yet another reason to doubt the national government's strategy and commitment to nationalizing the security forces: its lack of funding of the cantonment sites. The decision to restrict funding to the sites led many soldiers to desert and to join militias that could pay them more in bonus money from money collected from the illegal mining of gold and the sales of teak, mahogany, and charcoal. And yet, by incentivizing soldiers to rebel, the national government was helping to deplete natural resources while fueling more attacks on the civilian population. Its policies, then, were not only underhanded, they had also complicated the formation of the NUF and encouraged violence that violated the Cessation of Hostilities Agreement. The government's dubious strategy of speeding things up in this sense had actually slowed the pace of implementation.

Moral Accountability and Its Promises

Nowhere was this more evident than with the HCSS. Kiir, as we saw in Chapter 5, initially held up the EU's MoA in an apparent effort to block the court's implementation. He then issued his presidential decree on the number of states, which effectively muted discussion of the HCSS. On March 30, 2021, Kiir's cabinet finally approved the Commission for Truth, Healing and Reconciliation, the HCSS, and the Compensation and Reparations Authority.[23] The AU Commission soon announced its intention to work closely with South Sudanese authorities to review the atrocities committed during the civil war.

But many remained wary of their intention. The HCSS, after all, would be the first criminal court established by the African Union (and state). And there was concern if the African Union was ready and willing to help the court meet the fair and impartial standards of international criminal justice. The fact that so many of the perpetrators were current state leaders underscored the expected difficulties of the court's enforcing its arrest warrants. Why, then, would the African Union go to such lengths to prosecute when it still needed to work with some of the current leaders to enforce peace and security? Would the national government actually cooperate with court officials? With few assurances that the national government would follow through on its pledge to implement the court, it was not hard to see why the African Union was dragging its feet.

Still, the national leaders realized their precarious hold on power. Preserving their political survival was predicated in part on placating international authorities and donors, by making hollow pledges to promote accountability.

180 SOUTH SUDAN'S FATEFUL STRUGGLE

The question, however, was whether the ruling elite could agree to measures that would potentially lead to their being sentenced to prison. Ultimately, the solution, as we saw in Chapter 5, was to balance the dictates of their own political survival against potential prosecution. This is why human rights activists continued to insist that the African Union keep its skin in the game by retaining the option of administering its own ad hoc court to continue pressuring the government to implement the HCSS, while also making it harder for the leaders to survive politically.[24] The idea, in short, was to keep the option on the table until the leaders were literally forced to sign their own confession.

The African Union's other challenge was assigning equal priority to both the truth commission and war crimes court. This meant administering the truth commission first and the HCSS second, so that the HCSS could complement the work of the truth commission by drawing on its collected evidence (or testimony of victims) to prosecute the perpetrators. Another challenge was agreeing on the scope of the truth commission: namely, whether it would allow immunity for confession and have subpoena power like that of the South African Truth and Reconciliation Commission (SATRC). Would granting blanket immunity to some leaders preempt the HCSS's prosecutorial powers? As we saw in Chapter 5, Kiir seemed intent on using the truth commission to rule out the need for a hybrid war crimes court, and, in effect, gain immunity from prosecution. Machar, by comparison, expressed his conditional support for a hybrid war crimes court to advance long-term peace. Nyarji Roman, the deputy spokesman for SPLM-IO, stated that "If there is enough evidence that can link any one of our SPLM-IO members to any crimes against humanity, then we will hand them over to the court. We do not mind."[25] The words of "enough evidence" suggest that substantial evidence would be required to prove intent, particularly in the case of genocide—a crime subsumed under a state's plan to carry out the crime. The SPLM-IO in this case was counting on a claim of self-defense to justify its actions, a claim that assumed that any crime it had committed was intended to stop a regime from intentionally killing more civilians. But for some, this was nothing more than a bad faith effort to earn the trust of international actors and to gain legitimacy by politicizing justice.[26]

Kiir's eventual approval of the HCSS in January 2021 was thus seen as a ploy to placate international donors and to buy time—much like his decision to pass on signing the National Assembly's approval of the MoA. In this way, if he ends up getting cornered into implementing it, he can do what other abusive leaders have done in the past: default to state sovereignty and assert the state's right to be free of outside interference in hopes of mobilizing national opposition to the HCSS. The issue here is whether an approved and newly formed hybrid war crimes court can create the concurrent justification by a regional and national actor to meet the burden of administering hybrid justice. Several South Sudanese judges,

for instance, argued that the HCSS would infringe on South Sudan's sovereignty by violating R-ARCSS's chapter 5 provision stipulating that a majority of judges will represent "African States other than the Republic of South Sudan." Unlike the CTHR, in which South Sudan would sponsor the commission, the HCSS could bar the national government from overseeing the operations of the HCSS.

In sum, the CTHR alone cannot guarantee long-term peace and healing. The Security Council has made it clear that sustainable peace will come down to holding accountable those who have committed human rights atrocities. There is also evidence of strong civilian support for a war crimes court.[27] The hope, then, is that a war crimes court will finally help to isolate the guilt of leaders from the communities they had ravaged, and in doing so, deter would-be perpetrators from wantonly attacking their own civilians.

COVID-19 Crisis and the Government's Response

Like all other countries, South Sudan has had to confront the effects of COVID-19. In February 2020, as the COVID-19 infection rate surged in China, few (including myself) thought that COVID-19 could ever reach South Sudan. Everyone at this time was preoccupied with the fast approaching deadline of the 100-day extension of R-ARCSS. But by mid-March, COVID-19 had posed one of the gravest threats to South Sudan, which lacked the resources to mount a concerted response to the coronavirus. To help South Sudan meet some of its most basic needs, the US government provided nearly $17 million to assist South Sudan's government.[28]

In confronting the threat of COVID-19, the national government had adopted a zero-tolerance approach. This meant a national lockdown, or closing its internal and external borders, shops, offices, and Juba International Airport. It had hoped to avoid what many developed countries, including the United States, were facing at the time: a surge of COVID-19 patients into their hospitals. With its rudimentary healthcare system—where there were only four modern ventilators in the country, one less, as some joked, than the number of vice presidents in the national unity government—it stood little chance of ever recovering. In fact, there was fear that the government would soon collapse and trigger a mass exodus of national elites and prominent civilians. David Shearer pointed out that COVID-19 was bound to lead to a devasting number of deaths, "likely greater than the loss of life from COVID itself," given that it would disrupt the supply of medicine and vaccines for malaria and pneumonia.[29]

Unsurprisingly, South Sudan saw an increase in its infectious rate across the country. And it was not the sort of increase that developed countries had experienced. In fact, South Sudan's lack of infrastructure and technical expertise (in

182   SOUTH SUDAN'S FATEFUL STRUGGLE

terms furnishing reliable data), and severe poverty had the effect of suppressing the transmission rate of COVID-19. Undaunted, UNMISS took steps to head off any potential crisis by further equipping hospitals with the needed supplies in the ten states, while NGOs offered additional staff to support these efforts. The United Nations also took added measures to ensure the safety of peacekeepers and humanitarian workers. In striking a balance between offering hands-on care and keeping staff safe from the effects of COVID-19, the United Nations (and other agencies) relied on the government to collect the data on infection rates. The trouble, however, was that the national government lacked the resources to furnish accurate numbers. What's more, civilians risked being stigmatized by the disease which, in preventing them from working, would mean the loss of pecuniary wages and food insecurity. This may have explained the under-reported number of cases inside the country. In August 2020, for example, the number of reported cases stood at 2,200, which included such notables as Minister John Luk Jok, Machar, Angelina Teny, and James Wagi Igga.[30] A year later, there were only 10,400 cases reported, which led some to think that the actual number was much higher, especially given that testing was sparse and unreliable in the country.

In April 2020, Kiir established a High-Level Task force to address the risks and perils of the spread of the coronavirus. The committee was tasked with devising guidelines for containing the virus and redressing its effects. For some, the taskforce provided a welcome initiative to deal aggressively with the disease and to ensure that its effects did no unduly hinder the implementation of the RTGoNU. The restrictions included closing down houses of worship and restricting regional travel. Yet with pressure mounting, Kiir finally ended the lock down in early May 2020, lifting several of the restrictions on regional travel. Critics argued that he had reopened the economy too early. The South Sudan Doctors' Union, for example, contended that he had ignored scientific advice and catered to his political advisors on the taskforce, even though one of the stated objectives of the taskforce was to base its policy recommendations on scientific data and consensus.[31]

By late May 2020, Kiir replaced the taskforce with a second, high-level one—a reconstituted a High-Level Task Force consisting of national committee of 13 government officials, mostly ministers. The move helped to silence most of his critics and to placate international donors who had grown concerned about the threat posed by COVID-19 to their workers. Yet the revitalized task force did little to address the lack of transparency and faulty data gathering. South Sudan still lacked the mechanisms to enforce standard guidelines, such as social distancing, contact tracing, and masking.

To make peace with the virus, then, Kiir stressed the need for vigilance and resilience, insisting that "Covid-19 was here to stay with us."[32] But by the late summer of 2020, South Sudan found itself cash-strapped. It urged international

A TRANSITIONAL GOVERNMENT   183

donors to defray the costs of containing the coronavirus. The International Monetary Fund (IMF) responded by working through its Rapid Credit Facility to provide South Sudan a $52.3 million loan. Part of the loan was used to pay for the medical needs and the salaries of government officials (for June and July). An even larger portion was spent on auctioning US dollars to foreign exchange bureaus in the hopes of controlling the price on goods. In fact, the Panel of Experts on South Sudan reported that nearly 2 million dollars was being auctioned off weekly at "the exclusion of commercial banks from the weekly auctions has limited the effectiveness of the auctions in lowering inflation and closing the gap between the official exchange rate and the black market rate."[33] The black market, in short, was distorting the actual cost of fighting the spread of the coronavirus.

Reports also indicated an increasing black market for COVID-19 negative tests that involved travel through the country. An investigation conducted by the *New Humanitarian* found that "$3.8 million was awarded to a company to procure medical equipment and renovate the infectious disease hospital—work that was done but failed to meet the standards of an infectious disease unit."[34] With South Sudan still heavily dependent on international assistance, this seemed to confirm everyone's worst suspicion: that the national government could not be trusted to stop the spread of the coronavirus. COVID-19 seemed to collude with the system of corruption to create more government dysfunction in terms of an ineffective response to stopping the virus. More importantly, the struggle to contain the spread of the coronavirus helped slow down the implementation of R-ARCSS. But precisely how much of this delaying was due to COVID-19, and not the poor corrupt management of the leaders, remained uncertain. Yet what mattered for the parties of the RTGoNU was the political uncertainty and hardship caused by COVID-19. The coronavirus had ultimately become an unwanted ally in the struggle to stave off reform, an ally that threatened the political status quo.

Oil Revenue and Construction

There was little denying the economic impact of COVID-19 on South Sudan's economy. Not only did it drive down oil prices by reducing global demand, but it also greatly hampered plans for current infrastructure projects. The oil ministry stated that it would need nearly $1.5 million to invest in oil production machinery—much of which had been destroyed during the civil war—in order to make the oil sector more efficient and cost effective.[35] Prior to the civil war, South Sudan had been producing nearly 350,00 barrels of oil per day. But the war reduced pre-war production levels by over 60 percent. And it was not until

184   SOUTH SUDAN'S FATEFUL STRUGGLE

September 2018 that the oil industry began to recover by adopting plans to increase production from 150,000 to 175,000 barrels per day and to reach 400,000 by 2022.[36]

South Sudan's government continued to count on sustained levels of its oil revenue to fund its planned public projects. Yet the lack of transparency and shady practices, that is, prepayment for oil, forced it to sell much of its oil below market rates. The difference between market and concessionary rates resulted in the loss of millions of dollars and led the government to fall into arrears on several of its contracts.[37] The prepayment approach, as we saw in Chapter 4, required little oversight and was ultimately difficult to audit.

Still, the RTGoNU managed to return peace to many parts of the country and rekindle earlier plans for road construction hatched in 2012, which had called for investing $4 billion in roads that would stretch from Juba to Malakal and from eastern South Sudan to Kenya.[38] The money was expected to come directly from oil revenue.[39] In February 2019, the national government announced that it would allocate 10,000 barrels a day to fund roads from Juba to Terekeka, Yirol, and also Rumbek, thus connecting the Unity, Upper Nile, Western Bahr al Ghazal, and Warrup states.[40] Two months later, the number would increase to 30,000 barrels a day. Under the terms of the new contract, the national government would send the oil revenue directly to a Chinese account owned by the Chinese firm Shandong Hi-Sped Group. The plan was to deposit the money directly into a special account in hopes that it would provide an efficient and cost-effective transfer of money. While the direct deposit promised to reduce transactional costs, it violated R-ARCSS which stipulated that all oil revenue be deposited first with the Central Bank. The decision to send the revenue directly to a special fund thus renewed concerns about accountability and transparency, as outside observers remained unable to verify the transfers, or how the money was being spent.[41] Furthermore, the Chinese government's investment strategy in South Sudan still appeared to be based on maintaining the political status quo, not on R-ARCSS.

Another issue concerned the severe environmental effects of extracting and producing the oil. Since 2012, the government largely ignored the environmental impact of oil production facilities in the Greater Upper Nile and Unity states, including reports of oil leaking into the soils that contaminated the groundwater and released toxins into the White Nile (the reports stretched back to 2013). A 2013 environmental impact report, for instance, showed that the oil leaking from the pipelines was causing high concentrations of mercury and manganese in the soil. The high levels of the chemicals were believed to be the cause of the increasing number of miscarriages and still births in the Pibor Administrative Area and the Greater Upper Nile state.[42] Although the national government was aware of the oil leaks, it chose to ignore the problem. Eventually,

its inaction forced the people to drink from white containers with toxins residing in a chemical demulsifier used to separate crude oil from water. The truth of the government's neglect, though, would not remain a secret for long.

In April 2020, the Hope for Humanity Africa (H4HA) a South Sudanese NGO, filed an injunction against the government with the East African Court of Justice. The court determined that the government's neglect was responsible for the environmental damage caused by repeated oil spills in the northern part of the country and ordered the government to address the leak. The court's decision was closely followed by many in the area. In September 2020, local citizens living around the Palouch and Melut oil fields in the Greater Upper Nile came together to demonstrate Dar Petroleum's operations. They blocked access to their offices and the airstrip used by company officials and prevented the officials from leaving the facilities. Their stated aim was to call attention to the effects of the leaking oil on the water supply, which meant pressuring the national government to comply with the Petroleum Revenue Management Act, in particular the obligation to invest 3 percent of oil revenue profits in environmental security.[43] The 3 percent, however, was inadequate to cover the costs of damage and its impact on human life. As a result, frustration continued to mount toward the national government as well as the Chinese and Malaysian oil companies that had failed to aside the funds to help the government comply with the PRMC.

Of course, there is no easy fix to South Sudan's environmental problems. But the August protests exposed a growing sense of frustration with a national government that has done little to look after its people. The question raised by its insouciance was whether the GRSS was set up to promote the people's welfare and its country's public goods. What, in other words, was the core obligation of the GRSS to provide for such welfare; and how should we expect it to meet this obligation when its contract with oil companies take precedence over the people's welfare?

National Identity and a Social Contract

Since the CPA was signed in 2005, South Sudan has had to rely on powerful states such as the United States and international organizations to fund much of its people's basic needs, Many of the people I spoke to had given up on the national government and relied almost solely on NGO relief to meet their basic needs. Others talked about how the civil war enabled the national government to crackdown on its people, including the media. I asked Michael Duku, the Executive Director of Association of Media Development in South Sudan, about the repression of the media. He told me that "most of the people detained by the NSS for speaking out against the government had failed to follow basic ethics and

186   SOUTH SUDAN'S FATEFUL STRUGGLE

procedures of reporting, that is, checking sources, and knowing about libel laws."[44] Although following the basic rules and ethics did not offer any assurance against arrest, it did make such arrest less likely. The reason was that sound reporting raised the legal threshold of arrest and thus made arrests more arbitrary. Moreover, it suggested that civic awareness and participation still played a role in the country's broken justice system.

This may be why many South Sudanese have placed their faith in a permanent constitution to promote civic and political stability. Indeed, the feeling among many South Sudanese is that the Transitional Constitution's provisional status made it less binding and easier for the leaders to violate. For this reason, the permanent constitution remains crucial to promoting South Sudan's civic national identity. The importance of the permanent constitution returns us to the idea of a legitimate social contract rooted in the shared obligations and duties that bind the government to the people. So far, the people and civil society have played a marginal, outlier role in the government's formation. The ruling elite seem solely bound to the international donors and powerful states that offer them aid and legitimacy for their cooperation. This might explain why the government is always quick to deny the reports of international watchdogs such as the Sentry project, which rely on detailed reporting to expose the rampant corruption in South Sudan. It might also explain why many perceive South Sudan as a failed state in need of special international attention or even international protectorate status granted under UN Trusteeship—a measure designed to remedy the fundamental flaws of governance.[45]

Accordingly, the hope is that the permanent constitution, which is based on considerable consultation with and input by the people, will finally lead to binding duties and constraints. But to make the constitution binding, there also needs to be an idea of a social contract that articulates the mutual obligations to uphold the rights and principles of the constitution. The social contract must at least, as Oxfam affirms, "refer to the agreement by citizens to submit to the authority of government in exchange for protection of their rights, including access to public goods, basic services, security, justice, and development."[46]

In general, an effective social contract reflects the state's capacity to respond to the basic needs of its citizens and to integrate measures and mechanisms that effectively restrain the government from abusing these needs. Virtually everything we have learned of South Sudan points to a lack of restraint and an impulsiveness that inform the persistent warlike condition of the state, or the ruling elite's brute governance. For some, the underlying challenge is about conceiving of the resilient nature of the social contract, in which institutions and mechanisms are created to include the people, check the power of leadership, and to meet the basic needs of the people. As Luka Biong Deng Kuol argues, a lack of resilience may be attributed to number of past and present factors, including Dinka leadership

and the cleavage inside the ruling elite that reinforces the exclusionary norms/practices of public institutions. As he puts it, the leaders "produced a social contract that is neither resilient nor inclusive . . . it is one that had not generated mechanisms to address the core conflicts."[47]

This means that a resilient social contract should consist of the flexible mechanisms of governance designed to promote inclusion and accountability. A resilient contract should also reflect the role of federalism in promoting a checks and balance at the federal level and in devolving power to the local level to better manage ethnic strife and to work beyond the shortcomings of monetized patronage. The question, then, is how to integrate not just the separate institutions and functions of the current government (i.e., army and national assembly), but the ties between these institutions through a flexible checks and balances system that enables the state to work toward inclusion and accountability. As we saw in Chapter 6, federalism reflects a complicated issue that has divided parties and the people rather than integrating their will into the effective functioning of government. This is why some have looked outside South Sudan for comparative models such as Ethiopia's ethnic federalist model, which the Ethiopian People's Revolutionary Democratic Front (EPRDF) adopted in 1992, and which divided the country into 14 regional autonomous units, each with its assigned ethnic nationality. Although it remains a promising model, its focus on ethnicity and language risks further politicizing ethnicity inside South Sudan, unless there are guarantees at the regional level that power will be equally shared among the various tribal groups.[48]

The lesson learned from Kiir's presidential state decree is that the decision to decentralize power to the local government must come from the people. Otherwise, federalism is bound to polarize ethnic identities and diminish any positive link between tribal and national identity. "Under federalism," writes Douglas Johnson, "there must be a central government: however, its powers need to be defended. It will have presence wherever the capital is located, and it will also have a presence through various federal agencies in every state."[49] The fact that Kiir's presidential decree decentralized power to favor the Dinka in various local districts shows just how inflexible and non-resilient it was.

South Sudan's Democratic Aspirations and Regional Politics

Kiir has remained South Sudan's only president. His tenure is the product of broken. democratic and judicial system. Yet the revitalized peace process, as we saw in Chapter 6, did signal his willingness to compromise on a number of issues. In early 2022, for instance, he even reaffirmed his commitment to hold democratic elections in 2023, insisting that the lack of security sector reform,

188   SOUTH SUDAN'S FATEFUL STRUGGLE

that is, integration of the armed forces, should not justify any further delay. The opposition, though, feared that Kiir would try to rig the elections and perhaps take advantage of the lack of security by intimidating voters at the polls. An even more pressing issue of security concerned the millions of citizens displaced by the civil war, who still lived outside the country. Their absence meant that a large percentage of citizenry would be unable to vote. Many, in fact, expected the low voter turnout to hurt the opposition and benefit Kiir. Ultimately, the growing concern for free and fair elections led officials to delay democratic elections.

For many, the delay seemed inevitable. For our purposes, it can be understood in terms of the persistent nature of brute governance and the fear projected by its ruling elite. The embedded state of brute governance displaces and divides the will of the people and represses the ability of civil society to integrate the hopes for peace and justice within a functional, democratic framework of governance. As such, it fuels the uncertainty and instability that has slowed down the implementation of R-ARCSS, dampened the spirits of the parties and people, and turned normally celebratory events such as South Sudan's tenth anniversary into a subdued and "dismal" affair.[50] Not surprisingly, the RTGoNU as a whole, has done relatively little to fix the country's pressing problems, such as intercommunal violence and injustice, and to root out government corruption. So tainted is the corrupt national government that there are few good, trusted leaders left to lead the country out of its problems.

An integrative social contract, then, represents the project of rebuilding trust through a fully formed NUF, land reform laws, and the HCSS and truth commission, all of which are likely to counter the pervasive effects of corruption, militarized patronage, and armed conflict in the countryside. Yet the gap between the efficacy of these mechanisms and these structural factors speaks to a perverse commitment to manipulate justice and the rule of law by violent means—with the aim of staying in power indefinitely. Bridging the gap thus requires sincere legal and political commitments to assure the people of their basic human rights and to resolve the country's intractable problems.

Nowhere is this more evident than in the government's insincere commitment to control the intercommunal violence in the countryside. Over the years, farmers have been forced to take matters into their own hands to defend their property from cattle raiding. The absence of effective local land laws has essentially left the farmers with no other option than to kill the cattle herders and some of their own cattle (which still functions as commodity and cash currency in South Sudan). But in spurring revenge attacks, the killings have pitted one tribal community against another. And as Makuc Makuc Nyong, a member in the National Legislative Assembly, told me, "the reason why we need stronger, better controls for cattle grazing is that the humans can enjoy the number of protections granted to cattle."[51] Reforming local land laws will not be easy. Yet if

it is done properly, it might help to address this dehumanizing aspect by stressing the human right to property. The same promise applies to the justice sector, where tribal/customary law and a war crimes court might finally usher in a stable regime of victims' rights and moral deterrence. Neither of these strategic reforms alone will be enough to promote long-term peace and democratic stability, unless there is a comprehensive national reckoning with past wrongs.

Which brings us to the regional issue of whether South Sudan's predicament has been worsened by neighboring states and regional actors bent on keeping it weak and fragile. The civil war in Ethiopia, for instance, has forced South Sudan's government to toe a thin line between losing and maintaining outside support, while causing the IGAD to divert much of its attention away from South Sudan's transitional process to these conflicts. Abiy's decision to send troops into Tigray, it turned out, only heightened tensions between Ethiopia and the Sudan over the flow of refugees into Sudan (after Ethiopia, in February 2021, crossed into Sudan's border to attack Tigrayan soldiers), leading Sudan to declare the action as an act of aggression.[52] This followed an earlier IGAD emergency meeting held in December 2020, which sought to address the security threat posed by the refugees crossing over Sudan's southern border.[53]

In addition, Uganda's tumultuous 2021 elections saw Museveni strong arm his way to victory. But not before the United Nations and several human rights organizations accused him of tampering with election results and committing human rights abuses, including unlawfully detaining his main opponent. Despite international and local protests against his regime, Museveni was able to secure the nearly 1 million dollars in aid he received annually from the United States.[54] Museveni, as we saw in Chapter 2, is the main reason that Kiir remains in power and has done little to pressure the government to reform. For him, the status quo government of South Sudan remains the best opportunity to extend his geopolitical and authoritarian influence over the country.

South Sudan also faces the growing tensions between Egypt and Ethiopia over the completion of the Grand Ethiopian Renaissance Dam (GERD). Egypt, Ethiopia, and Sudan, along with other downstream riparian countries, were expected to settle on a timetable for the filing up of the lake located behind the Dam under an agreement brokered by Washington in November 2019. But Ethiopia refused to sign the agreement because of the GERD's expected economic benefits. In fact, the GERD, has become a source of Ethiopian national pride and its future development, even though for Egypt it represents an existential threat to its national existence. For his part, Kiir has had to assume a neutral role to balance the concerns of Egypt, Ethiopia, and Sudan.[55] In a meeting with el-Sisi held in Juba, in November 2020, for instance, he refrained from taking sides and encouraged more dialogue and compromise to reach a binding agreement that would resolve the crisis through trilateral talks and a negotiated agreement.[56]

190 SOUTH SUDAN'S FATEFUL STRUGGLE

Kiir still relies on the active support of his regional allies to maintain his power. They have, after all, saved him from defeat, while also taking in countless South Sudanese refugees. Yet South Sudan's political destiny as a peaceful, democratic country is not simply about ending Kiir's hold on power. It will ultimately be determined by the will of all parties to pursue an integrative social contract and the effective implementation of R-ARCSS. For South Sudan to overcome its fateful struggle for peace and justice, then, it will need to embrace an inclusive national identity that grows out of the reciprocal commitments to uphold the permanent constitution and to putting the basic needs and rights of its people first.

Notes

Introduction

1. See, for example, Alex De Waal, "When Kleptocracy becomes Insolvent: The Brute Causes of the Civil War in South Sudan," *African Affairs* 113, no. 452 (2014): 347–369; Øystein Rolandsen, "The Making of the Anya-Nya Insurgency in the Southern Sudan, 1961–64," *The Journal of Eastern African Studies* 5, no 2 (2011): 211–232; Douglas H. Johnson, *The Root Causes of Sudan's Civil Wars* (Bloomington, IN: Indiana University Press, 2003); Mahmood Mamdani, *Neither Settler Nor Native: The Making and Unmaking of Permanent Minorities* (Cambridge, MA: The Belknap Press of Harvard University Press, 2020).
2. Thomas Hobbes, *Leviathan* (Cambridge: Cambridge University Press, 1996).
3. Susan Faludi, *The Terror Dream* (New York: Metropolitan Books, 2007).
4. John Keegan, *A History of Warfare* (New York: Vintage Books, 1994)..
5. Peter Adwok Nyaba, "The Curse of Elitism: South Sudan's Failure to Transition to Statehood and Nationhood," in *South Sudan: Post-Independence Dilemmas*, ed. Amir Idris (Abingdon: Routledge, 2018), 19–37.
6. Jason K Stearns, "Rebels Without a Cause: The New Face of African Warfare," *Foreign Affairs*, 101, no. 3 (May/June 2022): 143–156.
7. Luka Biong Kuol, "South Sudan: The Elusive Quest for a Resilient Social Contract," *Journal of Intervention and Statebuilding*, 14, no. 1 (March 2020): 64–83.
8. Hobbes defined a social contract between the people and government as one in which the citizens renounced their freedom in exchange for the protection of their civil and political rights—and where the enforceability of such rights presupposed a sovereign power who Hobbes considered the "the author of all wills." Hobbes, *Leviathan*, 71.
9. Kiir, for instance, had to give the appearance of SPLA unity to show Bashir that it was a veritable threat to Sudan.
10. See Andrew S. Natsios, *Sudan, South Sudan and Darfur: What Everyone Needs to Know* (Oxford: Oxford University Press, 2012).
11. Salva Kiir and Riek Machar, "South Sudan Needs Truth, Not Trials," *New York Times*, June 7, 2015. Accessed July 15, 2020. https://www.nytimes.com/2016/06/08/opinion/south-sudan-needs-truth-not-trials.html.
12. For a discussion of hybrid justice in South Sudan, see Rachel Ibreck, *South Sudan's Injustice System: Law and Activism on the Frontline* (London: Zed Books, 2019).
13. Mahmood Mamdani, *Separate Submission to the African Union Commission of Inquiry* (South Sudan, 2014), 47–61.
14. See Christopher Zambakari, Targeet K. Kang, and Robert A. Sanders, "The Role of the UN Mission in South Sudan (UMISS) in Protecting Civilian," in *The Challenge of Governance in South Sudan: Corruption, Peacebuilding, and Foreign Intervention*, eds. Steven C. Roach and Derrick K. Hudson (Abingdon: Routledge, 2019), 95–130.

192 NOTES

15. Katherine Almquist Knopf, "Ending South Sudan's Civil War." *Council of Foreign Relations*, March 16, 2017.
16. The main set of issues facing the formation of ARCSS included: (1) the Joint Monitoring and Evaluative Commission (JMEC) to oversee the integration of security forces; (2) a timeline for integrating the army; (3) the adoption of a permanent constitution; (4) and transitional justice mechanisms to reconcile the nation.
17. Mahmood Mamdani, "Who's to Blame in South Sudan?" *Boston Review*, June 28, 2016. http://bostonreview.net/world/mahmood-mamdani-south-sudan-failed-transition.

Chapter 1

1. Oliver Albino, *The Sudan: A Southern Viewpoint* (London: Oxford University Press, 1970), 25.
2. At the same time, Egyptian Arabs played little role in political or military affairs; instead, they occupied the lower rungs of the clerical and financial administration, occasionally rising to become subordinate officials.
3. Robert O. Collins, *A History of Modern Sudan* (Cambridge: Cambridge University Press, 2008), 37–39.
4. Richard Hill, *A Biographical Dictionary of the Sudan* (London: Psychology Press), 54.
5. Robert S. Kramer, "Jihadiyya," *The Historical Encyclopedia of World Slavery*, Volume 1, ed. Junius P. Rodriquez (London: Hurst Publishers, 2009), 5–6.
6. Britain's 1807 anti–slave trade law did little to curb conscripted enslavement and the slave trade in parts of East Africa and the Middle East.
7. The price of ivory nearly doubled on the London market from 1840 to 1870.
8. Britain, for its part, relied almost exclusively on the ample supply of African slave laborers to help transport the ivory (mostly elephant tusks) downstream to the seaports.
9. Richard Gray, *A History of the Southern Sudan 1839–1889* (London: Oxford University Press, 1961), 6.
10. Adam Smith was one of the first economists to argue that slave labor worked at odds with capitalist supply and demand.
11. Collins, *A History of Modern Sudan*, 71.
12. On this point, see Øystein H. Rolandsen and Matthew Daly, *A History of South Sudan* (Cambridge: Cambridge University Press, 2016).
13. Mahmood Mamdani, *Neither Settler, Nor Native: The Making and Unmaking of Permanent Minorities* (Cambridge, MA: The Belknap Press of Harvard University Press, 2020), 205–206.
14. Garrett Gong, *The Standards of Civilization* (Oxford: Oxford University Press, 1984). European countries considered the Ottoman Empire, Egyptian, China, and Japanese civilizations as semi-developed civilizations.

NOTES 193

15. These standards included (1) the guarantees of basic rights, that is, life, dignity and property; freedom of travel, commerce, and religion; (2) the state existing as an organized state with some efficiency, and with some capacity to organize for self-defense; (3) the state adheres to the laws of war, while maintaining a system of courts, codes, and published laws which guarantee legal justice for all within its jurisdiction, foreigners, and native citizens alike; (4) the state fulfills the obligations of the international system by maintaining adequate and permanent avenues for diplomatic interchange and communication; and (5) the state conforms to accepted norms and practices of civilized international society, in which certain practices such as polygamy and slavery were not considered civilized.

16. Steven C. Roach, *Decency and Difference: Humanity and the Global Challenge of Identity Politics* (Ann Arbor: University of Michigan Press, 2019), 56–57.

17. See David Van Reybrouck, *Congo: The Epic History of a People*, trans. Sam Garret (New York: Harper Collins, 2010).

18. Muriel, E. Chamberlin, *The Scramble for Africa* (London: Longman, 1974), 85.

19. Norbert Elias, *The Civilizing Process* (London: Blackwell Publishers, 1981), 270.

20. Elias, *The Civilizing Process*, 270.

21. Collins, *A History of Modern Sudan*, 87.

22. The Khalifa, however, managed to escape to Kurdufan, where he would stay for several months.

23. Rolandsen and Daly, *A History of South Sudan*, 30.

24. The Anglo-Egyptian Agreement, Article II, 1899.

25. The civil servants would begin to arrive in Egypt in 1901.

26. Mamdani, *Neither Settler, Nor Native*, 213.

27. The 1902 Code of Civil Procedure provided the legal basis for governing the affairs in the North, particularly in the cities.

28. South Sudan has long been comprised of three major groups: The Nilotic, Nilo Hamitic, and the South Western Sudanic tribes. The two most dominant ethnic groups, the Nuer and Dinka, constitute over 50 percent of the present-day population of South Sudan (with the Dinka comprising 36 percent, and the Nuer 16 percent). Neither the Dinka nor Nuer can be considered a homogeneous group of Nilotic people, meaning that there is no one group of Dinka or Nuer per se, but rather smaller intraethnic or tribal groups, most notably, in the case of the Dinka, the Malwal, Awan, Tonj, Rek, Atwot, Ciec, Agar, Bor, Gok, Padang, Abyeilang, Ruweng, Ageer, Dongojol, Panaru, and Ngok; for the Nuer, it is the Lou, Jikany, Gaajak, Gaajuk, Dok, Bul, Lek, Nyong, Ador, and Gawaar.

29. By the 1890s, Social Darwinism had emerged to champion the survival of the fittest based on the social and racial traits of groups.

30. Mamdani, *Neither Settler, Nor Native*.

31. Rolandsen and Daly, *A History of South Sudan*, 42.

32. Sudanese administrators lacked the resources and political will to administer these provincial boundaries.

33. Rolandsen and Daly, *A History of South Sudan*, 42–43.

194 NOTES

34. See Mahmoud Mamdani, "Who's to Blame in South Sudan? *Boston Review*. Accessed June 28, 2016. http://bostonreview.net/world/mahmood-mamdani-south-sudan-fai led-transition.

35. Ziad Fahmy, *Ordinary Egyptians: Creating the Modern Nation through Popular Culture* (Stanford, CA: Stanford University Press, 2011), 138.

36. There was no mention of such control in the 1923 Egyptian constitution. The British would later pull out all Egyptian troops from Sudan after the assassination of the Governor General, Sir Lee Stack, in 1924.

37. See Eliza Griswold, *The Tenth Parallel: Dispatches from the Fault Line Between Christianity and Islam* (New York: Picador Press, 2010).

38. Decentralization was quasi insofar as there was no formal or official arrangement of governance between the British and tribal leaders, that is, security. Yet indirect rule, while informal, was as judicious as it was necessary, since large parts of Sudan were still unreachable throughout much of the year, such as the Bahr al Ghazal hinterland, where the Dinka and Nuer resided.

39. In keeping with arguments that tend to positively favor British indirect Rule, colonial administration as opposed to other forms of colonial rule, that is, French Direct Rule, the Republic of South Sudan, did make explicit mention at its independence that British policy played a positive role in protecting and promoting the indigenous African identity of southerners.

40. C. L. R. James, *In Beyond a Boundary* (Durham, NC: Duke University Press, 1983), 111.

41. Ann Mosely Lesch, *The Sudan—Contested National Identities* (Oxford: James Curry, 1998), 33.

42. Mansour Khalid, *War and Peace in the Sudan* (London: Routledge, 2003), 14.

43. There were still a few Turkish and Egyptian solders recruited.

44. Harold A. MacMichael, "Memorandum on the Southern Policy," SAD 397 (Sudan Archives: University of Durham).

45. Mamdani, *Neither Settler, Nor Native*, 213.

46. Mamdani, *Neither Settler, Nor Native*, 213.

47. Collins, *A History of Modern Sudan*, 48.

48. Christopher W. M. Cox, *Colonial Office and other departments: Papers of Sir Christopher Cox, Educational Adviser* (London: National Archives, 1946).

49. Rolandsen and Daly, *A History of South Sudan*, 53.

50. Quoted in Rolandsen and Daly, *A History of South Sudan*, 58.

51. Collins, *A History of Modern Sudan*, 75.

52. Quoted in Albino, *The Sudan: A Southern Viewpoint*, 25.

53. Steven C. Roach, *Cultural Autonomy, Minority Rights, and Globalization* (London: Routledge Press, 2016), 22–24.

54. The number of conversions reached nearly 650,000 in 1964, when nearly 500,000 flocked to the Catholic Church, and another 150,000 to the Anglican Church. See Rolandsen and Daly, *A History of South Sudan*, 77.

55. In 1936, for instance, after the British finally pulled all their troops from Egypt (with the exception of the Suez Canal), Egyptian authorities insisted that Britain recognize

King Farouk as the King of Egypt and Sudan. But Britain refused to concede. It was only in retrospect when the King conspired with Mussolini to take control of Sudan, that Britain's refusal seemed justified in the face of the spread of Fascism.

56. Fadwa A. A. Taha, "The Sudanese Factor in the 1952–53 Anglo-Egyptian Negotiations," *Middle Eastern Studies* 44, no. 4 (December 2008): 610–611.

57. Taha, "The Sudanese Factor in the 1952–53 Anglo-Egyptian Negotiations," 618.

58. The Anglo-Egyptian Agreement, 1953.

59. Collins, *A History of Modern Sudan*, 65.

60. Rolandsen and Daly, *A History of South Sudan*, 72.

61. Britain and Egypt recognized Sudan's unilateral declaration on January 1, 1956.

62. Quoted in Gray, *A History of the Southern Sudan 1839–1889*, 116.

63. Rolandsen and Daly, *A History of South Sudan*, 193.

64. The organization's name was later shortened to the Sudan African National Union (SANU).

65. The OAU was established in 1963 to promote African liberation, peace, and security on the continent.

66. The same rationale would be applied to later secessionist cases, such as the Biafran secession in Nigeria.

67. Øystein H. Rolandsen, "The Making of the Anya-Nya Insurgency in the Southern Sudan, 1961–64," *The Journal of Eastern African Studies* 5, no. 2 (Summer 2011): 221.

68. Organization of African Unity, *Charter of the Organization of African Unity*, 25 (May 1963). Accessed March 22, 2022. https://www.refworld.org/docid/3ae6b36024.html.

69. Southern Sudanese Liberation Movement Leadership Charter (Juba: National Archives of South Sudan, 1963), 391.

70. But the NTGSS failed to appeal to the South Sudanese and eventually was dissolved in 1970.

71. Øystein H. Rolandsen and Nicki Kindersley, "The Nasty War: Organized Violence During The Anya-Nya Insurgency in South Sudan, 1963–7," *The Journal of African History* 60, no. 1 (March 2019): 101.

72. Rolandsen and Kindersley, "The Nasty War," 103.

73. The Arab nations, including Egypt (with the support of Sudan) would eventually attack Israel to reclaim the Sinai Peninsula and the Gaza strip in the 1973 Yom Kippur War.

74. Addis Ababa Agreement on the Problem of South Sudan, 1972. Accessed at https://peacemaker.un.org/sudan-addisababa-southsudan72.

75. Selassie's compromise was that half of Southern Command would be comprised of insurgents.

76. Joseph Lagu, Pressing Briefing, February 27, 1972. Accessed at https://www.facebook.com/Hon.MangarAmerdid/videos/joseph-lagu-press-briefing-1972/1144297669006178/.

77. Nelson Kasfir, "Southern Sudanese Politics Since the Addis Ababa Agreement," *African Affairs* 76, no. 303 (1977): 153.

78. Kasfir, "Southern Sudanese Politics Since the Addis Ababa Agreement," 160.

79. Addis Ababa Agreement (1972), chapter II, Article 6.

196 NOTES

80. *The Nile Mirror*, 20, April 17, 1972, 5.
81. Rolandsen and Daly, *A History of South Sudan*, 99.
82. Abel Alier, *Southern Sudan: Too many Agreements Dishonored* (Exeter, NY: Ithaca Press, 1990), 212.
83. The Anyanya II' start can be traced to March 1975 when a mutiny at Akobo Garrison and National Unity Day occurred at a celebration honoring the Addis Ababa Agreement.
84. Robert O. Collins, "The Jonglei Canal Project: Illusion or Reality?" *Water International* 13, no. 3 (September 1988): 144.
85. The government anticipated an economic return that would help pay down its nearly $6 billion debt.
86. The Sudanese government would eventually resume construction of the project in 2000, but an independent South Sudan effectively put a stop to these plans, leaving the canal project in permanent abeyance. Recent studies estimate upstream development projects will reduce the flow of the White Nile into southern Sudan and the Sudd. See Miriam Allam, et al., "Jonglei Canal Project under Potential Developments in the Upper Nile States," *Journal of Water Management Modeling* 21 (2008): 26.
87. Luke Patey, *The Kings of Crude: China, India, and the Global struggle for oil in Sudan and South Sudan* (London: Hurst and Company, 2014), 34.
88. Patey, *The Kings of Crude*, 4.

Chapter 2

1. Douglas H. Johnson, *The Root Causes of Sudan's Civil Wars* (Bloomington: Indiana University Press, 2003), 60.
2. The Anyanya II rebels operated inside Western Ethiopia in early to mid-1983 to resist Khartoum.
3. The Anyanya II's operations broke down into four competing groups, the Adura, the Analaya, The Bilpam (from the Bentiu Nuer under the leadership of Gordon Kuang and Vincent Kuany), the Pakedio group (A student-led group), Itang camp, and the Buteng Camp of the National Movement (NAM).
4. The Anyanya II would become a looming and often threatening presence. What it lacked in terms of resources, it made up by with assistance from Nimeiri's government.
5. Johnson, *The Root Causes of Sudan's Civil Wars*, 92.
6. The Sudan People's Liberation Movement, "Manifesto of Sudan People's Liberation Movement," May 1983 (and updated in 2008). Accessed at www.theirwords.org.
7. Quoted in Johnson, *The Root Causes of Sudan's Civil Wars*, 64.
8. The Anyanya II meanwhile consisted of fighters with different tribal backgrounds.
9. See Frantz Fanon, *Black Skin, White Masks*, trans. Richard Philcox. Revised Edition (New York: Grove Press, 2009).
10. Frantz Fanon, *The Wretched of the Earth*. trans. Richard Philcox (New York: Grove Press, 1963).

NOTES   197

11. The Sudan People's Liberation Movement, the SPLM Manifesto.
12. Garang was trained by Rodney at the University of Dar es Salaam.
13. Walter Rodney, *How Europe Underdeveloped Africa* (London: Verso, 1972).
14. John Garang, "Identifying, Selecting, and Implementing Rural Development Strategies for Socio-Economic Development in the Jonglei Projects Area in the Southern Region, Sudan" (PhD dissertation, 1981).
15. He earned a master's degree in agricultural economics and later his PhD in economics from Iowa State University in the United States.
16. He even proposed replacing the colonial agreements of 1929 and 1959 which had allotted nearly and 85 percent of the Nile's flow to both countries.
17. In 2010 the NBI resulted in the Cooperative Framework Agreement and the end Egypt and Sudan's monopoly on the Nile's flow dating back to the 1959 Agreement between the British and Egypt and Sudan.
18. Even if Garang's quasi-Marxist views were meant to please Menjistu.
19. John Garang, "Speech Delivered to the U.N. General Assembly," July 12, 2005.
20. Garang, "Speech Delivered to the U.N.," 2005.
21. John Garang, "Speech Delivered to Soldiers in Bor," trans. Atem David Kuer Atem, 1986.
22. Garang, "Speech Delivered to Soldiers at Bor."
23. Jok Madut Jok, *War and Slavery in Sudan* (Philadelphia: University of Pennsylvania Press, 2001), 33.
24. When Nimeiri finally did respond to the effects of migration, he implemented policies in a harsh and often exacting manner. In the end, his policies managed to compound the effects of high inflation rates, rising unemployment, and diminishing wages in the cities.
25. Girma Kebbede, "Sudan: The North-South Conflict in Historical Perspective," in *Sudan's Predicament: Civil War, displacement and ecological degradation*, ed. Girma Kebbede (Aldershot: Ashgate Publishing, 1999) 20.
26. The delay resulted in the loss of much-needed relief to civilians.
27. Kebbede, "Sudan," 21.
28. Bashir would soon adopt the Criminal Act of 1991 which effectively reinforced sharia law to the South.
29. The NIF was founded in 1971 and began to gain influence in 1979.
30. Gérard Prunier, "Rebel Movements and Proxy Warfare: Uganda, Sudan, and the Congo," *African Affairs* 103, no. 412 (2003): 381.
31. Johnson, *The Root Causes of Sudan's Civil Wars*, 93.
32. Sharon Hutchinson, "A Curse from God: Religious and Political Dimensions of the Post-1991 Rise of Ethnic Violence in South Sudan," *Journal of Modern African Studies* 39, no. 2 (1991): 315.
33. Riek Machar, "The Nasir Declaration," August 30, 1991. Accessed July 3, 2021; 23 Years Later: The 1991 Nasir Coup—Paan Luel Wël Media Ltd—South Sudan, www.paanluelwel.com.
34. Machar, "Nasir Declaration."
35. Johnson, *The Root Causes of Sudan's Civil Wars*, 121–122.

198 NOTES

36. See Punier, "Rebel Movements and Proxy Warfare." Laurent Kabila, the President of the new Democratic Republic of the Congo (DRC), also, at this time, pledged his support of the SPLA-Mainstream.
37. Donald Petterson, *Inside Sudan: Political Islam, Conflict, and Catastrophe* (Boulder, CO: Westview Press, 1999), 53.
38. Johnson, *The Root Causes of Sudan's Civil Wars*, 118.
39. BBC News, "Hardtalk," with Zeinab Badawi, August 30, 2004. Accessed March 2, 2020. BBC, http://news.bbc.co.uk/1/hi/programmes/hardtalk/3704634.stm.
40. Johnson, *The Root Causes of Sudan's Civil Wars*, 93.
41. Girma Kebbede, "South Sudan: A War Torn and Divided Region," in Girma Kebbede (ed.) *Sudan's Predicament: Civil War, Displacement and Ecological Degradation* (Aldershot: Ashgate Publishing, 1999), 44–48.
42. The SPLM/A had, by now, organized into three core factions: The Dinka of Bahr al Ghazal, the Dinka on the eastern bank of the Nile, and the clusters of Nuer groups.
43. Hutchinson, "A Curse from God," 312.
44. Petterson, *Inside Sudan*, 187.
45. Hutchinson, "A Curse from God," 312.
46. Collins, *A History of Modern Sudan*, 63.
47. Wunlit Peace Conference, Dinka-Nuer West Bank Peace and Reconciliation Process, February 27 to March 8, 1999. Wunlit, Bahr El Ghazal. Accessed June 22, 2021. http://southsudanfriends.org/wp-content/uploads/2014/02/Wunlit-Documents-1.pdf.
48. Luka Deng Buol, "Social Capital and Civil War: The Dinka Community in Sudan's Civil War," *African Affairs* 109, no. 435 (2010): 249.
49. Deng, "Social Capital and Civil War," 241.
50. Mahmood Mamdani, "Who's to Blame in South Sudan? *Boston Review*, June 28, 2016. Accessed March 4, 2020. http://bostonreview.net/world/mahmood-mamdani-south-sudan-failed-transition.
51. Quoted in Adrian Blomfield, "Sudan Rebel Group and Former Rival Reunite," *Reliefweb*, May 28, 2001. Accessed June 22, 2021.
52. Quoted in Blomfield, "Sudan Rebel Group and Former Rivals Unite."
53. The adoption of this mandate led the agency to change its name from the Intergovernmental Authority on Drought and Development (IGADD) to the Intergovernmental Authority on Development (IGAD).
54. Khalid, *War and Peace in the Sudan*, 380.
55. John Young, *South Sudan's Civil War: Violence, Insurgency, and Failed Peacemaking* (London: Zed Books), 7.
56. It was its control of oil in the Unity State and South Kordofan region that provided continued revenue to finance its war activities.
57. Garang, "Speech to the U.N."
58. The United States would later admit that the intelligence was not as solid as it first thought, but conceded that there was not enough evidence to rule out the manufacturing of nerve gas.
59. Jaime Vicini, "U.S. Court Dismisses 1998 Sudan Missile Strike Suit," *Reuters*, June 9. 2001. Accessed June 21, 2021. The doctrine holds that in terms of national security, foreigners cannot question the US government's decision to retaliate against it.

NOTES 199

60. Vicini, "U.S. Court Dismisses 1998 Sudan Missile Strike Suit."
61. The United States' grand strategy overseas consisted of two primary objectives: the use of its military and economic mite to spread democracy and human rights overseas, and to help the United Nations to undertake nation building to counteract terrorism (e.g., Afghanistan and Iraq).
62. Young, *South Sudan's Civil War*, 46–47.
63. In 2004, he would sever all political contact with al-Turabi.
64. Young, *South Sudan's Civil War*, 51–52.
65. John Prendergast, "Senator Danforth's Sudan Challenge: Building a Bridge to Peace," The Center for Strategic International Studies, *Africa Notes* 5 (2002): 1–2.
66. Eric Reeves, "How Serious are John Danforth's 'Tests' of Khartoum's Willingness to Engage in Peace Negotiations," *Sudan: Research Analysis and Advocacy*, December 2003.
67. John C. Danforth, "Report to the President of the United States in the Outlook for Peace in Sudan." Accessed June 11, 2021. www.state.gov/p/af/rls/rpt/2002/10150.htm.
68. *Reliefweb*, US DOS Danforth report The outlook for peace in the Sudan, May 15, 2002.
69. At the same time, for the Islamists in the NCP, the SPLM/A's success had helped turn the South into an increasing political liability.
70. Young, *South Sudan's Civil War*, 54.
71. It should be noted that the meeting remained risky for both sides, since it symbolized a compromise that could be interpreted as surrendering to the other side. But in the end, the meeting showed the good graces of both sides, while helping to facilitate further compromises.
72. Ted Dagne, "Sudan: Humanitarian Crisis, Peace Talks, Terrorism, and U.S. Policy," CRS Issue Brief for Congress (Washington, DC: Congressional Research Service, Library of Congress, 2005), 7.
73. Øystein H. Rolandsen, "A Quick Fix? A Retrospective Analysis of the Sudan Comprehensive Peace Agreement," *Review of African Political Economy* 38, no. 130 (2011): 561.
74. John Young, "Sudan: A Flawed Peace Process leading to a Flawed Peace," *Review of African Political Economy* 32, no. 103 (2007): 101.
75. U.S. Senate, Congressional Resolution 467, "Declaring Darfur a Genocide," September 7, 2004. H.Con.Res.467—108th Congress (2003–2004): Declaring genocide in Darfur, Sudan.
76. Douglas H. Johnson, "The Helig Oil Dispute: Between Sudan and South Sudan," *Journal of Eastern African Studies* 6, no. 3 (September 2012): 14.
77. Johnson, "The Helig Oil Dispute," 16.
78. The Comprehensive Peace Agreement, Article III, Section, 2–5. Signed January 9, 2005. Accessed November 12, 2019.
79. Rolandsen, "A Quick Fix?" 559.
80. Small Arms Survey, "Human Security Baseline Assessment for Sudan and South Sudan, 2013." *Small Arms Survey*. Accessed June 10, 2021. https://www.smallarmssurvey.org/project/human-security-baseline-assessment-hsba-sudan-and-south-sudan/.

200 NOTES

81. As Article 67 of the Act, states: "Without prejudice to Sub-Sections (1) and (2) above, the parties of the CPA shall enter into negotiations aiming to achieve an agreement on post-referendum substantive issues to be witnessed by the organizations and countries signatories to the CPA such as: assets and Debts, oil fields, Production, Transport and Export of Oil; contracts and Environment in Oil Fields; water; property."

82. For a good discussion of these issues, see Kevin L. Cope "South Sudan's Dualistic Constitution," in Denis J Galligan and Milla Versteeg (ed.) *Social and Political Foundations of Constitutions* (Cambridge: Cambridge University Press, 2013).

83. Young, "Sudan," 109.

84. National Public Radio, "John Garang: A Conversation on Sudan," February 12, 2005. Accessed June 3, 2021.

85. In doing so, she emphasized that the crash was mostly likely an accident (which later evidence would prove). All of this helped to calm down the people and to focus their attention on the important task of implementing the CPA.

Chapter 3

1. Maria Gabrielsen Jumbert and Øystein H Rolandsen, *After the Split: Post-secession negotiations between South Sudan and Sudan* (Norwegian Peacebuilding Resource Centre, Report, December 2013), 3.

2. Kiir was born on September 13, 1951 to a family that herded cattle and other livestock outside the Akon village in the Gogrial District in the Warrap state.

3. Quoted in Simon Yel and Panuel Wel, *Salva Kiir Mayardit, The Joshua of South Sudan: President Kiir & Speeches After Independence* (Juba: The Center for Strategic and Governance Studies, 2016), 37.

4. Yel and Wel, *Salva Kiir Mayardit*, 67.

5. UN Security Resolution 1593, for example, delivered several thousands of peacekeepers to monitor and police certain areas. But the UN mission remained limited in meeting crucial benchmarks rather than extending its influence to other areas. On the challenges of implementing its terms, see Matthew LeRiche and Matthew Arnold, *South Sudan: From Revolution to Independence* (London: Hurst and Company, 2012), 137.

6. Steven C. Roach, "How Political is the ICC: Pressing Challenges and the Need for Diplomatic Efficacy," *Global Governance* 19, no. 4 (2013): 511.

7. Andrew S. Natsios, *Sudan, South Sudan and Darfur: What Everyone Needs to Know* (Oxford: Oxford University, 2012), 212. Natsios' concern was that the ICC's intervention was unwarranted given the fragile situation in Sudan. The ICC's arrest warrant, for instance, also limited Bashir's movement (i.e., the United States' refusal to allow him to come to speak at the UN General Assembly).

8. Bashir's government sent military supplies to the *Janjaweed*, the rebels responsible for conducting nightly raids of villages and killing countless women and children.

9. Yel and Wel, *Salva Kiir Mayardit*, 212.

NOTES   201

10. Juba Declaration on Unity and Integration between the Sudan People's Liberation Army (SPLA) and the South Sudan Defense Forces (SSDF). Signed January 8, 2006. Accessed March 24, 2020. https://peacemaker.un.org/sudan-juba-declaration2006.

11. Kiir, in turn, became chief commander of the SPLA.

12. Jason K. Stearns, "Rebels Without a Cause: The New Face of African Warfare," *Foreign Affairs* 1010, no. 3 (May/June 2022): 147.

13. Hereward Holland and Pascal Fletcher, "Special Report: In South Sudan, Plunder Preserves a Fragile Peace." *Reuters*, November 20, 2012. Accessed on February 21, 2021. https://www.reuters.com/article/us-south-sudan-governors/special-report-in-south-sudan-plunder-preserves-a-fragile-peace-idUSBRE8AJ08N.

14. This included his personal security budget that was separate from the defense budget and that had started with the Tiger Batallion.

15. Holland and Fletcher, "Special Report."

16. Cherry Leonardi, "Paying 'Buckets of Blood' for the Land: Moral Debates over Economy, War, and State in Southern Sudan," *Journal of Modern African Studies* 49, no. 2 (2011): 216–217.

17. Mohamed M. H. Salih, "The Ideology of the Dinka & the Sudan People's Liberation Front," in *Ethnicity & Conflict in the Horn of Africa*, eds. Fukui Katsuyoshu and John Markakis (Athens: Ohio University Press, 1994), 192.

18. Hereward Holland, "South Sudan Officials Have Stolen $4 Billion: President," *Reuters*, June 4, 2012. Accessed July 13, 2021. https://www.reuters.com/article/us-southsudan-corruption-idUSBRE8530QI20120604.

19. Holland, "South Sudan Officials Have Stolen $4 Billion."

20. Quoted in Panuel Wel, *The Genius of Dr John Garang: The Essential Writings and Speeches of the Late SPLM/A's Leader*, Vol. 2 (New York: Create Space Independent Publishing Platform, 2013), 56.

21. Yel and Wel, *Salva Kiir Mayardit*, 123.

22. Hilde F. Johnson, *South Sudan, The Untold Story: From Independence to Civil War* (New York: I.B. Tauris, 2016), 24.

23. Mugume Davis Rwakaringi, "South Sudan to Probe 'Dura Saga' Grain Swindle," Voice of America, May 15, 2013. Accessed May 5, 2021. https://www.voanews.com/a/south-sudan-probe-sorghum-dura-saga-corruption/1661994.html.

24. Kevin Watkins, *Basic Services in South Sudan: An Uncertain Future, in South Sudan: One Year of Independence* (Washington, DC: The Brookings Institution, June 2012), 36.

25. Watkins, *Basic Services in South Sudan*, 41.

26. Watkins, *Basic Services in South Sudan*.

27. In its 2010 budget, the GoSS provided $120.6 million for education, $70.6 million for health care, and $373.6 million for defense. See, Ministry of Finance of the Government of Southern Sudan.

28. Alex De Waal, "When Kleptocracy Becomes Insolvent: Brute Causes of the Civil War in South Sudan, *African Affairs*, 113, no. 452 (2014): 359.

29. CNN, Sudan, South Sudan Prepare for Peace Talks. May 28, 2012. Accessed May 23, 2021. https://www.cnn.com/2012/05/29/world/africa/sudans-talks/index.html.

202   NOTES

30. Government of Southern Sudan, "The Southern Sudan Audit Chamber Act 2011." Accessed June 27, 2021. http://www.mofep-grss.org.
31. *Sudan Tribune*, "Sudan's Ruling Partners Try to Resolve Consensus and Elections Results," January 14, 2010. Accessed May 13, 2021. https://sudantribune.com/artic le33584/.
32. Human Rights Watch, "Sudan: Government Repression Threatens Elections," March 21, 2010. Accessed April 8, 2018. https://www.hrw.org/news/2010/03/21/sudan-gov ernment-repression-threatens-fair-elections.
33. Outside observers such as the Carter Center had initially casted doubt on whether the elections met international standards.
34. John Young, *The Fate of Sudan: The Origins and Consequences of a Flawed Peace Process* (London: Zed Books, 2012), 36.
35. Young. *The Fate of Sudan*, 37.
36. The Carter Center (2010). "Observing Sudan's 2010 National Elections," April 11–18, Final Report.
37. Lotje De Vries & Mareike Schomerus, "Fettered Self-Determination: South Sudan's Narrowed Path to Secession," *Civil Wars* 19, no. 1 (2017): 38–39.
38. De Vries and Schomerus, "Fettered Self-determination: South Sudan's Narrowed Path to Secession," 39.
39. All South Sudanese Political Parties Conference document held that "(a) The South should be united as parties and people, to support the conduct of the referendum and completion of the CPA interim period on time; (b) . . . we must be mindful of the fact that the result of the referendum must not be a subject of dispute. A free, fair and transparent referendum, is a sine qua non for the recognition of the result. Therefore, more than anybody else, the South must be keen to ensure that the requirements of a conducive environment for the conduct of a free, fair, transparent and peaceful refer- endum provided in the Southern Sudan Referendum Act 2009, are met. In particular, all parties, including civil society organizations and individuals, must be free to prop- agate their preferred options in the referendum."
40. Kevin L. Cope, "South Sudan's Dualistic Constitution," in *Social and Political Foundations of Constitutions*, eds. Denis J. Galligan and Milla Versteeg (Cambridge: Cambridge University Press, 2015), 305–306.
41. Government of Southern Sudan, "The Southern Sudan Referendum Act," adopted February 21, 2009. Accessed March 23, 2020. https://reliefweb.int/report/sudan/ final-report-southern-sudan-referendum-9%E2%80%9015-january-2011-enar.
42. Article 101 holds that the President can "remove a state Governor and/or dissolve a state legislative assembly in the event of a crisis in the state that threatens national se- curity and territorial integrity; and appoint a state care-taker Governor who shall pre- pare for elections within sixty days in the state where the Governor has been removed or the state legislative assembly dissolved."
43. Mark A. W. Deng, "Defining the Nature and Limits of Presidential Powers in the Transitional Constitution of South Sudan: A Politically Contentious Matter for the New Nation." *Journal of African Law* 51, no. 1 (2017): 305.
44. Deng, "Defining the Nature and Limits of Presidential Power in the Transitional Constitution of South Sudan," 306.

NOTES 203

45. International Crisis Group, "Politics and Transition in the New South Sudan," *Africa Report* no. 172 (April 4, 2011). Accessed July 23, 2019. https://www.crisisgroup.org/africa/horn-africa/south-sudan/politics-and-transition-new-south-sudan.
46. Deng, "Defining the Nature and Limits of Presidential Power in the Transitional Constitution of South Sudan," 310.
47. International Crisis Group, "Politics and Transition in the New South Sudan."
48. Enough Project, "South Sudan," 2011.
49. On this point see Copnall, *A Poisonous Thorn in Our Hearts*.
50. Ethiopia decided to deploy several hundred troops to the area.
51. *Sudan Tribune*, "Sudan Announces Details of Contested Election Results," May 21, 2011.
52. It would not be until 2019 with Sudan's temporary transition to a democratic government in Sudan and Bashir's ouster, that the two sides would enter into peace negotiations that would end in a 2020 peace agreement recognizing Sudan as a multiethnic democracy.

Chapter 4

1. James Copnall, *A Poisonous Thorn in Our Hearts: Sudan and South Sudan's Bitter and Incomplete Divorce* (London: Hurst and Company, 2014).
2. Jason K. Stearns, "Rebels Without a Cause: The New Face of African Warfare," *Foreign Affairs* 101, no. 3 (May/June 2022): 150.
3. De Waal, "When Kleptocracy become Insolvent," 348.
4. IMF loans had propped up an agricultural ruling elite with ties to the state, which purchased land and drove out the subsistence farmers.
5. Jeffrey Gettleman, "Africa's Endless Wars: Why the Continent's Wars Never End," *Foreign Policy* 178 (March–April 2010): 73–75.
6. Many colonial wars were settled by a relatively efficient transfer of administrative power via the *uti posseditis* principle. The colonial wars of the mid-twentieth century were fueled by third would struggles for national determination. The United Nations addressed this by designing a system intended to accommodate the universalizing nature of these struggles, that is, the collective right of the colonized to determine their political destiny within existing legal boundaries. That system of course was decolonization. But it essentially left in place the colonial administration and boundaries that the new liberators or leaders of postcolonial states inherited to carry out their own form of divisive and dictatorial rule. It also failed to resolve the question of national minorities living within the postcolonial state, many of whom remained underrepresented and oppressed by the postcolonial state (e.g., the Hutus in Rwanda and the Amara in Ethiopia).
7. Stearns, "Rebels Without a Cause," 145.
8. Paul Collier, *Wars, Guns, and Votes: Democracy in Dangerous Places* (New York: Harper Collins, 2009).
9. Stearns, "Rebels without a Cause," 151.

204 NOTES

10. Sentry Project, "The Taking of South Sudan: The Tycoons, Brokers, and Multinational Corporations Complicit in Hijacking the World's Newest State". September 2019. Accessed June 24, 2020. https://enoughproject.org/about/the-sentry.

11. Sentry Report, "Making a Killing: South Sudanese Military Leaders' Wealth, explained," May 27, 2020. Accessed June 25, 2020. https://enoughproject.org/about/the-sentry.

12. Malong would eventually be removed from his position as military chief of staff in 2016, after bitterly contesting Kiir's support for the 2015 peace deal.

13. Alex De Waal, *The Real Politics of The Horn of Africa: Money, War, and the Business of Power* (London: Polity Press, 2015), 19.

14. Clemence Pinaud, "South Sudan: Civil War, Predation, and the Making of a Military Aristocracy," *African Affairs* 114 (2014): 193. Accessed June 23, 2020. https://academic.oup.com/afraf/article/113/451/192/13554.

15. Pinaud, "South Sudan," 201.

16. Peter Adwok Nyaba, "The Curse of Elitism: South Sudan's Failure to Transition to Statehood and Nationhood," in *South Sudan: Post-Independence Dilemmas*, ed. Amir Idris (London: Routledge, 2018), 31.

17. Conversation with Patrick Riruyo, Yambio, South Sudan, February 1, 2020.

18. Conversation with Riruyo, February 1, 2020.

19. Warren Strobel and Louis Charbonneau, "U.S. Was Slow to Lose Patience as South Sudan Unraveled," *Reuters*, January 14, 2014. Accessed January 9, 2019. https://www.reuters.com/article/us-usa-southsudan/u-s-was-slow-to-lose-patience-as-south-sudan-unraveled-idUSBREA0D08R20140114.

20. Republic of South Sudan, The Petroleum Revenue Management Act. Juba: Ministry of Justice, Article 7 (4 and 5), 2012.

21. Republic of South Sudan, "Petroleum Act" (Juba: Ministry of Justice, 2012).

22. Joseph Bell and Teresa Faria, "Critical Issues for a Revenue Management Law," in *Escaping the Resource Curse*, eds. Macartan Humphreys, Jeffrey D. Sachs, and Joseph Stiglitz (New York: Columbia University Press, 2007), 188.

23. Bell and Faria, "Critical Issues for a Revenue Management Law," 293.

24. Emily Savage, "South Sudan's Petroleum Revenue Management Act," Policy Brief, Sudd Institute, Juba South Sudan, December 13, 2013, 7.

25. This would be carried out by the Community Development Committee in 2012, comprising workers, leaders, and youth, who were expected to further direct or invest the funds in specific projects.

26. John Mukum Mbaku and Jessica Elaine Smith, "Efficient and Equitable Natural Resource Management: Using Transparency to Avoid the Resource Curse," in *One Year after Independence: Opportunities and Obstacles for Africa's Newest Nation*, ed. The Brookings Institute (Washington, DC: Brookings Institution, 2012), 10.

27. Emma Vickers, "Can South Sudan avoid the Resource Curse? Addis Talks Mark Tipping Point," *Global Witness*. March 20, 2014. Accessed August 20, 2019. https://www.globalwitness.org/en/blog/can-south-sudan-avoid-resource-curse-truncated/.

28. Global Witness, "Blueprint for Prosperity Report," Sudd Institute, July 2012, Juba, South Sudan.

NOTES 205

29. Quoted in Copnall, *A Poisonous Thorn in Our Hearts*, 136.

30. Kuol, "South Sudan," 65.

31. Michael L. Ross, *The Oil Curse: How Petroleum Wealth Shapes the Development of Nations* (Princeton, NJ: Princeton University Press, 2012).

32. Marcartan Humphreys, Jeffrey Sachs, and Joseph E. Stiglitz, "Introduction: What Is the Problem with Natural Resource Wealth?" in *Escaping the Resource Curse*, eds. Marcartan Humphreys, Jeffrey Sachs, and Joseph E. Stiglitz (New York: Columbia University Press, 2007), 11.

33. In a recent court ruling, the United States agreed to turn over nearly 200 million dollars of the money that had been allocated to US banks.

34. Terry Lynn Karl, "Ensuring Fairness: The Case for a Transparent Fiscal Contract," in *Escaping the Resource Curse*, ed. Macartan Humphreys, Jeffrey Sachs, and Joseph E. Stiglitz (New York: Columbia University Press, 2007), 270.

35. World Bank, "South Sudan," 2019. Accessed April 20, 2020. https://www.worldbank.org/en/country/southsudan/overview.

36. United Nations Security Council, "Final Report of the Panel of Experts on South Sudan," April 15, 2021, S/2021/365. Accessed August 30, 2021. https://www.securitycouncilreport.org/un-documents/south-sudan/.

37. United Nations Security Council, "Final Report of the Panel of Experts on South Sudan," 31. An estimated $400 million dollars in revenue was received from traditional companies.

38. United Nations Security Council, "Final Report of the Panel of Expert on South Sudan," 31.

39. Luke Patey, *The Kings of Crude: China, India, and the Global struggle for oil in Sudan and South Sudan* (London: Hurst and Company, 2014), 42.

40. Blocks 3, 7, and 1, for instance, produce just over 300,000 barrels a day.

41. Patey, *The Kings of Crude*, 126.

42. Jacob D. Chol, "The Reality of Petroleum Resource Curse in South Sudan: Can It Be avoided?" *African Review* 43, no. 2 (2016): 23–25. Accessed June 24, 2020. https://www.jstor.org/stable/45341720.

43. According to a 2012 World Bank report, supply would become negligible by 2035. The civil war, though, forced experts to recalibrate these figures upward, and in recent years, the government has taken the initiative to license its oil blocks consistent with the Petroleum Management Act to produce more oil.

44. Reuters, "South Sudan agrees to oil exploration deal with South Africa," May 6, 2019. Accessed June 24, 2020. https://www.reuters.com/article/us-southsudan-safrica-oil/south-sudan-agrees-oil-exploration-deal-with-south-africa-idUSKCN1SC0F3. South Sudan in fact still sat on large amount of unexplored oil. In 2013, it was estimated that South Sudan possessed nearly 7 to 9 billion barrels of crude oil, which could yield hundreds of billions of dollars on the global market.

45. See, e.g., John J. Mearscheimer, *The Tragedy of Great Power Politics* (New York: Norton, 2001).

46. Hilde F. Johnson, *South Sudan, The Untold Story: From Independence to Civil War* (New York: I.B. Tauris, 2016), 60.

206 NOTES

47. Johnson, *South Sudan*, 91.
48. De Waal, "When Kleptocracy becomes Insolvent," 363.
49. De Waal, "When Kleptocracy becomes Insolvent," 364.
50. Quoted in Gabe Joselow, "South Sudan Oil Shutdown Chokes Economy," *Voice of America*, June 30, 2012. Accessed January 23, 2019. https://www.voanews.com/a/south-sudan-oil-shutdown-chokes-economy/1352237.html.
51. Mirjam Donath, "South Sudan Humanitarian Aid Operations Are World's Largest," Reuters, August 10, 2014, Accessed June 20, 2019. https://www.reuters.com/article/us-southsudan-un-aid/south-sudan-humanitarian-aid-operations-are-worlds-largest-u-n-idUSKBN0G62DN20140806.
52. United States Agency for International Development (USAID), "South Crisis Fact Sheet #50," July 29, 2014. Accessed May 23, 2019. https://www.usaid.gov.
53. Energy Information and Administration, "Sudan and South Sudan," Washington DC, U.S. Energy Information and Administration, August 25, 2013. Accessed May 23, 2019. https://www.eia.gov/international/analysis/country/SDN.
54. United Nations Security Council, "Temporary Arrangement for the administration and Security of the Abyei Area," June 20, 2011. https://peacemaker.un.org/sudan-temporary-arrangements-abyei2011.
55. Between 2008 and 2013, the GoSS decreased security spending slightly to pay the salaries of security officials; a mere 28 percent was allocated to development-related projects. Most of the discretionary spending went toward modernizing Juba, which received 8.3 billion US dollars to construct paved roads.
56. Quoted in *Gurtong Focus Monthly*, 6 (2013): 14.
57. Interview with Stephen Dhieu Dias, Juba, South Sudan, August 3, 2013.
58. Johnson, *South Sudan*, 91.
59. *Juba Monitor*, "Kiir, Machar Fight Over SPLM Reshuffle" 3, no. 145 (August 5. 2013), 1.
60. Gabriel Bul Yak and John Deng Jok, "Was Kiir's Relief of Machar and Ministers an opportunity or disaster for SPLM?" *Juba Monitor* 3, no. 145 (August 5, 2014): 5.
61. Deng Mankok Ayuel, "A Tale of Juba and the Presidency," *Juba Monitor* 3, no.145 (August 5, 2013): 4.
62. Simon Tisdall, "South Sudan President Sacks Cabinet in Power Struggle," *The Guardian*, July 24, 2013. Accessed June 23, 2018. https://www.theguardian.com/world/2013/jul/24/south-sudan-salva-kiir-sacks-cabinet.
63. Interview with Tut Gak Tut, Addis Ababa, Ethiopia, August 6, 2016.
64. Mahmood Mamdani, "Who's to Blame in South Sudan?" *Boston Review*, June 28, 2016. Accessed June 21, 2018. http://bostonreview.net/world/mahmood-mamdani-south-sudan-failed-transition.
65. *Sudan Tribune*, "South Sudan Appoints Crisis Management Committee," January 11, 2014. Accessed July 21, 2019. https://reliefweb.int/report/south-sudan-republic/south-sudan-president-appoints-crisis-management-committee.
66. *Sudan Tribune*, "Huge Scandals Hit S. Sudan Crisis Management Committee." March 7, 2017. Accessed July 19, 2021. https://www.sudantribune.com/spip.php?article61828.

67. Republic of South Sudan, The Public Financial Management and Accountability Act, 2011.
68. *Sudan Tribune,* "Huge Scandals Hit S. Sudan Crisis Management Committee."
69. Al Jazeera, "Is Oil Money Fueling War in South Sudan," April 6, 2019. Accessed June 23, 2020. https://www.aljazeera.com/programmes/talktojazeera/2019/04/oil-money-fuelling-war-south-sudan-190405102202518.html.
70. United Nations Security Council, "Final Report of the Panel of Experts on South Sudan," 11.
71. United Nations Security Council, "Final Report of the Panel of Experts on South Sudan," 23.
72. The Sentry, "The Taking of South Sudan."
73. Much of this spotlighting was due to George Clooney, a sponsor of the report, who had already used his stardom to call further attention to the injustices in the Darfur conflict.
74. *Sudan Tribune,* "South Sudan Dismisses the Sentry's Report," September 25, 2019. Accessed July 25, 2021. https://sudantribune.com/article66314/.
75. Amnesty International, "South Sudan: Evidence of Violations and Illicit Concealment of Arms Must Spur UN to Renew Arms Embargo," August 30, 2020. https://www.amnesty.org/en/latest/news/2020/04/south-sudan-evidence-of-violations-and-illicit-concealment-of-arms-must-spur-un-to-renew-arms-embargo/.
76. United States Senate Committee on Foreign Relations, "Independent South Sudan: A Failure of Leadership," December 10, 2015. Accessed June 24, 2019. https://www.foreign.senate.gov/hearings/independent-south-sudan-a-failure-of-leadership-121015.
77. United States, Presidential Documents, Federal Register, 78, no. 66 (2014), Resolution #13664.
78. *Sudan Tribune,* "S. Sudan Urges US Leader to Reconsider Looming Sanctions," December 9, 2014. Accessed June 9, 2020. https://sudantribune.com/article51926/.
79. United Nations Security Council Resolution 2206, adopted by the Security Council at its 7396th meeting, on March 3, 2015. Accessed January 18, 2022. https://www.un.org/securitycouncil/sanctions/2206.
80. United Nations Security Council, "Security Council Sanctions Committee Concerning South Sudan Adds Six Individuals to Its Sanctions List", SC/11958, July 1, 2015. Accessed February 23, 2022. https://www.un.org/press/en/2015/sc11958.doc.htm.
81. United Nations Security Council, "Security Council Decides against Imposing Arms Embargo on South Sudan, Designating Key Figures for Targeted Sanctions," 7850th meeting, SC/12653, December 2016.
82. Voice of America, "UN Security Council Rejects Arms Embargo on South Sudan," December 23, 2016. Accessed February 21, 2022. https://www.voanews.com/a/un-security-council-rejects-arms-embargo-south-sudan/3648327.html.
83. Al Jazeera, "UN Panel Recommends Arms Embargo, Sanctions on South Sudan," January 26, 2016. Accessed March 1, 2020. http://america.aljazeera.com/articles/2016/1/26/un-panel-recommends-arms-embargo-sanctions-on-south-sudan.

208 NOTES

84. Radio Tamazuj, "UN Panel Accuses Ukraine of Supplying South Sudan with Arms," May 15, 2017. Accessed January 18, 2022. https://radiotamazuj.org/en/news/article/un-panel-accuses-ukraine-of-supplying-south-sudan-with-arms.

85. United Nations Mission in South Sudan (UNMISS), "Major General Chaoying Yanks Takes Responsibility as acting Head of UNMISS Force," November 11, 2016. Accessed December 12, 2021. https://unmiss.unmissions.org/major-general-chaoying-yang-takes-responsibility-acting-head-unmiss-force.

Chapter 5

1. *The Guardian*, "UN Peacekeeper Ignored "Rape and Assault of Aid Workers," August 16, 2016. Accessed February 02, 2020. https://www.theguardian.com/world/2016/aug/15/south-sudan-aid-worker-rape-attack-united-nations-un.

2. Mahmood Mamdani, *Neither Settler Nor Native*: *The Making and Unmaking of Permanent Minorities* (Cambridge, MA: The Belknap Press of Harvard University Press), 248.

3. See, e.g., Steven C Roach, "How Political Is the ICC? Pressing Challenges and the Need for Diplomatic Efficacy," *Global Governance* 19, no. 4 (December 2013): 507–523.

4. With 70 members drawn from the diaspora and across South Sudan, the group consists of doctors, lawyers, and economists, a network strong enough to influence the government.

5. Voice of America, "Diaspora Voices Missing in South Sudan Dialogue, Activists Say," January 21, 2018. Accessed, July 20, 2021. https://www.voanews.com/a/diaspora-voices-missing-south-sudan-dialogue-activists-say/4233632.html. The diaspora are those maintaining dual citizenship or who fled the country and left family members behind in South Sudan. The diaspora unofficially represents a sixth area inside the African Union, but in many cases, such as South Sudan, it has turned into an excluded area in which members have had little voice in the talks about peace and governmental affairs. The national government refuses to hear their concerns or demands.

6. This included John Bul Dau and Panther Dul, two of the main characters depicted in the documentary *God Grew Tired of Us*. The documentary chronicles Dau's and the other lost boys' journey from the desert of Sudan to the Kukuma refugee camp in Kenya. Their story reflected the plight and hope of these displaced children who had fled the attacks on their villages by government-backed military forces. Dau's words in the documentary highlight the difficulties transitioning from communal life to an individualist one.

7. In fact, 42 percent opposed independence and based their vote along cultural and tribal lines.

8. Cara Anna, "South Sudan Activist Flees to US, says Kiir Wanted Him Dead," *Washington Post*, July 23, 2020. Accessed, November 4, 2021.

9. Peter Biar Ajak, "South Sudan Deserves Better than Salva Kiir," *Washington Post*, October 6, 2020.

NOTES 209

10. Interview with Joseph Bakosoro, Juba, South Sudan, January 23, 2020.

11. Mamdani, *Neither Settler Nor Native*, 15.

12. Fanon, *The Wretched of the Earth*, 88.

13. Dave Eggers, *What Is the What* (New York: Vintage Books, 2006), 385.

14. Republic of South Sudan, The Transitional Constitution of the Republic of South Sudan, adopted March 2011 (Juba: Ministry of Justice).

15. United Nations Human Rights Office of the High Commissioner, "South Sudan: UN Report Contains 'Searing' Account of Killings, Rapes and Destruction," March 1, 2016. Accessed July 8, 2020. http://ohchr.org/EN/NewsEvents/Pages/DisplayNews. aspx?NewsID=17207&LangID=E#sthash.xkWt5VzL.dpuf.

16. Republic of South Sudan, "The Transitional Constitution of the Republic of South Sudan," Articles 145–146.

17. *Sudan Tribune*, "South Sudan Launches Human Rights Forum to Address Its Challenges," April 14, 2012. Accessed at June 14, 2021. https://sudantribune.com/ article42898/.

18. *Sudan Tribune*, "South Sudan Launches Human Rights Forum to Address Its Challenges," April 15, 2012. https://reliefweb.int/report/south-sudan-republic/ south-sudan-launches-human-rights-forum-address-its-challenges.

19. South Sudan Human Rights Commission, "Report on the Government's Suppression of the Media and the Hundreds of People Killed in the Streets by Government Forces and the White Army." March 2014.

20. *Sudan Tribune*, "South Sudan Human Rights Body Says that Violations Committed by Both Parties in the Conflict," *Sudan Tribune*, March 22, 2014. Accessed June 20, 2021. https://www.sudantribune.com/spip.php?article50386.

21. Republic of South Sudan, "The Transitional Constitution," Article 146. Accessed June 14, 2020. https://www.wipo.int/edocs/lexdocs/laws/en/ss/ss013en.pdf.

22. United Nations Security Council, "Panel of Experts on South Sudan addressed to the Security Council," April 9, 2019, S/2019/301. Accessed July 7, 2020. https://digitallibr ary.un.org/record/3801695?ln=en.

23. Republic of South Sudan, "The Transitional Constitution of the Republic of South Sudan."

24. United Nations Security Council, "Panel of Experts on South Sudan Address to the Security Council."

25. Human Rights Watch, "South Sudan: Government Forces Abusing Civilians," June 4, 2019, 2. Accessed July 20, 2021. https://www.hrw.org/news/2019/06/04/south-sudan-government-forces-abusing-civilians.

26. Unmarried girls, who become pregnant by a classmate or adult, are not allowed to attend school.

27. Human Rights Watch, "World Report 2013: South Sudan, 2015. World Report 2013." Accessed January 18, 2020.

28. Article 16 of the Transitional Constitution stipulates the equal rights of all people and equal gender pay as well as laws to combat harmful customs and traditions that undermine the dignity and status of women.

210 NOTES

29. National Democratic Institute, "Governing South Sudan," Washington, DC, March 22, 2012. 6. Accessed January 23, 2022. https://www.ndi.org/sites/default/files/Focus-group-governing-South-Sudan.pdf.
30. United Nations Children's Fund (UNICEF), "Some Things Are Not Fit for Children—Marriage Is One of Them," October 5, 2020.
31. African Union Commission of Inquiry on South Sudan (AUCISS), "Final Report", October 15, 2015, 194. Accessed June 24, 2019. http://www.peaceau.org/uploads/auc iss.final.report.pdf.
32. Interview with Joseph Mijack, Malakal, South Sudan, January 30, 2020.
33. Interview with James Aguer, Malakal, South Sudan, January 29, 2020.
34. Interview with Gertrude Callaway, Malakal, South Sudan, January 29, 2020.
35. Interview with Kari Oyen, Juba, South Sudan, January 23, 2020.
36. Interview with Judith Ruben, Yambio, South Sudan, January 30, 2020.
37. Interview with Edward Yaki, Yambia, South Sudan, on February 2, 2020.
38. AUCISS, Final Report of the African Union Commission of Inquiry on South Sudan, 210.
39. Interview with Daniel Makier, Malakal, South Sudan, January 29, 2020.
40. United Nations Security Council, "Report of Panel of Experts on South Sudan," addressed to the Security Council, April 9, 2019, S/2019/301. Accessed July 21.2021. https://digitallibrary.un.org/record/3801695?ln=en.
41. United Nations Office for the Coordination of Humanitarian Affairs (UNOCHA), "South Sudan: Humanitarian Snapshot," February 2020, Accessed July 10, 2021. https://www.unocha.org/south-sudan.
42. Many South Sudanese refugees in northern Uganda are given small plots of land to raise their food.
43. Elias Biryabarema, "Hatred Spills beyond South Sudan along with the Refugees," Reuters, December 15, 2016. Accessed August 2, 2021. https://www.reuters.com/arti cle/us-southsudan-uganda-refugees-idUSKBN1441QU.
44. Voice of America, "UN Appeals for 1.3 Billion for South Sudan Refugees," March 14, 2020. Accessed, July 24, 2021. https://www.voanews.com/africa/un-appeals-13b-south-sudan-refugees-host-countries.
45. Rachel Ibreck, South Sudan's Injustice System: Law and Activism on the Frontline (London: Zed Books, 2019), 6.
46. A number of judges in South Sudan's judicial system remain among the lowest per capita of developing countries.
47. Ibreck, South Sudan's Injustice System, 62.
48. Interview with Raimondo Geri Legge, Juba, South Sudan, February 8, 2020.
49. Interview with Legge.
50. After the South Sudanese pound was depreciated in late 2015, the national government slashed the salaries of full-time faculty from 3300 Sudanese pounds per month to 600, provoking mass protest. The national government would eventually relent to their demands by cutting salaries by half.
51. Nyagoah Tut Por, "South Sudan Academic Suspended over Opinion, Piece," Human Rights Watch, February 12, 2020. Accessed July 10, 2021. https://www.hrw.org/news/ 2020/02/12/south-sudan-academic-suspended-over-opinion-piece/.

NOTES 211

52. United Nations Security Council, "Panel of Experts on South Sudan addressed to the Security Council."
53. Amnesty International, "South Sudan: Missing File Blocks Justice for Terrain Hotel Rapes and Murder, September 6, 2019. Accessed July 18, 2021. https://www.amnesty. org/en/latest/news/2019/09/south-sudan-missing-file-blocks-justice-for-terrain-hotel-rapes-murder/.
54. Ibreck, *South Sudan's Injustice System*.
55. A UN Mobile Court had replaced the court's operations for a period between 12 and 18 months while the local government waited for funds to restore the High Court building.
56. Interview with Judge Aviel Nyong, Malakal, South Sudan, January 28, 2020.
57. Before it could complete its load, it had to suspend several pending cases.
58. United Nations Commission on Human Rights (UNHCR), "Report of the Commission on Human Rights in South Sudan, 24 February–20 March 2020 Agenda item 4," A/HRC/43/56.
59. Article 5 of the Transitional Constitution states these four sources: "The Constitution, written law, customs and traditions of the people, the will of the people, and any other relevant document." Accessed July 19, 2020. https://www.constituteproject.org/const itution/South_Sudan_2011.pdf.
60. Interview with Farouk Ismail, Juba South Sudan, February 5, 2020.
61. Ibreck, *South Sudan's Injustice System*, 69.
62. Joan Nyanyuki, "South Sudan: Missing File Blocks Justice for Terrain Hotel Rapes and Murder," *Amnesty International*, September 6, 2019. Accessed July 17, 2021. https://www.amnesty.org/en/latest/news/2019/09/south-sudan-missing-file-blocks-justice-for-terrain-hotel-rapes-murder/.
63. Human Rights Watch, "South Sudan Set Meeting on War Crimes Court, Lack of Communication and Clear Plan Impede Justice," October 9, 2019. Accessed July 24, 2021. https://www.hrw.org/news/2019/10/09/south-sudan/au-set-meeting-war-cri mes-court#.
64. African Union Commission of Inquiry on South Sudan (AUCISS), "Final Report", October 15, 2015, pp. 234–236. Accessed March 23, 2020. http://www.peaceau.org/uploads/auciss.final.report.pdf.
65. IGAD, "Agreement on the Resolution of Conflict in the Republic of South Sudan," Ch. 4, arts. 1–3.
66. Mamdani, *Neither Settler Nor Native*, 345.
67. United Nations Development Program (UNDP), "The Search for a New Beginning," a Nationwide Survey Conducted by the South Sudan Law Society. Juba, South Sudan, June 2015.
68. Kiir and Machar, "South Sudan Needs Truth, not Trials."
69. James Copnall, a BBC reporter for South Sudan, was able to verify Machar's claim that he had no knowledge of the op-ed, and that the opinion was probably released by Kiir's office without Machar's knowledge.
70. Amnesty International, "South Sudan: Crippled Justice System and Blanket Amnesties Fueling Impunity for War Crimes," October 7, 2019. https://www.amne

212 NOTES

sty.org/en/latest/news/2019/10/south-sudan-crippled-justice-system-and-blanket-amnesties-fuelling-impunity-for-war-crimes/.

71. China rejected the establishment of the ICC in 1998 and, like the United States, treated it as a threat to its sovereignty and overseas military operations.

72. Moreover, if the ICTR offers an important lesson, it is that the scale of crimes or the number of people who have committed them, would also require a local court perhaps similar to the Rwanda's gacaca courts, to address the hundreds, if not thousands, of other individuals who have perpetrated crimes.

73. The United States would eventually open up an investigation in Afghanistan 2019, only to see the Trump administration impose sanctions on the ICC Prosecutor.

74. Mamdani, *Neither Settle Nor Native*, 333.

75. Yel and Wel, *Salva Kiir Mayardit*, 284.

76. Yel and Wel, *Salva Kiir Mayardit*, 198.

77. Mamdani "Who's to Blame in South Sudan? *Boston Review*, June 28, 2016. Accessed July 3, 2019. http://bostonreview.net/world/mahmood-mamdani-south-sudan-failed-transition.

78. Sam Mednick, "South Sudan Paying US Lobbyists $3.7M for Better Trump Ties," *AP News*, April 29, 2019. Accessed September 23, 2021. https://apnews.com/11c96 fc87dc74750be72af91e9ea9474. The Contract stipulates: "(1) Open a channel of communication between President Kiir and President Trump with the objective of persuading President Trump and his administration to expand economic and political relations with South Sudan, and supporting American sector private investment in South Sudan in oil, natural resources, energy, gas, mining, and other areas; (2) Improve bilateral relations between the United States and South Sudan; (3) Persuade the Trump administration to reverse current sanctions and further block potential sanctions; (4) Delay and ultimately block establishment of the hybrid court envisaged in R-ARCISS; (5) Mobilize American companies to invest in the oil, natural resources, and other sectors; (6) Persuade the Trump administration to open a military relationship with South Sudan in order to enhance the fight against terrorism and promote regional stability."

79. Quoted in Mednick, "South Sudan Paying US lobbyists $3.7M for Better Trump Ties."

80. Holland Hereward, "Amid Criticism, South Sudan Signs New Deal with U.S. Lobbyists," Reuters, May 8, 2019, Accessed June 20, 2020. https://www.reuters.com/article/south-sudan-usa/amid-criticism-south-sudan-signs-new-deal-with-us-lobbyists-idUSL5N22K6EG.

Chapter 6

1. United Nations Security Council, "Final Report of the Panel of Experts on South Sudan."

2. In late August 2015, the three main parties, the SPLM-in Government, SPLM-IO and SPLM-A Former Detainee signed ARCSS.

NOTES   213

3. Simon Yel and Panuel Wel, *Salva Kiir Mayardit, The Joshua of South Sudan: President Kiir & Speeches After Independence* (Juba: The Center for Strategic and Governance Studies, 2016), 243.

4. Steven C. Roach, "South Sudan's Troubled Peace: How the Peace Deal Got Stuck?" *Foreign Affairs*, Council on Foreign Relations, April 3, 2016. Accessed November 13, 2019. http://foreignaffairs.com.

5. Brian Adeba, "Splitting South Sudan in 28 States: Right Move, Wrong Time?" *African Arguments*, October 7, 2015. Accessed December 3, 2019. https://africanarguments. org/2015/10/07/splitting-south-sudan-into-28-states-right-move-wrong-time/.

6. *Reliefweb*, "South Sudan Rival Peace Partners to Negotiate Solution to 28 States," January 12, 2016. Accessed April 12, 2021. https://reliefweb.int/report/south-sudan/ south-sudan-rival-peace-partners-negotiate-solution-28-states.

7. Quoted in Al Jazeera, "South Sudan's Riek Machar Sworn in as Vice President," April 27, 2016. Accessed March 24, 2021. https://www.aljazeera.com/news/2016/4/27/ south-sudans-riek-machar-sworn-in-as-vice-president.

8. Quoted in Al Jazeera, "South Sudan's Riek Machar Sworn in as Vice President."

9. Peter Martell, *First Raise the Flag: How South Sudan Won the Longest War but Lost the Peace* (New York: Oxford University Press, 2018), 247.

10. *Sudan Tribune*, "Machar in South Africa for Medical Treatment: Spokesperson," October 13, 2016. Accessed March 23, 2021. https://www.sudantribune.com/spip. php?article60513.

11. Steven C. Roach, "Down but not Out: What Machar's Absence Means for South Sudan's Peace Process," *African Arguments*, September 23, 2016. Accessed November 12, 2018. http:// africanarguments.org/.

12. Jok Madut Jok, "South Sudan's Elusive Peace: Between Local Drivers of Violence and the Actions of External Actors," in *South Sudan: Post-Independence Dilemmas*, ed. Amir Idris (Abingdon: Routledge, 2018), 75.

13. Statista, "Average annual crude oil price from 1976 to 2021." Accessed February 21, 2020. https://www.statista.com/statistics/262860/uk-brent-crude-oil-price-chan ges-since-1976.

14. Intergovernmental Authority on Development (IGAD), "Agreement on Cessation of Hostilities, Protection of Civilians and Humanitarian Access," High-Level Revitalization Forum, Addis Ababa, December 22, 2017. Accessed September 23, 2019. https://peacemaker.un.org/southsudan-cessation-of-hostilities-SPLM/AOpp osition.

15. Nyamilepedia, "Opposition Official Allied to Changson Reigns, Joins Josephine Lagu's Group," August 10, 2019. Accessed July 12, 2021. https://www.nyamile.com/ 2019/08/10/opposition-official-allied-to-changson-resigns-joins-josephine-lagus-group/.

16. European Union, "EU Sanctions South Sudan Militia Leader, Army Commander," Voanews.com. July 11, 2014.

17. Nyamilepedia, "NDM Says It Is 'Dismayed' over Government Role in Dividing SSOA," February 4, 2019.

18. The legal decree though was not incorporated into the peace agreement nor amended to the Transitional Constitution.

214 NOTES

19. The South Sudan Opposition Alliance (SSOA), "The Charter of the South Sudan Opposition Alliance," May 7, 2018. Accessed July 8, 2021. https://www.malakalpost.com/the-charter-of-the-south-sudan-opposition-alliance-ssoa/.

20. See, e.g., John H. McGarry and Brendan O'Leary, "Power-Sharing Executives: Consociational and Centripetal Formulae and the Case of Northern Ireland," *Ethnopolitics* 15, no. 5 (2016): 497–515; Nils A. Butenseøn and Øyvand Stiansen, *Power-Sharing in Conflict-Ridden Societies: Challenges for Building Peace and Democratic Stability* (London: Routledge, 2015).

21. Donald L. Horowitz, "Ethnic Power Sharing: Three Problems," *Journal of Democracy* 25, no. 2 (2014): 5–6.

22. International Crisis Group, Salvaging South Sudan's Fragile Peace Deal, Report N 270, March 13, 2019. Accessed July 9, 2020. https://www.crisisgroup.org/africa/horn-africa/south-sudan/270-salvaging-south-sudans-fragile-peace-deal/.

23. Museveni initially sought to recuse himself from matters related to the intervention of South Sudan, but in the end, he insisted on having an equal voice, jeopardizing any neutrality that IGAD claimed to provide.

24. Mahmood Mamdani, "The Trouble with South Sudan's New Peace Deal," *New York Times*, September 24, 2018. Accessed March 23, 2020. https://www.nytimes.com/2018/09/24/opinion/south-sudan-peace-agreement.html.

25. The NAS consisted in large part of Machar's SPLA-IO fighters, who had defected after government forces attacked Machar's military forces (and joined the NAS).

26. Sam Mednick, "Key Rebel leader in South Sudan's Civil War refuses to lay down arms," *Vice*, February 15, 2019. Accessed July 23, 2021. https://www.vice.com/en_us/article/mbz3wa/key-rebel-leader-in-south-sudans-civil-war-rejects-peace-deal-and-refuses-to-lay-down-arms/. The NAS had signed the Ceasefire Agreement, but not the 2018 peace agreement

27. Quoted in Mednick, "Key Rebel Leader in South Sudan's Civil War Refuses to Lay Down Arms."

28. *Sudan Tribune*, "13 Civilians Killed, 7 Soldiers Killed during Fresh Clashes in South Sudan's Equatoria: NAS," February 13, 2019. Accessed September 21, 2021. https://sudantribune.com/article65203/.

29. *Sudan Tribune*, "NAS claims obtaining evidences of War Crimes in South Sudan," June 14, 2021. Accessed November 23, 2021. https://sudantribune.com/article67778/.

30. United Nations Human Rights (UNHCR), "Report of the Commission on Human Rights in South Sudan," February 24–March 20, 2020. Agenda item 4, A/HRC/43/56.

31. Dimo Silva Aurelio, "MSF, ICRC Leave South Sudan's Pibor Area," Voice of America, June 25, 2020. Accessed April 23, 2021. https://www.voanews.com/africa/south-sudan-focus/msf-icrc-leave-south-sudans-pibor-area/.

32. Waakhe Simon Wudu, "What Is Causing South Sudan's Intercommunal Fighting," *Voice of America*, June 24, 2020. Accessed July 24, 2021. https://www.voaafrica.com/a/africa_south-sudan-focus_what-causing-south-sudans-inter-communal-fighting/6191679.html.

33. Anadolu Agency, "South Sudan's Vice President Guards Killed in Ambush," August 21, 2020. https://www.aa.com.tr/en/africa/south-sudan-vice-presidents-guards-killed-in-ambush/1948983/.

34. Jok, "South Sudan's Elusive Peace," 78.
35. Tom Ginsburg, "Constitutions as Contracts, Constitutions as Charters," in *Social and Political Foundations of Constitutions*, ed. Denis J Galligan and Mila Versteeg (Cambridge: Cambridge University Press, 2015), 182–206.
36. Vivien Hart, "Constitution-Making and the Transformation of Conflict, Peace and Change," *William and Mary Law Journal* 26, no. 2 (2002): 153–176.
37. See, e.g., Russell Hardin, "Why a Constitution?" in *Social and Political Foundations of Constitutions*, ed. Denis J. Galligan and Mila Versteeg (Cambridge: Cambridge University Press, 2015); Allen S. Wiener, "Constitutions as Peace Treaties: A Cautionary Tale from the Arab Spring," *Stanford Law Review* 64, no. 8 (November 18, 2011): 1–4.
38. Wiener, "Constitutions as Peace Treaties," 2.
39. Christof Hartman, "Limits of Constitutional Reform in African Conflicts," *Ethnopolitics* 15, no. 5 (2015): 523–27
40. The Reconstituted Joint Monitoring and Evaluation Commission (RJMEC), "The NCAC Hands over Constitutional Amendment to Constitution Minister," December 10, 2019.
41. Interview with John Natanga, Juba, South Sudan, December 18, 2015.
42. Interview with John Natanga, Juba South Sudan, February 8, 2020.
43. The Revitalized Agreement on the Resolution of the Conflict in South Sudan (R-ARCSS), signed December 9, 2018, Article 4(5). Accessed, February 8, 2021. https://www.peaceagreements.org.
44. Amir Idris, "How the UN Security Council Is Perpetuating South Sudan's Conflict," *Newsweek*, January 22, 2017. Accessed September 8, 2019. https://www.newsweek.com/south-sudan-conflict-civil-war-un-security-council-arms-embargo-544738.
45. The African Union Commission for Human and People's Rights defines civil society as formal and informal associations independent of the state through which citizens may pursue common purposes, participate in the political, social and cultural life of their societies, and be involved in all matters pertaining to public policy and public affairs.
46. Reliefweb. "In South Sudan, Nonviolent Action is Essential to Building Peace," February 22, 2019. Accessed May 9, 2020. https://reliefweb.int/report/south-sudan/south-sudan-nonviolent-action-essential-building-peace.
47. Johnson, *South Sudan*, 271.
48. Oxfam International, "Conflict, Poverty and Hunger driving Child Marriage in South Sudan," February 18, 2019. https://www.oxfam.org/en/press-releases/conflict-poverty-and-hunger-driving-child-marriage-south-sudan-0.
49. Ibreck, *South Sudan's In/justice System*, 179.
50. Interview with Simon Buony, Juba, South Sudan, February 9, 2020.
51. Denis Dumo, "South Sudan rebel leader Machar returns to mark peace deal," *Reuters*, October 31, 2018. Accessed March 30, 2021. https://www.reuters.com/article/us-southsudan-peaceconference/south-sudan-rebel-leader-machar-returns-to-mark-peace-deal-idUSKCN1N50LI.
52. Interview with Aysen Aler Jangroor, Juba, South Sudan, February 3, 2020.

216 NOTES

53. AUCISS, "Final Report of the African Union Commission of Inquiry on South Sudan."
54. United Kingdom Agency for International Development (UKAID), "South Sudan: The Perils of Payroll Peace." UKAID. March 2019.
55. Reliefweb. "South Sudan's NAS Establishes a Committee on Sexual Violence," February 6, 2020, Accessed March 23, 2021. https://reliefweb.int/report/south-sudan/south-sudan-s-nas-establishes-committee-sexual-violence.
56. Mamdani, "Whose to blame in South Sudan?"
57. Machar had earlier indicated his willingness to discuss a new number between 32 and 10.
58. *The New Humanitarian*, "South Sudan Peace Deal Looms as Questions linger on Financial Transparency," February 14, 2020. Accessed December 14, 2021. https://www.thenewhumanitarian.org/investigation/2020/02/14/South-Sudan-peace-fund ing-coalition-government-war-IGAD-displaced-NPTC-UN.
59. Interview with Joseph Bakosoro, January 23, 2020.
60. Conversation with Lorna Merekaje, Juba, South Sudan, February 12, 2020.
61. Radio Tamazuj, "Eastern Equatoria: Senior SPLA-IO officer defects to Cirillo's NAS," December 9, 2020. Accessed January 13, 2021. https://radiotamazuj.org/en/news/arti cle/eastern-equatoria-senior-spla-io-officer-defects-to-cirillo-s-nas.
62. Quoted in Siobhan O'Grady, "The African Rebel Leader Who's Stoked About Trump," *The Atlantic*, November 26, 2016. Accessed May 12, 2021. https://www.theatlantic. com/international/archive/2016/11/south-sudan-machar-kiir-trump-clinton/ 508499.
63. Quoted in Elise Labot,"Nikki Haley Issues Stern Warning in South Sudan," *CNN*, October 25, 2017 Accessed January 12, 2018. https://www.cnn.com/2017/10/25/polit ics/nikki-haley-warning-south-sudan.
64. Quoted in Michelle Nichols, "U.S. Warns South Sudan Government Against 'Deliberate Starvation Tactics,'" *Reuters*, March 23, 2017. Accessed January 18, 2018. https://www.reuters.com/article/us-southsudan-security-un/u-s-warns-south-sudan-government-against-deliberate-starvation-tactics-idUSKBN16U32C.
65. Nichols, "U.S. Warns South Sudan Government Against 'Deliberate Starvation Tactic.'"

Chapter 7

1. Quoted in *TRT World*, "South Sudan Declares 'End of War' as Rival Leaders form Govt," February 22, 2020. Accessed November 2, 2021. https://www.trtworld.com/ africa/south-sudan-declares-end-of-war-as-rival-leaders-form-govt-34026.
2. Nyamilepedia, "South Sudan Appeals to IMF World Bank to for Bailout as Economy Collapses," August 24, 2020. Accessed November 3, 2021. https://www.nyamile.com/ 2020/08/24/south-sudan-appeals-to-imf-world-bank-for-bailout-as-economy-collapses/.

NOTES 217

3. Jieng Council of Elders, "Breaking the Silence: The Way Forward." January 21, 2021.

4. Garang A, Malak, "South Sudan President, Salva Kiir names full Cabinet," *The East African*, March 13, 2020. Accessed August 23, 2021. https://www.theeastafrican.co.ke/tea/news/east-africa/south-sudan-president-salva-kiir-names-full-cabinet-1438518/.

5. United Nations, "COVID-19 Potentially Greatest Threat to South Sudan's Already Fragile Health System", Special Representative Warns Security Council, June 23, 2020, SC/42.

6. United Nations, "COVID-19 Potentially Greatest Threat."

7. Interview with Betty Sunday, Juba South Sudan, January 24, 2020.

8. *Sudan Tribune*, "South Sudan TGoNU Changed Constitution After Amendment by Joint Panel," March 29, 2020. Accessed July 12, 2021. https://sudantribune.com/artic le67270/.

9. *The East African*, "South Sudan: Kiir Stalls Appointment of Upper Nile Governor Olony." December 1. Accessed November 5, 2021. https://allafrica.com/stories/202012020044.html.

10. International Crisis Group, "Toward a Viable Future for South Sudan," February 10, 2021. Accessed November 2, 2021. https://www.crisisgroup.org/africa/horn-africa/south-sudan/300-toward-viable-future-south-sudan.

11. Radio Tamazuj, "Eastern Equatoria: Senior SPLA-IO officer defects to Cirillo's NAS," December 9, 2020. Accessed April 2, 2021. https://radiotamazuj.org/en/news/article/eastern-equatoria-senior-spla-io-officer-defects-to-cirillo-s-nas.

12. United Nations Security Council, "Final Report of the Panel of Experts on South Sudan," submitted pursuant to resolution 2521 S/2021/365. Accessed July 8, 2021. https://reliefweb.int/report/south-sudan/final-report-panel-experts-south-sudan-submitted-pursuant-resolution-2521-2020/.

13. United Nations Security Council, "Final Report of the Panel of Experts on South Sudan."

14. Al Jazeera, "Death Toll from South Sudan Soldiers, Civilians Clashes Hits 127," August 12, 2020. Accessed February 3, 2021. https://www.aljazeera.com/news/2020/08/death-toll-south-sudan-soldiers-civilians-clashes-hits-127-200812094926 256.html.

15. Voice of America, "No Deal on South Sudan States, Boundaries as Deadline Nears," February 7, 2020. Accessed April 4, 2021. https://www.voanews.com/a/africa_so uth-sudan-focus_no-deal-south-sudan-states-boundaries-deadline-nears/6183 851.html.

16. Voice of America, "South Sudan President Appoints 1 Woman Among 8 Governors, 3 Administrators," June 30, 2020. Accessed May 23, 2021. https://www.voaafrica.com/a/africa_south-sudan-focus_south-sudan-president-appoints-1-woman-among-8-governors-3-administrators/6192013.html.

17. Quoted in Voice of America, "South Sudan President Appoints 1 Woman Among 8 Governors, 3 Administrators."

18. Radio Tamazuj, Kiir appoints officials for N. Bahr el Ghazal, Warrap, Unity and C. Equatoria states, February 23, 2021. Accessed September 3, 2021. https://radio

218 NOTES

tamazuj.org/en/news/article/kiir-appoints-officials-for-n-bahr-el-ghazal-warrap-unity-and-c-equatoria-states.

19. BBC News, "South Sudan's President Salva Kiir Dissolves Parliament," May 9, 2021. Accessed September 4, 2021. https://www.bbc.com/news/world-africa-57046645.

20. Intergovernmental Authority on Development (IGAD), Communique of the 73rd Extraordinary Session, August 2021.

21. United Nations Security Council, "Final Report of the Panel of Experts on South Sudan."

22. United Nations Security Council, "Final Report of the Panel of Experts on South Sudan," 13.

23. Benjamin Takpiny, "South Sudan's Peace Deal under Serious Threat, *AA*," August 12, 2021. Accessed September 12, 2021. https://www.aa.com.tr/en/africa/south-sudans-peace-deal-under-serious-threat-warns-un/2442364.

24. Pur, "A Glimmer of Hope for South Sudan's Victims."

25. Jason Patinkin, "South Sudan's Machar Denies Opposing the War Crimes Court," *Voice of America*, June 10, 2016. Accessed June 23, 2021. https://www.voanews.com/africa/south-sudans-machar-denies-opposing-war-crimes-court.

26. Politicizing justice refers in this case to how a state or nonstate actor can use the legitimacy of a court to gain political leverage and to eliminate their political opposition by having the court target them. On this issue, see Steven C. Roach, "How Political Is the ICC? Pressing Challenges and the Need for Diplomatic Efficacy," *Global Governance* 19, no. 4 (2013): 507–510.

27. South Sudan Law Society "The Search for a New Beginning." 81 percent of the respondents supported reparations from the state for survivors of abuses.

28. U.S. Department of State, U.S. Relations with South Sudan, January 21, 2022. Accessed November 5, 2021. https://www.state.gov/u-s-relations-with-south-sudan/#:~:text=The%20United%20States%20has%20no%20significant.

29. Quoted in United Nations Security Council, "COVID-19 Potentially Greatest Threat to South Sudan's Already Fragile Health System, Special Representative Warns Security Council," June 23, 2020. SC/42.

30. United Nations Security Council, "COVID-19 Potentially Greatest Threat to South Sudan's Already Fragile Health System, Special Representative Warns Security Council."

31. Akot Emmanuel, "Kiir Dissolves Covid-19 Taskforce," South Sudan Eye Radio, May 16, 2020. Accessed November 2, 2021. https://eyeradio.org/kiir-dissolves-covid-19-taskforce/.

32. Quoted in David Ochieng Mbewa, "South Sudan's Kiir Hints at Reopening Churches in spite of Rise of Covid 19 Cases," CGTN. August 10, 2020. Accessed August 3, 2021. https://africa.cgtn.com/2020/08/10/south-sudans-kiir-hints-at-reopening-churches-despite-rise-in-covid-19-cases.

33. United Nations Security Council, "Final Report of the Panel of Experts," 27.

34. Paisley Dodds, "Inside Story: How We Broke the Story of Covid-19 Corruption inside South Sudan," *The New Humanitarian*, April 12, 2021. Accessed September 5, 2021. https://www.thenewhumanitarian.org/opinion/2021/4/12/how-we-broke-story-of-alleged-covid-corruption-south-sudan.

35. Associated Press, "South Sudan Oil Production Story", May 29, 2019. https://apnews.com/article/africa-sudan-international-news-south-sudan-juba-8bb3f5b30e444c0b807b3c73.

36. Victor Katona, "South Sudan Struggles to Boost its Oil Production," Oil Price.com, August 3, 2020. Accessed July 11, 2021. https://oilprice.com/Energy/Energy-General/South-Sudan-Struggles-To-Boost-Its-Oil-Production.html.

37. United Nations Security Council, "Final Report of the Panel of Experts."

38. Mading Ngor, "Road-Starved South Sudan Eyes a $4 Billion Road Network," Reuters, August 9, 2012. Accessed May 5, 2021. https://www.reuters.com/article/us-southsudan-roads/road-starved-south-sudan-eyes-a-4-billion-road-network-idUS.

39. The GRSS had already completed construction of a new airport terminal in April 2017.

40. Radio Tamazuj, "Government raises crude oil allocation to China," April 5, 2019. Accessed January 9, 2021. https://radiotamazuj.org/en/news/article/government-raises-crude-oil-allocation-to-china.

41. United Nations Security Council, "Final Report of the Panel of Experts on South Sudan."

42. Sam Mednick, "South Sudan Ignores Reports on Oil Pollution, Birth Defects," Associated Press, February 13, 2020. Accessed January 10, 2021. https://apnews.com/f2f06cfa70126ad179445720d7c60b8a.

43. David Mono Danga, "South Sudan Residents Protest Oil Facility," Voice of America, August 27, 2020. Accessed March 23, 2020. https://www.voanews.com/africa/south-sudan-focus/south-sudan-residents-protest-oil-facilities.

44. Interview with Michael Duku, Juba, South Sudan, January 23, 2020.

45. Katherine Almquist Knopf, "Ending South Sudan's Civil War." Council of Foreign Relations, March 16, 2017. Accessed April 22, 2020. https://www.cfr.org/report/ending-south-sudans-civil-war.

46. Oxfam, "Building a Social Contract in South Sudan," Oxfam Progamme Insights, October 6, 2014. Accessed April 9, 2020. https://policy-practice.oxfam.org/resources/building-a-social-contract-in-south-sudan-331967.

47. Luka Biong Deng Kuol, "South Sudan: The Elusive Quest for a Resilient Social Contract," *Journal of Intervention and Statebuilding* 14, no. 1 (March 2020): 73.

48. John Young, "Ethiopian Ethnic Federalism: A Model for South Sudan?" in *The Struggle for South Sudan: Challenges of Security and State Cooperation*, ed. Luka Biong Deng Kuol and Sarah Logan (London: L.B. Tauris, 2020), 124–143.

49. Douglas Johnson, "Federalism in in the History of South Sudanese Political Thought," in *The Struggle for South Sudan: Challenges of Security and State Cooperation*, ed. Luka Biong Deng Kuol and Sarah Logan (London: L.B. Tauris, 2020), 120.

50. Ero Comfort and Alan Boswell, "South Sudan Dismal Tenth Birthday: The World's Newest Country Needs an Overhaul," *Foreign Affairs,* Snapshot, July 9, 2021. Accessed September 9, 2021. https://www.foreignaffairs.com/articles/africa/2021-07-09/south-sudans-dismal-tenth-birthday.

51. Interview with Makuc Makuc Nyon, Juba, South Sudan, February. January 23, 2020.

220 NOTES

52. Quoted in *The Arab Weekly*, "Sudan Vows to Keep on Pushing for Peace with Ethiopia," August 16, 2021. Accessed October 21, 2021. https://thearabweekly.com/sudan-vows-keep-pushing-peace-ethiopia.

53. Al-Jazeera, "In Addis Ababa, Sudan PM Announces IGAD Summit on Tigray Crisis," December 14, 2020. Accessed October 11, 2021. https://www.aljazeera.com/news/2020/12/13/sudans-pm-visits-ethiopia-as-tigray-refugees-surpass-50000.

54. Max Bearak, "Tigray Rebels Announce Plan to Withdraw from Ethiopian Regions," *Washington Post*, December 20, 2021. Accessed October 4, 2020. https://www.washingtonpost.com/world/2021/12/20/tigray-amhara-afar-ethiopia/.

55. *Sudan Tribune*, "Ethiopia Completed GERD's Second Filling, Announce Abiy Ahmed," July 20, 2021. Accessed October 3, 2021. https://sudantribune.com/article67929/. Ethiopia has repeatedly insisted that any binding agreement upholding the status-quo colonial era agreements—which allowed Egypt to enjoy nearly 78 percent of the Blue Nile's flow—is unfair and unacceptable. After again refusing to reach an amicable solution with Egypt and Sudan in April 2021, which Uganda also supported (both Sudan and Egypt argued the UN Security Council to issue a resolution in support of a trilateral agreement), Ethiopia managed to complete the second filling of the reservoir in July 2021. As expected, Sudan and Egypt rejected the unilateral move.

56. *Egypt Today*, "South Sudan agrees with Egypt on necessity for reaching legal binding agreement on GERD operation, filling," November 28, 2020. Accessed October 9, 2021. https://www.egypttoday.com/Article/1/94734/South-Sudan-agrees-with-Egypt-on-necessity-for-reaching-legal/.

References

Abdin, H. (1985). *Early Sudanese Nationalism, 1919–1925*. Khartoum: Khartoum University Press.

Abushouk, Ahmed I. and Anders Bjorkelo (eds.) (1998). *The Principles of Native Administration in the Anglo-Egyptian Sudan, 1898–1956*. Omdurman: Abdel Karim Mirghani Cultural Centre.

Acemoglu, Daron and James A Robinson (2012). *Why Nations Fail: The Origins of Power, Prosperity, and Poverty*. New York: Crown Business.

Adeba, Brian (2015). "Splitting South Sudan in 28 States: Right Moved, Wrong Time?" *African Arguments*, October 7.

Adwok Nyaba, Peter (1996). *The Politics of Liberation in Southern Sudan: An Insider's View*. London: Fountain Publishing.

Africa (2018). "Clooney's The Sentry Says South Sudan Is Using Oil Cash to Fund Conflict," March 16. https://www.iol.co.za/news/africa/clooneys-the-sentry-says-south-sudan-is-using-oil-cash-to-fund-conflict-13619358.

African Union (2015). "Final Report of the African Union Commission of Inquiry on South Sudan," October 27. www.peaceau.org/en/article/final-report-of-the-african-union-commission-of-inquiry-on-south-sudan#sthash.evjg9lg8.dpuf.

Aggar, Malik and Eyre Gandof (2010). "SPLM Deputy Chairman Aggar Disapproves Elections Boycott in North Sudan," *Sudan Tribune*, April 7.

Albino, Oliver (1970). *The Sudan: A Southern Viewpoint*. London: Oxford University Press.

Al Jazeera (2020). "Death Toll from South Sudan Soldiers, Civilian Clashes Hits 127," August 12.

Al Jazeera (2020). "In Addis Ababa, Sudan PM Announces IGAD Summit on Tigray Crisis," December 14.

Al-Jazeera (2020). "Running on Empty: South Sudan Is Out of Foreign Exchange Reserves," August 20.

Al Jazeera (2020). "UNSC Extends South Sudan's Oil Embargo until May 2021," May 30.

Al Jazeera (2019). "Is Oil Money Fueling War in South Sudan," April 6.

Al Jazeera (2017). "Nikki Haley Blames Salva Kiir for Man-made Famine," April 26.

Al Jazeera (2017). "UN: South Sudan Forces Have Committed Capital Crimes," May 19.

Al Jazeera (2016). "South Sudan's Riek Machar Sworn in as Vice President," April 27.

Al Jazeera (2016). "UN Panel Recommends Arms Embargo, Sanctions on South Sudan," January 26.

Albino, Oliver (1970). *The Sudan: A Southern Viewpoint*. London: The Institute of Race Relations Oxford University Press.

Alier, Abel (1990). *Southern Sudan: Too Many Agreements Dishonored*. Exeter, NY: Ithaca Press.

Allam, Miriam, Hesham Bekhit, Alaa M. Elzewahry (2014). "Jonglei Canal Project under Potential Developments in the Upper Nile States." *Journal of Water Management Modeling* 26, 32–53.

222 REFERENCES

All Southern Sudanese Political Parties Conference (ASSPPC) (2010). "Southern Sudan United for Free, Fair and Transparent Referendum." Final Communique, held in Juba, October 13–17. www.southsudannewsagency.com/news/press-releases/all-southern-sudanese-political-parties-conference--final-communique.

Amnesty International (2020). "South Sudan: Evidence of Violations and Illicit Concealment of Arms Must Spur UN to Renew Arms Embargo," August 30.

Amnesty International (2020). "South Sudan: Thousands Still Missing," August 28.

Amnesty International (2019). "Do You Think We Will Prosecute Ourselves: No Prospects for Accountability in South Sudan," October.

Amnesty International (2019). "South Sudan: Crippled Justice System and Blanket Amnesties Fueling Impunity for War Crimes," October 7.

Amnesty International (2019). "South Sudan: Missing File Blocks Justice for Terrain Hotel Rapes and Murder," September.

Anadolu Agency (2020). "South Sudan's Vice President Guards Killed in Ambush," August 21.

Andreski, Stanislav (1968). The African Predicament: A Study in the Pathology of Modernization. New York: Atherton Press.

The Arab Weekly (2021). "Sudan-Ethiopia Mediation Gathers Steam," February 18.

Aurelio, Dimo Silva (2020) "MSF, ICRC Leave South Sudan's Pibor Area," Voice of America. June 25.

Ayel, Deng Mankok (2013). "A Tale of Juba and the Presidency." Juba Monitor, 3(145), 4.

BBC News (2021). "South Sudan's President Salva Kiir Dissolves Parliament," May 9.

BBC News (2015). "South Sudan Sanctions Blocked by Russia and Angola," September 6.

Bearak, Max (2021). "In Uganda, Museveni Steamrolls to a Sixth Term: Billions in U.S. Aid Help Him Stay in Power," The Washington Post, January 16.

Bell, Duncan (2007) The Idea of Greater Britain: Empire and the Future of World Order, 1860–1900. Princeton: Princeton University Press.

Biryabarema, Elias (2016). "Hatred Spills beyond South Sudan along with the Refugees," Reuters, December 15.

Blomfield, Adrian (2001). Sudan Rebel Group and Former Rivals Reunite," Reliefweb, May 28.

Bratton, Michael and Nicolas Van der Walle (1994). "Neopatrimonial Regimes and Political Transitions in Africa." World Politics 46(4), July, 453–489.

Burgis, Tom (2015). The Looting Machine: Warlords, Oligarchs, Corporations, Smugglers, and the Theft of Africa's Wealth. New York: Public Affairs.

Butenseøn, Nils A. and Øyvand Stiansen (2015). Power-Sharing in Conflict-Ridden Societies: Challenges for Building Peace and Democratic Stability. London: Routledge.

Carter Center (2010). "Observing Sudan's 2010 National Elections," April 11–18 Final Report.

Chamberlin, Muriel, E. (2014). The Scramble for Africa. London: Longman, 1974, 4th ed.

Chol, Jacob D. (2016). "The Reality of Petroleum Resource Curse in South Sudan: Can It Be avoided?" African Review 43(2), 17–60.

Christopher, Anthony J. (2011). "Secession and South Sudan: An African Precedent for the Future." South African Geographical Journal 93(2), 125–132.

The Citizen (2017). "Trump Delegation to Visit South Sudan," February 21.

The Citizen (2013). " 'Dura Saga' Probe Committee Urges Companies Involved to Appear or Face Legal Actions," August 4.

REFERENCES 223

The Citizen (2013). "SPLM-N, Ethiopian PM Discuss Peace in S, Kordofan and Blue Nile," August 4.

CNN (2012). "Sudan, South Sudan Prepare for Peace Talks," May 17.

Collier, Paul (2009). *Wars, Guns, and Votes: Democracy in Dangerous Places*. New York: Harper Collins.

Collins, Robert O. (2008). *A History of Modern Sudan*. Cambridge: Cambridge University Press.

Collins, Robert O. (1988). "The Jonglei Canal Project: Illusion or Reality?" *Water International* 13(3), 144–153.

Comprehensive Peace Agreement (2005). Available at: https://peacemaker.un.org/node/1369

Conflict Armament Research Organization (2018). *Weapon's Supplies into South Sudan's Civil War*. London: Conflict Armament Research.

Conflict Armament Research Weapons and Ammunition Airdropped to SPLA-IO Forces in South Sudan.

Cope, Kevin L. (2015). "South Sudan's Dualistic Constitution," in Denis J Galligan and Milla Versteeg (eds.), *Social and Political Foundations of Constitutions*. Cambridge: Cambridge University Press, 295–321.

Copnall, James (2014). *A Poisonous Thorn in Our Hearts: Sudan and South Sudan's Bitter and Incomplete Divorce*. London: Hurst and Company.

Copnall, James (2011). "Sudan: Why Abyei Is Crucial to North and South," BBC News, May 23.

Dagne, Ted (2005). "Sudan: Humanitarian Crisis, Peace Talks, Terrorism, and U.S. Policy," CRS Issue Brief for Congress, Congressional Research Service, Library of Congress.

Danga, David M. (2020). "South Sudan Residents Protest Oil Facility," Voice of America, August 27.

Danforth, John C. (2002). "Report to the President of the United States in the Outlook for Peace in Sudan." www.state.gov/p/af/rls/rpt/2002/10150.htm.

D'Estries, Michael (2015). "George Clooney Launches Sentry Project to Follow the Money from Africa's Wars," CNN, July 22, 2015. https://www.mnn.com/lifestyle/arts-culture/blogs/george-clooney-launches-sentry-project-follow-money-africas-wars.

De Vries, Lotje de and Mareike Schomerus (2017). "Fettered Self-Determination: South Sudan's Narrowed Path to Secession." *Civil Wars* 19(1), 26–45.

De Waal, Alex (2015). *The Real Politics of the Horn of Africa: Money, War, and the Business of Power*. London: Polity Press.

De Waal, Alex (2014). "When Kleptocracy becomes Insolvent: The Brute Causes of the Civil War in South Sudan." *African Affairs* 113(452), 347–369.

De Waal, Alex (2014). "Visualizing South Sudan: The Culprit: The Army." *World Peace Foundation*, 2014.

Deng, Francis (2006). "A Nation in Turbulent Search of Itself." *Annals of the American Academy of Political and Social Science* 603, 155–162.

Deng, Luka Biong (2010). "Social Capital and Civil War: The Dinka Community in Sudan's Civil War." *African Affairs* 109(435), 23–50.

Deng, Mark A. W. (2017). "Defining the Nature and Limits of Presidential Powers in the Transitional Constitution of South Sudan: A Politically Contentious Matter for the New Nation." *Journal of African Law* 51(1).

Dodds, Palsey (2021). "Inside Story: How We Broke the Story of Covid-19 Corruption Inside South Sudan." *The New Humanitarian*, April 12.

224 REFERENCES

Dumo, Denis (2019)."South Sudan Agrees Oil Exploration Deal with South Africa." Reuters, May 6.

East African (2020). South Sudan: Kiir Stalls Appointment of Upper Nile Governor Olony," December 1.

Eggers, Dave (2006). *What Is the What.* New York: Vintage Books.

Egypt Today (2020). "South Sudan Agrees with Egypt on Necessity for Reaching Legal Binding Agreement on GERD Operation, Filling," November 28.

Eisenstadt, Samuel N. (1973). *Traditional Patrimonialism and Modern Neopatrimonialism.* Beverly Hills, CA: Sage Publications.

El-Affendi, Abdelwahab (1992). *Turabi's Revolution.* London: Oxford University Press.

Elias, Norbert (1981). *The Civilizing Process.* London: Blackwell Publishers.

Elnur, I (2009). *Contested Sudan: The Political Economy of War and Reconstruction.* London: Routledge.

Emmanuel, Akot (2020). "Kiir Dissolves Covid-19 Taskforce, South Sudan," Eye Radio, May 16.

Energy Information Administration (2013). *Sudan and South Sudan.* Washington, DC: US Energy Information and Administration, August 25.

Englebert, P. and Hummel, R. (2005). "Let's Stick Together: Understanding Africa's Secessionist Deficit." *African Affairs* 104, 399–427.

Ero, Comfort and Alan Boswell (2021). "South Sudan's Dismal Tenth Birthday," *Foreign Affairs* (Snapshot). July 9.

European Union (2014). "EU Sanctions South Sudan Militia Leader, Army Commander," July 11.

Fahmy, Ziad (2011). *Ordinary Egyptians: Creating the Modern Nation through Popular Culture.* Stanford, CA: Stanford University Press.

Fanon, Frantz (1963). *The Wretched of the Earth.* Translated by Richard Philcox. New York: Grove Press.

Ferrie, Jared (2012). "South Sudan President Seeks Return of $4 Billion He Says Was Spirited Away," CNN, June 4.

Finnan, Daniel (2020). "South Sudan Elite Left Exposed as Covid-19 Strikes Government," *RFI*," June 4.

Fitz-Gerald, Anne M. (2013). "South Sudan," in Jane Boulden (ed.), *Responding to Conflict in Africa: The United Nations and Regional Organizations.* New York: Palgrave MacMillan, 307–326.

Garang, John (2005). "Speech Delivered to the United Nations in New York, July 12."

Garang, John (1981). *Identifying, Selecting, and Implementing Rural Development Strategies for Socio-Economic Development in the Jonglei Projects Area in the Southern Region, Sudan.* Ph.D. Dissertation, Iowa State University.

Gazibo, Mamoudou (2012). "Can Neopatrimonialism Dissolve into Democracy," in Daniel C. Bach and Mamoudou Gazibo (eds.), *Neopatrimonialism in Africa and Beyond.* Abingdon: Routledge. Ebook.

Gettleman, Jeffrey (2010). "Africa's Forever Wars," *Foreign Policy*, July 13.

Ginsburg, Tom (2015). "Constitutions as Contracts, Constitutions as Charters," in Denis J Galligan and Mils Versteeg (eds.), *Social and Political Foundations of Constitutions.* Cambridge: Cambridge University Press, 182–206.

Global Risk Insights (2021). "Hybrid War Crimes Court Promises Justice But Political Rivalry May Impede Pursuit," March 7.

REFERENCES 225

Global Witness (2013). "Blueprint for Prosperity: How South Sudan's New Laws Hold the Key to a Transparent and Accountable Oil Sector," November, 1–42.

Gong, Garrett (1984). *The Standards of Civilization*. Oxford: Oxford University Press.

Government of Southern Sudan (2009). "The Local Government Act", 2009. Juba, Sudan.

Gramer, Robbie (2019). "Former U.S. Diplomats Lobby to Stop South Sudan War Crimes Court," *Foreign Policy*, April 29.

Gramer, Robbie (2018). "How European and Chinese Arms Diverted to South Sudan Fueled Its Civil War," *Foreign Policy*.

Gray, Richard (1961). *A History of the Southern Sudan 1839–1889*. London: Oxford University Press.

Griswold, Eliza (2010). *The Tenth Parallel: Dispatches from the Fault Line Between Christianity and Islam*. New York: Picador Press.

The Guardian (2017). "Soldiers Accused of Rape and Murder Go on Trial in South Sudan," May 31.

The Guardian (2016). "UN Peacekeeper Ignored "Rape and Assault of Aid Workers," August 16.

Hartman, Christof (2015). "Limits of Constitutional Reform in African Conflicts," *Ethnopolitics* 15(5), 523–527.

Hassabu, Abu and Afaf Abdel Majid (1985). *Factional Conflict in the Sudanese Nationalist Movement, 1918–1948*. Khartoum: Khartoum University Press.

Hereward, Holland (2019). "Amid Criticism, South Sudan Signs New Deal with U.S. Lobbyists," Reuters, May 8.

Hereward, Holland and Pascal Fletcher (2012). "Special Report: In South Sudan, Plunder Preserves a Fragile Peace," Reuters, Nov 20.

Hill, Richard (1967). *A Biographical Dictionary of the Sudan*. London: Psychology Press.

Hill, Richard (1959). *Egypt in the Sudan 1820–1881*. London: Oxford University Press.

Hobbes, Thomas (1996). *Leviathan*. Cambridge: Cambridge University Press.

Holt, P. M. and M. W. Daly (1981). *The History of the Sudan: From the Coming of Islam to the Present Day*. London: Pearson Longman.

Horowitz, Donald L. (2014). "Ethnic Power Sharing: Three Problems." *Journal of Democracy* 25(2), 5–20.

Huliaras, Ateris (2012). "The Unanticipated Break-Up of Sudan: Causes and Consequences of Redrawing International Boundaries." *Commonwealth & Comparative Politics* 50(3), 257–270.

Human Rights Watch (2019). "South Sudan Set Meeting on War Crimes Court, Lack of Communication and Clear Plan Impede Justice," October 9.

Human Rights Watch (2019). "South Sudan: Government Forces Abusing Civilians," June 4, 2019.

Human Rights Watch (2010). "Sudan: Government Repression Threatens Elections," March 21.

Human Security Baseline Assessment for Sudan and South Sudan (2013). "Disarmament, Demobilization, and Reintegration," June.

Humphreys, Marcartan, Jeffrey Sachs, and Joseph E. Stiglitz (eds.) (2009). *Escaping the Resource Curse*. New York: Columbia University Press.

Hutchinson, Sharon (2005). "Spiritual Fragments of an Unfinished War," in Niels Kastfelt (ed.), *Religion and African Civil Wars*. New York: Palgrave MacMillan, 28–53.

226 REFERENCES

Hutchinson, Sharon (1991). "A Curse from God": Religious and Political Dimensions of the Post-1991 Rise of Ethnic Violence in South Sudan." *Journal of Modern African Studies* 39(2), 307–335.

Ibreck, Rachel (2019). *South Sudan's Injustice System: Law and Activism on the Frontline.* London: Zed Books.

Idris, Amir (2019). *South Sudan: Post-Independence Challenges.* Abingdon: Routledge.

Idris, Amir (2017). "How the UN Security Council Is Perpetuating South Sudan's Conflict," *Newsweek*, January 22.

Idris, Amir (2010). "Beyond 'African' and 'Arab' in Sudan," in Francis Deng (ed.), *New Sudan in the Making.* Asmara: Red Sea Press, 13–27.

Intergovernmental Authority on Development (2015). "The Agreement on the Resolution of Conflict in the Republic of South Sudan," August 17. Available at https://www.accord.org.za/conflict-trends/revitalising-the-peace-in-south-sudan/.

International Crisis Group (2021)."Toward a Viable Future for South Sudan," February 10, 1–33.

International Crisis Group (2019). "Salvaging South Sudan's Fragile Peace Deal." *Report N 270*, March 13, 1–42.

International Crisis Group (2011). "Politics and Transition in the New South Sudan," *Africa Report* 172, April 4.

International Crisis Group (2010). "Sudan: Regional Perspectives on the Prospect of Southern Independence," *Africa Report* 159, May 6.

International Crisis Group (2009). ""Jonglei's Tribal Conflicts: Countering Insecurity in South Sudan," *Africa Report* 154, December 23.

International Foundation for Electoral Systems (2013). "South Sudan's National Constitution Review," May 3.

James, C. L R. (1983). *In Beyond a Boundary.* Durham, NC: Duke University Press.

Jieng Council of Elders (2021). "Breaking the Silence: The Way Forward," January.

Johnson, Douglas H. (2019). "Federalism in the History of South Sudanese Political Thought," in Luke Biong Deng Kuol and Sarah Logan (eds.), *The Struggle for South Sudan: Challenges of Security and State Cooperation.* London: L.B. Tauris, 103–123.

Johnson, Douglas H. (2012). "The Helig Oil Dispute: Between Sudan and South Sudan." *Journal of Eastern African Studies* 6(3), 561–569.

Johnson, Douglas H. (2007). "Why Abyei Matters: The Breaking Point of Sudan's Comprehensive Peace Agreement?" *African Affairs* 107(426), 1–19.

Johnson, Douglas H. (2003). *The Root Causes of Sudan's Civil Wars.* Bloomington: Indiana University Press.

Johnson, Douglas H. and Gérard Prunier (1993). "The Foundation and Expansion of the Sudan People's Liberation Army," in Marten W. Daly and Akmad Alwed Sikainja (eds.), *Civil War in Sudan.* London: British Academic Press, 117–141.

Johnson, Hilde F. (2016), *South Sudan, The Untold Story: From Independence to Civil War,* New York: I.B. Tauris.

Jok Madut Jok (2018). ""South Sudan's Elusive Peace: Between Local Drivers of Vviolence and the Aactions of Eexternal Aactors," in Amir Idris (ed.), *South Sudan: Post-Independence Dilemmas.* Abingdon, UK: Routledge, 74–91.

Jok Madut Jok (2001). *War and Slavery in Sudan.* Philadelphia: University of Pennsylvania Press.

Joselow, Gabe (2012). "South Sudan Oil Shutdown Chokes Economy," Voice of America, June 30, 1–12.

REFERENCES   227

Juba Monitor (2013). "Kiir, Machar Fight Over SPLM Reshuffle" 3(145), August 5, 2–3.

Juba Monitor (2013). "South Sudan's New Government Must Quickly Enact Oil Law" 3(145), August 5, 4–6.

Jumbert, Maria Gabrielsen and Øystein H. Rolandsen (2013). *After the Split: Post-Secession Negotiations between South Sudan and Sudan.* Norwegian Peacebuilding Resource Centre, Report (December).

Kaplan, Robert D. (2000). *The Coming Anarchy: Shattering the Dreams of the Post-Cold War.* New York: Random House.

Karl, Terry Lynn (2009). *The Paradox of Plenty: Oil Booms and Petroleum.* Berkeley: University of California Press.

Karl, Terry Lynn (2009). "Ensuring Fairness: The Case for a Transparent Fiscal Contract," in Humphreys, Marcartan, Jeffrey Sachs, and Joseph E. Stiglitz (eds.), *Escaping the Resource Curse.* New York: Columbia University Press, 256–285.

Kasfir, Nelson (1977). "Southern Sudanese Politics since the Addis Ababa Agreement." *African Affairs* 76(303), 143–166.

Katona, Victor (2020). "South Sudan Struggles to Boost its Oil Production," *Oil Price.com*, August 3.

Kebbede, Girma (1999). "Sudan: The North-South Conflict in Historical Perspective," in Girma Kebbede (ed.), *Sudan's Predicament: Civil War, Displacement and Ecological Degradation.* Aldershot: Ashgate Publishing, 10–43.

Keen, David (2008). *The Benefits of Famine: A Political Economy of Famine and Relief in Southern Sudan, 1983–1989,* Second Edition. Oxford: James Currey.

Kenny, Charles (2012). "What Resource Curse," *Foreign Policy.* December 6.

Keppler, Elise (2019). "South Sudan's Cynical Bid to Block the War Crimes Court," Human Rights Watch, April 30.

Khalid, Mansour (2003). *War and Peace in the Sudan.* London: Routledge.

Kiir, Salva and Riek Machar (2016). "South Sudan Needs Truth, Not Trials," *The New York Times*, June 7.

Knopf, Katherine Almquist (2017). "Ending South Sudan's Civil War." *Council of Foreign Relations*, March 16.

Kramer, Robert S. (1999). *"Jihadiyya,"* in Junius P. Rodriquez (ed.), *The Historical Encyclopedia of World Slavery*, Volume 1. London, 377–388.

Kuol, Luka Biong (2020). "South Sudan: The Elusive Quest for a Resilient Social Contract." *Journal of Intervention and Statebuilding* 14(1), 64–83.

Labot, Elise (2017). "Nikki Haley Issues Stern Warning in South Sudan," *CNN* Politics, October 25.

Lederman, Daniel and William F. Maloney (2007). "Neither Curse, nor Destiny: Introduction to Natural Resources and Development," in Daniel Lederman and William F Maloney (eds.), *Natural Resources, Neither Curse Nor Destiny.* Washington, DC: The International Bank for Reconstruction and Development, 1–12.

Leonardi, Cherry (2013). *Dealing with the Government in South Sudan: Histories of Chiefship, Community and State.* Durham: BOYES6 Publishers.

Leonardi, Cherry (2011). "Paying 'Buckets of Blood' for the Land: Moral Debates over Economy, War, and State in Southern Sudan." *Journal of Modern African Studies* 49(2), 215–240.

Leriche, Matthew and Matthew Arnold (2012). *South Sudan: From Revolution to Independence.* London: Hurst and Company.

228 REFERENCES

Lerner, Helen (2011). *Making Constitutions in Deeply Divided Societies*. Cambridge: Cambridge University Press.

Lesch, Ann Mosely (1998). *The Sudan: Contested National Identities*. Oxford: James Curry Publishers.

Lijphart, Arend (1982). "Consociation: The Model and Its Applications in Divided Societies," in Desmond Rea (ed.), *Political Cooperation in Divided Societies*. London: MacMillan, 166–186.

Lyman, Princeton N. (2013). "Sudan-South Sudan: The Unfinished Tasks of American Foreign Policy Interests." *Journal of the National Committee on American Foreign Policy* 35(6), 335–378.

Lynch, Colum (2021). "Succession in South Sudan," *Foreign Policy*, July 7.

Malak, Garang A. (2020). "South Sudan President, Salva Kiir Names Full Cabinet," *The East African*, March 13.

Mamdani, Mahmood (2020). *Neither Settler Nor Native: The Making and Unmaking of Permanent Minorities*. Cambridge, MA: The Belknap Press of Harvard University Press.

Mamdani, Mahmood (2018). "The Trouble with South Sudan's New Peace Deal," *New York Times*, September 24.

Mamdani, Mahmood (2016). "Who's to Blame in South Sudan?" *Boston Review*, June 28.

Mamdani, Mahmood (2014). "Separate Submission to the African Union Commission of Inquiry," South Sudan.

Martell, Peter (2018). *First Raise the Flag: How South Sudan Won the Longest War but Lost the Peace*. Oxford: Oxford University Press.

Mbaku, John Mukum and Jessica Elaine Smith (2013). "Efficient and Equitable Natural Resource Management: Using Transparency to Avoid the Resource Curse," in The Brookings Institute (ed.), *One Year after Independence: Opportunities and Obstacles for Africa's Newest Nation*. Washington, DC: Brookings Institute, 10–13.

Mbewa, David Ochieng (2020.) "South Sudan's Kiir Hints at Reopening Churches in Spite of Rise of COVID-19 Cases," CGTN. August 10.

McCandless, Erin, R. Hollender, M. J. Zahar, M. H. Shwoebel, A. Rocha Menocal, and A. Lordos (2018). *Social Contracts: A Pathway to Preventing Violent Conflict and Sustaining Peace*. Oslo: UNDP.

McGarry, John H. and Brendan O'Leary (2016). "Power-Sharing Executives: Consociational and Centripetal Formalae and the Case of Northern Ireland," *Ethnopolitics* 15(5), 497–515.

Mednick, Sam (2020). "South Sudan Ignores Reports on Oil Pollution, Birth Defects," Associated Press, February 13.

Mednick, Sam (2019). "South Sudan Paying US Lobbyists $3.7M for Better Trump Ties," Associated Press, April 29.

Natsios, Andrew S. (2012). *Sudan, South Sudan and Darfur: What Everyone Needs to Know*. Oxford: Oxford University Press.

Nichols, Michelle (2015). "China Questions U.S. Threat of UN Sanctions on South Sudan," Reuters, February 28.

Ngor, Mading (2012). "Road-Starved South Sudan Eyes a $4 Billion Road Network," Reuters, August 10.

Nyaba, Peter Adwok (2018). "The Curse of Elitism: South Sudan's failure to transition to statehood and nationhood," in Amir Idris (ed.), *South Sudan: Post-Independence Dilemmas*. Abingdon: Routledge, 19–37.

Nyaba, Peter Adwok (1996). *The Politics of Liberation in Southern Sudan: An Insider's View*. London: Fountain Publishing.

REFERENCES   229

Nyamilepedia (2020). "South Sudan Appeals to IMF World Bank to for Bailout as Economy Collapses," August 24.

Nyamilepedia (2019). "Opposition Official Allied to Changson Reigns, Joins Josephine Lagu's," August 10.

Nyamilepedia (2019). "NDM Says It Is "Dismayed" over Government Role in Dividing SSOA," February 4.

O'Grady, Siobhan (2016). "The African Rebel Leader Who's Stoked About Trump," *The Atlantic*, November 26.

Oxfam (2014). "Building a Social Contract in South Sudan," Oxfam Programme Insights.

Patey, Luke (2014). *The Kings of Crude: China, India, and the Global struggle for oil in Sudan and South Sudan*. London: Hurst and Company.

Patinkin, Jason (2016). "South Sudan's Machar Denies Opposing the War Crimes Court," Voice of America, June 10.

Petterson, Donald (1999). *Inside Sudan: Political Islam, Conflict, and Catastrophe.* Boulder, CO: Westview Press.

Pinaud, Clemence (2014). "South Sudan: Civil War, Predation, and the Making of a Military Aristocracy." *African Affairs* (114), 192–220.

Politico (2017). "Nikki Haley Evacuates from Volatile South Sudan Camp," October 25.

Por, Nyagoah Tut (2020). "South Sudan Academic Suspended over Opinion, Piece," Human Rights Watch, February 12.

Pospisil, Jan, Oringa Christopher, Sophia Dawkins, David Deng (2020). "South Sudan's Transition: Citizens' Perception of Peace," United States Institute of Peace, March 19.

Prendergast, John (2002). "Senator Danforth's Sudan Challenge: Building a Bridge to Peace, The Center for Strategic International Studies." *Africa Notes* 5, 1–6.

Prunier, Gérard (2003). "Rebel Movements and Proxy Warfare: Uganda, Sudan, and the Congo." *African Affairs* 103 (412), 359–383.

Pur, Nyagoad Tut (2021). "A Glimmer of Hope for South Sudan's Victims," *Human Rights Watch*, January 31.

RJMEC (2019). "The NCAC Hands over Constitutional Amendment to Constitution Minister," April 23.

Radio Tamazuj (2021). "Kiir Appoints Officials for N. Bahr el Ghazal, Warrap, Unity and C. Equatoria states," February 23.

Radio Tamazuj (2021). "Peace Partners Write to IGAD to Extend Constitutional Committee Mandate," April 21.

Radio Tamazuj (2020). "Eastern Equatoria: Senior SPLA-IO officer defects to Cirillo's NAS," December 9.

Radio Tamazuj (2020). "US Appoints New Special Envoy to South Sudan," February 1.

Radio Tamazuj (2019). "Government Raises Crude Oil Allocation to China," April 21.

Radio Tamazuj (2017). "UN Panel Accuses Ukraine of Supplying South Sudan with Arms," May 15.

Reeves, Eric (2003). "How Serious are John Danforth's 'Tests' of Khartoum's Willingness to Engage in Peace Negotiations," Sudan: Research Analysis and Advocacy, December.

Reeves, Eric (2003). "Colin Powell's Bumpy Ride to Naivasha (Kenya): What It May and May Not Mean for the Sudan Peace Process," *Sudan Tribune*, June 4.

ReliefWeb (2020). "South Sudan's NAS Establishes a Committee on Sexual Violence," February 6, 2020.

ReliefWeb (2019). "In South Sudan, Nonviolent Action is Essential to Building Peace," February 22.

230 REFERENCES

ReliefWeb (2016). "South Sudan Rival Peace Partners to Negotiate Solution to 28 States," January 12.

ReliefWeb (2009). "Sudan's Elections to be Held on Scheduled Time: First Vice-President," November 21.

Republic of South Sudan (2017). "Approved Budget Tables Fiscal Year, 2016–2017," February 7, Juba.

Republic of South Sudan (2012). "Petroleum Act."

Republic of South Sudan (2012). "The Petroleum Revenue Management Act."

Republic of South Sudan (2011). "The Transitional Constitution of the Republic of South Sudan."

Reuters (2020). "South Sudan confirms first case of Coronavirus," April 5.

Reuters (2019). "South Sudan Agrees Oil Exploration Deal with South Africa," October 10.

Reuters (2017). "South Sudan's President Appoints New Army Chief," April 1.

Reybrouck, David van (2010). *Congo: The Epic History of a People.* Translated by Sam Garrett. New York: Harper Collins.

Roach, Steven C. (2021) "Bringing Cooperative Peace to the Nile Basin?" *Peace Review: A Journal of Social Justice*, 33(2):286-292

Roach, Steven C. (2019). *Decency and Difference: Humanity and the Global Challenge of Identity Politics.* Ann Arbor, MI: University of Michigan Press.Roach, Steven C. (2017). "Will Trump Help South Sudan," *Cairo Review of Global Affairs*, May 10.

Roach, Steven C. (2016). "Down But Not Out: What Machar's Absence Means for South Sudan's Peace Process." *African Arguments*, September 23.

Roach Steven C. (2016). *Cultural Autonomy, Minority Rights and Globalization.* Abingdon: Routledge.

Roach, Steven C. (2016). "South Sudan: A Volatile Dynamic of Accountability and Peace." *International Affairs* 92(6), 1343–1359.

Roach, Steven C. (2016). "South Sudan's Troubled Peace: How the Peace Deal Got Stuck?" *Foreign Affairs*, Council on Foreign Relations, April 3.

Roach, Steven C. (2013). "How Political Is the ICC? Pressing Challenges and the Need for Diplomatic Efficacy." *Global Governance* 19(4), 507–523.

Roach, Steven C. (2006). *Politicizing the International Criminal Court: The Convergence of Politics, Ethics, and Law.* Lanham, MD: Rowman and Littlefield Publishers.

Roach, Steven C. and Derrick K. Hudson (eds.) (2019). *The Challenge of Governance in South Sudan: Corruption, Peacebuilding, and Foreign Intervention.* Abingdon: Routledge.

Robinson, James A, Ragnar Jrvik, and Thiery Verdier (2006). "Political Foundations of the Resource Curse." *Journal of Development Economics* 79, 447–468.

Rolandsen, Øystein H. (2015). "Another Civil War in South Sudan: The Failure of Guerrilla Government." *Journal of Eastern African Studies* 9(1), 163–174.

Rolandsen, Øystein H. (2011). "A Quick Fix? A Retrospective Analysis of the Sudan Comprehensive Peace Agreement." *Review of African Political Economy* 38(130), 551–564.

Rolandsen, Øystein H. (2011). "The Making of the Anya-Nya Insurgency in the Southern Sudan, 1961–64." *The Journal of Eastern African Studies* 5(2), 211–232.

Rolandsen, Øystein H. and Matthew Daly (2016). *A History of South Sudan.* Cambridge: Cambridge University Press.

Rolandsen, Øystein H. and Nicki Kindersley (2019). "The Nasty War: Organized Violence During The Anya-Nya Insurgency in South Sudan, 1963–72." *The Journal of African History* 60(1), 87–107.

REFERENCES 231

Ross, Michael L. (2012). *The Oil Curse: How Petroleum Wealth Shapes the Development of Nations*. Princeton: Princeton University Press.

Sachs, Jeffrey D. (2007). "How the Handle the Macroeconomics of Oil Wealth," Humphreys, Marcartan, Jeffrey Sachs, and Joseph E. Stiglitz (eds.), *Escaping the Resource Curse*. New York: Columbia University Press, 174–197.

Sachs, Jeffrey and Andrew Warner (1995). "Natural Resource Curse: Abundance and Economic Growth," *NBER Working Paper* 5398, 1–25.

Saferworld (2020). "A Tale of Two Crises: Conflict and Covid-19 in South Sudan," May 27.

Salih, Mohamed M. H. (1994). "The Ideology of the Dinka & the Sudan People's Liberation Front," in Katsuyoshu and Fukui and John Markakis (eds.), *Ethnicity & Conflict in the Horn of Africa*. Athens: Ohio University Press, 76–94.

Savage, Emily (2013). "South Sudan's Petroleum Revenue Management Act." *Policy Brief, Sudd Institute*, December 13.

The Sentry (2020). "Making a Killing: South Sudanese Military Leaders' Wealth, Explained," May 27, Washington, DC.

The Sentry (2019). "The Taking of South Sudan: The Tycoons, Brokers, and Multinational Corporations Complicit in Hijacking the World's Newest State," September.

South Sudan Human Rights Commission (2014). "Report on the Civil War," March.

South Sudan Law Society (2015). "The Search for a New Beginning, a Nationwide Survey Conducted from March to November."

Specia, Megan (2019). "South Sudan Oil Consortium Funded Militias Accused of Atrocities," *The New York Times,* September 19.

Stearns, Jason K. (2022). "Rebels Without a Cause: The New Face of African Warfare." *Foreign Affairs* 101(3), 146–160.

Stiglitz, Joseph E, Macartan Humphreys and Jeffrey Sach (2007). "Introduction: What Is the Problem With Natural Resource Wealth?" in Humphreys, Marcartan, Jeffrey Sachs, and Joseph E. Stiglitz (eds.), *Escaping the Resource Curse*. New York: Columbia University Press, 1–20.

Sudan Tribune (2021). Ethiopia Completed GERD's Second Filling, Announce Abiy Ahmed, July 20.

Sudan Tribune (2021). "NAS Claims Obtaining Evidences of War Crimes in South Sudan," June 14.

Sudan Tribune (2020). "South Sudan TGoNU Changed Constitution after Amendment by Joint Panel," March 29.

Sudan Tribune (2019). "13 Civilians Killed, 7 Soldiers Killed during Fresh Clashes in South Sudan's Equatoria: NAS," February 13.

Sudan Tribune (2017). "Huge Scandals Hit S. Sudan Crisis Management Committee," March 7.

Sudan Tribune (2016). South Sudan President expands number of states to 28 as opposition accuses him of deal violation, October 2.

Sudan Tribune (2016). "Machar in South Africa for medical treatment: Spokesperson," October 13.

Sudan Tribune (2015). "South Sudan President Expands Number of States to 28 as Opposition Accuses Him of Deal Violation," October 2.

Sudan Tribune (2015). "EU Vows to Support Hybrid Court in South Sudan," November 15.

Sudan Tribune (2014). "South Sudan Human Rights Body Says that Violations Committed by Both Parties in the Conflict,", March 22.

Sudan Tribune (2014). "S. Sudan Urges US Leader to Reconsider Looming Sanctions," December 9.

232 REFERENCES

Sudan Tribune (2014). "South Sudan Appoints Crisis Management Committee," January 11.

Sudan Tribune (2012). "SPLA Top Generals Asked by Anticorruption to Declare their Assets," February 27.

Sudan Tribune (2012). "South Sudan Launches Human Rights Forum to Address Its Challenges," April 14.

Sudan Tribune (2011). "Sudan Announces Details of Contested Election Results," May 21.

Taha, Fadwa A. A. (2008). "The Sudanese Factor in the 1952–53 Anglo-Egyptian Negotiations," *Middle Eastern Studies* 44(4), 603–631.

Takpiny, Benjamin (2021). "South Sudan Approves Establishment of Hybrid Court, *Africa.*, January 3.

Tisdall, Simon (2013). "South Sudan President Sacks Cabinet in Power Struggle," *The Guardian*, July 24.

TRT World (2020). "South Sudan Declares "End of War" As Rival Leaders Form Govt," February 22.

UKAID (2019). "South Sudan: The Perils of Payroll Peace." March.

UNICEF (2020). "Some Things Are Not Fit for Children: Marriage Is One of Them," October 5.

UNOCHA (2020). "South Sudan: Humanitarian Snapshot," February.

United Nations (2022). "South Sudan: Political Violence on the Rise, UN Rights Experts Warn," February 11.

United Nations (2020). "COVID-19 Potentially Greatest Threat to South Sudan's Already Fragile Health System, Special Representative Warns Security Council," June 23. SC/42.

United Nations General Assembly (2017). "Children and Armed Conflict," General Assembly seventy-first session, August 24. A-72-361-S2017-821.

United Nations Human Rights Office of the High Commissioner (2020). "Report of the Commission on Human Rights in South Sudan," February 24–March 20, Agenda item 4, A/HRC/43/56.

United Nations Human Rights Office of the High Commissioner (2016). "South Sudan: UN Report Contains 'Searing' Account of Killings, Rapes and Destruction," March 11.

United Nations Human Rights Council (2020). "Report of the Commission on Human Rights in South Sudan," A/HRC/43/56, March.

United Nations Mission in South Sudan (2019). "Conflict-Related Violations and Abuses in Central Equatoria," September, July 3.

United Nations Security Council (2021). "Final Report of the Panel of Experts on South Sudan Submitted. Pursuant to Resolution 2521". S/2021/365.

United Nations Security Council (2021). "Resolution Renewing Arms Embargo," S/RES/ 2577, May 28.

United Nations Security Council (2020). "Security Council Welcomes South Sudan's New Power-Sharing Agreement, as Special Representative Briefs on Recent Events," March 4, SC 14135.

United Nations Security Council (2019). "Report of Panel of Experts on South Sudan," addressed to the Security Council, April 9. S/2019/301.

United Nations Security Council (2016). "Security Council Decides against Imposing Arms Embargo on South Sudan, Designating Key Figures for Targeted Sanctions 7850th meeting, SC/12653, December.

United Nations Security Council (2015). "Resolution 2206," Adopted by the Security Council at its 7396th meeting, on March 3.

United Nations Security Council (2015). "Security Council Sanctions Committee Concerning South Sudan Adds Six Individuals to Its Sanctions List," SC/11958, July 1.

United Nations Security Council (2011). "Temporary Arrangement for the administration and Security of the Abyei Area," June 20.

United States (2014). Presidential Documents. *Federal Register* 78, no. 66, Resolution #13664.

United States (2014). Presidential Documents. *Federal Register* 78, no. 66, Resolution #13664.

United States Institute of Peace (2015). "Independent South Sudan: A Failure of Leadership," Testimony of Princeton N. Lyman before the US Senate Foreign Relations Committee, December 10.

United States Institute of Peace (2007). "Sudan's 2009 Elections: Critical Issues and Timelines," November 1.

United States Senate Committee on Foreign Relations (2015). "Independent South Sudan: A Failure of Leadership," December 10.

US News and World Report (2017). "U.S. Warns South Sudan Government Against 'Deliberate Starvation Tactics,'" March 23.

Vertin, Zach (2019). *A Rope from the Sky: the Making and Unmaking of South Sudan's Newest Country*. New York: Pegasus Publishing.

Vicini, Jaime (2001). "US Court Dismisses 1998 Sudan Missile Strike Suit," *Reuters*, June 9.

Vickers, Emma (2014). "Can South Sudan Avoid the Resource Curse? Addis Tals Mark Tipping Point," *Global Witness*, March 20.

Voice of America (2020). "UN Appeals for 1.3 billion for South Sudan Refugees," March 14.

Voice of America (2020). "No Deal on South Sudan States, Boundaries as Deadline Nears," February 7.

Voice of America (2020). "South Sudan President Appoints 1 Woman Among 8 Governors, 3 Administrators," June 30.

Voice of America (2018). "Diaspora Voices Missing in South Sudan Dialogue, Activists Say," January 21.

Voice of America (2016). "UN Security Council Rejects Arms Embargo on South Sudan," December 23.

Voice of America (2015). "IGAD: More Mediators to be Added to South Sudan's Peace Process," June 12.

Vox (2021). "What Is Causing Inter Communal Violence in South Sudan," June 24.

Watkins, Kevin (2013). *Basic Services in South Sudan: An Uncertain Future, in South Sudan: One Year of Independence*. Washington, DC: Brookings Institute.

The White House (2014). "Blocking Property of Certain Persons With Respect to South Sudan," Executive Order 13664 April 3.

Willis, J. and el Battahani, A. (2010). "'We Changed the Laws': Electoral Practice and Malpractice in Sudan since 1953." *African Affairs* 109, 191–212.

Wudu, Waakhe Simon (2020). "What Is Causing South Sudan Intercommunal Fighting," *Voice of America*, June 24.

Wunlit Peace Conference (1999). *Dinka-Nuer West Bank Peace and Reconciliation Process*, February 27–March 8, Wunlit, Bahr El Ghazal.

234 REFERENCES

Yak, Gabriel Bul and John Deng Jok (2013). "Was Kiir's Relief of Machar and Ministers an Opportunity or Disaster for SPLM?" *Juba Monitor* 3 (145) August 5.

Yel, Simon Yel and Paanluel Wel (2016). *Salva Kiir Mayardit, The Joshua of South Sudan: President Kiir & Speeches After Independence.* Juba: The Center for Strategic and Governance Studies.

Young, John (2019). "Ethiopian Ethnic Federalism: A Model for South Sudan?" In Luke Biong Deng Kuol and Sarah Logan (eds.), *The Struggle for South Sudan: Challenges of Security and State Cooperation.* London: L.B. Tauris, 2020, 124–143.

Young, John (2019). *South Sudan's Civil War: Violence, Insurgency, and Failed Peacemaking.* London: Zed Books.

Young, John (2012). *The Fate of Sudan: The Origins and Consequences of a Flawed Peace Process.* London: Zed Books.

Young, John (2007). "Sudan: A Flawed Peace Process leading to a Flawed Peace." *Review of African Political Economy* 32(103), 99–113.

Zambakari, Christopher, Targeet K. Kang, and Robert A. Sanders, "The Role of the UN Mission in South Sudan (UMISS) in protecting civilian," in Steven C. Roach and Derrick K. Hudson (eds.), *The Challenge of Governance in South Sudan: Corruption, Peacebuilding, and Foreign Intervention.* Abingdon: Routledge, 95–130.

Index

For the benefit of digital users, indexed terms that span two pages (e.g., 52–53) may, on occasion, appear on only one of those pages.

Figures are indicated by *f* following the page number

Abache, Osanjo, 101
Abboud, Ibrahim, 37
Abdullah, Muhammad Ahmad bin, 18–20
Abdullatif, Ali, 28
Abyei, 90
Abyei Arbitration Tribunal, 90
Abyei Boundary Commission, 90
Abyei Protocol, 71, 90
activism, 117, 137
Addis Ababa Agreement, 41, 42, 44–45, 48
Afghanistan, United States invasion of, 68–69
African Union, 10–11, 153
    Hybrid Court for South Sudan, 140–41
    International Criminal Court and, 141
    Peace and Security Council, 139, 141
African Union Commission of Inquiry in South
    Sudan (AUCISS), 139–40, 166, 179
    report on human rights abuses, 10
African Union High-Level Implementation
    Panel (AUHIP), 91, 105
Agar, Malik, 91
Agar Dinka, 25
Agreement on the Resolution of the Conflict
    in South Sudan (ARCSS), 10–11, 112–13,
    115, 149–50, 152–53. *See also* Revitalized
    Agreement on the Resolution of the
    Conflict in South Sudan
Aguer, James, 127, 128*f*
Ajak, Peter Biar, 117, 120–21
Akec, Paul Mayom, 159
Aklab Dinka, 25–26
Akol, Lam, 56, 58, 60, 86, 154
Alenby (Lord), 26–27
ALF (Azania Liberation Front), 38–39
'Ali, Muhammad, 16, 17, 23
Alier, Abel, 42, 43–44
All African Conference of Churches, 40–41
All South Sudanese Political Parties Conference
    (ASSPPC), 87, 88
Alma, Abdul Fadil, 28
amnesty, 143–44

Amnesty International, 138, 141
Amum, Pagan, 101, 104, 105, 107
Anataban, 164
Anglican churches, 18
Anglo-Egyptian Condominium (1899), 22–23
Anglo-Egyptian Treaty (1936), 32–33, 34
Anok, Kon, 25–26
anticolonial resistance movement, 28
Anti-Corruption Commission Act, 85
Anti-Defamation League, 67–68
Anti-Slavery Society, 18
Anyanya, 6–7, 16, 38–39, 43–44, 78
Anyanya II, 6–7, 43–44, 47, 49, 58, 78
Arabs, as slaves and slaveowners, 23–24
ARCSS. *See* Agreement on the Resolution of the
    Conflict in South Sudan
al-Armani, Arakil Bey, x
armed conflict, profiteering through, 95–96
armed factionalism, 4
armed forces, 37. *See also* Sudanese
    Armed Forces
    reintegration, 79–82, 95
armed insurrection, educating masses for, 120
Around, Ahmad Muhammad, 91
Arrow Rangers, 158
Arusha Agreement, 160
asset freezes, 111–12
ASSPPC (All South Sudanese Political Parties
    Conference), 87–88
Atem, Akwon, 49
Ateny, Ateny Wau, 111, 178–79
AUCISS. *See* African Union Commission of
    Inquiry in South Sudan
Audit Chamber Act, 85
AUHIP (African Union High-Level
    Implementation Panel), 91, 105
autonomy in South Sudan, 37–42
Azande, 63–64
Azania Liberation Front (ALF), 38–39
Al-Azhan, 36
al Azhari, Ismail, 35, 36, 39–40

236 INDEX

Bakosoro, Joseph, 118–19, 154, 167–68
Bank of South Sudan, 99–100, 109–10
Bank of Sudan, 109–10
Bany, William Nyuon, 48, 59
al- Bashir, Omar Hassan, 55, 65–66, 69, 72–73, 142
  Agar election and, 91
  election results of 2010 and, 77
  International Criminal Court arrest warrant for, 88–89
  international pressure on, 77
  Kiir and, 78
  ouster and surrender to International Criminal Court, 167–68
  referendum of 2011 and, 77
  secession question and, 81, 87
Beir Patrol, 25
Benjamin, Barnaba Marial, 111–12
Bentiu child abuse, 124
Berlin Conference (1885), 20–21
Bidi Bid camp, 132–33
bin Abdullah, Muhammad Ahmad. *See* al-Mahdi, Muhammed
Bin Laden, Osama, 66
black-market rates, 98, 105
Blue Nile, 91, 106
Blueprint for Prosperity Report (Sudd Institute), 100–1
Bol, Kerubino Kuanyin, 62
Bol, Samuel, 62
border disputes, 90, 91–92
Bor Dinka, Murle attacking, 25
Bor massacre attack, 58–59
boundaries of South Sudan, 78
Britain
  as civilizer or savior, 15
  civilizing process of, 21–22
  divisions in South Sudan created by, 27, 28
  economic influence of, 19
  Egypt occupation by, 19
  Ethiopia concerns of, 19
  land policy of, 25–26
  Lou Nuer resistant to rule of, 24–25
  Mahdist forces overrun by, 20, 21–22
  modernizing North Sudan, 27
  neglect of South Sudan, 21
  Nile Basin control of, 22
  quasi-federal system under, 149
  racial and moral superiority of, 20
  secularizing education in Sudan, 31
  southern policy of, 29, 37
  Sudan governance plan, 27
  trade routes extended, 17

  treatment of natives by, 15
  veto power of, 23
Buol, Luka Deng, 186–87
Buony, Simon, 163–64
Burundi, 160
Bush, George W., 67–68, 72, 79

Callaway, Gertrude, 129–30
Camel Corps, Kordofan, 29
canal project, 44
Carr, Burgess, 40–41
Carter Center, 86
Catholic Church, 18
cattle raiding, 157–58, 188–89
census, 78, 85
Césaire, Aimé, 49–50
Cessation of Hostilities Agreement, 147, 153, 158
Changson, Gabriel, 154–55
Chevron, 44–45, 102–3
child abuse, 124, 126
Child Act (2008), 126
child marriage, 8, 125–26
Child Protection Unit, 124
children
  conscription of, 8, 124, 133–34, 157–58
  Transitional Constitutions and rights of, 124
China
  development assistance, 113–14
  oil contracts and, 184
China National Petroleum Corporation (CNPC), 102–3
Chol, Arthur Akuien, 82–83
Chol, Gordon Kong, 57
  Garang removal, 58
Christians, 18, 40, 131–32
  aid groups and, 129–30
  conversion rate to, 32
  Evangelical, 67–68
  missionaries, 27, 30–31
  toleration, 17
Chuol, James Koang, 112
"Circle," 67
Cirillo, Thomas, 147, 158, 174–75
civilization standards, 15
civilizing process, 21
civil society
  activism by, 117
  peace process and, 156–57
  United States engagement with, 168
civil society organizations (CSOs), 162, 163–64
Civil Society Referendum Taskforce, 162–63
civil war
  in Ethiopia, 189

law and, 130–31
  reemergence of, 140–41, 150–53
  refugees from, 132–33
civil war in South Sudan, 93, 94–95
clientelist networks, 82, 111
Clinton, Bill, 66
Clooney, George, 96–97
"Closed District Ordinance," 27
CMC (Crisis Management Committee), 109–10
CNPC (China National Petroleum
    Corporation), 102–3
Code of Civil Procedure Act (2007), 136
Code of Criminal Procedure Act (2008), 136
Collier, Paul, 96
Collins, Robert, 31–32
colonialism, 50
  national violence rooted in, 119
colonization, 15
Commission for Truth, Reconciliation, and
    Healing (CTRH), 115, 140, 179, 180–81
Common Ground, 164–65
Compensation and Reparation Authority
    Commission (CRAC), 115, 140
Comprehensive Amendment Bill, 174
Comprehensive Peace Agreement (CPA), 2, 62,
    69, 73, 78, 81
  armed conflicts after, 95
  conflict resolution championed by, 116–17
  elections and, 85–86
  ending oppression in South Sudan, 74
  forms of national unity of, 6
  oil taxes and, 104
  social contract underlying, 4–5
  toll of implementing targets of, 81–82
conscription
  of children, 8, 124, 133–34, 157–58
  managed, 16–17
constitutional processes, 159–65, 174
Constitutional Review Commission
    (CRC), 87–88
Convention on the Rights of the Child
    (2012), 124
corruption, 7, 97
  in Crisis Management Committee, 109
  in interim period, 82, 85
  oil revenue and, 84, 100–1
  pervasive, 11
  sanctions and, 111–14
  Troika and, 77–78
Council of Ministers, 171
courts, 133–34, 135–36
COVID-19, 172, 181, 182–83
Cox, Christopher, 31

CPA (Comprehensive Peace Agreement), 2005,
    2, 62, 71
CRAC (Compensation and Reparation
    Authority Commission), 115, 140
CRC (Constitutional Review
    Commission), 87–88
crimes against humanity, 70–71
criminal justice, 115–17
criminal punishment, 138–39
criminal tribunals, 141, 142
Crisis Management Committee (CMC), 109–10
Cromer (Lord), 28–29
CSOs (civil society organizations), 162, 163–64
CTRH (Commission for Truth, Reconciliation,
    and Healing), 115, 140
culture, 3
customary law, 135, 136–37

Dagne, Ted, 67
Danforth, John, 68
Darfur, 70–71
Darfur region
  International Criminal Court and, 78
  Western Arab Corps in, 29
Dar Petroleum, 102–3, 185
Dau, Stephen Dhieu, 106
DDR (Disarmament, Demobilization, and
    Reintegration program), 72–73, 166, 178
December 2013 civil war, 1
decolonization, 32
defense budgets, 80
De Mabior, Rebecca, 74–75
democracy
  reconstituting, 9–11
  regional politics and, 187–90
Democratic Alliance, 147
Democratic Republic of the Congo (DRC),
    Machar and, 151
Deng, Dominic Dim, 80
Deng, William, 37–39
deregulation, 95
devolution, 160–61
De Vries, Lotje, 86–87
diaspora in South Sudan, 117
Dinka ethnic group, 16–17, 24, 42, 47–48, 106, 109
  chiefs- attitude toward patrols, 25–26
  elders' role in, 82
  National Dialogue Committee and, 162
  peace process and, 148–49, 155–56
  state boundaries and, 149–50
Disarmament, Demobilization, and
    Reintegration (DDR) program, 72–73,
    166, 178

238 INDEX

disarmament efforts, 176
domination, 3
Dongalawi Sufi, 18–19
DRC. *See* Democratic Republic of the Congo
Dual, Simon Gatwech, 112
Duku, Michael, 185–86
Dura Saga, 84

East African Court of Justice, 185
East Equatoria, 59
Eastern Arab Corps, Kasala, 29
economic liberalization, 95
economy, war, 95–96
education
    for armed insurrection, 120
    of native population, 31
Eggers, Dave, 120–21
Egypt, 16
    Anglo-Egyptian Condominium
        (1899), 22–23
    Britain unequal partnership with, 22–23
    entitlement to Sudan rule, 33
    Grand Ethiopian Renaissance Dam project
        and, 189
    Ismail modernizing, 17–18
elections, 85, 87–88, 154
    Bashir and, 77, 91
    delays in, 171–72
    in Uganda, 189
electoral system, 85
environmental problems, oil sector and, 184–85
Episcopal Church of Malakal, 131–32
EPRDF (Ethiopian People's Revolutionary
    Democratic Front), 57, 187
Equatoria, 18
Equatoria Corps (Southern Corps), 29
Ethiopia, 19
    civil war in, 189
    displacement into, 91
    ethnic federalist model, 187
    Grand Ethiopian Renaissance Dam project
        and, 189
    UN peacekeeping force from, 90–91
Ethiopian People's Revolutionary Democratic
    Front (EPRDF), 57, 187
ethnic cleansing, 108–9, 119, 123, 158
ethnic factionalism, 166
ethnic federalism, 187
ethnic representation, 155
Evangelical Christians, 67–68
Evans-Prichard, Edward, 24–25
exchange rates, 98, 105
exchange reserves, 103–4

Expected Mahdi, 18–19

factionalism, 6
    armed, 4
    ethnic, 166
    rise of, 47–48
    Sudan People's Liberation Army and, 55–65
    in Sudan People's Liberation Movement, 96
Faludi, Susan, 3
Family of Nations, 20
Fanon, Frantz, 49–50, 119
Farouk (King), 33, 34
federalism, 149, 161
    ethnic, 187
    social contract and, 186–87
forced marriages, 125–26
forgiveness, 143–44
Francis (Pope), 171
Free State of the Congo, 20–21
"Friends of South Sudan," 67
Fuli, Severino, 38
Future Generations Funds, 99–100

Gaddafi, Muammar, 142
Gadet, Peter, 109, 154
Gai, Taban, 64, 113–14, 151, 152
    sanctions on, 168
Gainful Solutions, 144–45
Ganna, Kenneth, 164–65
Garang, John de Marbior, 4–5, 45, 72
    appointed President of Government of
        Southern Sudan, 73
    on corruption, 83
    death of, 75, 77, 78, 79
    Dinka identity and authoritarian rule, 57–58
    as liberal democrat, 65, 74
    as liberal reformer, 67
    on liberation, 52
    loyal army of, 52–53
    Machar and, 59–60
    militarism of, 95, 96
    militias and militaristic tensions, 52–55
    "New Sudan," 47
    solidarity for, 6–7
    South Sudan support of, 49
    SPLA-Torit of, 59, 62
    taxes levied by, 53, 54
    as third world, democratic socialist, 50–51
    troop loyalty toward, 56–57
    uncertain legacy of, 74–75
    understated and defiant, 57
    United States support of, 66, 67
    victories of, 54

vision of, 49–52, 120
Gastin, William, 44
gender-based violence (GBV), 130–31
gender representation, 130–31, 173–74, 177
genocide, 70–71
GERD (Grand Ethiopian Renaissance
  Dam), 189
Gettlemen, Jeffrey, 95–96
Gondokoro mission, 18
Gordon, Charles, 18, 19
Government of National Unity, Sudan People's
  Liberation Movement and, 78
Government of Southern Sudan (GoSS), 4–5, 73
  corruption and, 83, 84
  corruption investigations follow-up, 7
  defense budget, 80
  judiciary and, 136
  oil revenue, 84
Government of Sudan (GoS), 6–7, 59–60, 64
  Machar and, 61
Government of the Republic of South Sudan
  (GRSS), 94–95, 103–4
Graham, Billy, 67–68
Graham, Franklin, 67–68
Grand Ethiopian Renaissance Dam
  (GERD), 189
Gray, Richard, 17

Haley, Nikki, 169
Hardtalk (BBC), 60
Hassan al-Bashir, Omar, 55
HCSS (Hybrid Court for South Sudan), 115,
  133, 139, 141, 179, 180–81
HEC (High Executive Council), 42
H4HA (Hope for Humanity Africa), 185
Hicks, William, 19
High Executive Council (HEC), 42
Hobbes, Thomas, 3
Hope for Humanity Africa (H4HA), 185
How Europe Undeveloped Africa
  (Rodney), 50–51
human rights abuses, 10, 55, 68, 117
  accountability for, 5
  African Union Commission of Inquiry in
    South Sudan report on, 10
  conscripting children, 124–33
  Garang's alleged, 67
  legal activism and, 137
  of Machar and Garang, 59–60
  South Sudan, 122
  Trump administration priorities and, 145
Human Rights Council, 135–36
human rights gap, 121–23

Human Rights Watch, 124–25
Human Rights Watch Report (2013), 125–26
Hushek, Thomas, 169
Hussein, Seed Ahmed, "Al-Cardinal," 96–97
Hutchinson, Sharon, 56–57
Hybrid Court for South Sudan (HCSS), 115,
  133, 139, 141, 179, 180–81
hybrid justice, 8, 9, 116, 137

Ibreck, Rachel, 137, 163–64
ICC. *See* International Criminal Court
ICISS (Interim Constitution of Southern
  Sudan), 73, 87, 89–90
ICTR (International Criminal Tribunal for
  Rwanda), 142
ICTY (International Criminal Tribunal for
  Former Yugoslavia), 141
"Identifying, Selecting, and Implementing
  Rural Development Strategies for Socio-
  Economic Development in the Jonglei
  Projects Area in the Southern Region,
  Sudan" (Garang), 51
IDPs. *See* internally displaced persons
IGAD (Intergovernmental Authority on
  Development), 10–11, 65, 112–13, 152–53,
  162, 163, 189
Igga, James Wani, 109, 159, 177–78
Ilichev, Petr, 112–13
IMC (International Medical
  Corporation), 129–30
immoral behavior, pacification and, 26
immunity, 139–40
impunity, 116–33
In Beyond a Boundary (James), 28
inclusion, 159–60, 177
independents. *See* Sudanese Independent Front
indirect rule, 26–29
infant mortality, 41
infighting, 2
inflation, 105
infrastructure projects, oil revenue and, 183–85
Inside Tiger, 110–11
intercommunal violence, 157–58, 159, 171, 172,
  176, 188–89
interethnic solidarity, 6–7
Intergovernmental Authority on Development
  (IGAD), 10–11, 65, 112–13, 152–53,
  162, 163
Interim Constitution, 9, 87
Interim Constitution of Southern Sudan
  (ICISS), 73, 88, 89
interim period, 77
  border disputes in, 90, 91–92

240 INDEX

interim period (*cont.*)
  corruption in, 82–85
  divided loyalties and national identity
    during, 81–82
  judiciary during, 136
internally displaced persons (IDPs), 10, 131–
    32, 135
  census and, 85
International Committee of the Red Cross, 158–59
International Criminal Court (ICC), 78, 91
  Bashir arrest warrant by, 79
  Bashir surrender to, 167–68
  South Sudan and, 142
International Criminal Tribunal for Former
    Yugoslavia (ICTY), 141
International Criminal Tribunal for Rwanda
    (ICTR), 142
international justice, 140, 142
International Medical Corporation
    (IMC), 129–30
International Monetary Fund, 7, 172, 182–83
Islam, as "wicked religion," 67–68
Ismail, Farouk, 137
Israel, 39–40
ivory demand, 17

Jabal Ataka, 17
Jaden, Aggrey, 38–39
James, C. L. R., 28
Jangroor, Aysen Aler, 166
Janjaweed militia, 70–71
Jieng Council of Elders, 148, 155, 168, 172–73
jihad, against English speaking countries, 26–27
al-jihadiyya (slave soldiers), 16–17
Johnson, Douglas, 59–60, 71, 187
Johnson, Hilde, 83, 107
Joint Monitoring and Evaluation Commission
    (JMEC), 152–53, 162
Jok, John Luk, 84, 89–90
Jok, Jok Madut, 159–60
Jonglei, 58, 59
Jonglei Canal Project (1958), 44
Juba Declaration, 79–80
judiciary
  government neglect of, 137
  during interim period, 136
  Transitional Constitution and, 136
Judiciary Act (2008), 136
justice, 8, 9
  hybrid, 9, 116, 137
  peace and, 139–40

Kabara, Gichira, 160–61

Karl, Terry, 101
Kasha campaign, 54–55
Kenya
  imports from, 98
  refugees in, 132–33
Kenyatta, Uhuru, 142
Kerubino. *See* Bol, Kerubino Kuanyin
Kerubino Bol, Kuanyin, 48
Khalil, Sayed Abdallaah, 28, 36–37
Khartoum, 5
  Deng on, 63
  as Nasir faction's supplier of arms, 60
  repressive policies of, 37–38
  resentment against, 37
  Sudan People's Liberation Army as
    enemy of, 53
Khartoum Declaration, 39–40, 156–57
Khartoum Peace Agreement (KPA), 62
Khatmiyya, 36
Kibaki, Mwai, 105
Kiir, Salva Mayadit, 4, 9, 11, 62–63, 74–75, 115
  amnesty offers by, 143
  blanket immunity offer of, 7
  cabinet reorganization, 107
  civil war and, 93–94
  civil war reemergence and, 140–41, 150–53
  constitution and, 89–90, 174
  on corruption, 83, 85
  COVID-19 and, 182, 183
  Crisis Management Committee and, 109
  deflection by, 143, 146
  elections and, 86–87
  after Garang death, 77, 79
  governor appointments, 176–77
  human rights advocacy pressures on, 138
  Hybrid Court for South Sudan and, 180
  intercommunal violence committee formed
    by, 159
  Juba University and, 134–35
  Machar opposition to, 107, 108
  Machar vice-presidency and, 150, 171
  National Dialogue Committee and, 162
  Necessary Unified Forces and, 178, 179
  New Sudan and, 78, 79
  Obama meeting with, 99
  oil production negotiations and, 105, 107
  oil shutdown and, 106
  Olony and, 174–75
  peace negotiations and, 148, 155–56
  "peace through forgiveness" and, 139
  Reconstituted Disarmament,
    Demobilization, and Reintegration
    Program, 166

INDEX   241

reintegration of armed forces and, 79–
    80, 81, 95
Revitalized Agreement on the Resolution
    of the Conflict in South Sudan
    implementation and, 172–73
sanctions and, 111–12, 113
South Sudan Human Rights Commission
    and, 122, 123
states decree, 148–50, 167
Transitional Constitution views of, 9–10
transparency and, 100
on truth commission, 140
women appointed by, 126
kinship networks, 82
Kitchener, Horatio, 21–22
kleptocracy, 93–94, 137
KPA (Khartoum Peace Agreement), 62
Kuc, Akol Koor, 110–11, 176
Kuol, Luka Biong Deng, 4–5, 63, 186–87
Kwani, George, 38

Lagu, Joseph, 38–39, 40, 78
    negotiation strategy, 41
    under scrutiny, 43
Lagu, Josephine, 154–55
Lahure, Saturnino, 37–38
land laws, 188–89
Law Review Society, 8
League of Nations, 26–27
legal activist networks, 137
legal system, 133–34, 142–43
Legge, Raimondo Geri, 133–34
Leviathan (Hobbes), 3
LGA (Local Government Act), 136–37
liberation curse, 101
Libya-Egypt Initiative, 65
Likuangole attack, 159
Liyong, Taban Lo, 134
Local Government Act (LGA), 136–37
local land laws, 188–89
Lord's Resistance Army (LRA), 130–31
Lou Nuer, 24–25
loyalty identification cards, 39

Machakos Protocol, 69, 78
Machakos talks, 78
Machar, Rebecca, 162
Machar, Riek, 6–7, 56, 57, 82–83, 104, 107, 108, 148
    amnesty offers and, 143
    civil war reemergence and, 140–41, 150–53
    Democratic Republic of the Congo and, 151
    Garang and, 59, 60
    Garang removal, 58

human rights commission involvement, 122
on Khartoum collaboration, 64
Olony and, 174–75
Peace Charter signing, 61
rejoining Sudan People's Liberation Army, 64
security concerns of, 165–66
South Africa and, 151
Southern Sudan Independence Movement
    created by, 61
Trump and, 168
on truth commission, 140
as Vice President, 150, 171
MacMichael, Harold, 29, 30, 31
Magae, Festus, 162
al Mahdi, Abdal-Rahmen, 36–37
al-Mahdi, Muhammed, 15
al-Mahdi, Sadig, 55
Mahdiyya (Mahdist State), 19–20
Makier, Daniel, 131–32
Malakal, 126–27
    Protection of Civilians camp, 128f,
        129f, 131–32
    razed village in, 127, 128f
Malong, Paul, 96–97, 152
Mamdani, Mahmood, 11, 23–24, 63–64, 108–9,
    115–16, 119, 144
    on British categories of tribes, 29–30
Mandela, Nelson, 64, 140
Marchand, Jean Baptiste, 22
marriage laws, 126
Marxism, 51
masculinity, 3
Mate, Obuto Mamur, 109–10
Matip, Paulino, 65–66, 79–80, 95
Maximilian I, 16–17
Max Planck Institute, 73
Mayai, Augustino Ting, 177
Mayardit, Salva Kiir. See Kiir, Salva
Mayen, Gordon Muortat, 38–39
Mbeki, Thabo, 105
Mednick, Sam, 144–45
Mengistu, Haile Mengistu, 49
Merekaje, Lorna, 167–68
Mijack, Joseph, 126–27
militarized patronage, 11, 98
militia rebellions, 95
Milner Commission, 26–27
Ministry of Gender and Social Welfare, 126–27
Misseriya, 71
missionary schools, 32
modernization
    of Ismail Pasha, 17–18
    South Sudan and, 15

242 INDEX

Mondiri, Ezboni, 40–41
monetized patronage, 82, 187
moral accountability, 5, 179–81
moral deterrents, 120
morality, peace and, 9
moral reckoning, 7, 9
MSN, 158–59
Mubarak, Hosni, 67
Muras, George, 38
Murle, 25–26, 63–64
Museveni, Yoweri, 49–50, 59, 109, 122–23, 189
Muslim faith, 18–19
Myang Mathiang, 25

Napoleon III, 16–17
NAS (National Salvation Front), 4, 147, 153, 158, 171
Nasser, Abdul, 33
Natanga, John, 161
National Audit Chamber, 85
National Congress Party (NCP), 69, 77, 78
National Constitutional Conference, 87–88, 161–62
National Constitutional Review Commission (NCRC), 89–90, 161–62
National Constitution Amendment Commission, 9–10
National Constitution Amendment Committee (NCAC), 160–61, 174
National Constitution Review Commission, 9–10
National DDR Coordination Council, 72–73
National Dialogue Committee, 162
national disunity and insecurity, 6–7
national identity of South Sudan, 81–82, 185–87
National Intelligence Security Service (NISS), 110–11
National Interim Constitution, 88
National Islamic Front (NIF), 55, 152
National Movement for Change, 118–19
national resource fund (NRF), 99–100
National Salvation Front (NAS), 4, 147, 153, 158, 171
national security, non-state militias and, 157–59
National Security Service (NSS), 110–11, 117, 176, 185–86
National Security Service Act, 134–35
National Strategic Action Ban, 126
National Transitional Committee (NTC), 178
National Transitional Government of South Sudan (NTGSS), 38–39
National Unionists Party (NUP), 33
Nazari-Kangarlou, Soheil, 144–45

NBI (Nile Basin Initiative), 51
NCA (Norwegian Church Aid), 129–30
NCAC (National Constitution Amendment Committee), 160–61, 174
NCP. See National Congress Party
NCRC (National Constitutional Review Commission), 9–10, 89–90, 161–62
NDC (National Dialogue Committee), 162
Necessary Unified Forces (NUF), 6–7, 166–67
negligent behavior, pacification and, 26
Neither Settler Nor Native (Mamdani), 115–16
"new humanism," of Fanon, 50
"New Sudan," 47, 52
Kiir and, 78, 79
replacing racist "Old Sudan," 49
New Sudan Council of Churches, 62
Ngok Dinka, 71, 106
NIF (National Islamic Front), 55, 152
Nile Basin Initiative (NBI), 51
Nile Hope, 163–64
Nile Petroleum Corporation (Nilepet), 102–3, 110, 111
Nilotic Dinka, 30
Nimeiri, Muhammed Jaafar, 40–41, 48
Kasha campaign, 54–55
ousted from office, 55
South Sudan infiltrated by, 44–45
9-11 attacks, 68–69
NISS (National Intelligence Security Service), 110–11
non-state militias, 157–59
North Sudan, 27, 28
Norwegian Church Aid (NCA), 129–30
NRF (national resource fund), 99–100
NSS (National Security Service), 110–11, 117–18, 134–35, 176, 185–86
NTC (National Transitional Committee), 178
NTGSS (National Transitional Government of South Sudan), 38–39
Nuba Mountains, 16–17
Nuer ethnic group, 24, 30, 42, 47–48, 108–9
attacks on, 93
egalitarian traits of, 24–25
soldiers, 6
Western Nuer, 63
White Army, 61
Nuer West Bank Peace and Reconciliation Process, 62–64
NUF (Necessary Unified Forces), 6–7, 167, 171, 178, 179, 188
NUP (National Unionists Party), 33
Nyaba, Peter Adwok, 3–4, 98
Nyanyuki, Joan, 138

Nyong, Aviel, 135
Nyong, Makuc Makuc, 188–89

OAG (Other Armed Groups), 79–80
OAU (Organization of African Unity), 38
Obama, Barack, 91, 99, 111–12
Odong, Kennedy Ongie, 174–75
Oduho, Joseph, 37–38
oil pipeline plan, 104
oil revenue, 81, 82, 106, 183–85
  corruption and, 84, 101
  dependence on, 101–2
  missing, 82–83
  sharing, 103–4
  taxes on, 104
Oil Revenue Stabilization Account, 99–100
oil sector, 103–6
  civil war impact on, 94–95, 152–53
  COVID-19 and, 172
  environmental problems and, 184–85
  militarization of, 93–94, 110, 111
  shutdown crisis, 104, 106
  speculative contracts in, 102–3
  transit fees, 106
  transparency and, 99, 184
"Old Sudan," 6–7, 49, 50
Onek, Leonzio Angole, 134
Organization of African Unity (OAU), 38
Other Armed Groups (OAG), 79–80
Otony, Johnson, 174–75, 177, 178–79
Ottoman Empire, 16–17, 26–27
Outside Tiger, 110–11
Oxfam, 163, 186
Oyen, Kari, 129–30

pacification
  negligent behavior and, 26
  as official policy of Anglo-Egyptian
    Condominium, 22–26
  1920s, 24
Padang militia, 4, 110
Palau, 10–11
Panel of Experts. *See* United Nations Panel of
  Experts on South Sudan
paranoia, 121
Pasha, Abbas, 17
Pasha, Ali Kurshid, 16–17
  slave capture of, 17
Pasha, Ismail, 17–18
patrols, overt prejudice of, 25
patronage, 6
  militarized, 98
  monetized, 82, 187

networks, 3–4
PDF (People's Defense Force), 54
PDP (People Democratic Party), 36
peace
  justice and, 7–8, 139–40
  morality and, 9
  parameters of process, 155–57
  process, 187–88
  reconstituting, 9–11
  in state of war, 1–6
Peace Agreement of 2018, 1
Peace and Security Council (PSC), 141
Peace Charter (1996), 61
peacekeeping forces
  from Ethiopia, 90–91
  United Nations, 115
Pentagon attacks, 68–69
People Democratic Party (PDP), 36
People's Defense Force (PDF), 54
Permanent Ceasefire and Security
  Arrangement, 72–73
Permanent Court of International
  Arbitration, 90
Petroleum Act (2012), 99, 100
Petroleum Revenue Management Act, 185
Petroleum Revenue Management Bill (PRMB),
  99, 106
Petronas, 102–3
Petterson, Donald, 59
Pinaud, Clemence, 97–98
Pius IX (Pope), 18
PoC camps. *See* Protection of Civilians camps
Police Service Act, 160–61
Political Inclusion Act, 89
political marketplaces, 97–98
Powell, Colin, 69, 70–71
power sharing, 156, 159–60
predatory economy, 82–83
predatory warfare, 95–96
Prendergast, John, 67, 96–97, 111–12
Presbyterian churches, 18
Presidential armory break-in attempt, 108–9
Principle of Effective Occupation, 21
privatization, 95, 102
PRMB (Petroleum Revenue Management
  Bill), 99
procurement, 102
Production Sharing Agreements (PSAs), 103–4
Protection of Civilians (PoC) camps, 10, 128*f*,
  129*f*, 131–32
*Protocol on the Resolution of Conflict in
  Southern Kordofan and Blue Nile States*
  (2004), 71

Protocol on the Resolution of Conflict in the Abyei Area (2004), 71
provincial states, 148–49
PSAs (Production Sharing Agreements), 103–4
PSC (Peace and Security Council), 141
public trust, 42

al-Qaeda, 68–69
quasi-federal systems, 149

racial biases in South Sudan, 23–24
Raf'I (Aazande prince), 22
Ranneberger, Michael, 144–45
R-ARCSS. *See* Revitalized Agreement on the Resolution of the Conflict in South Sudan
rebellion in South Sudan, 2, 37–42
Reconstituted Disarmament, Demobilization, and Reintegration (R-DDR) program, 166
referendum vote, 87
refugees, attacks on, 133
regional autonomy, 42–45
regional politics, 187–90
Report on the Basis of the Upper Nile, 1904 (Gastin), 44
resource curse, 101
revenge attacks, 188–89
Revitalized Agreement on the Resolution of the Conflict in South Sudan (R-ARCSS), 1, 5–6, 118–19, 147, 154, 188
  agreement signing, 157
  election delays and, 172
  governor appointments and, 176–77
  Hybrid Court for South Sudan and, 180–81
  implementation delays, 167, 169, 172
  implementation of, 172–73
  inclusion and, 159–60, 177–78
  moral accountability and, 5–6
  National Constitutional Review Commission and, 161–62
  Necessary Unified Forces stipulated under, 6
  oil sector and, 183–84
  Transitional Constitution and, 160
Revitalized Transitional Government of National Unity (RTGoNU), 11, 148, 166–67, 170, 172, 174
  approval of, 171
  security challenges, 174–76
Revolutionary Command Council of National Salvation, 55
Rhodes, Cecile, 21–22
Rice, Susan, 67
Riruyo, Patrick, 98
road construction, 84

Rodney, Walter, 50–51
Rolandsen, Øystein, 39
Roman, Nyarji, 180
Rome Statute, 141
Ross, Michael, 101
RTGoNU. *See* Revitalized Transitional Government of National Unity
Ruben, Judith, 130–31
rule by law, 133–34, 135
rule of law, 135–38
ruling elite, 1–2, 3
  politicization of justice of, 11

SACDNU (South African Closed District National Union), 37–38
Sadat, Anwar, 33
SAF (Sudanese Armed Forces), 39, 42–43, 53, 55
Said, Mohamed Said Pasha, 17
Salafism, 17–18
Salih, Mohamed, 61, 82
sanctions, 111–14, 147–48, 168
  lobbying against, 144–45
SANU (Sudan African National Union), 38–39
SATRC (South African Truth and Reconciliation Commission), 7–8, 140, 180
Save the Children, 67–68
Schomerus, Mareike, 86–87
SDF (Sudan Defense Forces), 27, 29
secession, 77, 81
Security Council. *See* United Nations Security Council
security forces, national unity and, 6
Selassie, Haile, 40–41
self-determination, 6–7, 32
Self-Government Act, 33
Senghor, Leopold, 49–50
Sentry Project, 96–97, 111, 186
September 11, 2001 attacks, 68–69
"September Law," 48
Shab-e Field force, 25
Shaiqiya, 16
Shandong Hi-Sped Group, 184
sharia law, 48
  exemption, 69
  Mahdiyya based on, 19–20
  Nimeiri recommitment, 54–55
  September laws, 48
Shaykan, 19
Shearer, David, 173, 181
Shilluk, 16–17, 63–64
Shilluk Agwelek, 127

Sinopec, 102–3
el- Sisi, Fattah, 145, 168, 189
Sison, Michele, 169
slavery
  ivory demand and, 17
  modernization influence on, 17–18
  patrol presence and, 26
  in Turkiyyah period, 16
slave soldiers, 16–22
Slovakia, 111
small arms shipments, 111, 112–13, 158
social contracts, 4–5, 185–87, 188
sorghum, 84
South African Closed District National Union
  (SACDNU), 37–38
South African Truth and Reconciliation
  Commission (SATRC), 7–8, 140, 180
South African Truth Commission, 7–8
Southern Command, 41
Southern Corps, 29
southern guerilla movement. See Anyanya
Southern Liberal Party, 35
Southern Regional Assembly, 44–45
Southern Regional Government (SRG), 42–43
Southern Sudan Autonomous Region
  (SSAR), 41
Southern Sudan Defense Forces (SSDF), 79–80,
  95, 152
Southern Sudan Defense Forces-United, 62–63
Southern Sudanese Federalist Party (SSFP), 36
Southern Sudan Independence Movement
  (SSIM), 61
South Kordofan, 91, 106
South-South, axis of conflict, 48
South-South war, 62
South Sudan
  armed factionalism of, 4
  boundaries of, 78
  broken institutions of, 10
  civil war in, 93–95
  culture in, 3
  December 2013 civil war, 1
  lessons from history, 119
  national identity, 81–82
  national unity in, 6
  new social contract for, 4–5
  rebellion in, 2, 37–42
  state structure in, 148–49
South Sudan Churches Council (SSCC), 129–30
South Sudan Doctors' Union, 182
South Sudan Human Rights Commission
  (SSHCR), 122, 123
South Sudan Law Society, 8, 137

South Sudan Liberation Movement
  (SSLM), 40, 63
South Sudan National Dialogue, 112–13
South Sudan National Liberation Movement/
  Army (SSNLM/A), 143
South Sudan Opposition Alliance (SSOA), 153,
  154, 155–56
South Sudan People's Defense Forces (SSPDF),
  127–28, 152, 158, 176
South Sudan Sanctions Program, 111–12
South Sudan Young Leaders Forum
  (SSYLF), 117
South Transparency Initiative, 100
SPAFF (Sudan Pan-African Freedom
  Fighters), 38
SPDF (Sudan People's Defense Force), 65–66
SPLA. See Sudan People's Liberation Army
SPLA Act, 160–61
SPLA-IO. See Sudan People's Liberation
  Army-in-Opposition
SPLM. See Sudan People's Liberation Movement
SPLM/A. See Sudan People's Liberation
  Movement/Army
SPLM-IO. See Sudan People's Liberation
  Movement-in-Opposition
SRG (Southern Regional Government), 42
SSAR (Southern Sudan Autonomous Region), 41
SSCC (South Sudan Churches Council), 129–30
SSDF. See Southern Sudan Defense Forces (SSDF)
SSFP (Southern Sudanese Federalist Party), 36
SSHCR (South Sudan Human Rights
  Commission), 122–23
SSIM (Southern Sudan Independence
  Movement), 61
SSLM (South Sudan Liberation Movement), 40
SSNLM/A (South Sudan National Liberation
  Movement/Army), 143
SSOA (South Sudan Opposition Alliance), 153,
  154, 155–56
SSPDF (South Sudan People's Defense Forces),
  127–28, 152, 158, 176
SSYLF (South Sudan Young Leaders
  Forum), 117
starvation, 54–55
state boundaries, 148, 149–50
state governors, 176–77
state of war metaphor, 3
Statute of Self Government, 33
statutory law, 137
Stearns, Jason, 93–94
Sudan
  exclusion of South Sudan from Sudanese
    nationalism, 27

246　INDEX

Sudan (*cont.*)
　Grand Ethiopian Renaissance Dam project
　　and, 189
　independence declared by, 36
　irrigation projects, 54–55
　Khartoum Declaration and, 156–57
　oil revenues and, 103–4
　starvation, 54–55
　United States missile launch into, 66
Sudan African National Union (SANU), 38–39
Sudan Defense Forces (SDF), 27, 29
Sudanese Armed Forces (SAF), 39, 42–
　43, 53, 55
Sudanese Communist Party, 40
Sudanese Independent Front, 33
Sudanese nationalists, 32–33
Sudanese Socialist Union, 40
Sudanization, 35
Sudan Legislative Assembly, 33
Sudan Pan-African Freedom Fighters
　(SPAFF), 38
Sudan People's Liberation Army (SPLA), 52–
　53, 80
　factionalism and, 55–65
　formation of, 47, 78
　funding sources, 95
　Khartoum as enemy of, 53
　Nuer attacked by, 93
　oil sector and, 110–11
　reintegration and, 166
　United States aid to, 66
　United States support to, 65
　vision of, 48–55
Sudan People's Liberation Army-
　Government, 110
Sudan People's Liberation Army-in-Opposition
　(SPLA-IO), 110, 149–50, 153
　child recruitment, 124–25
Sudan People's Liberation Army-Nasir, 6–7, 58
Sudan People's Liberation Army-Torit, 7,
　58, 59, 62
Sudan People's Liberation Army-United, 59, 61.
　See also Southern Sudan Independence
　Movement
Sudan People's Liberation Movement (SPLM),
　1, 52–53
　constitution and, 88–90
　elections and, 86–87
　factionalism in, 96
　Government of National Unity and, 78
　infighting in, 107
　manifesto, 49
　militarism, 3–4, 96

　militarized patronage and, 98
　uncertainty of, 119
　unity-secession question and, 81–82
Sudan People's Liberation Movement/Army
　(SPLM/A), 2, 54
　as dictatorship, 56
　elections and, 86–87
　international pressure on, 77
　Machar and Akol ambition to control, 56
　reunification and Khartoum, 65
　secession and, 77–78
　splintering, 63–64
　split in, 2–3, 47–48
　United States securing ties with, 66
Sudan People's Liberation Movement/Army-In
　Opposition (SPLM/A-IO), 115
Sudan People's Liberation Movement-
　Democratic Change, 86
Sudan People's Liberation Movement-
　Government, 93
Sudan People's Liberation Movement-in-
　Opposition (SPLM-IO), 4, 6, 93, 95,
　150, 153
　amnesty and, 143
　federal structure and, 160–61
　Machar security concerns and, 165–66
　soldiers defecting from, 174–75
　war crimes court and, 180
Sudan People's Liberation Movement-North,
　91, 99, 106, 108
Sudd Institute, 100–1
Sufism, 17–18
Sunday, Betty, 173
Supreme Council of Armed Forces, 37
Symes, George Stewart, 31–32
Symington, Stuart, 168

Taha, Ali Osman, 70
Taha, Mohamed, 4–5, 54–55
Taliban, 68–69
TC Amendment Bill, 160–61
Tenth Parallel, 27
Teny, Angela, 173
Terrain Hotel invasion, 115, 138
terrorism, 60, 65–66
　Sudan support of, 68–69
　Trump administration priorities and, 145
Tier, Akolda Maan, 161
Tigray, 189
Torit Massacre, 35–36
Transitional Constitution, 8, 9–10, 88, 89–90,
　121–22, 173–74
　child rights in, 124

INDEX 247

judiciary and, 136
national identity and, 186
Petroleum Act and, 99
Revitalized Agreement on the Resolution of
the Conflict in South Sudan and, 160
state boundaries and, 149–50
transitional justice, 7–9
Transitional Legislative Assembly, 160–61
Transitional National Legislative
Assembly, 177–78
transitional period agreements, 87–88
Transitional Security Arrangement
(TSA), 171–72
transparency, 99, 100–1, 184
trauma, 118–19
travel bans, 111–12
tribal authorities, patrols relationship with, 24
tribal bonds in South Sudan, 3–4
tribal chiefs, pacification and, 22–26
tribal customs, 63–64
abusive nature of, 124–25
tribal identity, militia recruitment and, 165–66
tribe, defined, 24–25
Troika, 4–5, 10–11, 70, 73–74, 162
corruption and, 77–78
ending violence, 76
goal of, 9
Trump, Donald, 145, 169
truth commission, 8
TSA (Transitional Security
Arrangement), 171–72
al-Turabi, Hassan, 55, 60, 66, 67
Turco-Egyptian regime, 16
Turkiyyah period slave trade, 17
Tut, Samuel Gai, 49
Tut, Tut Gatlak, 108–9
Tutu, Desmond, 64, 140

Uganda
elections in, 189
Khartoum Declaration and, 156–57
refugees in, 132–33
underdevelopment, 50–51
UNICEF (United Nations International
Children's Emergency Fund), 126
unified military, 157–58
United Nations, 10–11, 38. See also specific
topics beginning with "United Nations"
critical of Israel's objectives, 39–40
Panel of Experts (see United Nations Panel of
Experts on South Sudan)
peacekeepers, 90–91, 115
PoC camps, 10, 128f

sanctions and, 111–14
Security Council(see United Nations Security
Council)
South Sudan recognition and, 91
Trusteeship, 10–11
United Nations Agreement on Temporary
Arrangements for the Administration and
Security of the Abyei Area, 106
United Nations Human Rights Council, 10,
121–22, 158–59
United Nations Interim Security Force for Abyei
(UNISFA), 90–91
United Nations International Children's
Emergency Fund (UNICEF), 126
United Nations Mission in South Sudan
(UNMISS), 10, 83, 113, 159, 173
COVID-19 and, 181–82
peacekeeping troops, 90–91, 115
United Nations Mobile High Court, 130–
31, 135–36
United Nations Panel of Experts on
South Sudan
on informal economy, 147–48
on National Security Service, 110–11, 134–35
on National Transitional Committee, 178
on peace process, 147–48
United Nations Permanent Court of
Administration, 71
United Nations Security Council
arms embargo and, 112–13
criminal tribunals and, 141, 142
International Criminal Tribunal for
Yugoslavia and, 141
Rome Statute and, 141
sanctions and, 111–14
United Nations Trusteeship, 10–11
United States
critical of Israel's objectives, 39–40
Evangelical Christians in, 67–68
foreign policy of, 65–69
on Garang as liberal democrat, 65, 74
Garang promotion by, 65
Garang support by, 66
peace process and, 147, 168
predatory economy and, 82–83
sanctions and, 111–14, 147–48, 168
shifts in priorities by, 145
South Sudan investments by, 94–95
South Sudan recognized by, 91
"The University Students African Revolution
Front," 49–50
UNMISS. See United Nations Mission in
South Sudan

248 INDEX

Vergee, Aly, 150
veto powers, 23, 156
Vickers, Emma, 100
victimization, 142–43, 144
violence
  of child abuse, 126
  gender-based, 130–31
  intercommunal, 157–58, 159, 171, 172,
    176, 188–89
  for political survival, 121
Von Bismarck, Otto, 20–21
VX nerve gas, 66

Waal, Alex de, 97
Wafd Party, 26–27
al- Wahab, Aba Ahmad Abd, 37
Wais, Ismail, 152–53
Wani, Beatrice, 173
Wara Wara Investment, 96–97
war crimes court, 5, 180, 188–89
  lobbying against, 144–45
war economies, 94, 96
Wars, guns, and Votes (Collier), 95–96
Washington Post, 118
Wealth Sharing Agreement (WSA), 84
Western Arab Corps, Darfur, 29
Western Nuer, 62–63

What Is the What (Eggers), 120–21
White Army, 109, 122–23
White Flag League, 28
White Nile region, 16–17
Wiener, Allen, 160
Wingate, Reginal, 28–29
Wol, Santino Deng, 178–79
women's advocacy groups, 130–31
World Bank, 7, 172
World Trade Center attacks, 68–69
Wretched of the Earth, The (Fanon), 50
WSA (Wealth Sharing Agreement), 84
Wunlit conference. *See* Nuer West Bank Peace
    and Reconciliation Process
Wunlit Dinka-Nuer Covenant, 62–63

Yac, Justin, 64
Yak, Peter Gadet. *See* Gadet, Peter
Yaki, Edward, 130–31
Yambio, child abuse in, 124
Yang, Chaoying, 113
Yau, David Yau, 107–8
Young, John, 65

Zaghlul, Saad, 26–27
Zenawi, Menes, 105
Zuma, Jacob, 151